Wendi Fox Pedicone

HANGING OUT WITH LAB COATS

Hope, Humor & Help
for Cancer Patients and their Caregivers

Published by:

Post Office Box 1601
Hockessin, DE 19707-5601
www.foxpress.com

First edition – November 2005.

This title may be available as a FoxPress™ audio product in the future. Visit www.foxpress.com for more information.

Photographs courtesy of G.Thomas Murray Photography©, Atlantic Portrait Studio, RhonJohn Communications, Inc., Colleen Burg, and Wendi Pedicone. Sketches by Anthony Carbone, Sr. Design, layout, graphics and typesetting productions of the book by RhonJohn Communications, Inc.

Last names of medical professionals, family, friends, and colleagues have not been used in this book for the purpose of maintaining individuals' privacy, and in some cases names have been modified.

Publisher's Cataloging-in-Publication
(Provided by Quality Books, Inc.)

Pedicone, Wendi Fox.
   Hanging out with lab coats : hope, humor, and help
   for cancer patients and their caregivers / by Wendi Fox
   Pedicone. – 1st ed.
   p. cm.
   Includes bibliographical references.
   LCCN 2005929249
   ISBN 0-9768997-0-1 (hc)
   ISBN 0-9768997-1-X (sc)

   1. Pedicone, Wendi Fox–Health. 2. Breast–Cancer–
   Patients–United States–Biography. 3. Breast–Cancer–
   Popular works. I. Title.

RC280.B8P343 2005   616.99'449
                                   QBI05-600089

Printed in the United States of America

MORE ENDORSEMENTS FOR *HANGING OUT WITH LAB COATS*

"This is a book written by an inspired person and a true survivor. When you are ready to combine the information in it with the inspiration you bring to it you will find yourself on the path to healing."

Bernie Siegel, MD
Author of *Love, Medicine & Miracles and Help Me To Heal.*

"Every man should read this book!"

John H. Molloy
CEO, Imaginis Corporation, "The breast health resource"

"Wendi Pedicone has done something unique and courageous by not only surviving breast cancer, but by connecting the dots of complementary healing and making the resulting picture work for her. By eating the purest natural and organic foods she could find, by adopting an unshakably positive attitude and by working with her health care providers, Pedicone won. This is a book of hope written with gratitude for a journey well traveled. Use it to inspire your own journey from illness to health."

Bob Kleszics
President
Harvest Market Natural Foods

MORE ENDORSEMENTS FOR *HANGING OUT WITH LAB COATS*

"Wendi has written an extraordinary account of her personal struggle with breast cancer. Because I shared some of the experiences described in her story, I found myself captivated by Wendi's description of her feelings from the other side of the "lab coat." Health care professionals like myself often view the obvious outward emotions of patients going through the experience of cancer diagnosis and treatment – the tears, denial, anger and ultimately acceptance – but Wendi reveals the inner details of her emotions in a way that few of us are able to express at all, much less articulate with such humor and elegance, in this tale of illness and coping.

Wendi describes her daily battle with cancer and her resultant particular demons and interweaves all of it within a tapestry of daily existence – mundane, yet somehow now not trivial, details of laundry, childcare, and marital relations. For those who need them she provides accounts of treatments and resources that are both practical and extensive. For those of us fortunate enough not to have gone through her experience, I cannot imagine a more compelling description of an illness and its aftermath or a richer narrative. To foster better understanding and emotional support for their patients, all oncologists should read this detailed portrait of one woman's reactions to her journey through treatment of breast cancer."

> **Christopher Koprowski, MD, MBA**
> Chair, Department of Radiation Oncology
> Christiana Care Health System
> Member of Radiation Oncologists, PA

"Wendi and her book are an inspiration to anyone dealing with cancer. Her strength, courage, and ability to keep her sense of humor shines thru each page, I cried and laughed out loud while reading *Hanging Out With Lab Coats* . It has been a true honor to be a part of Wendi's healing path and to watch her turn her fight with cancer into a challenge to gain back her health and vitality and to become a resource, teacher, and role model for her children, family, friends, and to other people with cancer."

> **Jennifer Workman, M.S., R.D.**
> Nutrition/Weight Management Program
> The Balanced Approach
> www.thebalancedapproach.com
> Author of *Stop Your Cravings*, (Free Press)

MORE ENDORSEMENTS FOR *HANGING OUT WITH LAB COATS*

"Inyengar yoga should be an important part of our lives. We enhance the ability to heal when we combine the eastern ancient philosophy with the western approach. The integration of both improves the ability for the body to heal itself. Somewhere along Wendi's journey Iyengar yoga helped her to get through the rough spots. Clearly Wendi has taken the bull by the horns and utilized the restorative Iyengar yoga sequences to increase her chances and eventuality overcome cancer, and the effect has been positive."

Donita Reitze
Certified Iyengar Yoga Instructor
The Iyengar Yoga Center of Denver

For 46 years, I have been Wendi's sister. Even though we had the usual sister "stuff" to deal with, things evened out and changed when we became adults. And things really changed when my little sister was diagnosed with cancer. Wendi has invited me to be an active part of her adventure while at the same time, she's given me the perfect opportunity to re-examine my own path through life, inspiring and propelling me into a totally different career as an ND (Doctor of Naturopathy) realizing that, through diet, yoga, meditation, --and with Ayurveda wrapped around it – I can make a difference in her life and in others' lives. I am proud of her courage and honesty and happy to be one of her sisters. In this relationship we never think small, and hopefully, you won't either after reading this book. Just don't lend her your softball glove . . . .

Deborah A. Fox
B.A., ND candidate

FOREWORD

A breast cancer diagnosis can trigger a host of reactions - denial, anger, apprehension, frustration, hopelessness, depression, fear. What should I do? Which doctors should I see? Which ones can I trust? What should I ask them? What tests do I need? What treatment is best for me? Should I get a second opinion? A third opinion? How do I read my pathology report? What exactly is a pathology report? Will I lose my breast? Will I lose my life? As editor of Imaginis.com, I have heard from hundreds of breast cancer patients and survivors who have confided that they didn't know where to begin to look for the answers to these and countless other questions. Wendi Fox Pedicone's *Hanging Out With Lab Coats: Hope, Humor, and Help for Cancer Patients and Their Caregivers* is that rare, exceptional resource that we are excited to add to our recommendations.

Ms. Pedicone asks, "Wouldn't it be magnificent to provide people with a wonderful reading experience and help breast cancer patients get through their treatment by telling my story?" And this is exactly what she does, with a wonderful balance of thoughtfulness and laughter. The reader is invited to take the journey right alongside her, from the clinical breast exam where a nurse first detects a lump to the mastectomy with TRAM flap reconstructive surgery to her hours of chemotherapy and then radiation therapy.

While Ms. Pedicone provides readers with hundreds of detailed tips on almost every aspect of breast cancer, from how to find reliable statistics on survival rates to how to locate a support group, her book is much more than a directory of information on the best breast cancer resources because each of her tips is framed within the context of her personal experience with the disease. Through her near daily account of what it's like to be a cancer patient, Ms. Pedicone covers the details that no one else talks about - how chemotherapy can give you gas, how prescription-strength fluoride toothpaste may be needed while undergoing radiation, how sometimes the best way to explain your illness to your three-year-old son is by sharing a dance. When Ms. Pedicone sends out periodic e-mail updates to her friends, family, and coworkers, we feel like one of the gang. We fight the battle with her, rejoice in the highs, suffer in the lows, and ultimately share in her victory over "the invader."

Users of Imaginis.com often tell me that there aren't enough reliable sources of information on the breast cancer experience available to the public. While Ms. Pedicone helpfully directs cancer patients, caregivers, and families to her favorite resources, it is Ms. Pedicone's book that is the real find.

Alissa H. Czyz
Editor,
Imaginis.com, The Breast Health Resource

A woman is like a tea bag.
You never know how strong she is
until she's in hot water.

Eleanor Roosevelt
America's Most Influential First Lady and wife of
32nd President, Franklin Delano Roosevelt
(1884 - 1962)

PROLOGUE AND NOTES TO READERS

Lately, I've been *Hanging Out With Lab Coats.* Actually, I've been hanging out with people who wear lab coats. I say things like, "Why don't we order liver function-ality testing with the CBC," and, "Let's determine the next steps in the treatment plan." I am neither a doctor nor a nurse. I am not a health care practitioner. My vocation has nothing to do with the medical profession.

My name is Wendi and I am a recent survivor of advanced stage breast cancer. I am a 46-year-old communications professional, wife, and the mother of three teenage daughters and a four-year-old son. My tumor was found during an annu-al clinical exam (and not a self-exam). I was complacent; I did monthly breast self-exams (BSEs) about twice a year. After all, I had none of the breast cancer risk fac-tors, breast cancer wouldn't happen to me. Yet, here I am, a breast cancer victim with a story to tell...

By chronicling my story, I hope to achieve several things: help people with breast cancer get through their treatment experience; help cancer caregivers and anyone who may develop breast cancer in the future (male or female); inform non-med-ical people in everyday language about some of the ways cancer is treated; and provide encouragement and inspiration to anyone facing something that threat-ens his or her quality of life or life expectancy. This is a story about facing fears, making decisions, living day-to-day, discovering comedy in unlikely situations and ultimately emerging triumphant. This book is my gift to everyone touched by cancer (which is just about everyone).

Some of the story is drawn from the regular written updates I had provided to friends and colleagues. Some of it is from notes I'd scribbled on bits of paper, nap-kins, and sticky notes. And the rest of it is the result of my time spent resting and recuperating with a notebook computer on my lap.

As you read the story, you'll find advice for cancer patients and caregivers in the form of underlined tips. However, read more than just the tips. There is practical advice throughout.

If you are a cancer patient or a caregiver looking for an understanding of what to expect and how to travel your cancer journey in an informed way, this book is for you. You can follow the story as you would a novel and get the timely tips as you read. I invested hundreds of hours of exploration into the cancer topic, so you don't have to. On the other hand, if you are the knowledge-hungry type, you can start with this book, and then proceed to the websites, pamphlets and books I suggest.

Prologue and Notes to Readers

This book is enriched with e-mails and comments from caring people and compassionate physicians who traveled this journey with me. I wrote about my journey. They wrote about me.

If you are a cancer patient and struggling emotionally, don't close the book because you think I'm too optimistic to be true. As you will come to find out, I hit my wall of gloom. The way I approached my ordeal was practical and positive. I am more optimistic than the average person; I don't expect cancer patients or their caregivers to be as positive as I was, but I anticipate that some of my ideas, attitudes, thoughts, and methods will grow in you and give you hope. Hope is powerful medicine. My path might not be your path, your stage of cancer might not be the same as my stage of cancer, but there are things in this book that will help you.

When I did my research, I separated the cancer books into two main categories: 1) informational resources and references guides, and 2) personal stories. This book is both.

Resource book: You'll notice that there are blank pages in the back for notes. This is to remind you that this book can be used as an informational source, and dog-earring pages is encouraged, too. Additionally, I suggest keeping a highlighting marker with your copy of this book so you can draw attention to information you want to remember or share with others, and sources you might want to investigate (such as books, websites, etc.). An important aspect of beating cancer is knowledge. Education is powerful medicine.

Personal story: You may be inclined to read the first few paragraphs of this book to compare your diagnosis with mine, and then jump to the last few paragraphs to see how I'm surviving. Let me save you some time. At the time of this writing I am doing extremely well. I've been told I am "cured unless proven otherwise." I've endured four surgeries, sixteen weeks of chemotherapy, and twenty-eight radiation treatments. It is my hope that my story will inspire you. Inspiration is powerful medicine, too.

And now, for the in-between part of the story…

TABLE OF CONTENTS

Hanging Out With Lab Coats: Hope, Help, and Humor for
Cancer Patients and their Caregivers

TABLE OF TIPS

*Hanging Out with Lab Coats: Hope, Help, and Humor for
Cancer Patients and their Caregivers*

CHAPTER 1

HOW LONG HAS THIS BEEN HERE?

[August 2001: (L to R) Mom Fox, Michele, Me holding Danny,
Christine, Dan & Andrea]

Photo courtesy of Atlantic Portraits

*We all have changes in our lives that are
more or less a second chance.*

Harrison Ford
Actor (1942 -)
*"Quoted by Garry Jenkins in
'Harrison Ford: Imperfect'"*

No one who discovers a lump or a mass on her body remains totally calm, outside and in.

I was scheduled for my annual mammogram in June 2004 at my employer's on-site facility. I work at AstraZeneca (AZ), a worldwide pharmaceutical company. Ranked by *Working Mother* magazine in the US as one of the "100 Best Companies for Working Mothers", AZ maintains a commitment to women and breast care. In fact, the company has been presented with the Celebrate Life Community Award by Crozer Regional Cancer Center in Pennsylvania and is one of the co-founders of National Breast Cancer Awareness Month. Working for a company such as this means I would never get breast cancer, right?

The Corporate Health Services (CHS) department coordinates on-site mammography screenings and clinical (hand to breast) examinations for its employees. All year long, female employees receive notices for periodic appointments, annual or every other year, via the intracompany e-mail and calendar system. I received mine.

My first mammogram, years ago, was my rite of passage to joke about what gets done to my chest during the procedure. I smile when other women tell comical mammogram stories; it is, after all, an odd kind of x-ray.

While I don't do my monthly exams nor believe there is the possibility of getting breast cancer, I have always viewed my annual mammogram as a gift and an opportunity. A gift, because an employer doesn't *have* to provide this screening for me. An opportunity, because I get to hear I've had another breast-healthy year.

> **Tip 1** A screening mammogram is a breast x-ray that can find early changes up to two years before they can be felt by a trained health care professional. It is often the best tool for diagnosing breast cancer early. When caught early, women have a ninety-seven percent survival rate (American Cancer Society). View your mammogram as an opportunity, to either get a clean bill of health or have something detected that you haven't yet discovered.

Somehow, I forgot to go to my appointment in June and it was rescheduled for July 28.

THE DAY OF THE MAMMOGRAM

The day arrived and I was determined not to miss it again. Even though I don't do the breast self-exams (BSEs), I always have yearly gynecological (GYN) visits and get annual mammograms. Why don't I do monthly exams? Because cancer won't happen to someone with zero risk factors and perfect attendance at annual exams, right? Wrong.

July 28, 2004: I walk from my office to the on-site branch bank to check on my home equity credit application. Then I proceed to the building where CHS is located. I expect to be in and out in ten minutes and back to my office in twenty. Home equity line, check. Mammogram, soon-to-be check. It's so rewarding to check things off my to-do list.

In typically warm fashion, the staff welcomes me. I complete the questionnaire that mostly queries any observed changes since my last mammogram. Afterward, I am taken into a cozy room so I can remove my clothes from the waist up and put on the patient gown. This is the clinical breast exam (CBE). The nurse comes into the room and introduces herself as Betsy. I've had annual exams at AZ for years, and even though I don't recall meeting Betsy, I feel that I am in good hands.

CLINICAL BREAST EXAM FIRST

I am lying on my back with my left arm over my head. Betsy is rubbing each breast in circular motions and up-and-down patterns. She tells me I'm cystic. No surprises there. Cystic means that my breasts are lumpy. Many women are cystic. It has always been difficult to feel for unusual lumps when my breasts are already lumpy, which is one of my excuses for being lax about doing a monthly BSE. I was often told that the fibrous tissue has its own texture and that I should get to know my breasts' textures - then feel for anything out of the ordinary. As I have aged and since I nursed four babies, the lumpiness in my breasts has decreased...*not to mention the fullness.*

Tip 2 Doctors recommend routine screening mammography because it helps find breast changes early. But not all changes show up on mammograms, which is why three things should be part of your prevention: studies have shown that using BSE, mammography, and a CBE by a doctor or nurse increases your chance for early detection and can reduce deaths from breast cancer (Breast Health, p. 6). Women between the ages of twenty and thirty-nine years old should have a CBE by a doctor or medical professional ever three years. Women forty and older should have a CBE and mammogram every year.

My thoughts drift. I'm not paying attention to the breast exam Betsy is doing because I don't need to. We already exchanged kind words and now she's doing something she knows how to do – she doesn't need me. *While I'm in this building, I'll stop for a bite to eat, swing by a colleague's office, and then back to my department for my next meeting. It's my turn to pick up little Danny (my three-year-old son) from daycare tonight. What shall I prepare for dinner?* Betsy's voice breaks in, "How long has this been here?"

..."Do you do a monthly self-exam?" Yes, I lie.

I lift my head from the pillow to look her in the eye. "How long has what been here?" I inquire. Betsy places the fingers of my right hand over hers where they are rubbing a hard lump, south of my nipple, under my left breast where the breast meets the chest wall. "Uh, hmmm, I don't know. I've never felt that before." The truth is, I wouldn't know how long it has been there because I can't recall the last time I did a BSE.

Betsy asks, "Do you do a monthly self-exam?"

"Yes," I lie. *Why lie about that?* If I told the truth, that I don't check regularly and I can't recall the last time I checked, would she be alarmed and would it make a difference? And when I actually do them, I am standing in the shower and neglect the on-my-back position. Oh well, I'll do them correctly from now on. *Famous last words.* Naturally, I preach to my teenage daughters about doing it at the same time every month, but I don't do it because breast cancer isn't going to happen to me.

...She places my breasts, one at a time, on the clear plastic tray portion of the large floor-to-ceiling machine.

Betsy calls in another nurse for a second touch, "Hmmm, un huh, I feel it. None anywhere else in this breast though...[pause]...or the other." The clinical examination is soon over and they both tell me not to worry, but see what the mammogram shows and see my GYN. I carry my personal belongings into the next room where the x-ray equipment is located.

The technician greets me. She is wearing a floral-print lab coat. I recognize her from last year and the year before. Whew, her hands are never cold. I stand in front of the machine. "Step here," she summons, "Move in a little closer and place your right hand here. Good." I proudly demonstrate that I know what to do in case she doesn't remember me. I can show her that I've done this before, because I'm good. I am smart enough to get annual mammograms. "Now, put your left hand over here. That's it."

She stands behind me and leans in. She places my breasts, one at a time, on the clear plastic tray portion of the large floor-to-ceiling machine. She continues to flop each one around a few times and smooth it outward in order to get the most breast tissue onto the tray. This is the part that some women feel put off by. It doesn't bother me since I know that the more breast that there is on the tray, the more tissue there is to examine. I always want the radiologist to see as much breast tissue as possible so I can get a true, clean bill of health.

The technician proceeds to move the upper tray downward using a foot pedal. The two trays coming together press my breast as flat as possible. We've all seen photographs and magazine spreads filled with lovely, perky, full breasts. In recent years, since plastic surgery and implants are on the rise, the phrase, "Those can't be real," has become synonymous with viewing marvelous cleavage. Even those large and perky breasts can be flattened and mashed into amazingly thin proportions. This is the part that almost all women are put off by. As the machine clicks to the technician's foot pedal signals, I watch the numeric counter and wince as the number goes lower, indicating the temporary thinness of my breast for the benefit of the x-ray. "I think last time I was able to endure two point something," I boast. *Whoa. It hurts a little.* As a young girl, I was told you could get breast cancer if someone or something hit your breast too hard and now my breasts are receiving intentional trauma. Ironic. She follows the same process for the upper-to-lower tray view for the other breast, then side-to-side tray views of each breast - four pictures in all.

She reminds me that a radiologist will read the films from the day's mammograms and CHS will get back to me. When I tell her about the lump under my left breast, she supports what the nurses said by suggesting a visit to my gynecologist even if the mammogram report comes back negative. I walk back to my office with only mild concern. I have a brief and strange thought: *If I stop to talk to someone and mention that I just came from CHS for my annual mammogram, that person might remember that information if they hear I have breast cancer, "Wendi has what? Gee, I just saw her on the way from her mammogram." Kind of like when you hear someone passed away and you say, " He died? I was just talking to him last week."* This lump will turn out to be nothing, yet I'll feel better when an expert confirms it. From my office, I call my husband, Dan.

Dan is my childhood sweetheart. When I was little, my neighbor and childhood friend, Nicki, invited me to her third birthday party. Nicki is Dan's cousin. Her parents have reel-to-reel home footage in grainy black and white of Dan and me eating cake and Neapolitan ice cream. When I was about ten years old, Nicki's family moved to a different neighborhood and I lost touch with Dan. When he and I were fifteen, and he was attending the local Boys Club with my brother, we reconnected. At fifteen, we saw each other through different lenses than when we were ten. Soon after, we began dating. We married when we were twenty-five.

With an intentionally casual tone, I tell him about my lump. *No sense in worrying him…he may want answers that I don't have.*

It is Wednesday.

MY HUSBAND, THE LUMP, AND ME

That evening, Dan is interested in seeing the lump. I lie on my back, place both hands on both breasts and move them upward in the direction of my collarbone. "Wow," he says, "You can see it when you are lying on your back."

"Really? Y'know something? You can see the lump and I can *feel* the lump while I'm on my back, yet it isn't visible when I'm upright and I can't feel it when I'm standing up." *Ah ha, I can let go of the guilt now. Even if I did do a BSE last month, I probably wouldn't have felt it since I usually did my infrequent examinations while standing in the shower.* I touch the lump whenever I think about it. It is hard, about an inch in diameter, and doesn't move around. My skin moves over top of it but it stays in the same place. It almost feels like a piece of my rib or that it is sitting on a rib.

"Does it hurt?" Dan asks.

"I don't think so."

"What kind of an answer is that?" he retorts, "Either it hurts or it doesn't." In retrospect, I know he was a little unsettled at this point. When he's looking for answers and can't get them, he gets frustrated.

I try to articulate what I meant, "Well, I mean, it didn't hurt before…at least I don't recall it hurting before the clinical exam. The under wires on my bra press against it and it was never sore, but I think it's getting sore now because I've been touching it a lot."

On Thursday, CHS called me to tell me that radiology contacted them about the "abnormal" films from Wednesday's mammograms and mine wasn't among them. *Okay, one hurdle cleared. The lump is probably nothing. But, it's there… so what could it be?*

I contact CHS on Friday. All films and reports were back and nothing showed up on my mammogram. *"Negative."* Yesss. They recommend I see my gynecologist.

> **Tip 3** Some lumps do not show on mammograms for various reasons. Do not ignore a lump. If it is a cancerous tumor, the size of it at the time of diagnosis is strongly associated with prognosis. According to The American Cancer Society the value of seeking care at the first sign of a new symptom can not be underestimated and could mean the difference in whether treatment is successful, as well as a greater range of treatment options. See your gynecologist if a lump has been detected.

I call Dr. C's office (Dr. C is my gynecologist). I am told that it would be okay if I schedule an appointment with her following my upcoming vacation. We schedule Tuesday, August 15.

In retrospect, I wish I'd scheduled with her sooner. Perhaps I could have come home from vacationing at our beach house for an appointment. I wonder, if I had progressed some steps faster, or not forgotten about the original mammogram, would I have found myself in an advanced stage of cancer?

WHY DO MONTHLY BREAST SELF-EXAMS?

Thinking back to my last annual GYN appointment, which took place just two months ago, on June 1, I recall Dr. C performing a routine clinical exam. She asked me, as she always did, whether I do the monthly exam. As you would expect, I fibbed and said, "Yes." I never thought I'd get breast cancer and so I didn't make the time to do the exams. Everyone stresses the importance of doing them and I didn't want anyone to think I neglected important things (*even though I did*).

At the June appointment, Dr. C found nothing in either breast and proceeded with my gynecological physical. Did I sabotage myself by saying "yes"? Could a small lump have been tangible, but since I said "yes" did she trust my exams and feel she didn't need to be as thorough? If I had said "no", would she have checked even more carefully and detected a small lump? I feel the guilt of telling an untruth.

If I had done my monthly BSEs I might have found my nearly one-inch lump sooner. If I'd found it sooner, the cancer might not have spread to my lymph nodes.

Tip 4 Do a monthly BSE a few days after your period ends. This is the time of the month when your breasts are the least complicated and least likely to be swollen and tender. Mark your calendar if it helps. If you are postmenopausal, do your BSE on the same day of every month. Use a day of the month like the 1st or 15th, or use a monthly marker, e.g., if you get paid once a month, do not open your paycheck until you've done your exam.

It is important that you get to know your breasts. Do your exams upright and on your back. In fact, go to www.breastcancer.org for specific instructions and positions. You may think that doing a BSE is daunting, but remember – you don't need to be responsible for knowing everything, just the changes. Sue C, a nurse at AZ, uses a car analogy: When you first learned to drive you concentrated heavily on every aspect of it. After awhile, you drove on autopilot because it came naturally, and you even talked on the phone or put on makeup while doing so. BSEs work the same way. The first few times you do them, you focus on every lump and bump. At some point, if you do them monthly, your breast patterns, lumps, bumps, size, and feel will register between your fingertips and your brain. You'll be able to do the exams and recognize changes. It is a good idea to recognize what is normal for you and then feel for changes. If you notice a change, talk to your doctor.

Did you know that men get breast cancer also? Most people think of breast cancer as a woman's disease, but men get it too. According to the American Cancer Society (www.cancer.org) about 1,300 to 1,500 new cases are diagnosed in American men each year. It is expected that, in 2005, almost 1,700 new cases will be reported. *Is it on the rise? Or, are more men finding breast lumps and going to their doctors than before?* Since breast cancer for men is rare, little research has been done. Many men do not know they can get it (Giordano, Gupta, et.al.).

Tip 5 Men, you should report unusual breast symptoms to your doctor. Common symptoms are enlarged breasts, a lump in the breast, or nipple inversion or discharge. And, as a precaution, report an enlarged lymph node to your doctor, especially if it is under your arm.

We drive to our beach house in lower Delaware on Friday evening. On Monday morning, Dan rises early and heads home for a few days of work (he doesn't have as much vacation time as I do). He is a construction manager for a general contracting company, EDiS. He manages the construction of buildings. He enjoys what he does and I am happy that he is doing something he not only enjoys, but also is quite good at.
My best friend, "Lisa from New York", and her family drive to their beach house too. Theirs is located a few doors from ours (we planned it that way). Dan and I met Lisa and her husband, Charles, when we were on our respective honeymoons in Hawaii. It was destiny; we became instant friends. We are from Delaware; they are from New York; we met thousands of miles away. We have always been very compatible; we mutually planned and raised our children. For years, Dan and I and the kids visited New York and they and their kids visited Delaware, for entire weekends. Typically, we take an annual vacation together. I always look forward to being with them. It is wonderful to be in good company.

Dan and I have three teenage daughters. Our firstborn, Christine is a brunette, like her dad, with a dark complexion and a pretty smile. She is an eighteen-year-old college freshman. "Teen" as we call her, is a nurturing young woman who rarely has an unkind word to say about anyone. Andrea is nineteen months younger than Christine. "Andge" is an energetic seventeen-year-old who is often told she looks like Kirsten Dunst, the actress in the Spiderman movies. She and I resemble each other (we are both blonde, except I don't look like the actress). Oftentimes, when she is organizing something, I see me in her.

Our youngest daughter, fifteen-year-old Michele, looks a lot like Christine (and Dan). "Shelly" has mastered the art of keeping her thoughts to herself, but whenever she does share them I am constantly astounded at how insightful and perceptive she is.

And then there's little Danny, our three-year-old. A few years back, Dan and I hit some bumps in the marital road. When we sorted them out, the girls convinced us to celebrate by having another child. (We enjoyed raising children, and I loved being pregnant, so the convincing was minimal.) When we found out our expected baby was a boy, Dan was beside himself. The girls were adolescents and Dan said on several occasions that, as much as he tried, he couldn't make heads or tails of the girls some days. While observing teenage daughter altercations, things that were crystal clear to me left him looking dumbfounded. Having a little boy around would ease his distress.

I have been thinking about something Andrea said a few days earlier. She said it was about time for our family to get a boat, like the one we had when she and her sisters were younger. She said little Danny should be able to enjoy boating in his childhood just as they did in theirs.

We recently received the home equity line approval and the upcoming college tuition payments were planned out. We can afford a little indulgence. I convince Dan, and I top off my case by saying, "Besides, you never know what could happen. We should have some fun now and not wait for later." How prophetic.

I walk in to a marine dealership at 8:30 in the morning on Thursday and say, "I want to buy the boat you have for sale outside and have it in the water by 4:00 this afternoon. Can we agree on a price?"

At 3:45 we are leveling-out on the surface of the Rehoboth Bay, feeling the salty spray on our skin. *A small piece of Heaven.*

Tip 6 Sometimes, doing something a little out of the ordinary is a nice treat, whether you're sick or not. Treat yourself. Oh, and use caution to avoid overspending on too many luxuries. Chances are you'll live through this and have to face the bills you incurred when you thought you wouldn't!

On the Tuesday following vacation, I hand an envelope to my gynecologist, Dr. C, now that I am in her examining room. It contains reports and x-ray films of past mammograms that the CHS Administrative Coordinator gave me. She reviews the information and does a clinical exam. Concerned, she writes down three names on a piece of paper. "I believe you should see a surgeon. There are many good ones out there, but I recommend these three. Each is good and kind. You'll like any of them. My husband and I met with this one last night [*she points to one of the names*]…Tom is doing my husband's surgery." She connects eyes with me and proceeds, "If you can't get an appointment by the end of next week, call me and I'll contact each one. I want you to see someone soon." She smiles a very reassuring smile and I am instantly reminded of why I chose her as my OB-GYN seventeen years ago.

Dr. C would tell my mother and me months later what it's like from her perspective as a physician:

> *It is difficult when you suspect something is amiss. And, it is truly devastating when you hear bad news from a patient or have to give bad news to a patient. You sit with the person in one room, and when you are finished you step outside, into the hallway, and try to put on a happy face in*

about three seconds for the next patient who's waiting in another examining room. Every patient expects you to have a smile on your face when you see her. That is the right thing to do, but in some circumstances it is not easy.

COORDINATING WITH MY GYN AND CONTACTING A SURGEON

I walk outside her waiting room and decide not to go back to work to make these calls. I will make them here. I am not thinking anything about cancer possibilities. I figure I'll have a little scare, it'll turn out to be nothing and life will go on as usual. All I care about now is contacting these surgeons and putting this "scare" behind me. If I don't get an appointment before next week, I'll walk back into Dr. C's office and tell her. I ask the receptionist if there is a phone I can use and a phone directory. The phone is being repaired and the directory is missing. "Thank you, anyway," I say to him. I sit down in a chair, whip out my trusty cell phone and dial a colleague, "Andréa, I need your help. Please look up three numbers for me."

Within minutes I have what I need. I call one who is the head of a breast center, or something like that. *Gee, Dr. C recommends the best. I hope she's right about their bedside manners.* He isn't available for an appointment until September 9. I call another on my list. She is an assistant or second-in-command or something to the head guy. She doesn't have an opening until September 8. *Oh dear. One more on the list. What are the chances?* "Hello. My name is Wendi. My GYN recommended that I call your office. I have a lump in my breast and she wants me to see a surgeon by the end of this week. A tiny white lie on my part. Can you please fit me in today or tomorrow?" Eureka, I have a scheduled time tomorrow morning.

Next, I call my husband to inform him. Now that I have a plan, I can return to work and get focused. On my way to my car, I see a coworker who's entering the medical office building that I am leaving. We exchange hellos. *Oh brother, here's another one who will say, "She has breast cancer? Gee, I just saw her the other day."*

On Wednesday, I go to Dr. M's office and find that my dear, sweet husband showed up in time for the appointment. "You didn't have to come today," I say. I'm really, really glad he did.

Once inside, I discover that the doctor is middle-aged and Indian. *Can't anything work in my favor here?* I have a phobia of middle-aged, Indian men. When I was ten or eleven years old, a neighbor's brother-in-law who was visiting from another country sexually molested me. He was middle-aged and had a very dark complexion. I'll never forget the details

...Can't anything work in my favor here?

of that occurrence, but I don't think about them unless I am reminded. And, I haven't thought about the incident in many years. Seeing Dr. M and knowing that I will need to put my trust in him is a reminder. *Ohmygosh, one of the things that man did over thirty years ago was touch my chest...what IS it about female chests and breasts?!! Oh dear, I wouldn't be here today if it weren't for my breasts. These darn things. Stop panicking.* I am acquainted with many women and men of Indian heritage, and they are wonderful and worthy of my respect and love. But I am still panicking. *Why is the phobia haunting me now? It must be my sudden vulnerability about my breasts that has returned me to that same helpless childhood place and I must get over my phobia quickly...QUICKLY...here comes the doctor.*

Dan, Diane (Dr. M's assistant), and I watch the doctor as he looks at the reports I brought. He does a clinical exam (I am a little uptight), feels the lump (I am tense), and then he covers me and offers his hand so I can sit up (and I relax). Amazing how a small humane gesture will put a person at ease. He puts the recent x-ray film in the light-up thing on the wall and flips the switch to the "on" position while I put on my shirt. I tell him that several years ago, before my son was born, a mammogram picked up possible calcification in the same area.. AZ recommended that I go to another facility to get a stronger mammogram. "Hmmm," he says. He looks closely at the film using a magnifying glass. "See this?" He puts his arm around me in a protective way and I relax. He urges me to look into the glass, "These tiny white dots look like calcification. They could be *something*. Do you see them?" I nod and say yes, but I can't actually see them because I'm too nervous to get close enough to see through the magnifying glass. "They are in the position of your lump. The lump doesn't show on the x-ray because it is not in the breast tissue that is on the film. These dots are worrisome."

Worrisome. Oh dear.

Excisional Biopsy (aka "Lumpectomy")

Dr. M tells us that a biopsy is in order. I need to have an outpatient procedure. "Doctor," I say, "If you find cancer when you are in there, please remove my breasts. I've always wondered why women, who find out they have breast cancer, think twice about removing them. Not me. If I had cancer, I wouldn't think twice."

"One step at a time," he says. "This is just a biopsy." *Oh good. I must not have cancer or else he'd take my request into consideration and acknowledge it.*

I'd probably have to sign some papers that state my wishes. He's not asking me to do that so he must not think I have cancer.

Marcia, his office assistant, makes a few calls while Dan and I sit in the waiting room. We can hear her conversations. She is sweet yet firm. In about ten minutes she tells us the details of my surgery that is scheduled for tomorrow. *Wow, GYN's office on Tuesday, surgeon's office on Wednesday, surgery on Thursday. Bing, bang, boom.*

I stop at the lab for presurgical blood work, and then Dan and I each return to our jobs.

In retrospect, I wonder if Dr. M suspected that my lump was cancerous. Since my diagnosis, I've read that a few breast cancer survivors observed some dimpling when they squeezed their lump. Did my lump dimple? Did it have any characteristics that cancerous lumps might sometimes have? Had Dr. M seen anything like it before? As a professional, he could not give me any indication of any speculation he may have had. He needed to do the biopsy first, and then wait for the pathology report.

I now know that Dr. M is a very kind man and I have no need to fear him because of one awful man I met over thirty years ago (and my irrational phobia). I think I'll take a leap of faith and put my trust in him. I am so sorry, Dr. M for being uneasy at first. I didn't mean to misjudge you... even though it was for only a minute or two...this is all so overwhelming and I panicked. Thanks to my cancer ordeal, I got over my phobia.

My manager and colleagues at AZ are very understanding about the urgency of my surgery. I call my sisters and brother from my office, and leave it up to Dan to contact his family. I intentionally do not tell my mom, because I don't want to leave her for the night with unanswered questions. I plan to tell her tomorrow, when the surgery is complete. I remember some feedback I had received about the way I handled something like this in the past and I didn't want to repeat the mistake. I want to inform other folks as efficiently as possible so I craft the following e-mail:

To all,

As you now know, the Christmas before last I was in the hospital, but didn't tell anyone. I felt bad when friends and colleagues heard about it from other sources, but when I was suffering from the symptoms of inflammatory bowel disease, it felt weird to tell anyone about it – ugh, and I didn't want sympathy or hospital visits. I wasn't quite sure what to say at the time, so I said nothing. I learned a lesson: Don't leave certain people out of the loop about important stuff.

Which brings me to the main point of this e-mail, I had my annual mammogram and examination at AstraZeneca Medical and they found a lump. I just came back from the surgeon about an hour ago who said it was "worrisome" and scheduled me to have it removed tomorrow at 2:00. After that, we'll wait to hear from the pathologist. I hope to be back to the office on Monday. Will keep in touch.

I clear my inbox and to-do list for tomorrow, record a voice mail greeting that says "I'm out of the office on Thursday" and head for home.

I take a shower before going to bed and touch the lump. *Gosh, I could be touching cancer! This could be it. They say cancer is something you can't see when it's in your body...a silent invader...but this could be it. I could be touching cancer.*

Thursday morning I constantly remind myself not to eat or drink. Habits are not easily interrupted and I reach for the coffeepot and the water cooler two or three times. Dan and I leave the house and go to the surgicenter where there are about twenty people in the room. *So, there must be ten people about to have outpatient surgery and each has a caregiver. Assembly line surgery. Interesting.* A kindly woman goes over my personal information, and then whispers something in Dan's ear. I later find out that she told him there was a coffee and beverage station nearby and that she didn't want me to feel put off because I couldn't have anything to eat or drink. "Mrs. Pedicone?" We are being led to a room where I will remove all my clothes, put on slipper socks and two gowns - one that opens in the back and another that opens in the front. *Two gowns, not one. Good. Now I won't have to walk the halls with one hand behind me holding the robe closed so no one will be privy to my awesome butt. Actually, I don't have an awesome butt. I just added that in because I'm getting a little nervous. I never had an awesome butt, unless you count the beauty-is-in-the-eye-of-the-beholder concept – only I'm not sure who the beholder is.*

I am given a black marker so I can place an X on the breast that is getting the excisional biopsy (aka lumpectomy). Doesn't "lumpectomy" sound like a fabricated word by someone attempting to speak surgi-talk, in the same way a person who doesn't know Spanish might attempt to communicate with a Spanish-speaking person by saying something hokey like, "Can I use your cell phon-o?" or "I have a flat tire-o." *Hmmm. On second thought...* "Lumpectomy" sounds like when a person describes a sickness from sitting a lot and they call it "butt-er-itus."

My vital signs are taken, and then we wait in another sitting room for a few minutes. Dr. M comes in to see us, fills us in on the details then says;

"I'll see you on the other side." He gives me a hug and kisses the side of my head. *Oh dear. He kissed my head. He knows something I don't know. He's taking pity on me. I'm dying, aren't I?*

...Oh dear... he knows something I don't know... I'm dying, aren't I?

I am told to say "so long" to Dan and put on the hair cap. A nurse walks me to operating room number seven. Two women wearing scrubs, hair caps, and face shields welcome me. One asks me a question but I can't understand her because my ears are covered, her mouth is covered, and the room is filled with some noise like air conditioning and metal implements being placed on metal trays. One tells me to step up on the stool and lie down on the table. I always wanted to see operating rooms, but this is a little intimidating. I am lying on my back, staring at the ceiling beyond the huge lights, which I know will be turned on to shine light on my chest once I am sedated. I can feel my arms being placed on outstretched table wings and strapped down. I feel my legs being strapped down too. "It's chilly in here," I comment, "Will I be able to keep my slipper socks on?

"We'll do better than that," a voice says, "We'll put warm blankets on you." *Ahhhh, they feel so good. I feel the intravenous being inserted. Ouch.*

One nurse asks me a question and I begin to chatter before going under. "If it weren't for my employer and the annual clinical exam, it would have been awhile longer before I would have detected this lump...Man, I've GOT to get better about doing my monthly BSEs...Shouldn't I be feeling woozy?...Don't start cutting until I'm under...Are you administering Diprivan...My best girlfriend works in an operating room and she says Diprivan is good stuff....It is an AstraZeneca product...That's the company I work for..." CLUNK! Next thing I know I am being awakened in post op. *How embarrassing.*

Done! What I previously referred to, as "assembly-line surgery" was simply efficient outpatient surgery involving many doctors and their patients, available operating rooms, and effective use of resources.

Tip 7 Be sure to have someone with you at this time. I've talked to several people who were informed during post-op recovery that cancer had been discovered during surgery. Sometimes, your head isn't clear enough to understand details. The value of having someone with you to listen or take notes is immeasurable. Not everyone is going to have someone, but you should try.

> If this is not possible, take a tape recorder and inform a nurse before surgery that you would like to have it available after surgery in the event the doctor discusses findings with you.

Dan drives me home and makes a few phone calls. I call my mother. She's eighty-two. I take her to the beauty salon every week to have her hair done. "Hey Mom, what's up? Oh nothing, just lying on the couch. I had some outpatient surgery today. No big deal. I'm fine. Sure, I'll take you to the hairdresser tomorrow, regular time. See you then." *No sense worrying her.*

My mom. She is one half of a parental partnership who raised me with love and a measure of frugality. She is outgoing, big-hearted and a good sport. Mom enjoys surprising people with happy things. She also doesn't mind being the center of our pranks. I have a plethora of wonderful childhood memories because of her. One is bike riding on the boardwalk in Wildwood, New Jersey on warm vacation mornings, and another one is home made eggnog. She would crack an egg and pour several ingredients into a special container, and then make me giggle by shaking her butt…and the container.

When Dad passed away, Dan and I invited her to live with us. She declined. It's just as well, I suppose. Had she lived with us, we would all be converted to believing that our toilet paper rolls were on backwards and that the best way to walk the stairs is to do it with our legs wide apart so we don't wear the carpet in the center.

Later in the evening, our neighbor, Cammy, is outside wearing summertime attire and she walks over to catch up with Dan. He is doing yard work. Cammy and her husband, Bob, have a daughter named Kala who is a best friend to our daughter, Michele. Through Kala, Cammy knew I had surgery. Dan proceeds to tell her about my biopsy. Racing into the house and looking frazzled, he says, "You know how when you are talking about a body part you tend to look at that body part?"

"Come again?"

"If you're describing something about your ankle to someone, you look at their ankle. Right?"

"Okaaaay…"

"Well, Cammy must think I'm a louse because I was telling her about your surgery and realized I was staring at her breasts the entire the time. *He might not have been embarrassed if she were older and less attractive, but she is our age, looks ten years younger, is extremely attractive, resembles Paula Abdul and, oh by the way, has fabulous cleavage. The first time I met her I said, "Those can't be real."*

The next day, Dan calls her on the phone and apologizes. I swear I can hear her laughter being carried by the summer breeze into my kitchen.

Friday morning I send a follow-up e-mail from home:

Hello everyone,

Thanks for your good wishes, prayers and kind words of support. Surgery went well and, aside from some tenderness at the site, I feel unbelievably good today. Next step is to receive favorable news from pathology, which will be by the end of next week (hopefully by Thursday). I'll be in the office on Monday. Have a good weekend.

It is Saturday and we are relaxing on the boat. The pier at The Rusty Rudder is a very popular place in Dewey Beach; we are seeing so many folks and old friends. Among them are Jack and Cheryl, a couple we came to know several years ago through our church. Cheryl is now an ovarian cancer patient. She is looking very relaxed and upbeat even though she is thin and wearing a baseball cap to cover her hairless head. She was always very beautiful, and looks beautiful still. My bandages cross the left side of my chest and can't be totally covered by my bathing suit. Since it is obvious I had surgery recently, I share my concern over the breast biopsy. I feel terrible that Cheryl is going through a cancer ordeal. Please don't let it be me, too. *I don't want cancer.*

THE FOLLOW-UP APPOINTMENT

I am scheduled to go for a one-week follow-up with Dr. M on Thursday, August 26.

On Tuesday, however I receive a call from Marcia. She tells me that the doctor needs to see me a day earlier due to a surgery he needs to perform Thursday. "Okay, we'll be there tomorrow afternoon at 4:00."

It has been almost a month since the CHS nurse at AZ discovered a lump in my breast. I've had it biopsied and I am fairly calm. *I dare not explore my inner feelings or think too deeply about it or else I might find some hidden fear. Perhaps I am not quite so calm on the inside.*

CHAPTER
2

DIAGNOSIS:
BREAST CANCER

(Danny and me)

The future is so bright I have to wear shades.

Author Unknown

Every cancer patient remembers the day he or she was diagnosed. August 25, 2004 is my diagnosis date. I will never forget it.

Wednesday, August 25 - I awake with a sudden feeling of butterflies in my gut. I haven't thought about the possibility of bad news much lately. *Why now?*

I am in a meeting to determine roles for this year's United Way campaign at AZ. I'm so flattered that my manager's manager, Nancy, believes I can drive a silent auction to raise funds. I want to say the proper things in this meeting so she will be confident with her decision, but the words aren't coming; I have something niggling in the back of my mind. *What is it? Oh, I remember, this afternoon's appointment.*

As soon as the meeting is over, I dash out to find an available phone. "Hello, Marcia? Hi, this is Wendi Pedicone. I have an appointment with Dr. M this afternoon at 4:00. Does the doctor have the results of the pathology report yet?"

"Not yet, but he will." She assures me.

"Will you call me if he doesn't get them in time? I don't want to come in if..."

"Don't worry."

"...If he doesn't have the report, only to get called back tomorrow or Friday. If you call me to come in another day, I'll know it's bad news and the drive to your office will be unbearable."

"You're worrying too much. We'll have the report by the time you get here."

It's 3:50 and I park my vehicle in front of Dr. M's office. I see Dan's vehicle. How wonderful, he's already here. Oh boy, do I love his dependability. We go into the examining room. I undress from the waist up. Diane and Dr. M smile when they enter the room. Dr. M peels the tape from the incision under the nipple of my left breast. He does a post-surgical site inspection and comments on how nicely the incision is healing. He places new tape over the top of the cut and offers his hand so I can sit up. I realize that I'd forgotten about my cancer fear. *I'll just get dressed and we'll go.* Dr. M places his hand on mine, looks into my eyes and says, "We found cancer. Get dressed and I'll meet you in the next room." With that, he

"We found cancer. Get dressed and I'll meet you in the next room."

walks out. I guess after twenty years of doing this, he found that delivering the news quickly and walking out is best.

I become conscious that Diane is already gone from the examining room. Where did she go? When did she leave? Dan and I are the only ones in the room. I am watching myself as an out-of-body-experience. I go about my usual routine of changing the table paper (my mother taught me to always make my bed). I stop, look at Dan and say, "Are you okay? I can't get a deep breath." *In through the nose. Ffffff. Out through the mouth, fffffssshhh.* He doesn't answer. He is blankly staring straight ahead.

I don't know how, but I am dressed. We are walking into a room that has a couch, chairs, lamps and a coffee table. My eyes become fixated on the breast cancer pamphlets arranged on the coffee table. *They knew. They all knew. They all knew before I did. They prepared this stuff for me. They watched me walk in...knowing that I have breast cancer. What did they think when they saw me? Did they feel sorry for me? Did they put their heads down and did each give me a 'tch, tch, tch, poor thing', under her breath? I feel betrayed.* Suddenly, the doctor is sitting on the couch. *I don't remember how he got here. Did he walk in with us, or after us?* Dan and I are on either side of him. I am missing in-between details. It's like we are moving under a strobe light, one moment we are in the exam room, then I see literature on the table, the next we are sitting with the doctor.

I would later realize that betrayal was an unfounded reaction...*how obtuse.*

For the next half hour, the doctor slowly and carefully takes us through information and explanations. "You have two kinds of breast cancer; invasive ductal carcinoma (ID) and ductal carcinoma in situ (DCIS)...when we removed the tumor we couldn't get clear margins." *I have what? TWO kinds of cancer? HelloOOoo, are there any long straws in the house? Am I pulling all the short ones, or what?* He draws and writes on lined paper as he talks. At some point, I sit on the coffee table to face him. "Please, doctor, I can't concentrate any more on what you are saying. I have a couple of questions in my brain that are stealing my focus from what you are telling us." He obliges me, gives me time to ask my questions and answers each one. My first question was, "Did I do something wrong?"

"No," he said, "but you live in Delaware and Delaware has a high breast cancer rate." Dan is sitting, silent.

While Delaware has many things to be proud of, its mortality and incidence rates of breast cancer are not among them (DBCC, Inc.). According to the American Cancer Society, in the year 2000, Delaware ranked in the country as follows:

- #2 for overall cancer mortality rates
- #1 for the incidence of in situ breast cancer
- #6 for the incidence of invasive breast cancer
- #6 for breast cancer mortality rates

And currently, as of December 2004, Delaware has the fifth highest cancer rate in the United States.

Breast cancer is the second leading cause of cancer deaths in women today (after lung cancer) and is the most common cancer among women, excluding nonmelanoma skin cancers. According to· the World Health Organization, more than 1.2 million people will be diagnosed with breast cancer this year worldwide (www.imagines.com/breasthealth, 4/11/2005).

This day, August 25, 2004, I was told I have breast cancer. The events are indelibly imprinted in my mind. Forever.

Later, I would look back and wonder what was going through my husband's mind:

"I was awestruck. Sure, I knew that cancer was an option. I felt like I was being pulled into a vortex. I had so many questions. Oh my. What if this… What if that… What can you say?"

My poor husband has married damaged goods. I used to worry that he might feel like he married a factory defect because of the way I suffered with migraines in the early years of our marriage. When they came they negatively impacted my interactions with Dan and our three little girls, Christine, Andrea and Michele, until I tried Zomig®. *Ah, I got my life back.* Then, almost two years ago, I had become increasingly sick in November and December. I took a turn for the worse on Christmas Eve. Dan drove me to the hospital Christmas morning after little Danny, then twenty months old, opened the last of his Christmas presents. I was in the hospital until January 3rd. Inflammatory Bowel Disease. *Ugh.* Another defect. Now cancer. *This stinks.*

I think I am a little too shocked, perturbed, or angry to cry. Then again, maybe I just want to get this problem fixed fast and there's no time for tears. Whatever the reason, the tears aren't coming.

COMMUNICATING THE NEWS

As a communications analyst, I help project teams and departments plan their internal communications (what, when, to whom, how, etc.). I look up at Dan and say, "We'll have to decide on our communication plan."

He looks at me strangely and says, "Wen, you aren't at work." *It did sound work-ish, didn't it?*

I smile. "I mean, when and how are we going to tell the girls, our sisters and brothers and friends?"

Dr. M is handing me his drawings and notes, plus the pamphlets. I realize we've been together for an hour and a half. *Don't he and his office staff want to go home for dinner?* Diane, Marcia and Dr. M are still here. It's 5:30 and they are still here. None of them made us feel that our time was limited. What humanitarians they are. Little do I know that I will become very close to each of them in the coming months. "Marcia will get all your tests scheduled. We need to know if the cancer has spread. Different cancers move to different parts of the body. We know that breast cancer tends to go to lungs, liver and bone, and then the brain. We'll check those places."

> **Tip 8** As soon as you get the chance, use the Internet to find out in plain language what in the world the "lab coats" are talking about. The Imaginis website (www.imaginis.com) is a good place to start.

Dr. M tells me he has done this surgery with a particular surgeon for years, but that surgeon's schedule can be difficult to coordinate with. There is another doctor that he likes to work with also. I tell him that time is of the utmost importance to me. I don't want to wait. So long as Dr. M is happy with either, I'll take whoever is available first.

Marcia is on hold while scheduling tests. I ask, "Would you mind if I step into the hallway to make a call?"

I step into the hall, take a deep breath and dial my sister Deb, who lives in Denver. I can describe her using several four-letter words: Amla, tofu, yoga and miso. She is an amazingly open-minded person. She'll handle this.

She knew I was having my follow-up appointment tonight. She's probably expecting good news. "Deb," I begin. "I have breast cancer. That's all I can tell you right now. I'm standing outside the doctor's office. He, Dan and I have been in his office for a while. He explained a lot to us, but my head isn't clear. I can't think, so please don't ask me any questions. [Pause.] Well, they are scheduling tests for me right now, and I better go back in." She respects my request and doesn't ask a thing. She tells me she loves me and we end the call.

Next, I call my other sister, Vicki. She inherited the worry-card from our Dad and this isn't going to be easy to tell her because I know she will be very concerned. She too knew I was going to the doctor tonight. There's no answer on her end and I don't think it's appropriate to leave a message. So, I don't.

I walk back in the doctor's office. Marcia gives me a paper with instructions for tests, test locations and instructions for each. She also gives me an appointment card with a day and time to see the plastic surgeon, Dr. D. "You'll have to meet with him and decide which type of reconstruction you want. Dr. M will remove your breast and Dr. D will build the new one." *Interesting.* She smiles reassuredly, "Call us anytime. We'll get you through this." I exit the office but not before smiling pathetically to each of them. I catch Dr. M's eye and say, "Don't worry doctor, I don't have to kill the messenger."

Dan goes back to work to close up shop for the day and pick up little Danny from daycare. We know our daughters will be out for a while, so we have a little time to get our thoughts in order before meeting them at home. "I'm going back to my office." I announce, "I'd like to finish out a few things, pack up my laptop and bring it home. I'll need to work from home tomorrow, in between my tests."

During that time, Vicki sees a "missed call" on her phone. She calls me and leaves a message. Later, Vicki told me, "Because you didn't leave me a message, I knew."

I leave Dr. M's and begin my trek back to AZ. I see that my phone shows a "missed call" from Vicki. I call her. "Vic, I don't have time to talk because I'm driving…I HAVE CANCER."

[Silence.]

Somehow, the familiar route to the office becomes a blur. I've worked at AZ for almost twenty years and lived in Delaware all my life. I can't believe I can't find my way back. Vicki asks, "Are you by yourself? "

"Yes."

"Are you okay?"

"No. I'm lost."

"Keep driving until you see something, then tell me what you see." Over the phone, she navigates me back to my office.

Vicki's reaction in her words:

I stood in my kitchen for a second; oh my God, my sister has cancer. I walked out onto the deck and started crying. I flagged Duke [my husband] down…he was on the tractor cutting the lawn. He took a look at me and knew. I can't believe this. He hugged me while I cried. 'Oh man, I inherited Dad's side of the family, I have a pessimistic outlook. How can I be positive about this?' Little did I know that I would be part of Wendi's optimistic journey.

> *…I stood in my kitchen for a second, oh my God, my sister has cancer. How can I be positive about this? Little did I know that I would be part of Wendi's optimistic journey.*

Later, I found out that Vicki and Deb immediately connected following our conversation and began consoling each other and planning how they would support me.

It is 6:30 PM; I am sitting in my office at work. On a piece of paper I write names of immediate family and loved ones. I will tell each directly (by phone or in person). Then I make a second list of extended family members, friends and colleagues. I am trying to notify people as swiftly as possible and even though using e-mail is not as warm as hearing my voice, it is either e-mail for them or nothing at all. There's little time. Here goes:

Hello all,

I promised I would keep you informed, so here it is: I have breast cancer. Isn't that crummy? The tumor that was removed was aggressive. The pathology report tells us that it has spread, but we can't tell how far.

I will undergo tests to see if the cancer is anywhere else in my body. If it is, the plan is to have chemo first and surgery second. If it is not anywhere else, I'll have the mastectomy first (to remove my breast) and chemo second. No, we didn't catch it early, but it's treatable. I'll keep you posted when I can.

In retrospect, I was creating my communication plan; who to tell, how, when, etc. The difference between doing it as a job and doing it now is that double and triple checking it is essential in my job, and I didn't have time to double check this particular plan. An hour or two after my diagnosis, my head was filled with emotion and the clock was ticking; there was no time to think it through. For all I know, I offended folks, or missed telling someone altogether.

Looking at my first list of names I place a check next to each one once I figure the best way to tell them. The kids, tonight, check. My sisters, done, check. My brother, tonight, check. My mom, tomorrow morning in person, check. Dan's mom, tonight by phone, check. Lisa, by phone tonight, check. Jill, Andréa, and Joseph, tonight by phone, check. Town Hall Planning Committee, after their planning meeting tomorrow, check. I freeze. Oh dear, how am I going to tell Kayla. There are two Kayla's in my life. One is Kala J, Michele's good friend and our next-door neighbor. The other is Kayla H who is an extraordinarily special person to me. She and I met through the Adopt-a-School program at AZ seven years ago. Through this program, employees get to choose ways to support the elementary grade students. I got paired up with Kayla via the mentoring component of the program. She was in fourth grade. She is now in eleventh grade studying to become a nurse. Kayla is very much a part of my family and my life. The sticky part about telling her is, her mother died of cancer when Kayla was eight months old. How do I assure her that this doesn't have to turn out the same way? *How do I know this isn't going to turn out the same way?*

I dial her cell phone number and leave a message to call me when she gets a chance.

GATHERING INFORMATION

What is breast cancer anyway? The organs in our bodies are made up of cells. Cells age and die, so healthy cells divide and replace them. Sometimes there is damage during this process and cells begin to duplicate incorrectly and uncontrollably. Impaired cells that are not killed off fast enough by our Natural Killer cells form tumors. Some tumors are benign, but others destroy surrounding tissue or parts of the body. These tumors are malignant.

There are three common kinds of breast cancer; The two I have, DCIS and ID, and IL (Invasive Lobular carcinoma). Then there are less common types; inflammatory breast cancer, Paget's disease of the breast, and Medullary, Tubular and Papillary carcinomas (Kaelin, C p. 6-11). I want to understand more about my breast cancer.

I look through three breastcancer.org pamphlets given to me by Dr. M, *Your Guide to the Breast Cancer Pathology Report, Your Guide to Breast Cancer Treatment, and Overcoming Your Fears of Breast Cancer Treatment.* Each is in plain English, has helpful pictures, provides places for hand-written notes and contains a glossary of terms. I select the first pamphlet and set the other two aside for the time being. With the help of *Your Guide to the Breast Cancer Pathology Report*, I attempt to read mine. The pamphlet helps me decipher some of the information. My pathology report says:

> *The specimen is received in two parts, both received in the fresh state on ice and labeled with the patient's name....left breast mass consists of a rounded piece of indurated yellow-tan fibroadipose tissue weighing 24.7 grams and measuring 5.8 (superior to inferior) by 4.1 (medial to lateral) by 2 cm. (superior to inferior)...Starting at the superior margin, the specimen is...revealing bands of thickened fibrous tissue and adipose tissue....poorly demarcated area of dull tan induration...greatest dimension is 1.8 cm...small foci of DCIS are present and widely scattered within the tissue relatively far from the main tumor.*

> *Diagnosis...Infiltrating ductal carcinoma...grade 3 extending to the margin...lymphatic invasion and DCIS are also present...hormonal and HER-2/neu studies are pending...portions of breast tissue with invasive...*

I understand some of it, but not all of it. *It's CANCER for goodness sake. I don't have to comprehend it all right now. I'll understand more as each day unfolds.* I write on paper, "Call Dr. M's office. Ask for my GYN, plastic surgeon, primary care physician and gastroenterologist to be copied on all correspondence and reports."

Tip 9 Get a copy of your pathology report. Understanding it is critical, especially if you are the inquisitive type and foresee the possibility of doing some research or being part of the decision-making process. Your treatment is dependent on the details of your pathology report; chemotherapy, adjuvant therapy, how aggressive or "busy" your tumor is (prolific index), and even predicting chances of recurrence; etc.

Tip 10 Once you have a biopsy or pathology report, you may want to visit the Breast Cancer Decision guide site: www.bcdg.org. It was developed by the U.S. Department of Defense for individuals diagnosed with breast cancer and their family members. Or go to the Women's Information Network Against Breast Cancer, www.winabc.org and search on "pathology report." This site contains a "decision-making checklist" that is very useful.

Tip 11 Some people prefer to know only the basics. However we are in an information era and many of us prefer to know more. We want to work with medical professionals and be contributors to our good health. You might want to go to www.imaginis.com and print out the "Proactive Patient Checklist" written by Dr. Schroeder and edited by Alissa Czyz.

Tip 12 Keep all of your physicians in the loop. Technology makes it easy to send copies of reports to your doctors.

Tip 13 Ask your doctor if he has any of the pamphlets I mentioned or go to www.breastcancer.org and request them. This particular website is a wealth of knowledge, and the information in it is delivered in a soothing, supportive and easy-to-understand voice. The illustrations are extremely helpful. You will feel less apprehensive about your situation once you find breastcancer.org. The site was developed by Dr. Marisa Weiss, a practicing oncologist at Lankanau Hospital in Philadelphia, PA. It provides opinions from experts, medical details about breast cancer, and information on emotional and financial matters. There is a twenty-four hour chatroom where visitors may go for around-the-clock support and guidance; many women use this area to build their support network. Also the site has a Celebrity Talking Dictionary. Celebrities like Courtney Cox, Celine Dion, Whoopi Goldberg, David Hyde Pierce, and Al Roker to name a few, have recorded personal messages about their participation in the dictionary, and made recordings of the words associated with breast cancer and their definitions. Consider this website a crash course on breast cancer.

Tip 14 Ask your doctor about a relatively new type of testing performed by Genomic Health in California USA called Oncotype DX". It is a diagnostic test that quantifies the likelihood of recurrence in patients with early stage invasive breast cancer (in particular - stages I and II, node negative, estrogen receptor positive). Oncotype DX" looks at the expression profile of a panel of 21 genes from a tumor specimen. It can determine risk of recurrence, that is, which patients with early-stage breast cancer could be the ones to develop distant metastasis, some of whom might not have been identified without this knowledge and would not have had the opportunity to get more aggressive treatment to improve their odds of survival over the long term. It can also tell which patients are unlikely to have their breast cancer return, giving these patients the opportunity to avoid aggressive therapy which might have little effect if they so choose (Paik). Genomic Health's Oncotype DX" could provide information to better individualize the odds. It might seem strange to consider recurrence even before the first occurrence has been treated, but your oncologist and you can make some treatment decisions based on this knowledge. More explanation and information can be found in breastcancer.org, search word: "Oncotype" or by searching www.genomichealth.com for "Oncotype."

Note: Doing a search on the word "oncogene" on the breastcancer.org site will take you to the definition of an "oncogene" (related to HER-2/neu testing looking at abnormal genes that control cell growth). Oncogenes are not really related to Oncotype DX".

Not in the United States? There are wonderfully informative international websites.

Tip 15 If you are in the UK, www.breastcancercare.org.uk/home seems to be a comprehensive site. It says that it is "The UK's leading provider of breast cancer information and support." It offers active forums and chat rooms, plus a toll free number: 0808-800-6000. AnotherUKorganization, www.Cancer BACUP.org. UK/Home provides good information for all cancer patients and all types of cancer. The site is easy to navigate and offers a toll free number for calls. Two others you may want to try are www.cancerhelp.org.uk/ and www.cancerresearchuk.org/.

And finally, the National Health Service, www.nhs.uk can tell you how medical treatment is coordinated in the UK. (It is different than how we do things in the US. I met a woman from Canada who talked about a Canadian standard of treatment, which led me to realize that different countries have different treatment protocols. This could be due to varied health care systems and services.)

Tip 16 If you are in Sweden, the Swedish Association of Breast Cancer Societies offers some information, www.bro.org.se/english.html, and so does the European Organization for Research Treatment of Cancers, www.eortc.be/About/links/htm, Europa Donna (the European Breast Cancer Coalition) http://www.cancereurope.org/europadonna/, and www.cancerworld.org. Sweden is not an HMO country like the US; it follows a program referred to as 'social medicine', which makes medicine/healthcare very different. There don't seem to be as many advocacy group websites in the Sweden as there are in the US, but there are many scientific organizations' websites. Marie, a Swedish colleague who speaks the language, requested information from her library and they were able to find some recent articles in which she found out more of what sites would be good forums. From what she could gather, these two sites are primary ones (written in Swedish): http://www.cancerfonden.org/ and http://www.bro.org.se/.

Tip 17 Canada has several good web sites. One I viewed; www.cbcf.org, Canadian Breast Cancer Foundation, toll free number, 800-387-9816, has recent health information for breast cancer and a monthly BSE chart that you can download. Use your Internet search engine to search for references to Toben Anderson PhD. She is the National Spokesperson for Canadian Breast Cancer Foundation and Canadian Cancer Society. Follow this link: www.cancer.ca to the Canadian Cancer Society website. You can choose to view information in English or French, and by province. French speaking people can also go to www.phac-aspc.gc.ca.

Tip 18 I looked at websites in Canada, the UK and Sweden because I have friends and AZ colleagues in these countries. If you are located in any other country, use your Internet provider's Web Directory or a search engine like Yahoo! or Google to search on "cancer+country", for example, cancer+Mexico.

In the United States but do not speak English? Janet, a colleague of mine, asked the Delaware Breast Cancer Coalition, Inc. and was told, "Pretty much anything the Susan G. Komen Foundation has they can get in Spanish as well, and fact sheets from the 'Komen' website can be downloaded in Spanish."

Tip 19 For Spanish-speaking cancer patients and caregivers, The National Cancer Institute and the Susan G. Komen Foundation offer breast health and breast cancer information; Lo que usted necesita saber sobre el cancer del seno (an NCI booklet), and ¡Buena Vida! ('Komen's' publication aimed at Hispanic/Latina women that addresses risk, screening, treatment and social support issues, recommendations, facts and statistics).

Tip 20 For Jewish women, www.sharsheret.org addresses culturally sensitive issues. The toll free number in the United States is 866-474-2774.

From the supply closet I get two folders. I mark one "Cancer Survivor" for saving uplifting e-mails. I mark the other one "Cancer Information and Contacts" for storing resources like website addresses, support group information, and contact information for people who have battled cancer. I pack up my laptop and folders, make a quick-glance inspection of my office, turn off the lights, and take a deep breath and leave. The world around me is about to change.

Tip 21 Decide which loved ones need to be told face-to-face.

Tip 22 For face-to-face discussions, consider telling each when they are with someone they are close to. That person can be a second set of ears for your loved one as well as an outlet for sadness or support needs.

Tip 23 If you are the caregiver, recognize the criticality of this new and evolving role. Communicate with the cancer patient. Don't make assumptions about what your loved one wants and needs. Ask her what she would like you to do or not do, for example in the telling phase, she may want you to inform family and friends, or be with her when she does. Going forward, she may want you to attend doctor visits with her, take notes, make phone calls, keep the appointment book, make telephone calls, do laundry, give her a massage; you get the picture.

Once home, Dan and I talk about the kids.

TELLING OUR TEENAGE DAUGHTERS AND THREE-YEAR-OLD SON

Our kids. All were planned, hoped for, and conceived in love. As parents, we don't want to see them hurt, and we certainly don't want to be the ones who hurt them. This news is going to hurt us all. And, we are going to be the ones to deliver the bad news.

First, we agree that an announcement to little Danny, who is just over three, is not necessary. We will help him cope all along, whenever he shows signs of needing help. Then we discuss how we are going to tell the girls.

We decide that it is important to tell Christine with her boyfriend, Andrea with her boyfriend, and Michele with her closest friend and next-door neighbor, Kala.

Christine and her boyfriend of several years walk in from having a farewell dinner together. He is leaving for college the next day; Christine is leaving on Saturday. Dan turns the TV off, "Mom and I have something to tell you."

That is my cue. *Say it fast.* "Jason, we are glad you are here. Mr. P and I have something to tell Christine and she'll need your support." They sit down on the hearth in front of the fireplace. "I have breast cancer."

Christine's back goes straight and her eyes open wide, "What? Mom! How do you know? When did you find out?" She begins to cry. "Are you sure?" I nod. "I'm not leaving for college on Saturday." Her head drops between her knees and her shoulders shake.

I address her slumped body, "Christine, we will take you to school this weekend, and you'll be fine. This is *my* life, not yours. It's just a part of your life. I realize I'm an important part of your life, but you need to live the other parts of your life. So, you'll go to Immaculata on Saturday. Besides, I'm not going anywhere and if I need you, I'll let you know." Dan hands her a box of tissues.

Little Danny asks me, "Why is Teenie crying?" He asks the same question of Dan, "Why is Christine crying?" Then he goes to her and pats her knees, "Why are you crying?" I see his bottom lip get full and his tiny nostrils begin to quiver. I stave off my own tears that threaten to come, so he can be reassured.

Christine lifts her head. Jason has his arm around her. The four of us talk, while Danny watches. I ask Christine if she has any questions, needs more information or wants to be left alone. She and Jason decide to leave.

Christine reflects:

> *I kind of had a burning feeling in the pit of my stomach. I knew it wasn't good news. You told us that you had breast cancer, and you're going to get everything worked out straight away because you already made some appointments. I was crying on the hearth with you. Jason and I had to get out of the house because Andrea and Michele were coming home and we didn't want to have to hear it all over again. I had questions, but not right away. I just wanted to get out of there. We left and went over to Jason's house. We walked in. I was teary-eyed. Mrs. B asked me, "What's wrong?" I told her. She hugged me. Mr. B was on their porch. He said, "I'm really sorry. I hope everything turns out okay."*

> **Tip 24** Tell your loved ones the basic facts of your diagnosis and give them time to react and absorb. Do not try to keep them in a conversation they aren't ready for or don't want to be in. Leave the door open to future conversations by telling them they can ask you questions as they come up. Assure them you won't keep anything from them. (And don't keep anything major from them.) Always be candid and open.

Andrea, Michele, and Kala walk in from the garage from evening-session marching-band camp. Andrea's then-boyfriend rings the front doorbell. Once all four are in the kitchen, Dan says, "Girls, we need to tell you something."

Michele and Kala are hungrily preparing a bite to eat. Michele looks up and says, "Why Dad, are we in trouble or something?" *You gotta love 'er.*

Dan looks at me as if to say, 'go ahead'. The kids turn in my direction.

Here goes. "Girls, I have breast cancer." I explain a few details without going overboard. Silence. There is silence and stillness as they listen. *Silence is far noisier than the chaos that's about to transpire...it speaks volumes to me.* When I am finished, I ask if they have any questions for me.

All at once there is a chaotic flurry of tears and questions. I begin answering as many as I can. My head is moving side-to-side like a person watching a tennis match. "Yes, we're sure" ..."Earlier tonight, at the doctor's office"..."Yes"..."No"..."Not yet"..."I don't know"... I look in Michele's direction and notice that she is quiet and statue-like. I look away from her frozen stance and watery eyes to respond to a question coming from Andrea's direction. When I am done talking, Kala asks, "Mrs. P, where's Michele?" An open can of tomato soup and a can opener are sitting on the counter where she had been standing, and no Michele.

"She must've run through the dining room and up to her room. Why don't you go to her if you think you are up to it."

Kala says, "Mrs. P, I don't know what to say." We hug each other, she leaves the kitchen and heads for Michele's bedroom.

Mom, I just can't listen to anything else you have to say...I need to get out of the house.

Andrea blurts out, "Mom, I just can't listen to anything else you have to say. Can I go out front? I need to get out of the house. I'm sorry Mom, but please..."

"Andge," I empathetically but quickly reply, "I'm not offended. Do what you need to do. I'll be here if you want to talk." The sounds of her anguish as she runs to the foyer and onto the front walkway are haunting and unforgettable.

"Mommy," Danny shouted as he grabbed my pant leg looking at Andrea, "Why's Eera crying?"

"Mommy," Danny shouted as he grabbed my pant leg looking at Andrea, "Why's Eera crying?"

Dan switches on the TV to mask the chaos and hopefully change the mood a bit. We say nothing more to each other about cancer for the remainder of the evening. After awhile I quietly exit the family room where Dan and Danny are sitting together.

By phone and from another part of our house, I inform my twin brother, Tim, and a few AZ team members, and then go to bed early.

Later, Michele steps one half step into my bedroom (keeping the most distance possible between her and me), "Mom, is it okay if I spend the night at Kala's?"

Dan is lying beside me and interrupts, "Don't you think you should be here with your mother?"

"No, no." I protest. "If she stays here, she'll lie awake in her bed and I'll lie awake in my bed and neither of us will discuss it. This way, she'll have someone to talk to. She'll have Kala and Cammy and Bob, [Kala's parents]. Sort of an outlet. And she won't be alone." I address Michele and smile, "Don't forget your toothbrush." My voice cracks and my fear is faintly revealed.

I would later be apprised by Cammy of Kala's admiration for me. "Mom," she said, "Mrs. Pedicone was so brave. You should have heard her."

Sometime during the night, I hear Christine come home and go to her room and later that evening, I hear Andrea come home and go to her room. I am not insulted that they do not come to me or say goodnight. *I am a pariah.*

So far, I have not seen my husband break down since we got this news. *Good thing because his tears would crush me.* I've seen Dan cry three times in my life. He doesn't shed tears often. He is not outward with his sad emotions. Maybe he has cried over this, but he wants to spare me from seeing him in a vulnerable state. Or, maybe he is simply taking a practical approach to his thoughts. I don't know.

There is no sleep to be had tonight. Most people in my situation would be crying right now. Perhaps I am too tired or wired to cry. Predictably, I lay awake. *Why did I get cancer? What did I do wrong?*

God gave me cancer. That's it. *Why would God do this?*

Oh dear, I think I know why. I am being punished for the terrible things I have done in my life. I have cancer...CANCER; it must be that I deserve to be raked over the coals. This horrific disease arrived at my doorstep to pay homage to the skeletons in my closet. *Oh, God, I'm sorry.* I did despicable things. I'm a bad person. I sinned. *I did, I did, I did.*

The older I get, the more I appreciate the value of truthfulness and ethics. Right now I am feeling especially guilty for the times in my life when I was dishonest or unethical. So, tonight I admit to my sins and misjudgments especially in my prayers to God. We all have indiscretions and I am not alone. Everyone has things they wish they hadn't done or that they are not proud of. A good number of my life's wrongdoings were of no major harm to others; yet some of them were and I am ashamed. *And now, it's pay-up time.* My mind is reeling. In the study of sociology, the concept *victimless crime* is false. Someone gets hurt. In economics, there's no such thing as free in a buy-one-get-one-free scenario. Someone pays, somehow. Someone got hurt, someone paid for my wrongdoings and now, it's my turn. Though it is not possible, I try to recall every offensive act I ever committed, large and small, even ones like the time I was in elementary school and I hit a boy over the head with my purse because I wanted to impress a couple of onlookers who were picking on him. I am being castigated for every wrongdoing. *Every single one of them.*

Breathe, Wendi. Take a deep breath.

Well, perhaps I got cancer because of what happened in high school. *Yes. That must be it.* When I was a teenager in ninth or tenth grade, I experienced severe stomach pains that doubled me over. Consequently, I was hospitalized for a few days. I truly don't know what the exact diagnosis was, but I doubt it was anything terribly serious. I think the spasms may have been attributed to nervous tension or teenage angst. A rumor developed as a result. Schoolmates heard I had cancer. I didn't do anything to stop that tale. In fact, whenever I described my hospital accounts and post-infirmary tests I unknowingly and knowingly fed the buzz. I am being rebuked for the *knowingly* part, for cultivating the gossip. *I asked for it, now I've got it. Why do teenagers need attention?*

In through the nose; out through the mouth.

Or, maybe I have cancer for a simpler reason. Maybe I got it because I ingested too much artificial sweetener and diet sodas. *Hmmm. Think, Wendi, think.* Maybe I got it from using my cell phone and cordless phones. *Don't they emit radioactive micro-waves or something?* Possibly I got cancer because I didn't move away from Delaware when, years ago, Dan told me he wanted to move to a warmer climate. Delaware has a very high cancer rate.

Getting cancer could be my payment for not doing my monthly BSEs.

Did God give me cancer? God wouldn't have given me cancer. Would he? What am I thinking? Oh dear. Why did I get cancer?

I inhaled helium from balloons. I went on weird weight-loss diets. I tried marijuana in high school. I breathed in the scent of gasoline, lighter fluid, and permanent markers. I drank from the garden hose. I drank from foam cups. I stood in front of the microwave. I ran with scissors.

I stepped on sidewalk cracks. I talked back to my parents. I called ex-boyfriends and hung up when they answered. I yelled at my kids. I looked at other men. *Oh God, help me, what have I done? I can't think clearly.*

I push my head into my pillow and stare at the ceiling. I allow thoughts to ebb and flow.

This I do know; I will allow myself to ask *why*, but I refuse to ask, why me. I believe it is valid for one to ask 'why', but I feel that for one to ask 'why me', one thinks it should happen to someone else. And if it should happen to someone else, then who? Who should get cancer if not me? Should anyone get cancer? I suppose someone should get it. We should all experience valleys as well as peaks in life. If we didn't come across bumps in the road, the smooth parts would have less meaning. The peaks are more meaningful because of the valleys. Right?

Never mind. I don't know why I got cancer.

BUILDING MY ARSENAL

Very early the next morning, before daybreak, I begin Day One of building a hefty assortment of anti-cancer artillery.

No tears yet. *Hmmm.* The way I am responding to my situation is almost too coherent. Most newly diagnosed cancer patients and their primary care givers (spouses, fiancés, parents, siblings, partners, etc.) would have cried through the night and awakened with swollen eyes and more tears.

Tip 25 Cry if you feel the need to. Crying is not a sign of a lack of courage. In this case it is shock. But if you are like me and don't feel the urge to cry, don't be concerned. It may come later when the news sets in.

Tip 26 Go to Amazon.com and search the Books section for *My Mother's Breast: Daughters Face Their Mothers' Cancer* published by Taylor Trade Publishing. Amazon.com allows you to view the Table of Contents and excerpts from books. Read the excerpts to see if this book, or any, will be right for you. You may want to consider buying this book and having it around for times when daughters, family members, and even spouses of daughters are facing their mother's cancer. I recommend for daughters to pick it up every so often throughout the cancer ordeal and read a few stories at a time.

Tip 27   There are books that address the cancer patient as a parent and the implications of the disease on family dynamics. The challenge of tracking down and obtaining supportive family reading materials compelled Hurricane Voices to create an annotated bibliography as a tool to help parents help their families. Go to www.hurricanevoices.org for the Family Reading List - a fabulous directory that is comprehensive, yet not overwhelming. There you'll see a summary of each book categorized as picture books, chapter books, books for young adults, ones at adult level, etc. Each listing shows a picture of the cover. (This can be important when choosing, especially for young children's books.) If you don't have access to the Internet, contact Hurricane Voices at 866-667-3300 and request a copy of the pamphlet called *Family Reading List*™. Mark the one(s) you want and ask a loved one to get them from your local library or bookstore. (Remember to rely on your support people.)

Constructing an arsenal will consume much of my time in the coming months. I start with the people aspect of my battle ahead. I draw my energy from people, so my line of defense is people first, information second. By now, many have read my e-mail from last night and they are aware. I write to them because I believe that people can send good vibes into the universe and the good vibes will make their way to me. I start with that and a note to people I know believe in God (and who haven't been notified yet):

> *To my friends in faith: Last night, at about 5:00 I got some crummy news: I have breast cancer...[details and explanation]...Please add me to your prayer chains. As you know, I believe in the power of prayer.*

I build a list of websites to visit and other resources to contact for information. Some that look promising are:

- **American Cancer Society**: www.cancer.org to learn about every major cancer type, treatment options, clinical trials and so much more. It includes an interactive cancer resource center, a directory of medical resources and links to other sites organized by cancer type or topic.

- **Susan G. Komen Foundation**, founded on a promise made by her sister, Nancy Brinker, after she (Susan) died of breast cancer at age 36. It has information for patients, survivors and co-survivors (family members). There is also a Marketplace to purchase educational materials and gift items (proceeds go to research and other invaluable programs) www.Komen.org, Toll free number: 800 I'M AWARE®.

- **Y-ME National Breast Cancer Organization**, a 24-hour, 365-day/year hotline. 800-221-2141 (English with interpreters in 150 languages) or 800-986-9505 (Spanish). www.yme.org. Two women with breast cancer founded Y-ME NBCO. Over twenty-five years ago these two amazing women began the Y-ME hotline by answering calls from their homes.

- **The Delaware Breast Cancer Coalition, Inc.**, a United Way agency that helps raise awareness of breast cancer: www.debreastcancer .org DBBC number is 866-312-DBCC.

- **Center for Advancement in Cancer**: www.BeatCancer.org, 610-642-4810. Information, counseling and referral agency that focuses on combining the body's natural healing potential with advances in medical science.

- **MEDLINEplus** for general cancer information as well as 34 specific cancers. It was produced by the National Library of Medicine. It includes health news, features by topic, drug information, a medical encyclopedia, a dictionary, databases and other resources. You can click on a link that will take you through an eight minute tour of the website complete with pictures and sound. It contains links to interactive tutorials and clearinghouses: www.nlm.nih.gov/medlineplus/breastcancer.html. This is a wond8erful site for all health information, not just cancer. And best of all, it is free.

Reading messages from friends and colleagues who responded to my news is uplifting. I reply to the abundance of e-mails I received since I sent the e-mail message last night.

Tip 28 It is your personal preference whether to inform people outside your close circle of loved ones or not. Some people have a strong need for privacy, but if others know, they can become your allies. There are ways to maintain your privacy once people know. But, think about what it is that would keep you from informing people. Is it your need for privacy or is it the process of telling? If it is the latter, enlist family members, friends and colleagues as points of contact. Let them tell others, if you prefer not to. And, let them keep the others informed of your needs and progress.

Somewhere in my head, the decision was made to tell my mother in person and that this morning (Thursday) would be better than last night. It would have been cruel to deliver the news last night and leave her to try to sleep on that, alone. It is 11:00 a.m. and I am sitting with her in her dining room. This is a place that holds many memories for me. It is the spot where, as a child, I hid my vegetables in the secret ledge under the table so I didn't have to eat them and where I muddled through elementary and middle school homework. It is the table where I argued with my parents during my adolescent years. A dining room table, like the walls if only they could talk, sees so many things. Here I am, at this very table, about to tell my mom I have breast cancer. I have a knot in my stomach. There is a knock at the door. "Who is that?" She asks.

"How should I know? It's your house, Mom." I go to the door and find Dan standing outside. *How supportive is that!?*

She looks surprised when we return to the dining room together. "Mom, Dan came over because he knew I'd be telling you something that isn't going to be easy to tell." I keep my eyes on her and watch her look at Dan, then back at me. "I had a lump removed from my breast last week. Last night I went for my follow-up with the doctor and he told me I have breast cancer."

I hear the faint and quick intake of breath, "Oh no."

"Mom, it's okay." We hold hands for a moment. She reaches for me and we hug briefly. The hug is nothing earth-shattering or overly moving, because I'm intentionally trying to minimize the emotional impact, for her sake. In my most practical and reassuring voice, I say, "I wanted to tell you today, in person, so you can see that I am okay." I tell her the details of the upcoming surgery, she asks some questions and we leave. On the way out the door I remind her to call me as questions pop into her mind. I will make certain to answer my phone as quickly possible whenever I see her calls, so I can allay her fears, because this is going to sink in later.

Standing out front of her house, we say "so long" before Dan returns to work and I go to the lab for some blood work.

I have no idea how I am staying focused and levelheaded. At this point in time it is very normal for a person to be in shock or crying. There are observed stages of traumatic news. I am not certain what they are, but I believe them to be; *first, you cry*, second, is anger, after that is acceptance. First you cry, by the way, is what Betty Rollins aptly called the book she wrote on this subject about 30 years ago.

Tip 29 Whether you are the cancer patient or a caregiver, remember that crying is not a sign of a lack of courage.

After my blood work, I arrive home. It is afternoon and less than twenty-four hours since my diagnosis. I walk in the house and notice Christine and Michele exchanging glances. I pick up on negative vibes. Michele rolls her eyes and leaves the room. I look at Christine, who shrugs her shoulders and says, "I asked her something about your cancer and she got mad at me."

I dash to catch Michele and see her on the way up the steps to her room. I delicately inquire, *"Are you angry with me?"*

It's funny how things that happened to you or you learned throughout your life, come forward in an instant. I once knew someone who told me that when a spouse passes away, the living spouse might feel resentment or anger toward the deceased spouse. For example, "Why did you leave me?" or feelings that if only the deceased spouse took care of himself he wouldn't have had a heart attack. That information popped into my head when I was addressing Michele's anger.

"Well? Are you?" She has no answer to my question, so I say, "I think it is normal and okay to be angry. I just want to be sure it's not with me."

"I'm not mad at you," she says, "I just don't know why everybody has to keep talking about it all the time." *All the time? It's been less than twenty-four hours! Oh dear. Reminder to myself - be sensitive towards Michele and watch for signs that indicate when she's ready to talk or hear about it. She's not ready now.*

Dan and I discuss Michele's reaction and he says, "I feel the same way. You are labeled now. He walks past me. "My wife has a big 'C' stamped on her forehead. Now, every conversation we have with people is going to be about cancer."

It is Thursday, August 26, 2004. Between now and September 9 (the day before my mastectomy) my life will become a whirlwind of undergoing tests, meeting physicians and specialists, and seeking information.

Tip 30 At some point, you will need to find out what insurance, disability and financial options are available to you. Start with your employer's Human Resources department (or your spouse's employer if you fall under his or her benefits). Breastcancer.org offers tips in their Financial Matters section about tax deductions for medical expenses. Imaginis.com, The Breast Health Resource, offers support and a directory of links to toll-free helplines, and non-profit or governmental organizations. Your caregiver can help you research financial impact, insurance implications and work arrangements. Search the Internet for "FMLA" and you'll find several sites with information on FMLA (Family Medical Leave Act), leave of absence options, ideas for flexible work arrangements, and more. Business & Legal Reports (www.blr.com) provides state HR answers and tools online.

After you contact your HR department, or if you are not employed and need assistance, look at pages 389 and 390 of *Holding Tight, Letting Go,* by Musa Mayer. These pages list organizations that can help you with financial and legal issues from treatments your insurance should cover and managed care bill of rights, to a directory of prescription drug patient assistance programs.

Tip 31 If you receive word from your insurance company that a specialized treatment you need is not covered, ask your oncologist if he knows about clinical trials you would qualify for. Clinical trials are funded. If that doesn't help you get what it is you need, your hospital may be able to help you get coverage from your insurance company by breaking down your uncovered specialized procedure into many parts (individual itemized expenses) that are covered.

Tip 32 If you are the patient and you have financial needs you or your caregiver can apply for grants to help with transportation, childcare, home care and more by going to the AvonCares Program as part of www.cancercare.org. Click on the Financial Needs section for more information or call 800-813-4673.

Friday morning I rise very early, take the laptop to my living room and log in to the company network. Before attempting some work, I write to a distribution list of people that I started building the night of my diagnosis:

Hello SPKS FOC team members, TH PC members, colleagues, and friends!

*Your supportive words have been **such an inspiration** to me...I used to be unsure if I should or should not approach someone who's been diagnosed with cancer. I'll never be uncertain again!*

Over the last few days, I've felt a sense of pride whenever I see doctors using Arimidex®, Faslodex® and Nolvadex® prescription pads, penholders and paraphernalia for AZ cancer drugs. Little did I know that I would become interested in the cancer drugs, not as an employee of AZ, but as a person with cancer.

Here's the latest: By this afternoon I will have had three important tests: Blood work to check my liver, a chest x-ray to check my lungs and nuclear meds to check my bones. I understand that after today I'll be radioactive for twenty-four hours. Aren't technology and pharmaceuticals fascinating! I will meet with a plastic surgeon on Monday and the oncologist on Thursday. (Geez, what a roller coaster ride.) The next hurdle is to hear good news from the three tests. To hear that it hasn't spread to any organs would be wonderful. Cross your fingers, or pray for that, because then we can get on with removing the defective part (my cancerous breast)!

I'll be teleworking on Monday and in the office on Tuesday. I will keep you posted mostly by e-mail (it's an easy-to-use vehicle I'm using to keep folks informed). I realize that everyone deals with something like this in his or her own way, so if you'd rather not be on my e-mail update list, let me know and I'll certainly understand.

Working toward adding the word "survivor" to my accomplishments,
Wendi

I care about the work I do and so I attempt to tie up some lose ends I left dangling yesterday. I find that I am fully able to channel my thoughts in the direction of my communications-analyst-to-do list. Perhaps this is because my cancer tests are scheduled; I'm on a path and there's nothing more I have to do but to go to the hospital testing locations on time today. By 7:45 a.m. I log off and leave the house.

BONE SCAN, BLOOD WORK, AND X-RAY - HOW FAR HAS THE CANCER GONE?

On my way to the hospital, I am stuck in traffic. *I can't even do the one thing I was supposed to do and that's to arrive on time. Oh brother.* There is a car accident up ahead that is causing the delay. There's no time to pull over and use the cell phone so I connect my headset and mouthpiece. I begin a barrage of cell phone calls to find someone in Nuclear Medicine. I reach a few voice mail greetings and leave frantic messages, "My name is Wendi Pedicone. I am scheduled to be in Nuclear Medicine on the fifth floor of the hospital at 8:30. It's already 8:20 and I am not certain if I'm going to make it in time. I'm not even certain if I've reached the right voice mail. Please don't turn me away from my test if I am late."

> **Tip 33** Ask someone to come with you for tests. I thought I could handle it on my own. I couldn't. It is important to have a second set of eyes and ears, in other words, someone to see, listen and take notes.

I arrive at 8:35 on the fifth floor after stopping at the lab to have my blood drawn. I am searching for someone to help me (no one is in the Nuclear Med office). Eventually, someone assists me and begins the process. She brings in a vial that looks formidable because of it's highly protective-looking encasement and the nuclear symbol that is stamped on it. Wearing rubber gloves, she carefully removes a tiny bottle, handles it with care and gives me an injection of liquid into my vein. It feels cold then hot going in. I do as I am told, and that is to walk around for two hours, eat food and drink fluids. The material has to weave its way through me and permeate my bones. I go to another floor to get my chest x-ray, then to the Whirling Top restaurant for breakfast. The eatery is a wonderfully preserved diner-style place located on the first floor near the gift shop. It was most likely here when the downtown Wilmington hospital was built some time ago. I'll guess, in the 1960's. I decide to forego healthy eating and order fried eggs, toasted white bread with butter, and sweetened full-fat cappuccino with whipped cream on top. *Heck, I've got cancer now, why guard my health!* I enjoy the repartee between the patrons and the very competent "Miss Eunice" who is serving the entrees.

I order fried eggs, toasted white bread with butter, and sweetened full-fat cappuccino with whipped cream on top. Heck, I've got cancer now, why guard my health?

Then, a fellow comes up behind me and engages in conversation with a young woman next to me. The lively conversation winds down when he says, "What's the matter with you? You didn't get a hug today or somethin'? I'm gawna give you a hug."

She turns to give him a mock-anger glare. He seems amused.

I look at her and say, "Take it. You can never get enough hugs."

"Ye heh," he shouts with enthusiasm. He hugs her, he hugs me, and she hugs me. *They are hugging me! This is a good omen.* We are so close that we become a mass of blonde hair, black ribbon curls, and Afro. Our cheeks are touching and I instantly know I was right when I said you could never get enough of these.

My tummy is full and I have time to waste. I walk the cavernous halls to energize my blood flow and enable the nuclear material to spread throughout my body. *We MUST get a good reading. I don't want anything to be missed.* The ubiquitous corridors of terra-cotta brick become my scenery for the next hour.

On my way back to Nuclear Medicine for the bone scan, the elevator opens on floor number two. It is not the floor I need to go to, but I spot my primary care physician (PCP). I immediately hop off the elevator and call his name, "Dr. K! I'm glad to see you. You probably haven't seen a copy of anything about me from Dr. M yet. Dr. M is a surgeon who did an excisional biopsy on me a week or so ago. I have been diagnosed with breast cancer."

The expression on Dr. K's face changes and his shoulder's slump, "Oh, no." He gives me a hug. We talk a few minutes; I fill him in on the details. We finish up with him saying, "Why don't you call the office and make an appointment. We can look over your path report and perhaps I can help answer some questions you might have. It'll be good for me to be in the loop in case you need to see me for any non-cancer reasons." *This is a good sign. Sometime PCPs take a backward step when a patient gets cancer. They'd rather leave care of the patient to the oncologists. For some, providing primary care to a cancer patient is too far out of their everyday practice. I understand. Happily, I've got an exceptional PCP.*

Tip 34 There are three disciplines for primary care. They are (and they treat): Pediatrics (infant to eighteen years old), Internal Medicine (adult population eighteen and up), and Family Physicians (infants to geriatrics). They are each a PCP role. Think of a PCP as a quarterback, the starting point to making referrals, and working with you and the specialists (oncologists being the specialists that deal with cancer care).

Dr. K writes:

The patient diagnosed with cancer is frequently confronted with an increasingly complex medical system and decision-making process. The Family Physician (FP) can be instrumental in assisting the patient to the appropriate oncologist and surgeon for further treatment and follow-up care. The role of the Family Physician oftentimes becomes secondary after diagnosis has been made, relying on the medical specialists to assist the patient through their oncologic therapy. However, it is paramount that the Family Physician continues to play an integral role in the assessment of the physical, psychological, and emotional well being of the patient.

In addition to confirming that the appropriate oncologic needs and services are being met, the Family Physician can provide treatment for non-oncologic disorders that may arise from treatment of patients with cancer. For example, dermatologic manifestations, respiratory infections, anxiety and mood disorders are conditions that may occur as a result of oncologic treatment. The FP is well trained to provide care for these disorders and others. Keeping a focus on the comprehensive care of the entire patient is a necessity when providing the highest quality care to a patient.

When faced with challenging decisions in the treatment of cancer including surgical, chemotherapy or radiation, a Family Physician can be available to help participate in the difficult and confusing decision-making process. Cancer treatment remains controversial, complicated and unequivocally frustrating. I would encourage all patients who are diagnosed with an oncologic disorder to use their PCP as a valuable provider of their health care, especially if the patient has a long-term pre-cancer relationship with the PCP. Working together with the oncology team, surgeon, support services, and others, the PCPs can contribute to this multi-disciplinary team of providers to help improve patient care, and hopefully improve patient outcomes.

Tip 35 Set up a consultation with your Primary Care Physician. Since during your cancer management he would be the one to treat you for non-cancer-related illnesses, he will need to see you and coordinate your care with your oncologist.

Jim, one of my cancer support group friends at the Wellness Community writes:

The PCP can also be a valuable resource for recommending who should give a second opinion. I found it very useful to ask the same questions of each of my physicians [and surgeons] and compare answers. You never can ask too many questions. Remember, you know your body better than anyone.

I return to the fifth floor for my test. I am told to lie flat on my back fully clothed and remove items in my pockets, especially coins and metal items. I ask the technician, "Will you be able to see if cancer is in my bones?"

"Yes."

"Will you be able to tell me?"

"No, a radiologist has to read the images." She detects my disappointment, "Don't worry, the radiologist usually has the readings back in the same day."

I move and hold my breath whenever she tells me to. As I stare at the ceiling, I feel a tear trickle from my eye to my ear. I cannot wipe it away for fear of moving and ruining a good image reading. I suspect she knows I'm crying. *What about the metal snap on my jeans? Will it block a cancerous spot? I should have insisted on taking my clothes off. I don't want any spot to be missed.* The computer images show bones and colors. They look beautiful, resembling infrared images in vivid yellows, reds and blues. I wonder which color is cancer?

Why did I get cancer? Oh brother, nothing to do but lay here and think. And, hold my breath when I hear the machine doing its thing.

All angles and imaging are complete; the technician comes close to me, bends forward, and puts her hands on her knees. She's about to tell me something. *Oh dear, what is she going to tell me? It can't be bad news, because she said the radiologist has to read the images and bad news would have to officially come from the radiologist. But, she can't tell me anything good either, because it's not her place. What is she going to tell me then?* Her mouth is near my ear and she softly says, "The radiologist is the expert so you have to wait for his reading, but I *will* say, nothing is jumping out at me."

I hear a quick and foreign sound come from me, "Hhheeeep." *A little relief.* Then I thank her profusely. She is my angel. *If the radiologist has bad news for me this afternoon, then I'll accept the idea of having a few hours of happy misbelief this morning.*

There's a lilt in my step when I leave. I entertain folks on the only working elevator that is overly full and very sluggish. (The other one is being repaired.) The doors open and I say, "Handbags and ladies accessories." There are smiles everywhere. How gratifying. Next floor. Ping. "Men's apparel." More smiles and some chuckles. Another floor. Ping. I place my fingertips to my lips, shift my eyes from side to side and lower my voice, "Lingerie and unmentionables." Several of us exit the elevator grinning and I am tremendously full of myself!

I walk to the car park and call Marcia from my cell phone. I report that I've completed my testing. "I know," she says, "the blood work came back negative and so did the chest x-ray. It sounds like your bone scan went well but I'll give you the official word as soon as I get it. Oh, and Wendi," she pauses, "I've walked in your shoes."

What did I just hear? Can it be true that she's had breast cancer and understands my plight? "What do you mean?" I hesitantly inquire.

"I had breast cancer when I was 30 and you can see... I'm a lot older than 30!" *I feel powerful. I also feel a glimmer of hope.* Before we conclude the conversation, she tells me that my blood work indicated a high INR factor. I should contact the blood bank and arrange for two autologous (self-donated) pints of blood as soon as I can before my surgery. INR is the blood test for velocity and clotting. Mine is a little thin, possibly from meds I was taking up until my biopsy for Inflammatory Bowel Disease (IBD). It would be too risky to postpone my surgery, but thin blood may complicate it. It will make for a messy operation so having some extra on hand will be helpful. I'll donate a couple of pints. *I'll get to it later today. Right now, I need to inform a few people about my good news.*

Wow. It is unbelievably reassuring to know Marcia and I are part of a sisterhood. A breast cancer club. I smile outwardly as I dial Dan's number from my cell phone. I am in the hospital parking lot telling him about all that's happened and he sounds nervous. I don't realize that I am so hysterically happy that I'm making no sense. He thinks I am crying. Later, he told me he was frozen in his spot waiting to hear what I had to say about whatever it was that had me so frantic. He was frightened. *I had no idea.*

Estimating the completion time of my tests, my sister calls my cell phone from Denver. I deliver the good news. She rattles off several things, "I've had buttons made that say 'We're here for Wendi' and I'm shipping them to people in Delaware...Dixie and Karen and Susan are wearing your name in the Breast Cancer walk out here next month...Next year, you'll get to wear a pink hat when you walk...That means you are a survivor...Karen is making you a hat...Call me when your surgery date is confirmed so I can get you a reading with my astrologist." She is feeling my relief. I'm crying and making joyful sounds. If she is too, I can't hear them. *She probably is.*

"Do you want to go shopping?"

"Not if people are going to see us and talk about cancer."

"Girls," I say as I walk into the house on Friday afternoon, "I know you each need a few things before your first day of school. Do you want to go shopping?"

Michele replies an honest reply, "Not if people are going to see us and talk about cancer."

"Okay, here's the deal, " I say, "If we run into anyone, I won't talk about cancer. It's that simple. Sound good?"

"And how about us," they ask. "Can we not talk about cancer?"

"We don't have to talk about cancer."

"Sounds good."

At the store, Christine and Andrea cling to me. I follow them to the accessories department and they start trying on hats. We are giggling over the ostentatious ones they put on. Michele and Danny join the fun. It is like the girls are small again and playing dress up. All along, I know that we are looking at hats to possibly cover a bald cancer head, but they would never admit it. For that matter, neither will I. At least, not yet.

LIFE CONTINUES TO GO FORWARD DESPITE A CANCER DIAGNOSIS

Ah, Saturday, wonderful day of the week. It is not a typical Saturday though; it is a milestone Saturday. My oldest is leaving for college. We have been preparing for this for months by following a process to give her more responsibilities and talk through what's to be expected. I am proud to say that, even with my diagnosis, Christine shows no signs of having qualms about leaving.

The temperature is in the 90's. *And it is only morning…the heat of the day is not yet upon us.* It is immensely hot inside and the dorms are not air-conditioned. *No air-conditioning? Oh, she is sooo gonna appreciate how good she had it at home. Oh, the realities of college hardships.* There are five of us and Christine, and three of her roommate's family members and her roommate, LaToya, moving furniture and unpacking. Ten of us in one room. *Man, it is hot!* The elevator is overloaded, the halls are crowded with people and many of the men are walking around with towels draped around their necks. *The sweat is aflowin' today!*

Because of my recent biopsy, it is recommended that I abstain from heavy lifting. *Noooo problemo! I'm happy not to help under these conditions.*

Before too long, Christine and LaToya are settled, and we celebrate by going to a nearby restaurant for an early dinner. We say our good-byes, and then we get in our vehicle and drive away. *It is done. My firstborn is in college. I thought about this day a few hours after she was born. I can clearly remember her first dry night without a diaper, how she didn't look back at me when she walked toward her classroom on her first day of kindergarten, and how she piled her prom dress in the passenger side of a car for her first formal dance. Tonight she is living on her own. Just like that. Mental snap of my fingers.*

The ride home is quiet. My mind explodes with sad thoughts and fear for the future. This is her first night at college. *Will I be here for her last? What does the future hold?*

Saturday night I log in to the AZ network and focus on work activities. *I don't want to fall behind.* My responsibilities are falling by the wayside. *I can't let this happen. I need to tie up loose ends.* After drafting a few communications that were on my to-do list, I read e-mail. *Stick to the work e-mail messages first, Wendi. Ignore the cancer e-mails, and do the work stuff first.*

I have accomplished more than enough for one evening, so I reward myself with time to read the messages that are of a more personal nature.

CONTINUING TO BUILD MY ARSENAL

People wanting to help suggest websites and resources. I add them to my list:

- Cancer Care Connection in Delaware offers ways to ease the burden of going through the cancer process: <u>www. cancercareconnection .org</u>, 866-266-7008. It is an organization that provides information, support, and referrals to people affected by cancer.

- A senior physician in the Oncology Department at AZ - An IS colleague who supports the oncology brand team believes that Dr. P may be able to give me an opinion on the treatment protocol since Dr. P was once part of an oncology practice. He may be able to serve as an additional resource for information.

  Living Beyond Breast Cancer offers educational conferences, opportunities to chat with others on message boards, as well as support after treatment: <u>www.lbbc.org</u>, 610-645-4567 or 888-753-LBBC.

- National Institutes of Health (NIH): www.nih.gov - The NIH knows where around the country experimental treatments are being tried. NIH distributes money for funding clinical trials; i.e., it funds individual institutions that are coordinating clinical trials and ongoing research to improve care for cancer. NCI does not handle patients other than those in Bethesda MD where the NIH federal agency operates. Bethesda is the largest medical research facility in the world. Clinical trials are for cancer metastases (pronounced, me TAS te sis); in the case of breast cancer they are for when the cancer has spread from the breast to another part of the body.

- National Cancer Institute (NCI), 800-4-CANCER (800-422-6237) or www.cancer.gov. NCI is a division of NIH. Call them for answers to questions about cancer, tips to prevent cancer, help with quitting smoking, information materials and other resources. You can order publications and talk to specialists by dialing the telephone number. I called the Cancer Information Service and provided the person on the phone with my personal and cancer diagnosis information. She mailed me information about cancer studies and clinical trials that I may be eligible for if my surgery, chemo and radiation treatment plan doesn't work. I want to know what options might be available to me if this doesn't work. They also provide an educational section on breast cancer and pregnancy on the website.

Tip 36 Folks will tell you about people they know who have had cancer. Write down the names of these cancer survivors, how you got their names, any additional particulars the person gave you about them and their telephone numbers. You may want to contact some or all of them when you get more information about yourself. Once your doctors determine what stage you are in (0 through 4: 0, I, IIa, IIb, IIIa, IIIb, IIIc, and IV), your Estrogen Receptor (ER) and Progesterone Receptor (PR) status (whether or not your cancer cells test positive or negative for hormone receptors and whether or not hormone therapy will be an option for you), the growth factor (HER-2/neu), and other particulars, you may want to compare yourself with others who were in similar situations. For example, once I found out I was in stage IIIc, I talked to many late stage cancer survivors on my list (stage III and IV) and felt hopeful about my life expectancy once I knew they were still alive and how many years they were cancer free.

Tip 37   For primary caregivers or anyone who lives with you: Get a cardboard box or large storage container for papers, pamphlets and miscellaneous things the cancer patient will receive and collect. Get a couple of bookends from an office supply store and determine a place for books and CDs. This is a confusing time. Seeing books, CDs and paperwork in every nook of your home will add additional stress and cause the patient and co-habitants anxiety. At least, if everything is in one place, you can always find it later, as well as organize it if you are so inclined.

It is Monday, the first weekday of a new week. *What will this week bring?*

Do we have a will? Yes, seventeen years ago we went to our attorney and had one drawn up. But, certainly, it would be considered out of date. Do we have a Power of Attorney? *We aren't so good at comprehending legal matters so I don't want to think about this right now.*

Recently, we saw an episode of *Larry King Live* on CNN. He was interviewing Terry Schiavo's husband and his attorney. Terry Schiavo is the young woman in Florida who was in a coma for years. A battle ensued because she didn't have a living will and neither her parents nor her husband could agree to pull her life-saving plugs or keep them. It became a national story. *Oh dear, I don't have a living will.*

Tip 38   It might feel morbid at this time to seek legal counsel to plan for loss of good health, but this is an important thing. If you don't have a will, living will, power of attorney and healthcare proxy, you should consider having your intentions documented. I recently read an article in *AARP Magazine* that explained reasons why these documents are imperative, and suggestions on how to avert tricky arguments amongst your loved ones after you are gone. Now might be too busy a time to do this, but when the dust settles and you are following a treatment plan, consider a visit to an attorney.

I donate the first pint of blood to be used during my surgery. They label it with a green card that says, 'autologous'. I receive a matching green card to take with me on the morning of my surgery.

Walking from the blood bank to my car, I dial Kayla's number. Her cell phone greeting finishes and I leave a message for her to call me. *I need to tell her my news.*

Marcia calls to tell me that Dr. M received official notification that all my tests are negative for cancer metastases to major organs. Additionally, she made an appointment for me to meet with the plastic surgeon that will do the reconstruction. *Wow, she's good. How is she getting all these tests and appointments scheduled so quickly, I wonder.* If the cancer had spread to my organs or bones, the surgery would be postponed until I complete chemotherapy.

Tip 39 People do not die of breast cancer; they die of breast cancer that has traveled to other parts of the body, which is why chemotherapy is important.

CONSIDERING RECONSTRUCTION OPTIONS WITH THE MASTECTOMY

Following Marcia's instructions, I go to Dr. D's office. Dan is already in the parking lot. *What a steadfast man I married.* Dr. D tells us that in the past, surgeons performed mastectomies and did reconstructive surgery a year or so later. Many women lived without breasts for that long and their self-esteem was compromised. Additionally, there were women who never returned for the reconstructive surgery. Once they finished with cancer treatment, they were ready to get on with their lives and disinclined to have another surgery. Nowadays, the removal and re-creation of a breast can be done together. This avoids the emotional pain of a woman seeing herself without a breast. *Thank goodness. I wouldn't want to wear a prosthetic breast until I get a new one.* Immediate reconstruction does

Tip 40 Ask your surgeon if he or she has prosthetics samples to show you ahead of time (to help you decide) and drains (so you know what to expect).

Tip 41 Consider other surgical options at this time. You may not need a complete mastectomy (modified or radical removal of the breast). Statistically, survival has nothing to do with what type of surgery one has. Breast surgery is for removal of the tumor, surrounding tissue and lymph nodes, if there is lymph node involvement. If, for example, your tumor is removed and margins around it are clear, more surgery may not be necessary except for aesthetic reasons. Go to breastcancer.org, plasticsurgery.org, some of the other websites I mention in this book, or your local library for resources on surgery.

not interfere with cancer treatments and has no known effect on the likelihood of cancer recurring.

Dr. D describes three reconstruction options: 1) TRAM flap reconstruction, *sounds like an elongated breast flapping in the wind,* 2) implants, *Ooh,
would I get the perky porno kind? Yowza. Or would I get rounded youthful
ones...the kind I never had even when I was youthful,* and 3) a reconstructed
breast mound using skin and muscle tissue from my back called Lat flap.

"I think I'd like implants. Tell me about that method."

Dr. D explains that I can get an implant in one or both breasts. After my
left breast is removed he will insert a temporary bag called a tissue
expander with about ten percent of the expected volume to start. Each
week or so I'll go back to have it gradually injected with more solution
until it reaches one hundred percent of the volume, and the skin and muscle is sufficiently stretched. The nipple and areola will be reconstructed in
a subsequent procedure, most likely following chemo and radiation. "Of
the three options, this one is the least painful and the most common." He
cautions that over time, however, women who go with the implants
option have to have several minor surgeries to readjust as they age.

I avoid learning about the flap option, because it sounds weird. Let's skip
to the other one. "Tell me about option number three."

Option number three is one where he will create a breast mound using
muscle and skin from my back. Like the implant option, a nipple and areola will come later.   I do not like this option because of the nasty-looking
scar I would have on my back because a Lat flap reconstruction uses tissue from the latissimus dorsi muscle under the shoulder blade. I want to
be able to wear a bathing suit and not have people gawk.

He tells me about option one. *The flappy-flap option.* Surprisingly, it inter-
ests me. *It should be renamed, for sure.* I now have to choose one of the
three. So, I consider them. And Dan and I talk. We ask questions of Dr.
D as we do so.

The decision making process I follow is akin to what I've seen contestants
go through on *Who wants to be a Millionaire*: The process of elimination.

I eradicate option three immediately because of the scarring to my back.

Then I consider option two. *Hmmm, what's behind door number two.*
Andrea told me last week that when I get my "boob-b-gone" operation I
should get implants. *Eeewww, I hate that word. I never use the B word for
such beautiful female anatomy, but I realize that many people do.... including my
teenager. This is Andrea we are talking about. She's very colorful. I hope she*

wasn't talking about porno boobs. I don't want porno breasts. She also suggested that I get a tattoo while I'm under. Such ideas! Let's just get the cancer taken care of, shall we? *Sheesh.*

I have a feeling that number two - the implants - would get me off easy for the mastectomy, but will inconvenience me over the long haul by having to go back, and back, and back again for saline injections into the tissue expander, a minor surgery to have the permanent bags implanted and alterations as I age. I don't think I want to do that. Besides, I hope to be aging for many years and I know I won't want the hassle of future procedures.

Okay; option one. It is the most painfully intense one. *Oh boy.* Basically, it is an alternative to implants. The surgeon creates a breast mound using skin, muscle and tissue from the abdomen. Because it is never totally disconnected from my body, it will retain its blood supply and gain and lose weight with me. *Cool.* This surgery also serves as a tummy tuck. *Very cool.* So, he will cut from hip-to-hip horizontally and under my belly button. He'll tunnel this tissue upwards under my abdominal skin and vertically towards my breast. (Dr. M would later describe this part of the procedure as 'lifting the skin up like an undershirt'.) He'll twist the muscle at a ninety-degree angle and bring it out of the opening from my removed breast. I'll be in the hospital for three to five days. The pain varies according to the individual and whether or not there's lymph node involvement. *I have a high tolerance for pain and I hope not to have lymph node involvement. I think I'll fare well with this option.* I tell Dr. D, "I am leaning toward the TRAM option. Schedule the surgery according to that option and if I change my mind in the next day or so, I'll contact you."

Dr. D writes:

> *I met Wendi in the office for the first time on August 30. She was accompanied by her husband. My initial impression from Wendi was that she was friendly. She had a nice big smile and a strong handshake. She did not have a sense of fear or excessive anxiety about her that is so common with breast cancer patients that I meet for the first time. It was obvious she was intelligent. We talked about immediate versus delayed reconstruction, pros and cons of implants, implant plus latissimus muscle flap and TRAM flap reconstruction. After my exam we looked at pre and post op pictures of various types of reconstructions.*

"...[Wendi] did not have a sense of fear or excessive anxiety about her that is so common with breast cancer patients that I meet for the first time..."

Later Wendi told me that she thought I should have more post op pictures of small women with small reconstructions to balance out the pictures in my file of larger women with large reconstructions. I thought that was reasonable. At the end of the consultation she was leaning towards the TRAM flap. I think it is good for patients to be "leaning" towards a particular method of reconstruction. That means they want to let the large amount of information sink in and not make a hasty decision.not make a hasty decision.

Once we arrive home, I sit at our computer and go to websites for more information and to get answers to my questions. I read the chapter called *Reshaping the Breast* (p. 150), in a book called *Living Through Breast Cancer*. I pay particular attention to the illustrations and explanation of how a TRAM is performed (p. 162-164). I call Dr. D with some questions and thoughts. I'm grateful that he patiently discusses each with me.

Dr. D adds:

As is common with modern information-hungry people Wendi went home and hit the Internet. She inquired about another reconstruction option. In general, it is a good microsurgical method, which requires less abdominal muscle to be borrowed. It is however, much more complex and not commonly done. My recommendation was to stick to basics and go with one of the simpler versions instead. She agreed.

It is confirmed; I've chosen the best option for me, the TRAM option. Dan agrees. Andrea is slightly disappointed. *I think she wanted to see what my breasts with implants would look like. This, coming from the kid who watched me nurse little Danny many times and teased, "Put those things away. Geez Mom, you have them out twenty-four, seven!"* To Christine, the reconstruction option I chose doesn't matter, and Michele is not ready to express an opinion.

> **Tip 42** Go to the website of the American Society of Plastic Surgeons: www.plasticsurgery.org for descriptions and pictures of breast reconstruction options. Also, ask the plastic surgeon if he or she has a recommended website or documentation that you can read through. This would also be a good time to view a twenty-four minute videotape made by Discovery Channel University called, *Donna's Story: Living with Breast Cancer*. Donna is a 47-year-old female considering surgical options and cancer fighting treatments. It shows the mastectomy and expander procedure (viewer discretion is advised). It also shows the drains that are surgically inserted to catch post-surgical fluid build up. All-in-all, an informative video.

Tip 43   There is a book called *Be a Survivor*™: *Your Guide to Breast Cancer Treatment* by Vladimir Lange, MD. It contains helpful illustrations and photos in color in the Reconstruction chapter. It also contains a CD-ROM. Call 888-LANGE-88 from the United States to order a 28-minute video for *Treatment Options For Breast Cancer*. The program, clearly illustrated with 3-D animated graphic, gives a step-by-step presentation of the treatment process, from needle biopsy to nipple reconstruction.

I understand that nothing the plastic surgeon (Dr. D) will do is life saving or can change my prognosis [*and that's okay*], but the reconstruction is a very important part of the procedure because it will make me a whole person again. Emotional strength is important. The mastectomy (Dr. M's role) is the potential life-saving, prognosis-improving part of the procedure. *Let's get it scheduled.*

Tuesday morning, I awaken before daybreak again…[*Am I detecting a pattern here? Hmmm, must be my brain's way of coping. I'm not crying, but my mind is too active to sleep.*]…I notify folks via e-mail:

Hello friends and colleagues,

Yesterday morning, we received wonderful news: The cancer has not spread to any organs! Ahhh, deep breath, what a huge relief. That means we can proceed with the mastectomy and immediate reconstruction. In the afternoon, Dan and I met the plastic surgeon who will perform my next surgery; a TRAM reconstruction…we learned that some parts of me will most likely look better in a few months…what a great perk. As a matter of fact, I now have a few "before" photos in my patient file! To those of you who yearn for a nip and tuck, eat your heart out!

All kidding aside, the target date for surgery is next Wednesday, September 8. I hope to get a confirmation on that, soon. Unfortunately, I'll be out of the office for four to six weeks afterward since it is major surgery (not like the excisional biopsy). As I am learning, I may miss a day or two here and there during the time of chemotherapy, but fully expect to be able stay focused at work most of the time.

To my Information Services colleagues: I am saddened that I will not be able to attend the IS Town Hall this year. Much of my energy over the last few months has gone into working with the TH Planning Committee to organize it. The 2004 TH Planning Committee, RhonJohn Communica-

tions, and IS Leadership will be delivering an important and memorable event on the 15th. Enjoy!

To all of you: My family and I are truly blessed to receive such remarkable support. I am receiving your wonderful e-mails, voice mails and phone messages at home. I have created a folder and optimistically labeled it, "Cancer Survivor." I have been saving everything you give me. Thank you, thank you, and thank you.

Little Danny goes willingly into daycare this morning. This is only his third week at Miss Sheri's daycare and he is adjusting well. I take a few minutes to tell her my cancer news and she assures me they will treat Danny with extra care. *I have faith that he is in capable hands. Miss Sheri, a mother of four, has been in the business of daycare for over fifteen years. In a few weeks, I already know that she, her husband and children are wonderful, and Danny will be fine with them.*

MY VISIT TO SEE THE CANCER CENTER WHERE I WILL BE TREATED

Thursday afternoon, just over a week since my diagnosis, Dan and I meet in the parking lot of the Christiana Care's Helen F. Graham Cancer Center in Newark on the Christiana Hospital campus. Helen F. Graham was employed by MBNA in their Support Services department, which, along with the Helen F. Graham Grants Program, provided meaningful employment to people with developmental disabilities. The Cancer Center has been dedicated in Helen's name.

According to the president and CEO of Christiana Care Health System, the cancer center and the entire organization strives to recognize that the delivery of health is fundamentally dependent upon the caring of one individual person for another (2004 Annual Report, p.1). The cancer center is accredited, has been awarded commendations, and is ranked among the best programs in cancer care. But what sets them apart from many, comes from the heart. *I already believe this to be true.*

All along and based on what I've heard, I expected to see a new state-of-the-art building with all the necessary resources inside. What I see is a *fabulous* new state-of-the-art building with all the necessary resources inside. The entranceway is inviting, people are welcoming us and there is a kindly looking, older gentleman with a bow tie playing music on a high gloss, grand piano. I know I am not on a cruise to a tropical port, so I conclude that we've found the right place. I am especially certain that we have, now that I see patients wearing scarves and hats. But all along I am thinking that I don't want to be here. *I definitely don't belong here. This place is for sick people...people with cancer.*

I remember reading about the Helen F. Graham Cancer Center when it was being built. I recall being in this area and watching the construction from the roadside. *I never thought I'd see the inside of it.*

We meet Dr. N, my oncologist and Kim, one of her assisting nurses, at 2:30. After her examination, I get dressed and take out my tablet that has over twenty questions written on it. I ask if I am a candidate for any of AZ's hormone therapy drugs for breast cancer (like Arimidex® - anastrozole, or Nolvadex® - tamoxifen) and she says "no". My hormone receptor status (ER - Estrogen Receptor and PR - Progesterone Receptor) tested negative for hormone receptors and therefore negative for hormone therapy. *Oh brother - one less treatment option if the standard treatments don't work.*

Tip 44   According to breastcancer.org, many breast cancers are hormone-dependent, like "ER-positive" – which means that estrogen stimulates their growth by "turning on" estrogen receptors in the cancer cells. Without estrogen, the cancer cells are not stimulated to grow. The same goes for "PR-positive" (cancer cells that test positive for Progesterone Receptors). The presence of at least some hormone receptors on breast cancer cells is associated with a better prognosis probably due to the success of adjuvant hormone therapies (tamoxifen, Arimidex®, etc.).

Then, there's HER-2/neu. Some breast cancers express high levels of a protein called HER-2/neu. This is a gene that makes the human epidermal growth factor receptor 2. The protein produced is HER-2/neu antigen, which stimulates growth. An excess of this protein is involved in the growth of some cancer cells. The presence of this protein indicates a favorable response to the drug, Herceptin® (trastuzumab).

Ask your doctor about your cancer status for these three traits, ER, PR and HER-2/neu, and what they mean for you.

I ask a few more questions. Dr. N answers each, but her answers are very clinical. It must be difficult to be in the profession of oncology and treat cancer. It can't be easy to talk with a patient who just found out she has this disease. I stop asking questions about a third of the way through my list. *I'll search the Internet and find other ways to get answers; I've taken enough of her time.*

As directed, Dan and I walk down the hall to the lab so I can have blood drawn. On the marquis in the hallway, we notice other departments list-

ed. Radiology and X-ray, to name a few. This place is one-stop-shopping.
Now that I've talked with the doctor I know more about the Helen F.
Graham Cancer Center. As I would come to find out, it is affectionately
referred to by some as "the Helen Graham." *So, this facility is where I'll be
getting CT scans, x-rays and weekly blood tests. Thank goodness I won't have to
wait in the queues of the in-network public labs anymore. This building is like
an all-inclusive resort - it's beautiful and has everything I need.* I feel less
apprehensive about what I am facing now that I've seen the place.

We've been here for a few hours and we get the impression that our stay
is concluded. After all, it is 4:30. Dan looks at me and asks, "Do you think
we are done? I mean, is there anything else you need me to stay for?"

We assume we are done and agree it is best that he goes back to his job to
close up. I say to him, "I'll go in a few minutes…I need to use the restroom first. I'll use the one outside Dr. N's office and will be right behind
you." He kisses me good-bye, tells me he'll see me at home tonight and
proceeds to his car.

When I am finished in the restroom I walk out, keys in hand, and hear a
voice, "Would you like to see the chemo room?" It is Dr. N's nurse, Kim.

"Okay," I say. *I am looking forward to this.* She takes me into a large open
area with a wall of windows overlooking a relaxing scene. There is a
pond with a fountain in the center sprinkling water. Watching it gives me
a hypnotic feeling. She motions; I do a full circle. I notice approximately
fifteen recliners, a television, and a pantry area with a microwave and coffee and tea. Some people are in the recliners. Next to many of them are
cushioned chairs (for companions, I suppose) and IV (intravenous) poles.
*My goodness, the people in the recliners look like shrunken cocoons. They are
wrapped in afghans and blankets. Some are sleeping. Ooh, I don't like this.*

Kim addresses me, "Now, you decided you'll get the medi-port implanted instead of receiving the chemo through an IV in a vein. Good choice.
The medi-ports really are better. Chemo can burn the smaller veins that
are in your arm. When you get the meds through your port, they go in
through the vena cava and directly to your heart. Let me see if I can find
someone here who has a medi-port." She looks around the room. *What
does she mean "burn" the veins? Burn - like tingle and feel heat? Or, burn - like
blacken and shrivel?*

The vena cava is a large vein that returns blood directly to the right atri-
um of the heart; perfect for directing medicine to the body. Receiving
chemo via the vena cava is an efficient process (versus receiving chemo
through an arm vein) because the medicine, after it reaches the heart, is

circulated from head to toe within a minute.

We walk over to an African-American woman who looks a little older than me. She is sitting upright and reading a magazine. *I wonder why she's awake and the others aren't. Why isn't she wrapped in a blanket? She looks unruffled and healthy.* Her rows of braids have tiny gray hairs in them so I assume the hair is her own, "You haven't lost your hair yet?" I inquire.

"This is my first treatment," she replies. She opens her blouse enough so that we can see her chest. A few inches below her collarbone, under her skin is a device about the size of a quarter. The IV tube is sticking out of it. Weird. *I'll be walking around with a quarter on my skin? Will the tube be hanging out too? What if I knock it by accident? Can it fall off? Will it leak or does it have a valve to close it? Will people be able to see it? How will I shower?*

"I've seen enough, thanks." Kim shows me the way out.

The next moment, I'm in my car. *How did I get here? I wish Dan were here.* I am sitting in my car, unable to start it. *Put the key in the ignition and turn.* I am paralyzed. Unexpectedly, I cry hysterically. This is the first time since my diagnosis last week that I am crying…really crying. It's uncontrollable. The floodgates are open. My hands are on my face and my head is turning from side to side. *Are the odd sounds that I hear coming from me? Are those my feet stomping on the floor? My nose is running…can't find tissue when I need it. I won't be able to drive like this. Dan. Call Dan. No, I can't call Dan. He'll feel awful about not being here for me. I can't compose myself. Lisa. I'll call Lisa.* My best friend, Lisa, is always my calming influence.

Lisa is an operating room nurse who works in a hospital in New York. She is there for twelve-hour stretches at a time. It's sheer fortune that I reach her. Somehow, amidst my hysteria, she comprehends what I'm saying, "Yes, Wendi, it's lousy. It stinks to have cancer and it's okay to be mad. I'm mad. I want to stay on the phone with you and get you through this. I am driving right now though, and I have to turn off the turnpike to drop Caitlin [her daughter] off to work. Hold on. I am putting the phone down."

I'm still sitting in my parking space. I am still crying. She comes back on line, "I'm back." She talks some more. I don't hear what she's saying at first, but I hear the reassuring tone of her voice. It comforts me. Then, her words reach my ears, "You've had a great life so far. You're 45. Think about how you'll feel if you see a teenager or a kid in the chemo room." *Wham!* That sobers me. Instantly, I am extraordinarily calm. We talk a little more, and then conclude the conversation. I think I'll drive home.

Labor Day weekend is approaching and I look forward to seeing her at the beach. I owe her BIG.

Someday, I'm certain that I'll look back on this day and, aside from my madness, I'll recall and appreciate this wonderful cancer center that has so much to offer people in need, like me. People who belong here, people with cancer, people like me.

Tip 45   If you haven't already, now would be a good time to consult, Dr. Susan Love's Breast Book, by Susan M. Love, M.D. It is 700 pages of vast knowledge that Dr. Love candidly delivers to her readers. It is comprehensive and can be used as a reference book. There are 34 chapters (I am tempted to list them, so you can see how all-inclusive it is). The chapters are separated into seven parts: The healthy breast, Common problems of the breast, Diagnosis of breast problems, Prediction and prevention of cancer, Diagnosis of breast cancer, Treating breast cancer, and Living with breast cancer. Part six (Treating breast cancer) is almost 200 pages of treatment options.

Tip 46   I recommend two more really useful books; you can choose which might be helpful for you.   One is called 100 Questions & Answers About Breast Cancer by Zora Brown and LaSalle D., Leffall, Jr., MD with Elizabeth Platt. A colleague in the oncology department at work gave this one to me when I was well into my treatment.   If I had known about it sooner, I would have picked up a copy very early on. It has seven parts. 1 - The Basics, 2 - Risk Factors, 3 - Prevention, 4 - Diagnosis, 5 - Treatment, 6 - Changes Cancer Brings, and 7 - Coping with Treatment and Side Effects.

The second one is called Living through Breast Cancer by Dr. Carolyn M. Kaelin.   A breast cancer survivor and a doctor at Harvard Medical School, Dr. Kaelin takes you through from soup to nuts. It is divided into three parts. I - Getting your Bearings: Diagnosis, Treatment, and Drawing Together Your Medical Team, II - Preserving Your Sense of Self: Responding to Treatment Challenges, and III - Regaining Your Balance: Exercise, Nutrition, Sexuality, and More.

Tip 47   With a colored highlighting marker, highlight the books that I suggest (in the text and at the end of the book in the *My Favorites* sections) that you think you may want to read. Call or go to your local library to get them. You might want to call ahead and ask if the library specialist will set them aside for you. Explain that you are a cancer patient; an extended trip to the library might tucker you out or expose you to viruses. Alternatively, take this book or your book list to one of the large bookstores like Barnes & Noble or Borders. Both stores provide seating and allow you to look through books. Do this before you buy so you can choose the ones you want rather than spending an exorbitant amount of money on books you may not get a chance to read. (Your time in between treatments, appointments, resting, and day-to-day living will be limited.)

The six of us go to our beach house for the Labor Day holiday weekend with Charles and Lisa, and their kids, Shaun and Caitlin. On Saturday, we boat over to the local waterfront restaurant and dock at the pier. Relaxing and listening to the steel drums and Caribbean songs of the Island Boys is immensely therapeutic. This weekend will be the last time in awhile when we can be together in full complement, because Shaun and Christine have started college, Andrea, Michele and Caitlin are back to high school and the autumn routine will begin.

We are sitting on the boat; Charles is building an audience as passers-by see him mixing virgin piña coladas and strawberry banana daiquiris. "How are you doing that?" they eagerly inquire.

He proudly shows off his bar-tending skills and the smoothie maker that is powered by a generator. In time, the kids are doing kid things, the men are doing men things and Lisa and I are relaxing. In a quiet moment she asks, "Did you bring the path report?"

"Yep." I pull it out and hand it to her. She reads it quietly and says something ambiguous. Since she's an OR nurse, she likes reading this stuff, so I don't expect any comments from her that I would be able to understand. Months later, she told me what she was thinking when she read it:

Most of what I read confirmed what you told me except for one thing, 'lymphatic system involved'. I didn't think it was my place to say anything and I didn't say anything to Charlie but I knew what it meant. I kept thinking, did they not say anything to her? She doesn't know. That's why she got this boat. She knew something was wrong.

Donating My own Blood for My Surgery

On Tuesday, I attempt to donate a second autologous pint of blood. These have to be spaced out by at least three days, the idea being that surgeons do not want patients with low blood counts caused by over-donating. I am running out of time. "I'm sorry, you can't donate another pint. Your hematocrit is 9.0. It has to be at least 12.5." *Dang, I'm going into surgery a pint low of autologous blood and with a low red blood cell count too. Can't anybody throw me a bone here? I'm wagging my tail and panting. I'll sit up and beg.* I leave the Blood Bank of Delaware feeling dejected.

Marcia calls the next day and says I'm confirmed for Friday for surgery. *Not Wednesday?* She reads my mind, "Two days won't make a difference, Mrs. Pedicone." *Oh, she's good.*

Folks Appreciate Knowing What I Really Need

As I listen to answering machine and voice mail messages, and read my e-mails and cards, I am thankful that people did not try to spare me by not telling me how my diagnosis is affecting them. I am grateful that they are telling me, expressing their sadness; I need their candor.

To all,

Thank you, again for your support and for being interested in my progress. To think I was afraid that folks might avoid me. I had a wonderful holiday weekend with family and friends, and that was extremely important as part of my emotional preparation for the road ahead.

My surgery has been scheduled for this Friday, September 10, not Wednesday as we'd originally planned. Heck, what's two more days? I will be in the Wilmington Hospital location of Christiana Care. I am scheduled to be in surgery from noon to 5 to have the mastectomy and lymph node biopsy performed by Dr. M who is surgeon number one, and then the breast reconstruction by Dr. D, the plastic surgeon, surgeon number two. The reconstruction will be done using tissue from my abdomen...that's the pseudo tummy tuck I will get out of this...what a bonus, hunh! I'll be in the hospital for three to five days, and then home to recuperate. Dan will contact Brenda and my sister, Vicki, and they will send the post-surgery e-mail update in my stead (Brenda - to a distribution list of AZ colleagues, and Vicki to a distribution list of friends and family).

The next important hurdle to clear is, upon waking from the surgery, receiving news that the sentinel node biopsy shows the lymph node under my left arm is clear. If it isn't clear, the lymphatic system that is attached to the sentinel node will be removed. If that is the case, I will have a minimum of two months of chemotherapy added to my current chemo treatment plan, and some minor arm problems that I may have to deal with (something called Lymphedema). Therefore, I am visualizing myself clearing that hurdle! It'll be great to wake up and hear the good news, "Lymph nodes are clear."

At the risk of sounding presumptuous, I have a request; please do not feel compelled to send flowers. Your good vibes and prayerful thoughts are enough to sustain me...honestly. Besides, if we receive more flowers than we already have, my teenagers won't have places to toss their back packs, keys, lip gloss, and bits of paper!

I know people will want to do something, but I don't want an overabundance of flora and greenery to have to maintain or dead flowers to have to toss. I didn't know when I wrote this paragraph just how important it would be that I diplomatically said 'no flowers please'. Looking back, my family and I were truly amazed at the creative gifts people sent and the things they did instead. We were taken aback by the books and gifts that arrived in our mailbox. And, we were amazed at the meals and treats that appeared in our kitchen. I can sum them up in one word - Mmmmm.

I conclude the e-mail with next steps:

Four to six weeks following the mastectomy Dr. N, the oncologist, will coordinate with the surgeons to schedule the start of my chemotherapy. It is my understanding that coordinating the timing is critical, since the chemo drugs would interrupt healing from the surgery, yet we do not want to delay chemo longer than we have to. Also, I'll be scheduled to have a medi-port implanted, which is a device that looks like a quarter and placed under the skin on my chest (under sedation, thank goodness). Behind the device will be a catheter going directly to the heart. It will provide a place to receive the chemotherapy drugs. (This is truly fascinating.)

At some point after the chemo, I will undergo another surgery to finish the reconstruction of the left breast and touch-up scarring on the torso. Thank you American Medical Association and anyone else who recognizes that breast cancer clean up is important.

Well, that's all I have at this point. Thanks for listening; if you didn't read this e-mail in its entirety because it is long, it's okay and I understand. Writing it was very cathartic for me.

And now, my family and I begin a major journey....

Tip 48   Think deeply about what you may need and make a list. You may be pleasantly surprised to find that people truly want to know, specifically, what they can do to help. Some people actually have a fear of asking for help. If you are one of them, get over your fear. Do not deny friends and loved ones the opportunity to do something.

I list things I'll possibly need, like rides for my mom since she doesn't drive, play dates for Danny in case we need to keep him occupied, research on specific topics and rides to medical appointments for me during times when I won't be able to drive. I make another list of names of people whom I would like to appoint to a specific role, for example, Brenda and Vicki to send updates, Deb to do some fact-finding, and Tim to leave me wonderfully obnoxious voice mails. My brother, Tim…he was a class clown in school. He has such an ability to entertain a room full of people. He is also quite good at crafting voice messages complete with music and background sounds. The first time I saw McCauley Caulkin's clever character in Home Alone, I knew he had nothing on my brother.

About Brenda, she is a friend outside of work and a colleague at AZ. Our career paths have continuously crossed for about sixteen years. She and I and our families see each other socially, outside of work. She is saintly (only she's the last to know it). I am certain there are times when she glows, though the glowing hasn't been confirmed.

Ultimately, I communicate with everyone on my list. Each seems genuinely pleased that I have assigned them a responsibility that is aligned with his or her strength and my needs. *My instincts were correct. People really do want to know the best way to support me.*

Dan and I are in bed, discussing the day's events and he says, "I went to A.I. today [Andrea and Michele's high school, Alexis I. duPont]. I talked to Dr. Ln and asked him to inform the girls' teachers. He agreed that they'd need to know. I just want them to support the girls in case they miss assignments or get to school late in the mornings. Did you know Andrea is taking Danny to daycare each morning? Dr. Ln said 'their understanding and assistance won't be a problem'. He'll take care of it."

"That's nice of him. Yeah, I know Andrea's the one taking Danny to daycare. I hear her in the mornings pluck him out of a sound sleep to go. They have to leave so early and it makes me sad. Poor little guy. His world is turning upside down."

Tip 49   Even if you are an immensely private person, consider the benefits of telling people. Notify the schools your children attend. Ask them to understand if the children seem out of sorts. And when something actually does happen that requires their school's support, remind them in a note or conversation. For example, if you are addressing tardiness in a note, start out by saying something like, "Thank you for agreeing to be supportive in my family's time of need." Then go on with the rest of the note; "Please excuse [my daughter] from being late to school each day this week. She has been taking her little brother to daycare for me and the daycare doesn't open until 7 a.m." An example of a phone conversation could be, "We could really use your support right now. Would you give [my child] another day to turn in her assignment? She spent most of last night with us in the hospital." It is okay to remind a teacher that this is precisely how you need him or her to support your children.

Tip 50   When your kids panic over something that happens at school, as they would under normal conditions if you weren't facing a crisis at home, remind them that you asked for the school's support and it'll be okay. (Caregivers, you may want to keep your finger on the pulse and watch for signs that they aren't taking advantage of the support that's been promised, because that might point to an emotional situation that could possibly be addressed through the school's guidance counselor.)

It is late one evening, most of the house is asleep, and I am lying in Andrea's bed with her. She is telling me about a pain in her side that has been getting worse over the last few days. "Why haven't you told me about this before?"

"Because Dad said not to bother you."

I decipher Dan's directive, "Dad probably said to do as much as you can without me and not to bother me with little things that you can do on your own. BUT, when it comes to something like this, naturally you should tell me." She tells me what things she's been doing to make it better, but the pain has become excruciating.

Tip 51 Caregivers, it is very noble to ask others not to burden the cancer patient with things he or she would normally worry over (and shouldn't have to at this time), but recognize that the patient may not want to be excluded from certain things within her immediate family. It may be tricky at times to recognize when to and when not to involve her, so keep the lines of communication open. Ask her how she wants you to act upon everyday happenings and unusual events, and how she sees herself fitting in.

I bring the portable phone in Andrea's room and dial her physician's number. The doctor in the group who is on call is mine. Dr. K is not only my doctor, he's someone Dan and I know socially. A few minutes after I left a message with the answering service, he calls. I describe the symptoms and history, then add, "Dr. K, you know what I'm going through. Don't ask me to take her to the ER unless you absolutely think it's necessary."

He replies, "I think it's necessary. It could be appendicitis. It may not be, but it could be. You'd better take her."

I press the "end" button on the phone and turn my head to look at Andrea, "I'll get dressed; let's go to the emergency room."

It is 5:00 a.m. and we've been here for about four hours. After several tests to rule things out, the doctors are thinking kidney stones or a nasty case of a urinary tract infection (UTI). She is in a twilight sleep and scratching her arm where the IV is. I ask the attending nurse about the scratching. "Oh, that's the morphine, it makes you itch. Itching is better than the pain, though."

In the semi-dark room, I stand by her bedside and gaze at her. I recall my terror when she was three-years-old and got lost on the beach. And I recollect my relief when she came walking up, flanked by two lifeguards and swinging her long blonde hair from side to side. Now, she lies perfectly still. I run my fingers through her hair as I used to when she was little, and as my mother used to when I was little. Exhaustion overcomes me. I haven't slept much in the last week and not at all since yesterday. I feel like I am carrying 300 pounds of something on my shoulders and my eyelids are heavy. After a slow and deep breath, I pull my chair up to the bed and lay my head by her legs. "God, please give me strength." *9-1-1 to*

God: My children need me. "God, please don't let me die." *I cannot die from cancer. It's going to be a crummy road ahead for a while, but I must live through it.* I drift off until the next medical professional dressed in a lab coat appears in the room.

"A CT scan is scheduled for 6:30 a.m.," he tells me, "which is when that department opens. We are not staffed to do round-the-clock scans." So, if we want one immediately or, at the very least, sooner than 6:30, we'll have to go to the Christiana Care/Newark hospital. *Hmmm, by the time we leave here, go there and wait in their queue, it could be later than 6:30. Andrea is resting comfortably and appendicitis has been ruled out.* I elect to stay.

"We'll stay." I inform him.

I need to go home and get Danny so that Dan can go to work. He has several meetings today, and if he misses them, that would make his next few work days complicated. I am sensitive to his work ethic and do what I can to enable him to be there. On a subconscious level, I know that keeping him in his work routine will help him feel safe and in control. Cancer is taking everything else out of his control…and mine.

Since Andrea is under eighteen, the 6:30 CT scan can't be done if I'm not present. *I'd better hurry. I can get back in time.*

I return at 6:15, with Danny, some toys, and two-dozen doughnuts in tow. I give one box of doughnuts to the nurses' station. It feels wonderful to bring smiles to people's faces. The second box, I take into Andrea's room. Danny and I sit by a sleeping Andrea and make small messes with cream filling and sugary glaze. A staff member arrives to take her for her test. He wheels her out of the room. *Oh brother, I could use some sleep.* I prepare to make an attempt: I wash Danny's hands in the sink and turn on the television hoping to get him interested in a cartoon. I sit him on my lap so he won't be wandering around and touching things. I move my chair close to the closed door and place my foot in front of it so I can doze and he can't leave without me waking up to prevent it. *I've got all bases covered. Right? Wrong. There are no cartoons and television doesn't interest him.*

Tip 52   If you are the type of person who gets a rise from doing things for others, continue to do so when it's convenient. It will make you feel wonderful and give you a taste of normalcy. Alternatively, don't do anything that will add pressure at this hectic time. The good feeling you get may not be worth the anxiety you cause yourself.

At some point, Andge returns from x-ray. A doctor gives us the diagnosis of a UTI, a prescription for an antibiotic, and a document of information. A nurse removes the morphine IV. We wait a little longer for the proper dismissal procedure, and then Andrea is taken to the front door in a wheel chair. Meanwhile, I walk to the car with Danny on my hip. The cool morning air makes my breath appear like smoke and my ears feel numb. They feel as they used to when I'd leave a nightclub on a wintery night after listening to a rock band. I recall the muffled sounds in the parking lot that reminded me that I was standing by the speaker all night until last call. *Or maybe it's the exhaustion.*

The three of us head for the pharmacy before going home. Reclined in the passenger seat of the vehicle, Andrea is woozy and scratching her arm. I pull into a parking space at the store and unbuckle Danny from his car seat. He and I approach the counter and I am like a gorilla, knuckles dragging on the ground. Actually, I think I am walking, neck deep in a swimming pool of water. Danny actively hops and skips around me, and asks for just about everything from the beginning of the aisle all the way back to the pharmacist's counter. *What energy. This is definitely going to be a daycare day for him.*

EVERYONE AROUND ME THINKS ABOUT CANCER NOW

It's Friday night and Christine is home! I'm so happy to see her. I'm proud that she completed her first week of college. *Is it my imagination or does she really look different? Older? More mature? Hmmm.* She asks about my cancer activities, but mostly we talk about her school activities. I don't want all our discussions to be about cancer.

We have a long and relaxed conversation before turning in for the night. She assures me she's not worrying about me and I vow to tell her everything going forward (so she won't have to wonder, ever, if I'm holding anything back). In other words, if I hear significant news, at any time, I promise her that she'll be one of the first to know. "Good night Mommy. I love you," are the last words I hear her say before she goes to bed. I'll never grow tired of hearing those words from any of my children.

Dan and I go to bed, too. The room is dark and quiet. I am wondering how I will quiet the cacophony in my head. I suspect it is going to worsen with time. Moments later, a light shines through our partially opened door, and then I see a silhouette. It is Christine. She walks in holding one of our cats, Genesis. "Mom," she begins, "Feel this." She places my finger on hers, which is kneading something on the cat's rib cage. It is a tiny lump. "Do you think Genesis has cancer?"

Cancer is definitely on all our minds now, *and it is beginning to tick me off.*

"...Mom, do you think Genesis has cancer?"

...It is definitely on all our minds now...

Life is a bowl of pits.

Rodney Dangerfield
Actor / Comedian (1921 - 2004)

CHAPTER
3

MASTECTOMY FIRST, CHEMOTHERAPY SECOND

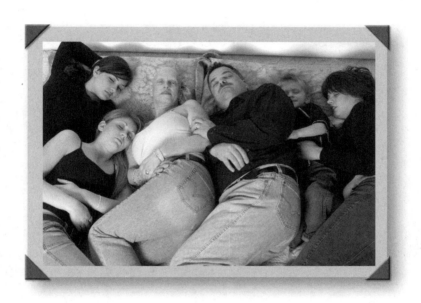

*When we are no longer able to
change a situation, we are challenged
to change ourselves.*

Victor Frankl
Holocaust Survivor and Author
(1942 - 1997)

Some women who are diagnosed with breast cancer do not need a mastectomy. I do.

CAREGIVERS (NOT JUST CANCER PATIENTS) NEED SUPPORT TOO

I am at home and wearing comfy clothes. Totally relaxed, I am having a no-make-up-who-cares-how-I-look day. Dan stops home to grab a bite to eat and check in on me. He looks at me from head to toe and says, "So, are you just giving up? Are you throwing in the towel? I guess you're going to just lay down and die from cancer, right?" *You've got to be kidding me. I look that bad?*

I realize in an instant that this is simply an expression of his fear. He is expressing his fear to me, his wife and friend. He forgets that I'm also the cancer patient. *My pillar of strength has sounded his alarm. I think I'm a little less brave than I was five minutes ago.*

He and I may, down the line, need some support or counseling to get us through this.

Tip 53   Caregivers, you can't be the be-all end-all for your loved one. Get support.

Tip 54   Look in the phone book, call a cancer center near you and check with your doctors' offices for nearby support centers that offer cancer patients and caregivers information, education and creative opportunities, such as nutrition sessions and stress reduction programs. These are just as helpful as support group discussions.

Tip 55   Check for local cancer support avenues, particularly ones that are run by professionals (very important). For example, the Wellness Community in Delaware offers free professional support to people whose lives have been touched by cancer who live within driving distance. They offer support group sessions, specialized sessions by topic, cooking classes, and complementary therapies like yoga and Reiki, and so much more. With any Wellness Community, there are no boundaries; everyone dealing with cancer in some way is welcome (cancer patients, relatives, friends and caregivers). The Delaware locations serve nearby states; New Jersey, Pennsylvania and Maryland. You can check www.wellness-delaware.org or call 877-892-9355 to determine if the ones in h any Wellness Community, there are no boundaries; everyone dealing with cancer in some way is welcome (cancer patients, relatives, friends and caregivers). The Delaware locations serve nearby states; New Jersey, Pennsylvania and Maryland. You can check *www.wellnessdelaware.org* or call 877-892-9355 to determine if the ones in Delaware can help you. Alternatively, visit the national website: www.wellnesscommunity.org and you will find a list of twenty-five cities across the country where Wellness Communities exist (as of September, 2005).

Tip 56   Go to the library or bookstore and read anything by Bernie S. Siegel, M.D. (Love, Medicine & Miracles, Prescriptions for Living, and Help Me To Heal.) He is a retired general/pediatric surgeon who is now involved in humanizing medical care and medical education. Additionally, buy his CD called Getting Ready by Hay House, Inc. There are three sections of a series of visualization exercises to help you mentally prepare. I listened to two of them over and over; Getting Ready for Chemotherapy, and Getting Ready for Radiation. There is also one for surgery. I would have listened to this section too had I known about the CD in September. Hay House CDs are not intended as substitutes for medical care, but they are powerful, energizing and life-changing tools to supplement your care. Louise Hay, the founder, has all kinds of self-help books, workshops, and opportunities to offer. For a free catalogue call 800-654-5126 in the USA or visit www.hayhouse.co.uk (UK), www.hayhouse.com.au (Australia) or write to orders@psd-prom.co.za (South Africa). Dr. Siegel's books and CDs are also comforting for caregivers. My husband listened to the CD, and my daughter Andrea read excerpts from one of his books.

THE TRANSITION OUT

It is two days before surgery. My manager, Jill, and I go over a checklist I created of things that will need to be done in my place over the next six weeks and my suggestions for who should do each.

Jill. Picture someone who is the most compassionate, open-minded and effective manager you've known and you'll know what Jill looks like.

Jill was my friend before she became my manager. We separate the two. We successfully change hats when appropriate. So, now that we are finished talking shop, she removes her "manager" hat and dons her "friend" hat. She gives me a wrapped box filled with Thank You cards. She took the time to select three kinds (for three types of thank yous). Oh, she knows me well. The seals on the packages are all broken. I realize that she put a postage stamp on every envelope. The item I gravitate to, however, is the get-well card to me. On the front of it is a print of a renaissance woman dressed in a gossamer gown and resting in a floral garden. She says it reminds her of what I may be like in a few days; resting peacefully and looking serene and beautiful.

Tip 57   Go to the Women's Information Network Against Breast Cancer, www.winabc.org and click on the "Help Through Surgery" tab. This section of the site contains tips to help a breast cancer patient prepare for surgery and get through the surgical experience as smoothly as possible.

It is one day pre-surgery and I am overcome with an unanticipated emotion – sadness. I am sad because I am about to lose something that provided for all my children when they were babies. I watched them drink milk from my breast thousands of times. I can see each, frantically searching for the nipple while hunger cries consume them. I vividly recall the white line of mother's milk where their infant lips touched my breast. The sounds they made when the calming effect of warm milk settled their tiny tummies were miraculous. Then, they would succumb to blissful sleep and I would feel the intermittent vibration of suckling...of my breast. To a nursing mother, this is heavenly. I thoroughly enjoyed nursing. I would have missed the beautiful experience were it not for my breasts, both of them. I have been thankful for them and now it is time to let one go.

I've been at work for an hour and a half and cannot seem to stay focused. I contact my life coach and tell her about my emotional state. She says it is normal grief, and then asks me to consider answers to some questions, "In addition to what they did for your babies, what did your breasts do for you?" *For me?* "Haven't they made you feel beautiful when you made love with your husband? Do you remember the first time your husband touched them? Do you remember how old you were and what it was like when you got breasts? Did you ever stuff your bra? Tonight, why don't you celebrate your breasts? Get some body paint and paint them, take pictures of them and discuss answers to the questions with Dan."

Wow! I feel better. And, I look forward to tonight. I contact Dan and reiterate the conversation with my life coach. I punctuate it with the telling of the celebration. "Sounds good to me," he says. *He's all man. Would he have declined my party invitation? I think not.* The conversation concludes with him saying to me, "I'll see you at the doctor's office in a little while."

Tip 58   Celebrate your breasts before your surgery. Look at favorite pictures you may have of your breasts and talk about breast milestones and special events.

REMOVAL OF BOTH BREASTS?

An associate comes into my office and greets me. She was diagnosed a year ago, had a mastectomy, chemo and radiation. She tells me that she went back to have her other breast removed and wished she'd done that first. It is an option she thinks I should consider. We talk about it a bit. She wishes me well. Next stop after finishing a few e-mails and discussions, the doctor's office.

I walk in to Dr. M's and see Dan in the waiting room. Marcia and Diane cheerily say hello. I smile and sit down next to Dan. "I've been thinking. I'm going to ask Dr. M if he can remove both breasts and use my abdominal tissue to create two A cups instead of one B. What do you think?

He looks extremely troubled and inquires, "Why would you do that?"

"So I won't ever get breast cancer again. If I have no breasts, I can't get breast cancer. Do you remember me telling you about Mary? I had lunch with her about six months ago." He shakes his head yes and I continue, "She went back to have her second breast removed. She feels *that* strongly about it."

"But," he cautions, "This is going to change everything. It'll delay your surgery." He pauses a moment and says, "It's your body; you should do what you want to do. I'll support you."

"Are you upset with me?" I ask.

"No, just surprised. I wasn't expecting this. I thought we were here for a pre-op visit, last minute details."

When in the examining room with the doctor (the same one where he delivered the news I was hoping I wouldn't get) he explains that we have breast tissue not just in the round part of the breast, but under our arms and as far up as a few inches under our collarbones. To remove the breast doesn't prevent breast cancer. "Mrs. Pedicone, you can't cut away body parts because you are afraid of getting cancer. If you were afraid of lung cancer, you couldn't cut out your lungs. Cutting things away is just not the best way to prevent disease." He further explains, "It is your choice and if you want to have both breasts removed, I can not do it. It goes against my ethics."

Tip 59   Having both breasts removed does not mean you cannot get breast cancer again. You could have breast tissue as far up as your collarbone and as far out as your armpit. And, it certainly won't prevent breast cancer from recurring or spreading in other places of your body (like bone, liver, lungs or brain). Having both breasts removed may help you to live with less fear, and that is important, however you may be putting yourself through unnecessary surgery while giving yourself an unrealistic sense of security. Ask your doctors and other breast cancer survivors (if you have access to any), and go to a live chat on some of the cancer websites I recommend to help you make this decision.

I trust him. I believe him. Tomorrow, I'll have one breast removed. I'll have the left breast mastectomy and TRAM flap reconstruction. Tomorrow is the first day of the rest of my life.

THE EVENING BEFORE

In the afternoon, my OE core team at work meets for our quarterly meeting. We do not follow the agenda. Instead, we take advantage of the lovely Indian summer day and meet outside where AZ has adirondack chairs. Squirrels and birds hum around us. The air smells sweet and woodsy. Things fall from the trees and hug the sides of the brick walkways. Our voices sound muted and without the echoes they would have if we were talking in a corporate sitting area of the building. Each of the four of us discusses what we envision in the workplace in the next six weeks. Naturally, I say nothing about my workload. I say, "recovering." They ask me what they can do for me during my recovery time until I return to work. *What they can do for me?*

It would be months later when I realize that the things my manager and coworkers did to transition me out of my role (to begin treatment), and then transition me back into my role (when the main course of my treatment was complete) were in response to my decisions. If you are a cancer patient, don't make assumptions about what is expected of you. Think about the things you will need for yourself, and in order to be an effective employee. Discuss them with your manager or someone in your HR or Medical department. For example, once I was diagnosed I set the priority to begin my treatment ASAP and my department doled out my responsibilities so I could leave, knowing things were going to be taken care of. Later, when I set the priority to not return following surgery and move onward to chemo and radiation, my manager found a temporary back-fill person for my job. And when I was ready to return, my colleagues followed my wishes when I said I needed two weeks to absorb information about where the company and my department was before I could begin to deliver on projects and against timelines.

I leave work late and there's no time to stop for body paint for tonight's celebration, but Dan and I can still rejoice and commemorate the part of me that I'm about to lose.

At the end of the evening, when we are behind closed doors, I ask Dan to take a few pictures of my breasts. I will not look at the images now, but might want to at some point in the future. I don't want to alter the mood. We talk about the first time he touched me, where we were, and what the circumstances were.

I tell him an anecdote about how I felt when my neighbor, who was two years younger than me, got a training bra soon after I did. *Why do we get training bras? What is there to train? What do trained breasts look like? And, what do untrained ones look like?* It didn't seem fair that she got a bra so soon after I did, because she didn't have to wait as long as I did to begin wearing one. I liked her, but her breasts became my breasts' archenemies. This was warfare and I began to wear see-through shirts to show off my real bra. You see, hers was only a half undershirt, so if she employed the same strategy, the world would see the difference. Checkmate! Yes, I did try stuffing, for only about a day. I soon realized that no cotton balls, nylon ankle socks or tissue would compare to the real things, even if they were only budding things. Dan and I conclude our celebration with the natural joining of two lovers. We are sated.

After a short time, I stroll to the bathroom. I look in the mirror and say to Dan, "I want to write a message on my breast and abdomen. I asked Lisa if ink would be a problem in the OR. She told me it would mean an extra few minutes to clean it away with Betadine, but the minutes would be worth the fun. What do you think?" *If everyone in the OR has a smile in their hearts, I win and we all win.*

"I think you should do what you want to do, dear." *Whatta guy.*

There's nothing more I need to say to Dan, the kids, and my extended family that I haven't said already and there's nothing I need to do in the way of a will or a document of our accounts and assets. So, we try to have a normal no-cancer evening. I turn the ringer of the phone to the off position and ignore all calls for the evening. I secure a ride for my mother (to go to her weekly hair appointment) for tomorrow and next Friday. I play with little Danny in his domain, the den floor, and the girls come and go as they usually do.

Tip 60   When you are facing cancer, you have to be a little selfish and think about you. Take time to give yourself the things you need, like time with your family, rest, relaxing baths, reading, time for talking on the phone and time for phone-abstinence.

Tip 61   Men: Go to MenAgainstBreastCancer.org for issues pertaining to you.

Tip 62   Caregivers: This might be a good time to get the book called *The Breast Cancer Husband* by Marc Silver. I have not read it myself, but have had many caregivers (not just husbands) recommend it for my family. It offers tips on coping, and becoming active in the cancer patient's care.

I would think there would be information about sexual intimacy in his book, as well, because Mr. Silver has done interviews for magazines on the topic. For example, I recall a bit of sage advice he offered on the topic: He suggested that you should assume your wife with cancer wants to continue a sexual relationship and that she might turn it down whenever you offer it, but if you never offer it she may feel worse.

Tip 63   The website www.cancercare.org offers online support circles with open forums for friends and family. Another great feature of CancerCare; you can have private group discussions (ten people or less) online that are facilitated by an oncology social worker.

Centuries ago, women who fought in battles used to remove a breast in order to shoot their arrows with precision. *Hmmm. I can remove mine. I can do this.* I pray to God for safe delivery and strength on the road ahead, and we go to bed.

SUPPORT FROM COLLEAGUES

Sue S is the Administrative Coordinator in our group. You've met her. She's the one person on your team, in your group, or in your family who thinks she has little to offer when she is actually pretty remarkable. She sends out an e-mail using my AZ distribution list:

We have received many questions from Wendi's friends asking what they could do that would be most meaningful to Wendi and her family. In an attempt to try to make this easier on everyone, I am volunteering to be the point of contact.

One of the things that Wendi is most concerned about is getting her family decent meals. Therefore, if anyone is interested in supplying a meal, please let me know. I will keep track of this information.

Sue F and Joseph have graciously offered to deliver meals and other things to Wendi's home. They would be more than happy to take them out to Wendi's home between Monday and Thursday either at noon or after work during Wendi's absence. If it is a food item, please be sure it is properly wrapped or containerized and bring it to our location by 11:00 a.m. We have a refrigerator/freezer here, so the food will be kept fresh until it gets delivered. If it requires cooking/reheating, please be sure to tape instructions on the wrapping so the girls/Dan will know how to handle it. Also, write your name and a little note on it so Wendi knows you were thinking of her since she may not be awake when it's dropped off. Wendi also mentioned donations of gift cards to local take-out restaurants and/or other places (i.e., a restaurant that has take-out) so that her family could have somewhat 'real' meals.

If you're interested in doing something other than food, knowing Wendi, she would appreciate anything and everything. We could possibly collect money donations that her family could use as they feel necessary towards medical expenses such as a wheel chair or specialized bed rental, etc. or any number of other things. Please feel free to make any kind of suggestion. Thank you very much for caring.

Sue F, the person Sue S mentioned in her e-mail, is a colleague at AZ and has been a friend of mine outside of work for several years now. I'll bet you can think of someone you know who tries to maintain a tough façade. *But, the warmth from within always shines through.* Sue is a caring mother and mother-in-law, loyal to her friends, and charitable. Little do I know at this time, that over the next few months she would be visiting us often and making lots of food runs to our home.

Joseph joined our team at AZ in January. I wonder how he will react to being tossed into this whirlwind. My cancer diagnosis is drastically changing the way our team interacts and what the "day-to-day" is.

Vicki sends out an e-mail using my distribution list for folks outside AZ:

Wendi is scheduled for surgery tomorrow, Friday, 9/10. At 9:00 am she reports to the Wilmington hospital location on Washington Street and surgery starts at noon. It will last at least 5 hrs plus recovery so I won't see her until Saturday.

While under, they will check her lymph nodes. If clear, she will have two months of chemo (not sure how many applications). If they are cancerous and have to be removed, an additional two months of chemo will be added on.

Thanks for asking.... I'll keep you all posted.
Please say a prayer. V.

THE MORNING OF MY MASTECTOMY

Today is the day. This day, I will have a skin-sparing modified radical mastectomy with a TRAM flap reconstruction. *To say that is a mouthful, isn't it?* I awaken before the alarm, pleasantly surprised that I slumbered heavily. Dan has gone to work. Andrea and Michele wish me luck before they leave for school. Christine calls from her dorm at Immaculata (IU) and does the same. *I hope I appear brave and unworried. Kids have sonar that detects parents' fears.* I give Danny extra squeezes as I leave him at daycare. *I feel sad to leave him. What will it be like when he comes home tonight and I'm not here?* Miss Sheri assures me that he'll be all right and can stay as long as we need him to. Even though that won't be necessary, I am thankful for the contingency plan. Andrea is picking him up in the afternoon and taking him to my brother's house. He will have a blast with Tim and Mary's sons, Nathan, who is eight, and Evan, who is a few months younger than Danny. Dan will be with me until I go into surgery. He will leave for a few hours, and then return to the hospital when I am in recovery.

I call my mother-in-law and my mother. I remind both that there is no need for them or anyone to sit in the waiting room for hours upon hours today. *Who would want to sit in a waiting room during a five-hour surgery and two-hour recovery?*

Since I've known Dan for the better part of my life, his mother has been many things to me. While I was growing up, she was "Aunt Helen," and his father was "Uncle Sammy." When Dan and I started dating, she became "Mrs. Pedicone." And, when we were engaged, she became "Mom." (Dad Pedicone passed away nine years ago.) Mom Pedicone is patient, understanding, and unassuming; I don't have any bad mother-in-law stories.

Talk to the kids. Check. Talk to my moms. Check. Talk to my sisters. I exchange cell phone instant messages with my sisters. Check. I am surrounded by love. I am ready.

There's still time to kill. I set about doing some last minute paperwork and bill paying. While I am on our computer, I download the digital images from last night. My left breast looks odd. I can see what I couldn't see from above, what Dan saw from the angle of the camera. The biopsy slightly deformed my breast. It is misshapen. Gee, a good bit of breast tissue is gone from underneath the nipple. It looks ugly. Dan has been seeing and touching it and has never said a word. *How wonderful.* I pity partners of women who are in similar situations to mine who cannot see past the lack of physical beauty in a maimed or missing breast.

In my bathroom, pen in hand, I stand in front of the mirror. My backward writing expertise is tested. I write a note for Dr. M on my left breast and one for Dr. D on my abdomen. *Oh, I'm goooood.* Won't they be surprised!

Dan has just walked in the door from the garage. I am in the kitchen. He keeps himself busy for a minute or two and, I know, is watching for my signal to leave. "Are you ready?"

I catch myself as I reach for the water cooler. "Yep, I gotta get outta here. Let's get this show on the road."

I've got a small overnight case, purse, pictures of the kids, cell phone, portable CD player, and other miscellaneous belongings. I also have in my possession the card with the resting woman on it that Jill gave me.

Thanks to Dan, we arrive safely and on time at the Christiana Care/Wilmington hospital campus. The surreal nature of being here has me tense. The caffeine headache I am experiencing doesn't help. Did you know that some people have such a problem with caffeine withdrawal that doctors will order a caffeine drip in their IV? My headache is mild, as is my caffeine dependency.

"Good morning. I am Wendi Pedicone and I am scheduled for surgery at nine with Drs. M and D," I say to the receptionist.

"Yes, good morning," she says, "Have a seat. We'll be ready for you in a few minutes." She looks in Dan's direction and addresses him; "You may help yourself to coffee or tea located in the corner. When Mrs. Pedicone is in recovery, someone will call you on this phone." She points to a red phone on the counter. It is a means of communication between the recovery room and the waiting room.   I suppose any person-in-waiting answers it near the time of the expected surgery-end-time. *Perhaps the receptionist leaves at the end of the shift and anyone waiting after that can be reached via the bat phone.*

What may be perceived as composure and focus on my part is utter dread. The thought of what is going to be happening to me in an hour makes me shudder. *Don't think about it. Think happy thoughts.*

Next stop, vital signs and prep. We go into a small room with a curtain separating us from the medical staff. I change my clothes. *More hospital gowns and slippers. Sheesh. I'm getting too good at this. Matching the ties on the robe is a piece of cake!* A nurse tech says something and I assume she is talking to someone else because she doesn't make eye contact with me. She repeats what she said in a louder tone and both Dan and I realize she's talking to me. "Pardon me?" I ask. I make eye contact with her.

She rolls her fore finger from me to her in a come-here gesture. Loudly, she says, "Step here." Her foot points to the scale on the floor, "You get weighed." *Well, now I know.*

We have a similar experience when she takes my blood pressure and pulse. "Your arm."

"I'm sorry?"

"I need your arm." *Is it because I am inwardly panicking that I do not understand much of what she's saying? Or is she not speaking clearly?* "I'm gonna take your blood pressure and pulse, for real." *For real? Is she for real? I think she missed the class on etiquette. Or, maybe she's having a bad morning…she's only human. Make a mental note; remind Kayla, who is studying nursing, that people are people at all times and nurses should treat them as such, and nursing is an everyday job to a nurse, but being a patient is not an everyday occurrence for people. It can be extremely difficult for patients when nurses have bad days. I know Kayla will treat patients compassionately.* I smile as a way to overturn the direction of our interaction, and she saunters away. Dan and I look at each other and shrug our shoulders. *Oh, well.*

A sweet, African-American woman who is older than me softly says, "Time to go now." The three of us walk the hall toward pre-op. She lumbers a bit, so the walk is slow. I am grateful. About every fifth step she looks at me and smiles. She reminds me of a child's grandmother who slips her candy when her mother is not looking. *Everyone should have a sweet grandmother who lovingly bends rules. How pleasant. She's pleasant. I'm frightened and I draw courage from her pleasantness.* She is facing forward when she says, "See the brass plate on the floor where the double doors are propped open?" Then she looks at Dan, "That's where you kiss her good-bye." *My heart begins to beat wildly. I can hear it in my head. Good-bye. We have to say good-bye.*

> *"...Time to go now...see the brass plate on the floor where the double doors are propped open...that's where you kiss her good-bye..."*

Raised on respect for rules, the dreaded brass threshold is upon us and we know what to do. We don't need a reminder. We stop, she stops and he and I kiss. It is a very practical kiss. An I'll-see-you-on-the-other-side kiss. The high degree of my fear is downgraded to a mild level. My lovable pseudo-grandma and I step over the brass line, and leave my husband behind. After a few steps, I look back one last time to see a forlorn Dan, standing in the place where we kissed, clutching to his chest the brown paper bag containing my belongings. One side of his mouth turns upward, he waves a half-hearted wave, turns on his heal and retreats. *I'll bet he thinks he looks brave. I know he is trying to be. Please God, deliver me back to this man tonight.*

My precarious position on the table, with curtains dividing me and the other pre-op patients, gives me a feeling of vulnerability. I am in the inner sanctum, a place where no one who loves me is allowed. I watch the multitude of people move about the area. Some are staff and others must be concerned family members. In what appears to be the alcove where provisions are kept, there are a few men wearing scrubs, going through the cabinets and organizing glass bottles and tubing. One is rather handsome. Despite the baggy green cotton outfit I can see he's all firm muscle underneath and in perfect proportion. He has attractive hands. His eyes are intensely focused. *Oh great, I'm checking out guys. I'm about to undergo major surgery and I'm checking out guys. What is wrong with me? What am*

I thinking? I'm not a teenage girl. I'm a 45-year-old mother of four. Egads.

GENERAL ANESTHESIA AND AN EPIDURAL

An IV is placed in my arm and an anesthesiologist introduces himself. He begins with something that will relax me. *Thank you.* Then he asks me if I want an epidural.

What? We're not having babies here. "I've never had an epidural. I delivered all my children naturally." I uneasily replied. "Do I need an epidural for this? I thought I was going to be under general anesthesia." I'm getting edgy. *Did I miss something? Are they going to do this under local anesthesia? They can't possibly do this under a local.*

His eyes open wide and he senses my mounting angst. "Oh yes, of course you will be under general anesthesia." He is distracted for a millisecond. "Hold on, your doctor is here. Let me check with him. I'm so sorry to have upset you. I'll explain it all to you after I talk with him." Just then Dr. M walks by on his way to scrub. "Doctor," he says. "Do you want Mrs. Pedicone to have an epidural?

Dr. M looks delighted, "Really, you will give her an epidural? That'd be great." He looks at me and says, "I'll be back in a few minutes."

Somehow, his delighted response reassures me and I look at the anesthesiologist and say, "Yes."

In a sitting position I am holding my breath. I do not feel the needle being inserted between the vertebrae in my back. I do, however, feel the tape being applied to hold it in. *Feels like a lot of tape.* "Thank goodness I'll be asleep when all that's being pulled off, otherwise it would hurt." I say.

"Actually, the morphine epidural will stay in for a few days and so will the tape, but you'll be numb so you won't feel the tape being pulled." He explains more about the pain treatment plan. "You'll have morphine in your IV and your epidural. The first will keep you under light sedation; the second will anesthetize your torso. With TRAM flap surgery, you'll be glad for that. One side effect of morphine that people complain about is itching. I'd rather itch all over than be in pain." *Sounds like a plan to me.*

I find myself alone and I talk out loud but softly, "Please God, bring me out of this surgery. Don't take me from Dan and the kids. I have too much life left to live. Bless the surgeons. Bless the nurses. Bless me, Lord."

Tip 64   Remember, there are thousands and thousands of surgeries that are performed in the country on a daily basis. People rarely die in surgery. According to the American Society of Anesthesiologists, deaths attributed to anesthesia occur in only one in 250,000. Those are excellent odds; in the 1970's the odds were one in 10,000. Have faith in science, medical technology and patient safety standards. You have puh-lenty of things to think about; not making it out of surgery is definitely not one of them.

My head is beginning to spin and I feel like I am rocking on a boat. Dr. M is talking next to my ear, "You're in good hands." *Did he hear what I said to God?* He opens my gown and looks at my left breast. I hear him chuckle when he sees what I wrote, "Heh heh heh, 'steady hands Doc'. That's funny." He looks me in the eye, "You're funny." He turns serious and with gloved hands and syringe, he injects something into the areola of my left breast. Unless I'm delirious, it looks like the dark pink area surrounding my nipple is shriveling. I think I hear crackling sounds like *Pop Rocks* candy makes when placed in your mouth. *Weird.*

> *He opens my gown and looks at my left breast. I hear him chuckle...*

I recall a quote I read recently, from Betty Ford, former first lady and breast cancer survivor. She said, "I made it, and so can you." *Well, treatment begins today. Here I go. I hope that someday I can say I made it.*

Oh my head...spinning, swirling... Someone switches off the lights.

A second later, someone switches them on. Dan and his mom are standing at the foot of my bed. It is moving. I am moving. I am being wheeled into a room. *It's over. The surgery is done. The only thought that comes to my mind is that about cancer in my lymph nodes.* I reach for Dan's hand. My mouth feels full of cotton, but I manage to ask, "Was it in my lymph nodes?"

Dan hesitates for a nanosecond and I pick up on it. "Yes." He knows *exactly* what I'm thinking and follows it up with, "But the doctor says you could outlive me."

"What time is it?" I inquire tiredly. "Nine?" *Really?* "What took so long?" I do not hear the answer. A drifting feeling overcomes me. The rest of the night is a blur.

Dr. D writes:

The surgery went extremely well without a glitch. Wendi's sense of humor and positive spirit came through at the start of the case with her written message on her abdomen stating "Dear Doc D. Take more than you need from here." You gotta love it. She was already asleep and prepped. It is common for patients to tell me before a procedure, 'Doc, if you slip and take out some more fat somewhere else that's okay with me.' Only one patient that I know of actually put that in writing. That would be Wendi! I wish all my patients could be so positive. A great attitude, for sure.

THE HOSPITAL STAY

At 6:00 a.m. the next morning I am awake and alone so I check voice mail at work. As I had hoped there would be, there are messages from colleagues. Hearing voices helps me to feel grounded. I switch on my cell phone. Sure enough, there's a message from Tim. The chanting of Gregorian Monks is the first thing I hear. Next, his voice, and the monks fade to the background. "Wendi, how you doing? Wait...ah, these guys are so loud...hold on..." He pulls away from the mouthpiece and shouts, "Hey guys, can you keep it down?" The monks fall silent (Tim must've turned the volume down). He says a few supportive things to me, then shouts, "Okay guys, you can do your thing." The monks are chanting again, for a minute or two, then the message disconnects. *My brother, what a knucklehead.*

I turn the cell phone off to save my battery. I reach for the hospital phone and turn the ringer to silent. Dan and I pre-agreed that I would do this to keep my phone from ringing constantly. A ringing phone feels invasive. It makes me stop what I'm doing to answer it. I expect to be dozing in and out and don't want to be interrupted.

Tip 65   Encourage people to leave messages for you. They are comforting to listen to when you are awake in the wee hours of the morning and there's no one else awake to talk to.

I lay my head back on the pillow. *What do I do now?* I press the button on the bed and tilt my upper body upward. As the bed hums and my head is lifted I see what my body looks like. *Holy cow, there are cords and tubes everywhere.* I see huge leg cuffs that are squeezing and massaging my legs and an electrical cord coming from the cuffs to the side of the bed. *That's one.* I have two small tubes from my right arm to the IV pole. *Two, three.* One is clear and the other is deep red. On the pole are three bags. One that is going in my arm is clear, probably saline, nourishment and the morphine they told me I'd have. Also on the pole is a bag of blood. I suppose that's my autologous pint. I'm scanning my body again and see a clear tube coming from the vicinity of the top of my legs. I know what that is. A catheter. *Four.* I guess I won't be going to the potty or using a bedpan. The fluid in the bag at the end of the tube is blue. *My urine is blue, just as Dr. M said it would be.* I reach down to touch my genitals. *Wow, that tube feels big. Glad I was unconscious when they put that in.* Oh, the thought of what gets done to you when you are out. I squeeze my eyes shut... I refuse to think about it and return to what I was doing before I had that thought. There is a swollen part of my genitalia. It feels cool to the touch. What is that, I wonder. I later find out it is a balloon of water just inside me that is attached to the catheter and keeps it from slipping out.

A nurse comes in to empty my drains. *Do what?*

Tip 66   Do not be concerned if you are in a similar situation and you discover blue or green urine. During surgery and as part of the sentinel node biopsy, radioactive dye is injected into your lymph nodes. Cancer-positive nodes hold the dye, which is how they know which ones to remove.

"Empty your drains," she repeats. "When you were in surgery the doctor put drains in, so you won't have internal bleeding or bloating. The fluid has to go somewhere. It's best that it exits through the drains." She holds up a bulb that looks like the one used as a hand pump on the end of a blood pressure cuff. Only this is transparent. It is filled with yellowish fluid and blood that stays separated like oil and water. *Gross!* There are several of these coming out of me. *Five, six, seven, eight.*

She pulls a tiny plug from each bulb. The plugs look like ones you'd see on an inner tube or swim ring. She squeezes the fluid from each into containers that are marked one through four. I notice that each drain is marked one-two-three-four also. Before she replaces the plug, she squeezes the bulb to create a backward suction. *Eeewww.*

As she empties each one and records the amount of fluid in each, I follow the tubing from the bulb back to my body. Two are stitched in under my left armpit and the other two are stitched in at the top of my pubic hair. For the first time I get a good look at the doctor's handiwork.

I wonder what the third bag on the IV pole goes to. I trace it from the pole to the bed and behind my back. Oh, it's my morphine epidural. *Nine.*

The oxygen tube in my nose makes ten. Ten tubes. I wonder how many post-surgical complications there were through the years before people invented these preventatives. *Amazing.*

A phlebotomist arrives with her tray of supplies. She's here to take some blood. After several attempts to get a drop from a finger prick, she prepares to draw some with a needle. "Your blood pressure is really low and I can't find a good vein." She eventually gets what she needs and says good-bye.

"Hello sweetie," The first of many wonderful, compassionate nurses that I will meet over the next few days greets me. She's wearing a commemorative FDNY shirt. I stare at the embroidered image, squint, and try to recall where I've seen it before. *That is so familiar.* "Today is 9-11," she says. *Oh yeah, it's the Fire Department of New York emblem. Man, this morphine has my head cloudy...I would never forget 9-11. I remember exactly what I was doing, where I was and who I was with when I heard about the first plane that hit the World Trade Center.* She takes my vitals, checks my tubes and catheter and says before leaving, "If you need anything press the call button, dear."

Alone at last. I open my hospital gown and see the magnitude of the surgery. There is no gauze. Nothing is covering the stitches. I can see everything. *Everything.*

My nipple is gone. I knew it would be, but I'm still a little surprised. The stitches go in a circle around where my nipple was and then wider and lower to where the lump was removed. From what I can see the incision is in the shape of a bell and my new breast mound looks a lot bigger than I expected. My belly button is scabbed and there's a lot of surgical tape from hipbone to hipbone. *Eeesh.*

Dan arrives. He's holding a gift. *I wonder what he's thinking. What kind of a night did he have?* I hear the distant sounds of breakfast trays being delivered but I do not get one. I do not have much of an appetite, anyway. I receive a paper so I can make my selections for tomorrow's meal, but I won't be eating for a few days. *I'll get to it later.* He tells me that the surgery lasted a little longer than expected, and that while he was in the waiting room he got a call on the red phone and was told that I'd be in recovery awhile. He and his mother went out for a bite to eat and were back before I was awakened.

Tip 67   Seeing members of your immediate family or extended family as soon as you arrive from recovery is important to your emotional well-being. If someone offers to be there, don't tell him or her not to come, as I did. (I didn't want to inconvenience anyone by expecting them to stay in the hospital from morning until evening; I denied my mother, sisters, daughters and close friends the right to decide to come to the hospital. Any one of them could have come at the hour I was expected to be out of the recovery room.)

Tip 68   Receiving visitors during your hospital stay is important too; however, people who are curious and want to hang around for long periods of time are not helpful. A close family member or friend who is willing to sit quietly with you, rub your back or keep you company when you are awake is encouraging, especially if you are the type of person who prefers to have someone near. That person can serve as your gatekeeper by diplomatically suggesting to long-period visitors that they leave so you can rest. All visitors should be supportive and upbeat, willing to stay for short periods of time and be able to understand that you will most likely drift off to sleep during their visits. Mine certainly were.

Mom and her neighbors come in soon after. The neighbors leave and Vicki walks in. We are doing an excellent job of keeping quiet. Then, Andrea and a few friends enter. That's the last thing I remember. *Zzzzzz.* Andrea snickers as she reflects:

You didn't talk at all. You were sleeping the whole time. Me and Dad took change from your purse and got candy from the candy machine. We walked around and he showed us things he built, like he always does. Someone gave you a present of chocolate candy and I ate it all because we didn't have food at home and I was hungry. But then, you woke up when I was leaving. You tried to show my friends your boob. Dad kept yelling, "No, it's not for the whole world to see." But then we moved closer to your bed, my friends left the room and you said you would show me. Mom-Mom and Aunt Vicki were in the way so I couldn't see anything. Then you went back to sleep.

I wake up to the sound of Mom and Dan murmuring. *How long have I been asleep? Oh, I'm thirsty.* At Dan's request I receive crushed ice from a nurse.

The doctors want to keep my fluids low until they see how much is flowing from my kidneys to the bag.

Dr. M visits, meets my visitors and looks at me. "How are you feeling?"

"I'm okay."

"You were in surgery longer than we expected."

"I was? Why?"

"You bled like a steak!" He says. "Your blood is thin, so surgery was messy." I am told that the blood on the IV pole is the sixth bag from the Blood Bank. *Eeps.* "Do you remember seeing me last night?"

"No."

"I didn't think so." He pats my leg, "You'll be all right. Dr. D will be in to see you, too. We work together to make sure you're okay, so you'll see both of us while you're here."

The hospital stay following my surgery is expected to last four or five days. In my case, until Tuesday or Wednesday, the 14th or 15th.

The girls are taking care of the household responsibilities and Danny. The brunt of the weekday tasks falls to Andrea as the other driver at home (Christine is only home on the weekends). Each morning, she starts her day by taking Danny to daycare at 7 a.m. Sometime after school she brings him home. She and Michele do what they can to keep him busy, fed and entertained while I'm in the hospital and Dan is either at work or with me. They prepare dinner and pack lunches. In the evenings, the two of them switch off to be at home with Danny or at the hospital. This doesn't sound like much to have to do, but most teenagers already have overfull plates; they go to school, do homework, get involved in sports and extracurricular activities, volunteer in their communities, hold part time jobs and have social lives.

While I am in the hospital some of my colleagues write to my distribution list.

From Jill:

> *I just got the call that Wendi made it through the surgery okay today. There were no complications and according to the doctors she did great.*
>
> *Dan said that there will be some bad news for Wendi when she wakes up — The sentinel node biopsy shows that the sentinal lymph node was not clear. According to Wendi's earlier e-mail this means that the lymphatic*

system that was attached to the sentinal node under her left arm was removed and she will have a minimum of two months of chemotherapy added to her treatment plan.

Wendi will be in the hospital for at least five days. Please continue to send your good vibes and prayerful thoughts to Wendi & her family.

Take Care,
Jill

From Sue F:

I plan to stop in to see Wendi tomorrow (Sunday) and may have more news to report on Monday. Dan did say that Wendi will be extremely sore – and probably more from her abdomen area than the breast area due to this surgery.

Wendi is at Christiana Care Wilmington Hospital and, if you'd like to send her a card or note, here is her address for the next few days: [hospital address]

Her home address is: [home address]

I know our words of encouragement, love and prayers mean so much to Wendi. She really needs us now so, if you haven't already done so, we need to be driving God crazy with our pleas for her full recovery. Wendi is the sunshine in everyone's day; her thoughtfulness in those small, creative gestures continues to lift our spirits. I know, that when she is fully awake, her first thoughts will be for her family and her second thoughts will be for us.

The second night, after everyone has gone home, I see that the clock says 10:20 and I drift to sleep. I awaken after about what seems like a dozen hours. My mouth is dry and my chin is wet. *Great, I've been drooling. Un hunh, I've been sleeping with my mouth open. Hope I didn't do the ol' capital 'Q' (mouth open, tongue hanging out). Yep, I think I have been. I'm a real beauty. It's 1:00 a.m. What? That's all it is? I'm rested for the night? Why can't I sleep very long? It feels like it should be about 8 a.m. Now, what do I do?* Generous folks gave me books on CD and I could start one, but my arms are weak. I don't have the energy to reach into the nightstand, find my belongings and my CD player, and get it set up for listening. I don't even know if I am in the mood to hear a story. *Odd. I love books and stories.* All I want to do is scratch. Oh dear, my legs and feet itch like mad. *Arrrgh.* So do my arms. So does my back. *What a nuisance.* I lay and scratch for

...All I want to do is scratch...

almost half an hour. *Ahhh, blessed relief.* I go in and out of sleep and fits of scratching all night long. I have a slight fever and I am so woozy. My urine is less blue and more green. *Oh joy.*

> **Tip 69**   Have some Gold Bond Triple Action Relief Body Lotion in the green bottle on hand. It will provide some relief for your itchy skin.

Today is Sunday and I receive several phone calls and visitors. I have a 100% drop off rate; I doze off on every one. Sue F stops in. I later find out that I insisted upon showing her the doctor's handiwork, but I don't recall doing so. Brenda and her husband, Frank, visit too. *Did I show them my new stuff? I don't know.* Enter Lisa and her family. The room is a little crowded, so Dan and the menfolk retreat to the solarium. I am too tired to say much to Lisa. *She understands. They all understand.*

> **Tip 70**   You do not have to act happy when others are around just to make them feel comfortable. Your *true* friends will be revealed to you during this time – the ones who are there for you and don't expect anything in return. Believe in your heart that you've been good to your friends and that now it is time to take what they have to offer you.

A doctor arrives and tells me he's going to write the orders for Clonidine. *Clonidine? That doesn't sound familiar. Who is this guy?* Lisa addresses him. "She doesn't have problems with high blood pressure, are you sure you've got the right patient?"

He looks at my chart and his paperwork and chuckles, "Oh, you are correct. Wrong patient, wrong room." *Thank goodness for Lisa. Did I get to show him my doctors' handiwork?*

Dr. D appears in my room. I ask, while pointing to my abdomen, "Doctor, did you get my note?" He chuckles so I've got the answer to my question. I move on to the next topic. While pointing to my left breast I say, "You gave me a "C" cup, I'm only supposed to be a "B" cup." He explains that there is swelling, it will eventually go down, and the "C" will be reduced to a "B." As my brain moves through the mental inventory I took when I first examined the surgical work, I ask, "What happened to my belly-button pierce?" *My daughters and I did some bonding a year or so ago when we got these.*

"The skin on your stomach was pulled downward and smoothed out. We cut a new hole around your belly button so the pierce is gone." I'd already looked at my stomach. It definitely looks goooood. It is smooth and tight. He adds, "You have a Goretex® patch on the right side of your torso inside. It is there to replace the muscle.

"Oh, that's right! Did you give me Janet Jackson squares?" *I'd love to have Janet Jackson squares. I like sexy abs.*

"No," he says as he is smiling. "No squares or fancy abs, just a flat patch." *He must think I'm so greedy. On second thought, nah, he's a plastic surgeon for Heaven's sake. He knows, better than I, how much women are willing to pay for decent looking breasts and a tummy tuck.*

Dan has three siblings, twin sisters Tina and Terri, and an older brother, Vincent. Vincent and his son Patrick come in. Vincent is jovial and upbeat, but Patrick is quiet. What can a thirteen-year-old young man say to a woman who just had breast surgery? *I hope he's not too uncomfortable.*

Thankfully, everyone and Dan go to a local restaurant together for munchies and drinks. *Good, he needs a social break from this mess.* They leave and I call home to check on the girls and Danny. We have an unspoken decree not to tell Danny that I am on the phone. It might make things too difficult for him to accept that I am not there.

> **Tip 71**   Caregivers, take time for yourself to eat, sleep, exercise, socialize, etc. Remember to do the things that were right for you before your loved one got cancer.

Things are quiet. I am alone. I decide to disconnect these darn massage boots. I need to....[*hmmmm*]...get to my...[*unh*]...legs and scratch...[*ah, yessss.*] That's the last of them! I spend a good bit of time, thirty to forty five minutes, scratching. I scratch my legs and arms, I rub my hips and scratch my feet....*eek, how I itch.*

It is Monday early evening and someone arrives to remove my epidural. *Oh gosh, is this because I removed the boots? Do you think I don't need any painkiller? What will happen if the pain becomes too great...I don't want another epidural.*

All in all, I am glad to have a tube pulled, because it represents one step toward going home, but I am fearful that it's going to hurt. Dan has not returned yet, so I call Vicki for some moral support.

The removal is quick and not painful, as I had anticipated. *Surprise. What a chicken I am.*

Dan returns to sit with me while I scratch and doze, when a nurse visits: The next order of business; pull the catheter so I can urinate on my own. *And, it is neither blue nor green, it is yellow…yay.* It turns out that pulling this tube is another painless procedure. *And so, I wait to feel a sign of biological urgency.*

Later in the evening I am given Percocet, for discomfort. It seems to help, but it makes me dream the strangest dreams! So much so, that I am afraid to go to sleep. Eventually, I succumb.

WALKING, COUGHING, AND OTHER IMPORTANT POST-SURGICAL EVENTS

I awaken to hear a straightforward nurse talking to me, "We got to get you out of that bed and walk." *What? Is she crazy? I can't walk.* "We're going to get you to walk to the door and back." *Ohmygod…unthinkable.*

Walking to the door and back looks to be an enormous, impossible task. She tells me, quite confidently, that I can do this.

Somehow, I am out of bed. "What about my drains?" The nurse clicks her finger and exits my room. Meanwhile, I get an idea and pull two safety pins from my overnight bag. *Who knows why I had safety pins in it, but I did…A regular Mary Poppins, I am.* I pin the two drains that are attached to my abdomen, by their tabs, to my hospital gown. Then, my lifesaving nurse returns holding string that looks like a tie from a hospital gown. We rig the two drains that come from my underarm, onto the string and tie the ends together. I pull them onto my left shoulder. *Have purse, will travel!*

> **Tip 72**   If you are having the TRAM reconstruction, pack a few safety pins and a shoestring in your bag. You'll be able to pin the lower drains to your robe and the upper ones to a string that you can wear over your shoulder. While you are walking, you won't want drains dangling or pulling on your incisions.

Adorned with my new purse and the nifty safety pin accessories, I am ready to go. When I attempt to stand I feel Dan's hands on my hips. He asks, "If you begin to fall, where shall I grab you? Is there anywhere I can touch you?"

"NO," I say rather loudly. "There's not a place that doesn't hurt. If I begin to fall, just let me go!"

To my horror, I can't get past a 90-degree angle. So here I am, feet on the floor, hands on the handle of the IV pole, which is located waist high, and my forehead resting on the back of my hands. I take my first step. Then, my second. I walk to the door of my room and back to my bed. *Eureka. I've done it!* I feel the urge to cough, but the thought of it is unbearable. The pain in my torso is unbelievable. But, hey, I'm walking. I think I'm gonna make it. The nurse and Dan help me into bed.

The nurse leaves and I drift to sleep. She returns, it is 3 a.m. and Dan is gone. She has a plastic device used to measure my lung capacity. She tells me to "suck in through the mouthpiece, as hard as you can and bring the blue indicator up to this point." She draws a line on it with a marker. "There's gunk in your lungs and you've got to move it around. You've been lying still for too many days." *Walking. Clearing my lungs. Sweet recovery. I am winning.*

"Let me see that," I bravely react. I attempt to impress her with my ability to suck, "Huuuuh...uh...uh...oh." *Don't cough! I mustn't....uh, uh, ah...cough! Oh, I'm gagging on the phlegm. Foul.*

"Here," she says as she folds a pillow and pushes it into my abdomen. "You won't break any stitches, now COUGH." *Oh geez. I'm revolting. Ah, ahem, ahhhh, huh, huh...owww."*

From Brenda to the AZ distribution list:

> *I received an e-mail from Wendi's sister, Vicki. She writes:*
>
> *Wendi just called me. Still extremely tired but sounds a lot better. Said she couldn't talk long because the telephone was very heavy... she wanted to talk to me while they removed the epidural and she was concerned that pain would be setting in. Her fever finally broke, which was a relief to all. She has walked a few times and is pushing to go home. Dan has a bed set up in the family room.*
>
> *Sue and I will keep you updated as we learn more.*
> *Brenda*

The next morning, Vicki writes to the non-AZ distribution list:

> *I saw Wendi last night and she looked much better – color was back in her face. She has the IV for nourishment. She was in lots of pain but took a pain killer and as she put it "Wow – it was gone." She did fall asleep,*

which was great. I left about 8pm and she said she was going to walk around. Although she is on the mend, the doctor wanted her to stay at least through Wednesday.

She told me she put in a rough night. She could not sleep as her allergies were causing a problem. Wendi did not want to cough but the nurse said that if she didn't, it would cause her lots of problems with her lungs. Finally at 3am, she did eat a little of a turkey sandwich, took a Percocet, held the pillow against her stomach and COUGHED. She said it really hurt but it cleared her lungs. She got back in bed and had a well-needed great night's sleep.

This morning, we only talked a minute, as she gets tired quickly. Her left arm is numb and she can't bend the right. The phone is still very hard to work with. Mom spent the day with her yesterday and Dan is picking Mom up this a.m. to take her in. Wendi is working hard on getting out and getting home.

Wendi said she can't wait to get home to clean herself up and I told her my idea of how we are going to wash her hair. She laughed, although I just got "the look"' when I said I was going to bring my camera!! Guess that wasn't a good idea.

I've received lots of e-mails back from friends and passing them on to Wendi. She has a great support group! When over the house the other night, Dan said PLEASE MAKE SURE THAT EVERYONE KNOWS HOW GREATLY APPRECIATED EVERYONE AND EVERYTHING IS.... EVERYONE HAS BEEN SO HELPFUL!!

Day three, Monday. Dan brings my mom in. After he leaves for work, Mom and I get comfy. "C'mon Mom, pull your chair up to the bed, take your shoes off and put them on the bed next to mine. She takes a nap. I reach down and spread my blanket over her feet. *Just me and my mom.* My back itches so much. "Mom, will you wash my back?" *Oh my, aren't moms wonderful?*

Sometime in the middle of the night, out of boredom or desperation I'm not sure which, I decide to get out of bed on my own. With a great deal of coordination of the remaining appendages, I manage. *Woo hoo!*

Another nurse tells me to use the call button when I am ready to use the bathroom. Later, I decide I am so good at hanging my drains on my gown, getting out of bed on my own and walking that I decide to take the adventure...unaccompanied. Solo. Single-handedly. Advice I'd gotten from John, an associate, before I left work was to look at minute achievements as small victories. So, I'm sitting on the toilet all by myself envisioning colonial minutemen and wounded soldiers playing musical instruments, limping and carrying the American flag while celebrating their conquest. Furthermore, I see WWII infantrymen pushing Old Glory into the soil to stake their ground and commemorate their win. Me? I am peeing on my own and rejoicing by giving myself a mental high-five.

...Small victories...I'm sitting on the toilet all by myself envisioning colonial minutemen and wounded soldiers playing musical instruments, limping and carrying the American flag while celebrating their conquest.

Furthermore, I see WWII infantrymen pushing Old Glory into the soil to stake their ground and commemorate their win. Me? I am peeing on my own and rejoicing by giving myself a mental high-five.

Lynne, who is on the distribution list, replies:

Well, guess who just called me – the girl who is supposed to be resting! She said the hospital has been pulling her plugs (drains, epidural painkiller, etc.). Her mom came in today and gave her a sponge bath, which she said felt so good. We only got to talk for a minute because they came in to do blood work.

She sounded in pretty good spirits. I dropped off a ham and all the fixings for Dan and the girls on Sunday. I will be happy to drop things by the house on my way home from work. I live close by Wendi's so it's not a problem any day. Let me know if I can do anything else, and thanks for keeping the progress reports coming in!!

Sue F wrote on Tuesday:

Wendi called me at 7:30 this morning. She sounded so much better and said she actually slept four straight hours last night because they gave her something for the pain. She is able to cough, which is reducing the fluid in her lungs. Unless her insurer kicks her out today, she expects to go home tomorrow.

Focusing on John's advice, Wendi is counting the small things: she was able to go to the bathroom by herself this morning!

About her surgery, Wendi said that, since the doctor found a cluster of cancerous nodes and he decided to take them all out, her scar goes all the way up to her armpit. That arm (left side) will be weak for some time, swelling may occur periodically and her arm will need to stay covered in the sun in the future. The condition is called lymphedema.

Wendi will be going home to recover and will probably return to work, I'm guessing, around the end of October. As I understand it, her next step will be the outpatient procedure to insert a device for chemotherapy, which will begin after she fully recovers from the surgery – probably in November.

I am grateful for people who visited me during my hospital stay and equally grateful that none of them stayed very long. I got weary very quickly.

It is the final evening and I know I am leaving in the morning. I am pretty sure I'm ready. If this was a hospital stay with nothing but healing that awaits me, I would certainly be ready. But there is more to healing from surgery that is in store for me. I am a cancer patient. *Geez. I am a cancer patient. I have to have chemo. Unbelievable.* I am startled from my position as a ceiling-tile-starer. Dan has materialized. Standing at the foot of my bed he cheerfully says, "Let's take a walk."

I think he is feeling resourceful. When I was hospitalized the Christmas before last, he would take me for slow and long walks on the fifth floor of the hospital, a few times each day to regain my strength. Those walks were helpful for my physical and emotional healing. That's what he's going to do tonight; take me for a walk.

Our first stop is the nurses' station just outside my room. He steps up to the counter and to the staff on the other side says, "There's something wrong here. Every time I place my order and leave money at this bar, the beers never come." The nurses' quiet laughter makes us all feel good. And we continue walking to the solarium. It takes me awhile; he doesn't rush me. I round the bend and see a pair of knees. Someone is sitting in one of the chairs. I take another step and realize that those knees belong to Michele. She has come to see me. I sense that she is not keen on seeing me in pain, yet she is here. I love her.

One more step and I see little Danny sitting in another chair. For an instant I see him move when he sees me, but then he catches himself. His hands grip the arms of the chair. I realize he's been ordered to stay put. *Poor little guy.* He turns backward in the chair that looks way too big for him and he faces me once again with two bunches of flowers.

"Awwww, isn't he cute," and, "What a good boy," say the nurses who are standing behind me.

Danny still doesn't leave the chair despite the fact that his body language is screaming for release. *Poor little fella.* Michele, who is now at my side, kisses me on the side of my face, but doesn't reach out to touch me. She comes near me like I'm a breakable piece of glass. She tells Danny, "Come see Mommy, but don't touch her."

Several more nurses have been tipped off to the visit from my family and they arrive in the solarium.

Very carefully, Danny gets off the chair and comes close. I am already bent over so I don't have far to go to reach him. I pucker my lips to taste a sweet kiss. Oh, what I wouldn't do to feel his tiny arms around my neck. He comes close and rubs his cheek against mine.

With one hand on my IV pole and the other extended as a shield to guard my body, I engage in a non-verbal tête-à-tête with my lovable little boy. I close my eyes and feel our cheeks touching. I marvel at the softness of his skin and breathe in his scent.

I know exactly how Dumbo's loving mother, in Walt Disney's animated movie, *Dumbo*, felt when she was unable to cuddle with her baby. Dumbo was visiting his mother who had been imprisoned in a circus wagon cage. The only way she and her baby could touch was for her to extend her trunk through the bars. She reached and curled her trunk around tiny Dumbo, who was outside the cage. While he rested peacefully in her appendage, she cradled and rocked him gently back and forth to the tune of *Baby of Mine*. As I nuzzle with Danny I swear I can hear the melody: *Baby of mine don't you cry. Baby of mine dry your eyes. Rest your head close to my heart; never to part, baby of mine... You are so precious to me, baby of mine.*

The magical connection between Danny and me remains intact even in the crowded and noisy room. I am so overjoyed to be with my son that tears begin to fall and I am gasping for air. I am shaking. "What's wrong Mommy," he asks.

I recover myself and say, "I'm so glad to see you. Let's go see my room."

He stays put. Cheerlessly, he says, "Miss you Mommy. Can you come home?"

Attuned to my feelings, Michele answers for me, "Mommy will be home tomorrow, Danny."

Sleep is not to befall me this night. It is after 2:00 a.m. and I am wide-awake. A nurse brings ice water, at my request. She brushes some hair from my face and says, "Hey, sweetie. I used to work on the cancer floor before the Helen F. Graham Cancer Center was built. While you are having chemo, gargle with baking soda and warm water a few times each day. It'll keep the mouth sores from getting too bad." She gave me a few other tips, wished me well and left after she said, "I'll keep you in my prayers."

I believe that these wonderful nurses treat all patients well, even those who are grumpy. *I was never grumpy.*

Tip 73   I believe we get back what we give. Remember, even though you feel down on your luck, don't forget your pleases and thank yous.

After 7:00 a.m. shift change, another nurse stopped by. "You still here? Mm, mm, I thought you'd be gone by now seein' as how you were walkin' so well the other day. You gooood." We cheerfully chatted and she motioned to exit the room. Before doing so, she said, "I'll check your release paperwork. Girl, you got family waitin' on you. Mm, hmm, I heard all about your kids. You got to go! Got to get outta this place!"

That's exactly what I am doing. It is Wednesday and I am going home! I've been here since Friday. The first phase of my recovery, the hospital stay, is almost over. While I wait for my official discharge, I check voice-mail at work. I don't expect any messages since today is the 15th and the day of the annual Information Services Town Hall when 300 or so IS colleagues will be offsite. I spent months facilitating a committee and planning this important, informative and fun event. As I listen to the messages, tears spring to my eyes, my nose begins to run and my stomach begins to quiver (happily, but painfully so). There are several messages from people who are at the event. They compliment my work and tell me how great the day is so far. Then, l hear our CIO's voice in a voice-mail message to me. *Our CIO. Wow! True, the event that I helped to plan is done in support of the CIO and his leadership team, but a personal message from the Chief Information Officer? Wow. Wow. Wow.* He tells me that the morning's events are being received extremely well and he knows I would be satisfied with the committee's efforts and the culmination of a successful delivery. *Job satisfaction…what a rush! What a way to end my hospital stay. I'm on top of the world.* In life, people do seemingly simple things that can have surprisingly colossal impact. That's what's so great about life and people.

I am informed that my drains will not be removed before I leave. *Gross. I'm taking these things home with me.* Since the ones that drain my abdominal tissue are located at the top of my pubic hair, I can't imagine wearing my jeans or underwear. Since the ones under my left arm dangle and need to be pinned to something I decide it will serve me well to wear a button-down robe and go commando. I sit on a blue pad on the wheel chair with a blanket across my lap. *Here we go!*

I will never forget the incredible nursing staff at this hospital. All week long, Dan, Vicki, and I captured the name of each one on a napkin. I will write to Christiana Care Health System and inform the appropriate person about their personnel. In the meantime, I ask to talk to the head nurse or team lead. I tell her something that each one said or did that helped me through these last few days.

HOME SWEET HOME

Tip 74   Look at your surgery recovery in phases. Phase one is the hospital stay where you will be in bed for a few days, then walking very slowly with help. Phase two is the first week or two at home where you will sleep with pillows under your knees or in a recliner, move around your home on your own or with the help of a walker, and work your way toward standing straight. Phase three is when the drains will be removed (if they haven't been removed by this point already) and you will be able to lie flat in a bed and drive a vehicle. Try not to stress about going home with drains. They are, *believe it or not,* your friends. They are extremely helpful in your recovery because they minimize internal draining, possible internal bleeding and infection. The discomfort from the drains is very mild.

Phase three is usually during the third week following surgery. Three weeks is a small amount of time compared to a lifetime. If chemotherapy will be prescribed for you, many women begin treatment as early as four weeks following the surgery. The sooner the better to start the fight I say!

With extreme care, Mom P drives me home. She pulls into the driveway and takes a walker out of her trunk. *I don't think I need a walker. Walkers are for old people and invalids.* "I don't need it just to walk in through the garage," I say. But she is an awesome person and if it takes pushing it along to help her to feel good about bringing the walker, I'll do it.

By the next morning my lower back is sore. I am compensating for my inability to stand straight. I try the walker. It takes the strain off my lower back and enables me to ambulate using the strength of my arms and legs. *Mom Pedicone is my savior.*

Dan and the girls brought a single bed downstairs. It is in the den. The first night, I realize that lying in the bed with pillows tucked under my legs and head is no different from lying in a recliner. Except that someone has to pack the pillows under me. From the second night onwards, I sleep in the recliner and a family member sleeps in the bed. I assume it is reassuring for each to be near me. Michele and I, for example, don't talk at all about cancer or my surgery, so I was pleasantly surprised to awaken in the middle of the second night and discover that she is the first one to sleep in the bed, about five feet from me. I guess I'm not a pariah to her after all. *A warm smile spreads across my face when I realize this.* My kitties want to be near me too. I place a pillow across my midsection. Good thing I did.

Tip 75   Wherever you decide to sleep (bed or recliner), if you have pets or small children who may invite themselves onto your lap and torso while you are sleeping, place a pillow on top of your torso to avoid pain in case they surprise you. If a cat, for example, jumps up on you while are asleep, there is no risk to the surgical work that was done to your torso, but it will surely cause you immediate (albeit temporary) discomfort. With a pillow on my torso, one of our cats, which loves to curl up with me, was able to lay on the pillow and I felt close to normal by having him there.

I realize that for most of my hospital stay, I did not think about cancer very much. Not today, but another day I will honor my feelings of loss, vulnerability and defenselessness. *Not today though.*

Now that I am home, I get to face wonderfully minor annoyances; my skin under the tape that is covering my abdominal incision is blistering, badly. Dr. M's office gives me a great tip: Mylanta. I am told that I can begin removing the tape in sections, especially where there are blisters underneath.

Tip 76   Use a topical antibiotic ointment such as Neosporin,, or Mylanta, liquid on the newly exposed or blistered areas to soothe and heal. Use a hair dryer (low heat) or sit in the air and sun for a few minutes to dry.

My mother-in-law and I sit on the back deck in the mornings and relax. I appreciate each day I get. We watch a little TV and read the newspaper before we get ready for the day. I may not be going places, but getting washed and dressed makes me feel less like an invalid and more like a person.

Tip 77   I recommend having an extended family member or friend stay with you most of the time to help with cooking for your family, cleaning and laundry, etc. This is helpful especially since women tend to want to provide for their families, and easily forget that this is a time to rest and heal.

Kayla and I keep missing each other's phone calls. She maintains a very rigorous schedule. She is in a vo-tech high school taking college prep courses and works as often as she can to earn money for a car and insurance. She manages homework and only a little bit of a social life. Trying to pin her down is not so easy. I contact her grandmother, Sharry. I know that delivering my news to her is not going to be easy, since she lost her daughter (Kayla's mother) sixteen years ago to cancer.

We have a wonderful conversation. I am amazed at how her faith in God gives her such strength. She assures me she will tell Kayla in a loving way. I trust her. Kayla is in good hands.

Sue F begins wearing a path to our doorstep. *I just love her.* She stops by for the first time (of many). I am so glad to see her. She and my mother-in-law meet. She brings soup, main dishes, gifts, books and pink ribbons from colleagues. Along with the loot, she brings cookies she'd gotten from the Hotel duPont. They have a distinctive look. You know how when you know you shouldn't say something you are thinking, the little person over your shoulder reminds you not to? Well, mine didn't make a sound…

"Hey!" I said, "They look like tiny nipples."

"What?" Sue asked.

"The cookies. They look like nipples." *Nipple cookies. I'm going crazy, for sure.*

Sue and Mom have a good laugh, and I begin munching nipples. *I mean, cookies.*

A day later she updates the troops:

> *Good morning. I got back to my desk yesterday after a training session and had a phone message from Wendi wondering about a few things that had nothing to do with surgery or breast cancer. I thought perhaps she was delirious until she explained that she was helping Andrea research her homework assignment! Perhaps it's a sign that she's able to focus some energy on her "mom" activities.*
>
> *I saw Wendi on Thursday evening. I was greeted in the front yard by a 3-year old dirtball who, through all the mulch, looked surprisingly like Danny. As Dan was building a garden around two large boulders, Danny was throwing himself off the boulders into the mulch pile. There was nowhere on his body unmulched.*
>
> [Sue shares some details of my progress.]
>
> *While Wendi hasn't logged on yet, she wants everyone to know how much she appreciates all the support. Additionally, the kids love all the surprises in the refrigerator and the home-baked goods. The soup (boy, did it look good!) was enough to last three days. They have eaten all of the food provided by relatives and friends, so I think I will begin to cook a meal every weekend for the next several weeks. If you are also planning to supply a meal for the Pedicones but are waiting because of the initial deluge of food, consider something over the next few weeks.*
>
> *Wendi had a visit from Rhonda and John who brought her the tape from the IS Town Hall and shared the event with her. She was so thrilled, not just to see them, but to see the event on which she worked so hard and to*

hear their descriptions of the day's events. She was so touched and teary by Rob's recognition of her at the beginning of the session.

So, that's my update. Also, now that she's feeling better and beginning to sleep through the night, I believe it would be okay to call her at home. She will probably be logging on within the next week.

Somewhere along the line, I was given a three-ring binder from Christiana Care. It is called a personal treatment journal, but it is far more comprehensive than just a journal. It is designed with tabs to get information and record observations by category; e.g., Appointments, Notes, Side Effects, Tests, etc. It even has a section for organizing business cards. I found two resources for scarves and head apparel. One was *Simply You,* a store that has two locations in Delaware; one is on the first floor of the Helen F. Graham Cancer Center. I am pleasantly surprised to read the name of the owner. She's my cousin! Next time I go to the cancer center, I will visit her and buy headwear. I am too sore to go to the cancer center today and I'm in the mood to shop, so I'll catalog shop from my kitchen table. I have a booklet from the *American Cancer Society,* called *TLC.* I call 800-850-9445 and order several scarves for when I am hairless. *The scarves are pretty. I just may enjoy the fashion side of this cancer thing.*

Tip 78   When you buy scarves and hats, consider buying two things, especially if it is wintertime: a nightcap and a headliner. The nightcap is a soft cotton covering to be used at night. It has lace around the borders that can be pulled down over your ears and won't roll up when you sleep. It is more comfortable to sleep in than a turban or ski cap. A headliner is a cotton covering that looks like a skullcap, designed to be worn under your hat or scarf. A scarf isn't enough to keep your head warm on a brisk winter day.

LYMPH NODE INVOLVEMENT

Additionally, I will need a medical alert bracelet for my left arm, the one that is at risk of lymphedema. I order one from TLC, the scarf catalogue. I wear it on my left arm. It says, "Do not use this arm for IV, IM, BP or finger stick."

Tip 79   If you had lymph nodes removed, the arm on the side they were removed from is at risk for lymphedema. Lymphedema is a side effect that can begin during, immediately following, or years after breast cancer treatment. It isn't life threatening, but it can last over a long period of time. This condition involves swelling of the soft tissues of the arm or hand caused by lymphatic fluid build up. The swelling may be accompanied by numbness, discomfort, and sometimes infection. (www.breastcancer.org) In some cases, the affected extremity (arm, wrist, hand, fingers) is visibly larger than the other. Educate yourself on how to minimize your risk (click on Preventions at www.lymphnet.org to view a list of eighteen ways to prevent lymphedema) and consider wearing an American Medical Identification bracelet. Visit www.american-medical-id.com for the online store of medical jewelry. Additionally, the Online Medical Registry at www.medicalregistry.net offers storage of and access to your medical information.

Tip 80   If you had lymph nodes removed, you will need to stretch the armpit-chest area before radiation. At this point, you have several months, but do not neglect this area – during radiation you may be placed in a position with your arm over your head so that the beams can reach the places where your lymph nodes were removed (your armpit being one of them). You'll need to have full range of movement. Open up that area as much as possible so that your arm can be positioned over your head for a period of about ten minutes. The American Cancer Society offers a Reach for Recovery program of exercises and aids (for example, a ball and string, and instructions to use it). Additionally, I understand they will arrange to meet with you to help you with full-mobility training.

Tip 81   Check out a lymphedema specialist, go to www.nln.org, or go to a yoga teacher to help with stretching. Inquire of your PCP or oncologist about treatment; there is physical therapy and specialized massage to aid lymph drainage. This is critical if you begin to encounter problems, because there are things that can be done early-on. Many women I've met did not know this and now have permanent swelling; one hand, or a portion of an arm is visibly larger and more taut than the other.

BEGINNING TO EXPLORE WELLNESS OPPORTUNITIES

It is no coincidence that cancer centers and wellness centers offer yoga classes. Yoga does for the body what meditation does for the mind. Through Iyengar yoga you can build a memory of a relaxed sense, so you can identify when your body is getting in a stressed state (and stress is unhealthy). Learning relaxation and body and breath awareness through Iyengar yoga helps us to get to know our bodies and then learn to know how our bodies are speaking to us.

Tip 82 Go to www.bksyoga.com (BKS Iyengar), www.journal .com or www.yogafinder.com where you can find Iyengar yoga classes and events in your area, yoga products, poses, music, ask-the-experts, and more. In the case of the Yoga Finder web site, you can click on any country, then drill-down to find teachers, classes and events in your area. In the case of the BKS Iyengar web site, you can resource certified teachers within your area and their scheduled classes.

Our daughters are in the A.I. high school band and on one afternoon, two weeks following surgery I feel up to attending a game. Here I am, with my walker in front of me and Dan by my side, working my way toward the bleachers. I hear the music of the band as it processes into the stadium. The music fills my soul. I sob, unashamed. It is a warm, sunny September day and I am alive.

...I sob, unashamed. It is a warm, sunny September day and I am alive.

Tip 83 Once you leave the hospital (phase two), walk slowly, and use rails and furniture for support. Use a walker for a few weeks, if you have access to one. It will ease lower back discomfort that sometimes occurs when you inadvertently use your lower back to accommodate for the bent over position due to the surgery. It allows you to walk and get exercise while easing the pain. Walking improves circulation, the respiratory function, and overall healing. The important thing to remember is that you should be ambulatory, but only when you are feeling up to it.

After the field show, when the band members are in their seats, Andrea comes and takes me by the hand. The bandleader, the assistant bandleader, administrators and students come by and wish me well. This very cool band, nicknamed "the jock band," has traveled to England, Ireland, and Canada, and performed in the Rose Bowl parade. They've done interesting things. Their supporters are gathering around me as if I am interesting. *I feel like a celebrity.*

Sunday afternoon; my mother-in-law is here to spend the night and take me to a follow-up appointment with one of the surgeons tomorrow. She insists upon taking me to my physician visits. This arrangement serves dual purposes; I get the help I need without pulling Dan from his work routine, and she gets to be close to me. She is a second mother to me. How comforting I imagine it must be for a mom to be able to see firsthand that her daughter (or daughter-in-law) is okay.

TEMPORARILY LIVING WITH (AND REMOVAL OF) THE DRAINS

I hope the doctor will tell me that I can take a shower or hop in the hot tub. I miss both.

> **Tip 84**   To reduce the risk of infection it is recommended to avoid baths, hot tubs and showers for the first few weeks after surgery. Full immersion in water usually happens when the incisions around the newly constructed breast and along the torso are free of infection and the operative glue around the belly button has done its job.

Today, I have an appointment with Dr. D at 11:00 a.m.   Before getting dressed, I am carefully and deftly sponge bathing. I look in my bathroom mirror and see my body. I scan the area below my belly button where the tissue was taken to build my breast. I have a seventeen-inch incision from left hip to right hip that will hide nicely under the bottom half of a two-piece bathing suit. My stomach looks smooth. My belly button looks different. *No love lost there.* And I look at my breast. I see a pinkish brown mark on it. *How long has that been there?* I am surprised and I panic. I do not want to call the doctor…I'll be seeing him in a little more than an hour. Meanwhile, I ask Mom P to come into my bathroom and look at the blotch on my breast. "Oh no," she says. We look at each other and say nothing, but I suppose we are thinking the same thoughts. *The tissue is dying. The reconstruction is failing. The cancer got to my new breast. The &#@% cancer is spreading!*

By the time I get into Dr. D's examining room and sit on the tissue paper covered table naked from the waist up, I am shaking, my palms are sweaty and my thoughts have spiraled out of control. As soon as he walks in I blurt out, "Doctor, what's this spot on my breast?"

He calmly looks at it, and then looks downward. His hand forms a loose fist with his forefinger sticking out. My eyes follow the forefinger for what seems like a full minute. It goes from my breast, lower and lower as he says, "That's a mole that used to be riiiiiiight [lower] there." And his pointer finger lands on a spot on my right hip. *I remember that mole!*

He tells me that two of the drains are ready to be removed. I had taken Percocet, minutes before walking into his building for this very reason. I am afraid of the pain of removing the drains. *Am I bad.* As he is preparing his tools and wheeling the tray close to me I hear the music from the movie, *Jaws. De-da, de-da, de-da, bah dah dah!*

Snip. He cuts a stitch. *No pain, just a pinch.* He pulls the tube. *Three inches…six inches…ten inches…unbelievable! I can't believe how much tubing is inside me.* It doesn't hurt to have the tubes removed, but it is a very, very strange feeling. *I'll take pain meds before I go to see Dr. M next week to have the other two removed…. just in case.*

Tip 85   When you are doing weekly post-surgical follow-ups, ask both surgeons (the one who did the mastectomy and the other who did the reconstruction) if you can coordinate your schedule so you don't have to make two trips to see both each week. After all, they are both surgeons and assisted each other: Surgeon number two assisted number one during the mastectomy, and surgeon number one assisted number two during the reconstruction. Either can see you for follow-ups.

A week later, Dr. M removes the other two drains. No pain, no problem. During my visit he and I have a profound conversation about life. He, like many quality physicians, is treating more than just the physical aspects of my illness; he is talking to the emotional aspects too.

Tonight I have difficulty falling asleep.

Sue F writes to the distribution lists:

I stopped by Wendi's on Saturday, but was unable to see her because she was getting ready to go to the A. I. football game at William Penn; her girls are in A. I.'s band.

She called me last night with a progress report, and I can't get her out of my mind. If you have a little time this afternoon, please say a quick prayer. She is going to the oncologist soon.

The reason I have been thinking of her so much is that she revisited the surgeon who removed her remaining drains. He said some unusual things, which worried Wendi. While I can't quote her, he said things like: There is no set time that each of us dies; you could die the day after you are born – The progress of medicine can be compared to a dog's age in relation to a human, so that for every year we age, medicine advances by seven years in new products – With the advancement of medicine these days, people are living much longer than previously expected. Wendi was frightened that he might be trying to tell her some bad news. I'm hoping that he just was trying to tell her not to worry.

On a brighter note, Wendi is driving a little (Sue S describes this as the little hunched-over old lady whose head isn't much taller than the car seat.) around the neighborhood, is doing the stairs, is blow drying her hair, and her spirits remain high.

Wendi hopes to log on within the next week and thank all of you for the wonderful support you have given. I think she's starting to get antsy and wants to get back into action.

MORE INVOLVEMENT FROM MY SUPPORT SYSTEM

Our mailbox is stuffed with mail, and delivery services stop by almost daily with gifts from people. Some of my favorites are pink-ribboned items (a robe, slippers, a pillow, pins), hats, scarves, books, bracelets, fruit baskets, plants, gift cards to restaurants, candles, stuffed animals, body and hand lotion, and flowers (yes, I love flower arrangements, I simply didn't want too many).

Mary Ellen, a colleague, sends us several books for small children with hope that Danny will be able to comprehend. He especially likes *Sammy's Mommy has Cancer*. It has simple language and wonderful illustrations.

Even though I talk with my mom several times a day, it is not the same as seeing me. We bring her to the house to sit with me about once a week. I believe it is important for her to see for herself that I am okay.

Tip 86   Caregivers: If there are extended family members who cannot drive or are elderly consider bringing them into your home for a relaxing visit.

It is a beautiful September morning. The television is on. Breaking news on major network channels: Melissa Etheridge, 43, has breast cancer. Ms. Etheridge is a recording artist famous for her raspy rock voice and soulful lyrics. *Gosh, cancer touches people from all walks. Breast cancer has long arms.* I like Melissa's songs (Come Through my Window, Just to Meet You). I appreciate her celebrity persona and the way she stretches the boundaries of life. *I feel a bond to her now that she has breast cancer, but I can't decide if this makes me feel better or worse.*

Night after night of wonderful meals, greeting cards, and gifts makes the thought of writing thank you cards daunting. I believe strongly in thanking people, but I do not have much energy or inclination to write at this time. My creative juices flow and I come up with two ideas: For the fine folks where I work, I leave voice mail messages. In a two-minute message, they are able to hear my voice and my gratitude. For people who sent food in to-be-returned containers and dishes, I put candy bars wrapped with the following message in them, "My family and I can't thank you enough for your generosity and support. The only way we can repay your kindness is to pay it forward to others in need…and we will! Gratefully, Wendi and Dan, Christine, Andrea, Michele and Danny"

The remainder of people to thank is now a smaller list. The task of writing thank you cards does not seem so overwhelming. So, I begin.

My mother-in-law brings in the mail. Among the cards, there is one from my cousin, Lorraine, who is exceedingly committed to God. She wrote a Christian message, signed her name and included her telephone number. I contact my cousin immediately. Also, there's a package from a colleague and his wife. In it are handmade gifts from their four young children and papers with phonetically spelled words from scriptures written on them by tiny hands. The gifts are so dear to me that I place them on my kitchen windowsill so I can see them often and be reminded of these small beings and their huge faith. Their parents remind me that I am blessed, and they conclude their note with their telephone numbers. I call David and Connie soon afterward. During my cancer voyage we left a few phone messages for each other. Even though we didn't talk 'live' as often as we all would have liked, it's okay. Knowing they were praying for me was invaluable.

God did NOT give me cancer. Instead, He put people in my path to help me through it. Albert Einstein knew this when he said, "God doesn't play dice." People like David, Connie, my cousin, and a few others were, at the time, seemingly coincidental encounters. And folks like Fi, who found herself on a team I was leading, Edna who turned me on to a bible group (that meets at lunch time, periodically), Keva, who has been studying the Bible, and others...at first I thought these were coincidences, now I believe differently.

Tip 87   From this point forward, whenever you write get-well cards to others, include your phone number. People who have been diagnosed with a serious illness are understandably disorganized for a time. Placing your number in a card you send enables them to call you immediately if they want to and are up to it. Otherwise, contacting you later when they locate your number becomes a task on their to-do list that they may not get around to doing.

I wonder when I will be able to wear a bra. During TRAM flap reconstruction, the tissue and muscle is moved up along the torso and stomach under the skin, and then turned at a 90-degree angle under the breast that was removed. At the point where the muscle is turned, it is puffy and tender. Tight bras or bras with underwires can put pressure on the turned muscle and decrease blood flow to it.

Tip 88   Wear shirts with bras built in or close-fitting undershirts to hold both breasts firm but not constricted, for any of the surgeries but especially if you chose TRAM surgery.

Jill and another friend and colleague named Joann (who is on the "Heaven express"), visit for lunch. Other than being hunched over (I am not able to stand straight yet), I look okay. I haven't started chemo so I've got hair. I can wear day clothes versus PJs and a robe. It is so good to see them both. They bring good tidings from AZ folks and a book from the town hall meeting. When folks found out I had cancer, they were invited to sign a book. I read each entry. I will treasure it for the rest of my life.

This afternoon, Andrea comes home from school and tells me that her friend's mom (Mrs. S) had breast cancer about two years ago and it recently recurred. I do not know the details of her first bout of cancer nor her second bout. *I wish I did.*

"Can we order some buttons for her?"

I contact my sister. "Deb," I ask, "How can I order some buttons like the We're-here-for-Wendi   ones   you   got   for   me?"   From www.oneinchround.com I order 100 for Andrea to give to her friend. Together, they establish a goal to get as many people in their schools to wear their mothers' buttons. *Cool beans. A common goal for both girls. A positive goal. This will be good for Andrea.* I worry about how my daughters are going to fare over the long haul.

I have a post-op visit with Dr. N so she can see how I am healing from the surgery and decide how soon to start chemotherapy (generally four to six weeks after surgery). Chemotherapy drugs might slow down the healing process. She informs me that I am in stage IIIc. I know that this news means I will have four additional rounds of chemo, but what does it mean in the way of a prognosis? According to Lee, Zava and Hopkins, once cancer has invaded the body (meaning, once it has metastasized, or traveled to the lymphatic system or organs) – stopping its growth becomes more complicated. The good news is that breast cancer is a disease of long duration, and we have daily opportunities over a lifetime to treat it (p. 61).

> **Tip 89**   Caregivers need to understand the details and prognosis as much as the cancer patient, and the patient may not be able to fully comprehend or explain what the doctors tell them about staging. I recommend page 23 of *Living Through Breast Cancer* by Dr. Carolyn Kaelin to learn more. The section is about breast cancer staging using TNM classifications (Tumor, Nodes and Metastases).

Many evenings, our daughters come home to goodies on the kitchen counter and I hear exclamations like, "Yesssss", "All right", and "Awesome." And when a neighbor dropped off a favorite dessert with a dinner, I heard Andrea say, "Mrs. H rocks!"

I prepare my first written update to everyone: September 29, 2004

It has been almost three weeks since my surgery. I am doing well. Now that I am on the other side of the intensive procedure, I must say, science and technology is certainly fascinating. Thank goodness for the men and women who become trained in medical professions, and for the bright people who are courageous enough to explore possibilities. The incisions and reconstruction from my left armpit to my chest and stomach, and down to my lower abdomen are healing. I am not yet fully able to stand up straight (one ability I appreciate more now than before, since it has been temporarily taken away); however, happily I have been able to set aside the walker and am almost upright! 5' 3" here I come!

Through this ordeal I've counted the smallest of steps toward full recovery as "small victories." Some of them have been quite amusing. Heck, if I can't laugh at myself, how can I ever expect anyone else to laugh at me! I owe so much to my mother-in-law, mother and sister Vicki for helping Dan, the kids and me to keep the household running. Y'know, the usual stuff; laundry, cleaning and ensuring that we eat wonderful meals as a family at the kitchen table...the very meals that so many of you have been providing. I am humbled. My brother supports me by leaving comical messages du jour on my voice messaging systems. (It's no wonder that he earned the senior superlative in high school as funniest person/class clown). Another sister has been supporting me in truly creative ways given that she lives two time zones away (she's the one who ordered the buttons that many of you are wearing). I am grateful.

Our oldest daughter comes home from school on weekends; she and our two high school daughters help me to feel like a Mom, even when I'm not always physically and emotionally up-to-par. And, our delightful three-year-old son continues to ask me, "Is your surgery better yet so I can hug you?"

Monday afternoon, we received sobering news from the oncologist based on the pathology report from the surgery. My cancer is very advanced. How did that happen? With breast cancer, there are stages 0, I, IIa & b, IIIa, b & c, and IV. I am in stage IIIc! Oh dear. "Stage IV is treatable, but not curable," she told me. I'm not in stage IV...that's good news. She said, "Is it possible to live to raise all your children and retire with your husband? Yes. Is it probable? I don't know." Hmmm, it is difficult to think positive thoughts after hearing that. Dan and I spent precious little time sleeping that night. We talked, prayed, researched materials at hand and on websites, and then got on with a new game plan for a new ballgame. By morning, I had created a to-do list of inquiries to make and people to contact. I spent the day following the to-do list. Structure, yes, structure will keep me focused. I also dedicated time on Tuesday to engaging in phone conversations with people who had news that they had once been worse off than me and survived! By mid-morning we were feeling somewhat optimistic and by the time we went to bed I was back on track as the glass-half-full person that most of you know me to be. The last thing I did before I fell asleep was to be inspired by Lance Armstrong's ordeal and survivorship. I'll never forget pages 70 to 155 in his first book, It's Not About the Bike: My Journey Back to Life. In them, his day-by-day cancer nightmare from discovery to state of being cancer free is explained in ways that affected me deeply. Whew, got over that emotional setback quickly.

Other tasks from my to-do list were to schedule more tests, scans and procedures. Beginning Thursday and onwards-through next Friday, I have at least one appointment a day. This Friday, I will undergo my third surgery to have the medi-port installed in my chest. It will enable me to receive the chemotherapy drugs through it versus an IV. On Wednesday, I will start chemotherapy. I will take an antiemetic (to help avoid nausea) and start with two drugs, Adriamycin® and Cytoxan®. The first will be the one to take my hair. I have decided to take control of that myself; I will be the one to decide when the hair goes, not the cancer or the treatment. So, on the Sunday beforehand, my family and I will shave my head. This step is symbolic and will require the purely mental metal that I know we are made of!

After a few months of those two drugs, I will have a third one called Taxol®. I will receive this one in addition to the first two, because the cancer was in and outside my lymph nodes. The extra nodal diagnosis means that micro-metastases (microscopic cancer cells) are somewhere in my body, but we do not know where. Hence, more combatant chemo! Since this will knock down my immune system through to February, I'll be educating myself on how best to avoid germs, colds, flu, etc. I told my surgeon that if I have to post a sign outside my office door, avoid hugging well-wishers and shaking hands with professionals, and wear a mask, I'll do it!

Meanwhile, I have more people to contact (thanks to you who have offered names and numbers of survivors) and success stories to surround myself with. I have a short-term strategy in place. The long-term strategy will be to arm myself with knowledge of the possible treatments or clinical trials available beyond the chemo and radiation, in the event they are not successful enough to wipe out the cancer in me. I will succeed. Got that right!

My team of physicians is working with the nurse at AstraZeneca who is handling my short-term disability case. They will decide when I return to work. I am hopeful that it is at the end of the six-week surgery recovery period, which is the end of October. I truly look forward to contributing to the objectives of the company I am proud to work for, having a routine and enjoying a sense of normalcy in my life beyond my home.

Final thoughts for you: Be proactive in checking your body's signals for help (something I didn't do before), live life to the fullest each and every day, discover and follow your purpose in life, find your spiritual direction, and smile! Those are some of the things I am going to do more often.

THE CATHARSIS OF REVEALING MY ORDEAL

Revealing my ordeal has been extremely satisfying for me as a cancer patient. It makes my family and me feel like we have company on this journey, and it helps to know that I'm sharing information with people who do or may need it in the future. I am sharing every aspect of my life so folks can reach the peaks with me and feel the glory whenever I do. In turn, I receive cards with sincere and heartfelt letters.

Tip 90   Keep a journal, even if no one reads it but you. According to Joan Leof, a communications consultant and certified English teacher, who has taught a "Write to Heal" journal-keeping workshop where I work, research has shown that writing has the power to help maintain physical and mental health. It boosts your immune system, improves your sense of balance, and even decreases symptoms of certain illnesses.

I get some useful advice from Gin, a colleague, who tells me what her sister did with all of her cards: She saved them and revisited them in an interesting way. From this day forward, I do the same. I revisit those cards where they reside, in a large decorative basket in the kitchen.

Tip 91   Place your get-well and greeting cards in an attractive container somewhere in your house. Whenever you or your caregivers are feeling low, reach in the basket and pull one. Read and reflect on the message it conveys. You will be surprised how enriching and timely the messages sometimes are.

THIS ONCOLOGIST OR ANOTHER ONE?

Lisa and I are talking on the phone. She tells me what's happening in her life, I tell her about what's happening in mine (non-cancer stuff). I eventually get around to the cancer topic. "What do you think I should do; should I switch oncologists?" I explain to Lisa that emotionally, I didn't get any positive vibes from my oncologist when I first met her, but that clinically I trust her. I went on to say why I trust her, "I checked with survivors who were in the same stage as me and had similar types of breast cancer and they received the same treatment Dr. N is planning for me. Also, she came highly recommended. I verified my treatment plan at www.nccn.org and with the senior physician in the Oncology Department at AZ, who used to be part of an oncology practice. I am able to determine that my protocol is a good quality standard. Besides, the biggies, like Sloan-Kettering and Johns Hopkins, don't have silver bullets. Right? They aren't keeping secrets about cancer cures. And there's no need for me to go out of state. There's a market here in Delaware...a big market! Yipes, have you seen our stats...so we aren't going to be kept in the dark."

I continued, "And she scared me when we talked about the stage I am in. Sheesh, she told me the news and didn't follow it up with anything positive. There were no buts. There should always be buts. After the bad news, she could have said, 'but there are always people who do better than expected.' Nothing. She gave me nothing." *By now, I'm a little worked up.*

"Now Wen," Lisa began, "Statistically, oncologists lose patients," she said. "Yours probably *can't* get emotionally connected. How *can* she when eventually many of them won't be with her anymore? I've seen it happen at Horton [hospital]. They've got to maintain a distance, for their own emotional well-being." Then she added, "You researched her. You know she's one of the best there is in the area and the same with the treatment. It sounds like you trust her expertise. Believe me, you *want* her expertise. And you are going to get your emotional boost from your other doctors and from the people in your support network."

Lisa and I talked about what a difficult night it was when Dr. N and I talked about my prognosis. Lisa said, "Okay, so she didn't sugar coat it. She couldn't give you a false sense of hope. She laid it on the line for you and you had to deal with it. Nobody can deal with your diagnosis other than you. You could've pulled the covers over your head, moaned and said 'why me' the entire time. *She did you a favor!*...Because immediately you started talking to people, researching, writing, and now you are getting benefits of that. No platitude she could have given you would have done that."

Tip 92   Recognize that when you first hear the "C" word, you may not be your usual tolerant, patient self. Anger is a classic reaction and a bona fide stage of the process, from diagnosis to completion of treatment. As for me, perhaps I was in a frame of mind such that I was not open to what my oncologist had to say (or didn't have to say). Perhaps I was angry about having cancer on the day I went to meet her. My suggestion is that if a medical professional on your team does not give you answers that you want to hear, maybe it is because you aren't ready to hear them. You are only human, you know. If a physician on your team does not seem as compassionate as you think he or she should be, ask yourself, "What do I need from this physician?" and "Can I get whatever this physician may not have to offer from one of the other physicians on my team?" Using a scale analogy, I would rather have a physician who is heavier on the side of technical expertise and lighter on the other side, than the reverse.

Switching physicians is occasionally done, and in some cases entirely necessary. If that is your case, the main thing is not to delay your treatments looking for physicians. But I suggest that you give it another try. The next encounter might be much better for any number of reasons.

Tip 93   Go to www.talkingwellness.org and look in the Learning About Cancer section. You'll find suggestions for how to better communicate with doctors and other health care professionals. Also available at this website are helpful basic information about cancer and advice on how to cope with cancer.

Tip 94   According to the United Health Foundation and the National Health Council there are ways you can make the most out of a visit to the doctor's office: 1. Take a friend, someone who will help you remember important information, 2. Educate yourself. Seek trustworthy information about conditions that affect you, 3. Be up-front. Tell your doctors everything, or they might miss something important, and 4. You have to ask in order to receive. If you want answers, you have to ask questions (UHFtips.org).

Tip 95   You can look at treatment protocols (what should be done for each type of cancer) at www.nccn.org. There are decision trees for every type of cancer. The information and menu of drugs for specific cancers can be found in MS PowerPoint slides. It seems technical enough for oncologists to use this site to verify patients' treatments. Additionally, I found an interactive treatment wizard: NexProfiler Treatment Option Tool for Breast Cancer. It offers full disclosure of treatment options, assistance understanding options and side effects, questions to ask your doctor, complementary and alternative therapies (also known as integrative medicine), person-alized reports using published medical research papers, and more. Cost?   Free!   The Internet is wonderful so be sure to use it. Remember when I said that having your pathology report is important?   Here's an example of why; get yours and go to www.cancer.nexcura.com/Secure/InterfaceSecure.asp?CB=266, or go to your search engine (Yahoo!, Google, or your own internet provider; AOL, Comcast, etc.) and type in 'NexProfiler'. If you are a 'wizard' user, you will appreciate entering the information and getting a report.

Muga-Scan to Measure Heart Strength

Today is September 30 and I am scheduled to have a muga-scan. This is a necessary preliminary to Adriamycin®. Adriamycin® is a cardio-toxic drug; it is hard on the heart. I am sitting in the waiting area with Mom Pedicone when a staff member comes to talk to me, "I saw your name on the chart and had to come see you. Why does your name ring a bell?"

We exchange ideas and then it hits me, "You did my bone scan after I was diagnosed! You made me feel so good when you confided that nothing was jumping out at you." I explained a little more, and she recalled.

She notices I am sitting in a slumped fashion. "How long ago was your surgery?" I tell her that it has been almost three weeks. She reminds me to straighten up as much as I can, so I will heal properly.

"I knew you looked familiar, I always remember my special patients," she says. "Good luck with chemo." And she leaves.

Tip 96   If you are recovering from a TRAM reconstruction, walk with your hands clasped behind your back. This will eliminate the ability to hunch forward and heal incorrectly. A bonus; it will give you a wonderfully non-chalant look that may actually help you to feel casual in your very intense world.

Tip 97   If you had lymph nodes removed, and your arm is stiff, try walking your fingers up the wall, a little farther up each day.

Another nurse takes me around the corner and injects my arm with dye, and then returns me to the waiting room. A few minutes later, a technician calls my name and I follow her to what looks like an x-ray room with a curtain pulled in front of the entrance. I remove my clothes from the waist up and lay back on the table. She puts several electrodes on my chest (like the ones you get when getting an EKG), covers me with a sheet, positions a machine over top of my chest area and walks to her computer. While the scan is happening I watch it on the computer. *Cool. I'm watching my heart. I can see it beat.*

Fifteen minutes later we leave the hospital. I'm sure my heart is strong enough to withstand chemotherapy.

As I stand in the now familiar spot on the patient side of Marcia's desk, she hands me paperwork so I can get my pre-operative blood work done – I passed my test; my heart is strong. It's time to have my medi-port implanted. Marcia is on a phone line confirming that today's lab results will reach the doctor in time for tomorrow's surgery, while Diane is on another phone line with the surgi-center. Both are confirming and coordinating details for tomorrow. Dr. M walks in the room, observes the scene and says, "Someday we'll be able to do phone-in surgery. All of us will call in at the same time and it will be done over the phone." *Wouldn't that be nice? Perhaps we can pay surrogates to feel the postoperative discomfort…they will make money, we will feel no pain and everyone wins. It's the American way. I chuckle, but you never know; in the last century people laughed when they heard about an oddity called television.*

Tip 98   Ask your surgeon if he or she has a medi-port to show you ahead of time (if you are interested). Also, discuss placement of the port. It can be placed slightly higher or lower on your chest to accommodate your clothes to ensure it will not be irritated by your bra strap or a shirt neck-line.

Diane writes:

Wendi is not a marshmallow. Of course she was devastated when the diagnosis was confirmed, but she did some investigation and was prepared to fight. "What do we do now?" "What is the next step?" "Can we do that today or tomorrow?" "Why not?" "Who do I see next?" She asks and she listens. All the while she is gathering information, because it seems less scary if you understand what is happening. Her personality is upbeat and kind. It is a pleasure to know her. Yeah Wendi!

MEDI-PORT FOR CHEMO

It is Friday, October 1 and I am ready to have my medi-port implanted. *I don't like the idea of going under the knife again so soon, but I am ready for chemo, hence I am ready for the medi-port.* Dan has a meeting in the morning, so his mother drives me to the surgi-center. I'm getting used to surgical procedures. In fact, I'm growing very accustomed to medical facilities. When I go back to work I might have to readjust. I fear that every time I walk into a small office and hear someone crinkling printer paper, I will feel the urge to remove my clothes from the waist up. *Won't my colleagues love me!*

This facility is newer than the one at the Christiana Care Newark hospital location where I had my biopsy. It's open and airy. I am relaxed…. mostly. I am really not in the mood to have more surgery now… *Geez, I can't even stand up straight yet. How are they going to lay me flat on the OR table?* My name is called and, just in time, Dan appears. Both Mom P and Dan come in now that I am prepped. They are wearing nametags with my name written on them. *My name? Not their own names? So, if they pass out and are resuscitated, they'll remember whom they were here with? Yeah, like I'm gonna be able to help them.* I am wearing a gown and hospital socks. Before I go into the OR, I'll put on the spiffy surgical hair cap they gave me. *It's a fashion risk I am willing to take.* I declined the felt tip marker to mark the side I'm having the port implanted on, because I've already written a note, "Doc, hit me with your best shot." Oh, and I marked the spot with a bulls' eye. *Get out the Betadine; Wendi's in the house.* The IV is in my arm, and I'm ready to roll. I am summoned and I walk with the OR nurse to one of the operating rooms.

Afterward, I am awakened and driven home. *I am port code 0602270 from lot number 22E04618.* I sleep in the recliner for a while. I have a pillow covering my chest. *Mustn't forget my loving cats.* When Danny is brought home from daycare, he sees me in the oh-so-familiar position on the recliner and picks up the signals, "Did you have surgewee, Mommy?"

I still wonder if there was anything I should have done to avoid getting cancer. Should I have eaten more fruits and vegetables, and less chocolate? Perhaps I shouldn't have had a thirty-year love affair with diet soda. If I did my monthly BSEs would I have found the lump sooner? Would cancer not have invaded my lymph nodes? Not doing exams reminds me of that dumb jerk...what's her name...oh, me!

> *"...what's done is done, and beating yourself up about it only affects your self-esteem - and negatively at that."*

I receive sensible advice from my friend and colleague, Brigid (who is another person on the "Heaven express"):

Wen...it feels like you're being really hard on yourself at this point. The truth is that what's done is done, and beating yourself up about it only affects your self-esteem – and negatively at that. Perhaps you want to think about forgiving yourself for the lapse. I know you, Wendi, and your answer to that question is yes. Stop berating yourself.

Tip 99   Stop blaming yourself or focusing on should have, could have, and would have. Start the forgiveness.

Saturday morning I wake feeling rested. As Dr. M promised, I am up for a wedding today. A friend and colleague is marrying his girlfriend and I'm not only going to get to see them, I'm going to see other AZ colleagues. This will be the first time since September 10 that I attend a social function.

I am pleased to discover that my black dress is no longer snug. In fact, it's roomy. I went from 155 to 145. *A perk.* I wear a lace sweater over the sleeveless dress to hide the white patch of surgical tape on my chest; it may make others feel awkward.

It is so therapeutic to see folks and have fun. Dan is relaxed and has a few drinks. Before I get too tired, I'd like to have a dance with him. A slow song is playing and he walks me to the dance floor. I am still walking old-lady-ish, that is, I am hunched over a bit, but we dance. Actually, we kind of rock from foot-to-foot in place. *Good enough for me.* We say our so longs and depart early.

SHAVE IT OFF

Today is the last time I will be seen with hair. I want to take control over *something*. I will be the one to decide when my hair goes and not the cancer nor the treatments.

So, Sunday morning, Christine, Andrea and I gather in the kitchen. It is time. I call to Michele who is in another room, "It's head shaving time. Are you sure you don't want to be part of this? I wouldn't want you to have any regrets."

"Mom," she says, "Eeeewww." *Right then. Gotcha.*

Dan and Danny are in the den; Andrea sits at the kitchen table and watches Christine begin the procedure. "Mom, do you want to save any of your hair?" *Nah. Let's just get on with this.*

> **Tip 100**   For cancer patients, who know they're going to lose their hair, consider donating it. It may help some underprivileged kid get the wig that's so desperately needed. Locks of Love has a website: www.locksoflove.org. For some, this could be a constructive, positive undertaking.

I feel the pulsation of the electric sheers against my scalp. *Weird.* I hope it doesn't hurt. *I've been cutting Dan's hair like this for years. Why am I jumpy thinking it's going to hurt?*

Halfway through, the girls switch places and Andrea shaves the other half of my head. I see a huge pile of light brown and blonde hair on the floor. *Clean up in aisle seven!*

Finally, Andrea hands the clippers to Christine and she does a few touch ups. Andrea is sitting with her elbow on the table and her chin resting in her hand. She is smiling at me. I think she is about to crack a joke to keep the mood light. "Andge," I start out, "I know I wanted this, but I'm a little anxious. This is not the time for joking."

"I wasn't going to joke, Mom." She answers. "I'm smiling because you look nice. You have a nice shaped head."

"So, I won't be having any bad-hair-days for awhile, will I?"

"Mom," she says, "you won't be having *any* hair days...no, you'll be having *no*-hair-days!"

Danny stands on the chair next to her and says, "You're bootiful Mommy." *Thank you, God, for that boy!*

When all is done, we clean up and I go upstairs to shower. As I am walking, it feels like there are imaginary people walking with me, waving their hands, fanning my head and blowing on it. It's a strange sensation. *Chilly too. I never felt such a draft!* I avoid looking in the mirror until after I am done showering. When at last I look at it, I think I look kind of cool. I put on my wig and a little make up, dress and go downstairs where my fan club awaits my arrival.

Having no hair is not so bad. Having cancer is bad. I have decided to give my cancer a name; "the invader." It has invaded my life and my body. It was uninvited. An invader is sly. An invader creeps up on you under cover or in the darkness. It knows it is not welcome. It has come to me and I need to send it packing.

Each day I am more comfortable in my new bald state. But, I always keep something handy to place on my head, should someone walk in. I am never quite sure how others would feel. Like Michele, for example: I watch her walking by me holding a paper in front of her. "Michele, is something wrong with your face?"

"No."

"Then why are you hiding it behind a piece of paper?"

"Mom. Put a hat on." *Gotta love her candor.*

Another day Michele comes in through the garage earlier than I expected her to. I am sitting on the couch with nothing on my head. "Hi Mommy!" I hear her cheerily shout. When she comes into the kitchen and sees me, she hesitates a moment, rolls her eyes and walks out of the room. *I figured there was bound to be someone who would be uncomfortable with me, but my own daughter?*

Teenagers speak English as a second language. Their first language is eye rolling. I understand this phenomenon, but I don't always accept it.

"Michele?"

"What?"

"Is there something wrong?"

"I hate seeing you look that way...y'know, without hair." She walks away. *Conversation over. I asked, and she was honest with her reply. She'll come around.*

Later that evening I walk by her as she sits at the computer and, without looking at me she calls, "C'mere Mom." She shows me an image on the Internet of the pink ribbon in Times Square. This is the first recognizable sign that she wants to support me.

"Would you like to go see it?" I ask.

"What do you mean?"

"Would you like to take a day trip to New York together and see the pink ribbon?"

"Sure! There'll probably be lots of breast cancer survivors there, you know."

The day she and I went to New York City was the day I realized she doesn't mind being with me. In fact, I think she may even like to be with me – even when I am bald. As it turned out, she invited three girlfriends, I invited their moms, and the eight of us had a truly memorable mother-daughter day together. *And I got to know a few more women that I can call 'friend'.*

In a conversation with a friend named Diane, I learn that her nineteen-year-old daughter recently discovered a lump in her breast. *Nineteen? Ugh.* They had the lump surgically removed, but it reminds me to caution my daughters against omitting their monthly BSEs.

> **Tip 101**   If you have daughters, go to KidsHealth.org, in particular the Parents' Q&A section and an article, Medical Care and Your 13 to 18-Year-Old.

INTIMACY

I have been wondering when I will feel ready to make love with my husband. I haven't felt particularly amorous in a physical way until now. The doctor told me that all systems are go as soon as I am able. Other than the discomfort from surgery, there's no reason to abstain.

Sleeping in our bed (Dan's and mine), upstairs where the bedrooms are located, will feel like a step toward the next phase of recuperation. Since I am not certain how he'll feel about the changes to private parts of my body, I'm nervous. Sure, we've talked about this. His view is, "It doesn't matter to me if you are missing a breast or have scars all over you, so long as you are living. That is what matters." *But, will he balk when it's time to stand by his words?*

I know he likes my wig so I put it on and freshen up. I move to his side of the bed and hint that I am ready. His body signs suggest he is ready also.

While we make love, Dan, in a seemingly subconscious gesture, reaches for my wig and gently pulls it off. I see this as prophetic; I inherently know at this moment that everything will be all right.

Afterward, as I drift off to sleep, I hear his breathing become slow and even. It is not the most wonderful sex we've ever had, to say the least, but the sheer meaning of the act, and the fulfillment we now have, is enormous.

My final thought before I go under is that I am sleeping in our bed for the first time in weeks.

Tip 102   Caregivers, remember to touch your loved one. If you are not ready for sexual intimacy, hold hands, snuggle or hug until you are.

Tip 103   There are books with information on the topic of sexual intimacy. I recommend reading some. Understanding what is typical at this point would be helpful to a married couple, as well as for a woman who does not have a current sexual partner. Therefore, I recommend *Bosom Buddies* by Rosie O'Donnell and Deborah Axelrod, M.D., FACS with Tracy Chutorian Semler for the topic of sex (and many other topics, too). *Bosom Buddies* is informative and fun to read (it's by Rosie O'Donnell for goodness sake, how can it not be?). Another is *Living through Breast Cancer* by Dr. Carolyn M. Kaelin (Sexuality, chapter 16). (If the Internet is your mecca, an entire section is dedicated to intimacy in www.breastcancer.org.) No time for books? Go to MayClinic. com's Cancer Center. Specifically, www.mayoclinic.com/ invoke. cfm?id= SA00071 and read about female sexuality after cancer, vaginal dryness, orgasms and sexual satisfaction, fertility, and more.

Tip 104   I discovered a website for lesbians called The Mautner Project, www.mautnerproject.org. It is named for Mary-Helen Mautner, a lesbian who died of breast cancer in 1989. The website offers support group information for caregivers. This could be a valuable venue for practical support regarding lesbian intimacy. For more information, call 866-MAUTNER from the United States, or e-mail: jhall@mautnerproject.org.

The next day Dan, his mother, and the girls do not waste any time removing the bed from the den and carrying it upstairs where it belongs. A small part of me will miss sleeping in the recliner with one of them in that bed, next to me. *But, only a small part of me, because I'm happy to be upstairs in a bedroom.* Graduating from the recliner means I am officially out of phase two and three of my recovery from surgery.

Another message from Brenda:

I had a few voice mail messages from Wendi over the weekend and this morning. Her surgery went well on Friday...three down, one to go.

She said she went to a wedding on Saturday and felt great. Got all dressed up and had a great time. Sunday, the girls and Dan shaved Wendi's head. Then she donned her new wig, got dressed up in new clothes, put makeup on and even wore jewelry and went to her nephew's birthday party at her brother's house. She said she felt very pretty!!

And, she slept in her own bed last night!

So, our girl is doing just great. What a courageous person with such a positive attitude!

Lynne, another colleague and friend, responds:

I was at the wedding Saturday with Wendi, and I was very happy to see her doing so well too. The reception was at the Delaware Creative Center

of the Arts on the Riverfront. They have an artist's rendition of a minia-
ture golf game in one of the rooms, and Wendi joined in the game! She
truly had a great time, and seemed to be able to put her illness out of her
mind for a little while. It really was great to see her doing so well and feel-
ing happy.

Here are some beauty tips:

Tip 105   A baldhead requires special care. If you are in the sun, be generous with sunscreen. Treat yourself to some of the beautiful scarves and hats that are available. And when your hair falls out (mine did around the fifteenth day after chemo began which was a few days after the second chemo treatment) use a shampoo that is "formulated for chemotherapy-radiation hair loss." My cousin, owner of *Simply You* in Delaware, gave me a bottle of *Brian Joseph's™ Formula 1 shampoo.*

Tip 106   Consider pampering yourself in the months ahead with new ways to look beautiful. *Facing the Mirror with Cancer* by Lori Ovits with Joanne Kabak offers tips on how to simulate natural-looking eyebrows (in case you lose yours) and modify your make-up regimen to improve your complexion, especially when chemo makes it pale or ruddy. The makeup artists' ideas can give you a real boost, and the before, during, and after photos of cosmetics' applications are helpful and fun to look at.

Tip 107   I found a pamphlet at the cancer center that introduced the *Look Good...Feel Better*, (LGFB) program. They offer free make-up sessions that teach beauty techniques to female cancer patients that will improve your self-esteem. Bonus: They give you a nifty kit of high quality cosmetics. Inquire at your physician's office or cancer place where you could be treated to a program like this one in your area. Alternatively, you could use your Internet service provider's search engine (or Google or Yahoo!) and search on any of the three sponsors of the LGFB program I mentioned. The American Cancer Society, CTFA (Cosmetology, Toiletry, and Fragrance Foundation), and NCA (National Cosmetology Association) sponsor the LGFB program in Delaware and Maryland.

Tip 108   Have any needed dental work done before you begin chemo. Chemotherapy drug products attack fast growing cells. Cancer cells are fast growing, and so are the ones in your hair follicles, your digestive system, and the lining of your mouth. The latter is a good reason to see your dentist before you begin cancer treatment. Dr. G, my dentist, told me that cancer patients should not leave their dentists out of the loop – chemo could hasten a current dental problem or slow down healing from a dental restoration done during treatment.

It has been a few days since my port was implanted and I am able to remove the tape. It looks odd. My sister Deb would describe it this way; "Your doctors must've been partying in the OR 'cause they left a bottle cap under your skin."

I am glad I had the mastectomy and very pleased with the TRAM reconstruction. Would I do it again? You bet I would. My head is shaved and I am ready to start fighting "the invader" with chemotherapy.

CHAPTER

CHEMOTHERAPHY: ADRIAMYCIN® AND CYTOXAN®

·4

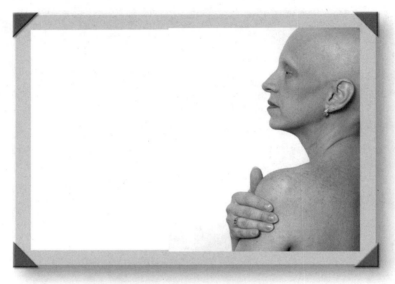

Photo courtesy of G. Thomas Murray Photography

Life is a long lesson in humility.

Sir James M. Barrie
Creator of Peter Pan
(1860 - 1937)

On the evening prior to my first chemotherapy treatment I arm myself with support. I pull out my phone list of names I created over a month ago. I contact folks and get tips about what to wear, what to eat on the morning of, how I'll feel, what it may be like; etc. I also read through the pamphlet, *Chemotherapy and You*, NIH Publication No. 03-1136, and two of the three I received when I was first diagnosed: Breastcancer.org; *Your Guide to Breast Cancer Treatment*, and *Overcoming Your Fears of Breast Cancer Treatment*.

Cytotoxic chemotherapy is commonly known as "chemo" or "chemotherapy." It is a systemic (total body) treatment with drugs that attack and kill cancer cells and rapidly growing normal cells.

Earlier today, Dan and I met with "Betsy the chemo nurse" as I call her…[*my nickname for her sounds like a new release of Mattel's Barbie™, doesn't it?*]. She is a nurse specialist who thoughtfully and calmly described for us what side effects I could possibly experience, and what to do about them. We discussed the one that unnerves me the most and is commonly associated with chemo, nausea. I now know what to eat before and after my infusion to minimize the possibility, and I am armed with Decadron® as a preventative (as I understand it, an alternative preventative is Zofran®). I also have a prescription script for Compazine® tablets (for adhoc nausea). Dan and I have knowledge, and knowledge is power. I have emotional support and now I am ready.

Tip 109   Write in a journal or notebook. Keep track of your chemo appointments, symptoms, side effects, lab test results and any medications you are taking. This information may be helpful for your oncologist to know.

Apprehensive doesn't half convey how I am feeling this morning. Today, October 9, I will have chemo. *I am really a cancer patient. Now I'm going to look like a cancer patient.* I eat a cup of oatmeal and drink some herbal tea. I take my purse and a small canvas bag that Danny made at daycare – I proudly display his handprints in blue and yellow paint. In it I have some reading material, Emend® prescription pill pack, my port identification card, a portable CD player and a few relaxation and visualization CDs, *For People with Cancer,* by Belleruth Naparstek and *Getting Ready,* by Bernie S. Siegel, M.D. Dan and I head for the cancer center. I am nervous the entire fifteen-minute trip. *My heart is beating rapidly. Will the chemo go through my system too fast if my heart is beating wildly? Will it work? Surely, everyone who starts chemo does so with an elevated, nervous heartbeat.*

Now that we are here, my anxiety is decreased. *Why is that?* I choose a recliner away from people [*I don't want to talk to anyone*] and in view of the TV. Dan pulls up a chair next to me. The nurse approaches. I remind her that the area around my port is still a little tender from surgery. She delicately and quickly inserts the specialized needle into my port. Surprisingly, it doesn't hurt.

Tip 110   A non-coring needle is used with a medi-port to prevent holes in the rubberized front of it (that is under your skin). A cored needle (one with a hollow opening like the type used when you have blood drawn) would take out tiny bits of the rubber, leaving it open to infection or leakage under the skin. A non-coring needle enables the hole in the port under your skin to reseal immediately upon removal of the needle. Also, some facilities are prepared to do your weekly blood work using your port, versus an arm vein. This is to preserve your vein. Many people are unable to use one arm for blood work due to lymph node removal. Preserving the veins in the remaining arm can be crucial if you are a cancer patient who needs regular blood draws for months or years.

The nurse starts the first bag of antiemetics and I relax. Dan opens his newspaper and reads. I send a few text messages from my cell phone to my daughters and my sisters. Knowing that they are thinking of me at the precise time I'm receiving chemo is comforting.

So far, so good. I don't feel any differently. Will I start getting sick? Will my hair stubs start falling out? I sit and listen to my CD.

After awhile, I feel the urge to go potty. *Badly. It must be all the fluid going into me.* I wheel the IV pole to the bathroom, because I can't wait until I am disconnected from it after the rest of this bag drips! *Hurry! Don't I look silly waddling – I have to do two things urgently; go right away and figure out how to walk quickly with an IV pole and tubing. Ooh, ooh, ooh.*

As I turn to flush the toilet I see the pretty color of peach-ish orange. They warned me that the red syringe of Adriamycin® would turn my pee orange or red. *Oh, the indignity. Good grief.*

Once I am back in my recliner and all the IV bags have emptied into me, the nurse pulls the needle from the port. I am disconnected, no longer plugged in. Dan and I gather my things and I stand. *Ooooh, steady going. I feel woozy.*

That Wasn't so Bad

Dan gets me settled into my seat in the car and drives me away from "the Helen Graham."

The day new parents bring their newborn baby home from the hospital, there's a great deal of ceremonious attention given to the event. Once there, the baby goes into the bassinet, falls asleep and parents wonder, "Okay, now what?" The hours following become quiet and typical.

Like that event, Dan and I go into our home and wonder what we should do next. *What does a person do after chemo?*

Hello all,

Yesterday (Wednesday), I underwent my first chemotherapy treatment. It was a cakewalk! I wish I hadn't spent so much time feeling anxious.

> *...I underwent my first chemotherapy treatment... I wish I hadn't spent so much time feeling anxious.*

Dan and I went to the Helen F. Graham Cancer Center in Christiana and entered the "chemo room." Once relaxed, the nurse attached a needle into my medi-port, which is just under my skin on the right side of my chest (opposite from the surgical work that was done on the left side). She visited us several times during the two hours. In between each IV bag, the nurse injected a small syringe filled with saline to "flush" the vein, and after the last bag, another syringe of a substance to protect the port from clogging until the next treatment. The protocol began with oral antiemetics (Emend®) and a steroid IV bag (to prevent nausea and vomiting), flush, a red syringe filled with Adriamycin®, flush, a Cytoxan® bag, flush and the last substance from a syringe to clean the opening. So, the chemo plan is; two hours, once every two weeks for eight weeks on these two drugs, and then once every two weeks for eight weeks on Taxol®. Barring complications or delays, I hope to be finished by mid-January. During this treatment process I'll receive weekly blood work to check the levels of my white blood cells, among other things. If the white blood cells drop too low, I'll be highly susceptible to catching nasty things like infections, colds or the flu. During these times I'll need to take extra precautions. The day following each chemo treatment I will return to the center to receive an injection of a product that will tell my bone marrow to step-up production of white blood cells and search out immature ones, and then hasten the maturation process. It is called Neulasta® I may feel bone achiness, but all will be well.

During the two-hour chemo drip, Dan and I chatted, read and watched some discussions about the Vice Presidential debate on TV. Thanks to the advice of my life coach, that my sister Deb put me in touch with, I dedicated some time to envisioning the chemo products searching out the cancer cells and attacking them. I listened closely to the sounds of ahhhhh, and heeelllpp! By the way, I've nicknamed the cancer, "the invader" so I can speak about it with revulsion. When all was complete and I stood up, I'd felt as if I had a few glasses of wine. Once home, I was wiped out for a few hours. I slept in the recliner that recently served as my bed.

So far, I've experienced minimal side effects through the night and this morning.

My guardian angel (my mother-in-law, Helen) has been staying with us during the week on weekdays to do the things I would normally do to run the household, and driving me to appointments, picking up prescriptions and more. I'm lucky to have her. After the chemotherapy treatments, I'll undergo radiation treatments once a day, for five consecutive days, for 5-8 weeks (to be determined). My mom is eighty-two. She told me that she wished this were happening to her instead of me. I told her that I would rather go through this than watch a loved one go through it. Besides, since I have it, and I have access to e-mail, which she does not, I have the opportunity to communicate to a fairly wide group of folks, so they can understand cancer and one of the ways we fight it. Hopefully, this knowledge will reach someone who may face the same thing one day. If I can help diminish someone's anxiety by telling my story, then I've done well.

What are my new passions? Asking God to allow me to show people that miracles do happen, and becoming an advocate for fighting cancer.

I enjoy keeping you informed about my progress and of the details because it is my way of keeping a journal, connecting with you and telling folks who may be curious about how this particular cancer is treated. I hope I'm not overstuffing your Inbox. A bonus for those of us at AZ; it will hopefully serve to humanize what our company does for patients.

Love to all,
Wendi

The next day, I write an update: October 10, 2004

Shortly after I send the e-mail, I leave with Mom Pedicone to get my 'day-after' shot, as I call it, of Neulasta® (to boost my white blood cells). By the time we come back home, I feel crummy.

The inability to be involved in others' lives as I used to be or I would like to be makes me feel torn. I am totally preoccupied with my chemo.

Now that I am officially a chemo patient, I take better care of myself. I exercise, rest, eat better than I did before and listen to what my body tells me.

> **Tip 111**   Mouth care during chemo: Use children's fluoride toothpaste (I switch between Sponge Bob Square Pants and Winnie-the-Pooh!). Children's toothpaste provides fluoride and is not as astringent or strong as adult toothpaste. Also, gargle several times a day with baking soda and water. It'll neutralize the acid in your saliva caused by chemo and cut down on mouth sores. There are prescription drugs available for mouth sores, so ask your doctor if they become bothersome.

The Philadelphia Eagles sell and distribute pink hats at their stadium in honor of Breast Cancer Awareness Month. I receive three from friends. Each is different from the others and I plan to wear all three in the coming months. *When the Eagles get to the playoffs and the Super bowl this year, I just may have to share two of the hats with my family.*

I SPOKE TOO SOON

Update: October 14, 2004

Hello all,

On the morning following my first chemotherapy treatment last week I wrote about my experience. I stated that my encounter with chemo was a "cake walk." Well, I had spoken too soon. I was wrong. At the time, I documented my first experience for folks who may be curious to learn about chemo and the ups and downs of having breast cancer. I e-mailed the journal entry to Brenda and Vicki to kindly distribute, then went to the Helen F. Graham Cancer Center for my "day-after' injection. By noon, I'd arrived home and said to Dan and my mother-in-law, "Gee, the couch looks very good to me right now, I think I'll take a NNNAAAaaaappppppppp." The next few days were hazy. I'd felt like I'd come down with the flu. I had "chemo face" for starters. My cheeks, neck and shoulders were pink and I appeared to have mild sunburn. I had a slightly elevated temperature and body aches. Through to Sunday, I didn't sleep well. My skull, neck, shoulder blades and ribs hurt. Lying on my back was uncomfortable, but I had no choice; lying on either side or face down was difficult too because of the two surgeries. Still, I said to myself, "Don't be a weenie, there are people who are worse off than me."

Some folks have asked and I'm happy to report, I didn't get sick or nauseous. The antiemetics are very effective. For the heck of it I decided to tempt fate and skip the third-day pill (I have a strong stomach). No nausea...a personal triumph...oh boy, am I living on the edge!

Thank goodness for pharmaceutical advancements, new medications and target therapies. In the case of chemo, my quality of life without pharmaceuticals would be very diminished. So glad I don't have to spend endless hours vomiting like people did before antiemetics were developed.

Dan sat with me for chemo treatment number one. My second treatment is scheduled for Tuesday and my very close friend, Lisa, will sit with me. Then, Deb will arrive from Denver on Wednesday. She'll bring our mother to my house to stay for a bit. If I feel as lousy as I did the last time, I suspect that we won't have many words to say out loud, but sitting quietly together will speak volumes. I am surrounded by so much love that I ask myself, "What did I do to deserve all of this kindness and support?" I mean, I believe that I've been kind to people and kindness comes back, but it's coming back tenfold...a hundredfold, no, a thousandfold.

Under my wig, I have hair stubble from when the girls shaved my head. So far, I can detect only a hint of a receding hairline. A tiny bit of fear creeps in; if the chemo hasn't made my hair fall out, has it reached the cancer in my body? Trust science and chemotherapy Wendi...move on to positive thoughts. I smile whenever I think back on my wig-buying experience. I was told to "see the oriental guy at the Farmer's Market." We went to the market in New Castle and inquired about the location of the wig shop. Andrea and I went in the shop while Dan kept Danny busy in a toy store nearby. At the time, I was getting around with a walker. I am certain I looked pathetic and old. Once inside the shop, we were having fun trying on long, blonde wigs when suddenly we heard a loud voice, "YOU CHEMO PATIENT?" The walker must've been the giveaway.

"I, ah, will be soon," I answered.

"You come back in fifteen minute," he said, "Somebody already here," he added. Before I had the chance to leave he was touching my head and face while staring into space. "Hmmm, you have very small head, yehhh, come back, I fix you up." As we walked out I heard once more, "You come back in fifteen minute."

When we returned, he took us behind a partition and motioned for me to sit in front of the mirror. We grimaced when he showed us a wig. "No," I said, "it's too short, too close to my face and not the color I am looking for."

I sat in a beauty chair in front of a mirror while Andrea and selected several hairpieces. The Asian man was nearby and quiet. We then came upon a very nice, short styled, reddish blonde wig. "Dats first one I show you!" He said excitedly (and loudly – yeesh, Andrea nearly dropped it when he spoke up). "Red is very nice new color, many women in New York City wearing red now." He obviously knew what he was talking about. By the time we left, I had a wig and accessories and knowledge of the dos and don'ts of synthetic hair care. I will always remember, fondly, the direct yet kind Asian man nodding his head as we exited his shop saying, "You be alright, you be fine, be strong, good luck."

One recent morning, one of my daughters, Michele, was about to leave for school. I got out of bed hurriedly to tell her something. Now, keep in mind that upon rising, it takes me awhile to stand up straight due to the surgical work on my torso. It has gotten better, but I get stiff in the mornings. This particular morning, there was no time to waste; I was certain she was about to leave. I didn't think to put something on my head. I stood hunched over in the shadows and poked my head out of my bedroom door. I still laugh out loud when I recall her sleepy but startled reaction. Think about a time when you were a kid and you jumped from the darkness to scare someone and you'll laugh too. "Michele," I called. Her head swiftly turned upward. In her underwear she did this arms-flailing kind of thing and a sort of hop-skip-jump across the hall and into the bathroom. "Geeeeez, God, Mom!" I could practically hear her heavy breathing from where she stood in the bathroom. Oh, it was golden. Ahhhhh, I must've looked like a little alien standing in the dark hallway. I'm still grinning... Oh, and she's probably gonna hate me for writing about that.

The human mind is amazing. The ability to forget pain once it's over is wonderful. Ask any mother if she truly remembers the pain of childbirth. The days following the mastectomy seem very long ago. The memories that come to my mind are the sounds of squirrels eating black walnuts from the tree in our backyard, sitting on our deck allowing warm air and sunshine to heal my incisions and the expressions of support from colleagues, friends, neighbors and family. That's the stuff I remember.

I have figured out that I could attend a school function with my daughters for a short time, then rest. I could shop at a clothing store, then sleep in the car for ten minutes. I was able to go to my brother's house for a birthday party, leave early once I became tired and Tim seemed grateful that I had been there. I could read a book to my three-year-old son, then close my eyes so he could go off with Christine to put up Halloween decorations. It's all about understanding and following my body's signals. We go about our day-to-day lives, and the girls bring home their teenage friends as they always have. Their friends immediately see that this is not a sad place with a cancer patient in it, rather a lively household. Thanks to you, I can feel somewhat normal and say, "There are goodies on the counter and food in the fridge, help yourself." I always enjoyed being able to offer kids comfort foods when they visit. Right now, none of us has time or energy to shop for and prepare anything. Thank you, because the meals you've prepared and sent to my house not only nourish my family, but they help me to feel nearly like my former self.

Throughout all of this, I actually do think about other things, like the company I am proud to work for, the people I enjoy working with (and miss), IS communications planning, Exanta®, Corporate Health Services, Rob and the ISL, Dr. P and the oncology department at AZ, Crestor®, SPKS, mySAP, BIS Ops & Finance, a strong finish for 2004, the United Way campaign, next year's objectives, UK colleagues, Swedish colleagues; etc.

PLEASE KNOW that I'm not self-absorbed and that I do think about the events in your life, like miniature golf with Lynne, newly married friends Mike and Clavel, Kim who just lost her father, Bill and Lucy who became grandparents this year, Keva's ambition, Kayla's nurse-tech studies, Andréa's faith and her new husband, Joseph's recent presentation and his incredible focus, Ronya's job, Jill's trip, Sue's garden, Gin's sister and cousin, the Jamisons, Cole's new look – hair and clothes, Jess's new look – haircut and color, Nancy's mother, Maggie's mother, Rob and Chirag's babies on the way, Tina R's arm, Tina M's bracelet, Denise and Greg, Diane and Jeff, Paula and Dan, Cheryl and her family, Joann, Janet, ISACs, RhonJohn, Ray and Peggy, Ron and Cindy, Roseann, Uncle

Johnny, Uncle Earl and Aunt Lue, my professors, my Denver resources, my doctors and their staff, my Florida friends and family, Karen and my other class of '77 chums, Caitlin's new job, Shaun at WVU, the Hanus girls, the Gillette boys, Terri's family, Dottie's grandchildren, Heidi and Tim, Harry and Jean, Diane K's veggie regimen, Diane P's daycare, Miss Sheri's daycare and Miss Amy...the list of my thoughts goes on and on, so even if I didn't mention something about you, DON'T THINK YOU AREN'T ON MY MIND.

Am I glad I have breast cancer? Of course not. However, I would not have witnessed the depth of human kindness, my spirituality and strength of character, nor my family's ability to balance a life-altering event with day-to-day living if I didn't have it.

We all have gifts and talents. Many of us don't realize what they are, because the talents are effortless to individuals. Remind yourself that your particular talent, or what comes easy to you, is not effortless to others. Utilize your talents. I'm trying to discover mine; perhaps one of mine is writing my personal communications throughout this ordeal. I am hoping that they will help others in some way.

My body is on the mend from surgery and I'm thinking that when all of this is over I'm gonna look pretty darn gooood by summertime. Whether I will or won't, here is a motto I think I'll live by: "Life should NOT be a journey from start to end with the intention of arriving safely in an attractive and well-preserved body, but rather to skid in sideways, chocolate in one hand – chocolate martini in the other, body thoroughly used up and totally worn out, and screaming WOO HOO! – what a ride!"

Dan comes home from work one evening and asks me if I am up to going out for a bite to eat. Mom P, Danny, Dan and I take a ride to beautiful, historic Kennett Square. We are seated in a restaurant and place our orders. A thick, juicy Swiss cheese and Kennett mushroom burger arrives and I take a bite. It is so rare that it is only mildly warm in the center. It tastes funky and I am tempted to spit it into a napkin. But I don't. *Spitting it out would be unbecoming.* I swallow it instead. My mother-in-law is horrified at how uncooked the burger is, especially because we saw a health channel documentary last night about a young boy with eColi bacteria that was literally attacking his organs. He nearly died several times over the course of a few days in the ER. He contracted eColi by eating a raw piece of ground meat when on a camping trip. He was too embarrassed to spit it out so he swallowed it. *Just like I did.* I ask the waitress if she will take the meal back. On the way home I recall that TV documentary and my fear begins to mount. *If I have eColi, will the chemo that is in my body destroy it?* When we arrive at the house I announce that I am going upstairs to change my clothes. I lock my bathroom door and force myself to vomit. *I hope it's not too late. I hope the raw meat came up with the french fries I ate and the yummy chocolate cake the restaurant gave me for my inconvenience.* Then I take a senna laxative, cross my fingers and hope that it will move my dinner through me by morning. *I am scared. Before, eating a raw burger wouldn't have bothered me. Now I am terrified.*

> *...If I have eColi, will the chemo that is in my body destroy it? ...I lock my bathroom door and force myself to vomit.*
>
> *...Before, eating a raw burger wouldn't have bothered me, now I am terrified.*

This is going to be a long winter. I am blue. I receive a card from Gin; she sends me one about every other week. *She is so kind. She's been through this with her sister and her cousin and knows fighting cancer is not a once-and-done thing...it is ongoing.* I read what she wrote at the precise hour I was thinking about the winter that looms:

> *This card makes me think of spring and you being well, whole, and happy. So keep the thought of bulbs lying dormant through cold, hard, freezing days of winter, only to thrust slowly through the earth to grow and bloom and be a beautiful, resilient flower.*

Potent stuff. Powerful coincidence. Kismet.

Tip 112   You and your family may feel better if some parts of family-life-before-cancer remain. Try turning off the ringer of your telephone during times when they (and you) need uninterrupted interaction (like family movie night or for a family discussion). Or, if you get these well-intended phone calls while you are involved in an important activity, ask callers to call you during hours when you have more free time.

Tip 113   Ready for a little humor? Try reading *Why I Wore Lipstick to My Mastectomy* by Geralyn Lucas. She struggles to find her sense of self and the significance of her breasts in unique ways. I treasured the chuckles I got when I read about her experience in a strip club and with a New York cabbie who confided that he had one testicle.

Also, check out *Not Now...I'm Having a No Hair Day!* By Christine Clifford (University of Minnesota Press). It is a book about the humorous side of the cancer experience. Ms. Clifford took cartoons from the book and turned them into calendars and greeting cards and T-shirts and coffee mugs. Use your favorite Internet search engine and find The Cancer Club.

Doing something kind for others will give me a lift. Telling the flattering truth about people who deserve my sincerity will be good for me also. I write a letter to the CEO of Christiana Care Health System and include it with my feedback form. On the form, I am honest in my comments about the HVAC system in this particular location, the Wilmington Hospital building. Telling them that the rooms could use some dressing-up and the air quality needs improvement not only gives them information they can use, it lends credibility to my positive statements about their staff. If I didn't include it, they might think I see the world through rose-colored glasses only.

My letter to the CEO of Christiana Care Health System regarding the "Quality Care of the Staff":

Dear Dr. Lsk:

On September 10, I had a mastectomy and TRAM reconstruction. Dr. M and Dr. D performed the surgery at your Wilmington Hospital location. I knew then that I was in capable hands, and my husband and I trusted their expertise. Since the surgery, I have come to know them as extremely compassionate individuals. I would rank the "bedside manner" of each, on a scale of one-ten (with ten being the highest) as eleven. They are sympathetic, supportive and always give me the time I need to discuss concerns. Additionally, each has a caring and responsive office staff, all of whom are essential to my emotional welfare as I strive to beat breast cancer.

From Friday evening September 10 until Wednesday, I was in Wilmington Hospital room 546A. During that time, I received exceptional care from the nursing staff. Every woman who provided care for me was extraordinary and unique. Though I was administered pain medication and my thoughts were not always clear during the hospital stay, I remember at least one distinctive thing about each.

Please recognize the following nurses for their compassion:

Bonnie 1	Bonnie 2
Bonnie 3	Margarette
Valerie	Sunita
Michele	Melanie
Laurie	Christine
Jada	Alice
Beth	Natalie
Loretta	Sophia

Please ask the nurse manager to check her records from 9/10 to 9/15 in case I neglected to name a nurse who cared for me. If I did miss a name, it is only because I was recovering from surgery and not always fully awake or lucid. A nurse that didn't get mentioned in my letter should get recognized too.

This letter is about far more than just technical expertise and capabilities. It is about the other side of care giving; the people side. It is rare indeed to encounter members on any team who demonstrate consistently high quality output (every person, every shift, every day). Christiana Care must have an amazing training program with daily incentives for nurses, because each seems to sincerely look into the souls of patients and possess incredible human kindness. I am humbled.

Gratefully,
Wendi Fox Pedicone

The goodies I have been collecting for my return trip to visit the fifth floor nurses are in a large bag in my dining room. It's time for a visit to see them. The large decorative gift bag is filled with fruit, candy, nuts, cookies and a bag of pink M&Ms (a portion of the proceeds from the sale of the specially-packaged candy goes to breast cancer research). On the outside of the box, just under the ribbons, I attach a copy of the letter to their CEO and a picture of my family with a circle around me that says, "I'm the patient who was in room 546A." *How can they possibly remember their patients?*

When I arrive at the hospital I stroll around the fifth floor to find my old room and the nurses' station. I walk past the Nuclear Medicine rooms where I received my bone scan in August. Wow, it is located about fifty paces and around the corner from where I spent phase I of my recovery. *I hadn't known that. An interesting coincidence.* The nurses' station that I am looking for is the one I went crying to when I thought the nuclear med nurse would not be able to do my bone scan since I had arrived late.

"Heeeyyyy, look who's here," one of them exclaims. I recognize her as "Bonnie to the third power." Using an algebraic reference, I nicknamed all three of them [with the same name, Bonnie]. *But, I can't believe she recognizes me. They must see so many patients, how can they remember one?* "Well, how've you been? Did you start your chemo yet?"

A few of us talk for a bit, and I give them their thank-you gift before I depart. The joy of seeing them was great. *And now I need a nap.*

My First Breast Cancer Event as a Breast Cancer Victim

Last year, Michele joined the Lady Colts Rugby Club. Her coach calls and says that the team has its first team event of this year; walking together in the American Cancer Society breast cancer walk. And they are doing it for me. *Wow.* So, it is a cool October morning and we meet at the event. Volunteer walkers wear tags with names written on them of people who have, or had, breast cancer. The girls are wearing their team sweatshirts and my name!

It is a non-chemo week for me, so I feel that I can do this. Christine is home for the weekend and joins us. We are headed for the Wilmington Riverfront together. As soon as we get out of the car, I am fighting back tears. I am so glad to be here and grateful to everyone else who is. I hope that every single cancer patient feels the way I do; I want to walk up to each of the five thousand people in attendance and say 'thank you', since they are here because of me. *Thank you. Thank you.*

I sign in and one of the attendants tells me to sign the survivor board. "But I'm not a survivor yet. I just started chemo," I say.

"Nonsense," she says as she hands me a marker. She walks me to the board and smiles as she says, "You're here aren't you? So, sign it."

Misty-eyed, I sign the board.

> **Tip 114**   If you are a breast cancer patient or survivor, join a walk
> if you are up to it or attend the kick-off to a walk! It can be very
> exhilarating just to be there. There are many year round (and not
> just during breast cancer awareness month, October). Look for
> *Race for the Cure* advertisement of an October walk near you, or
> contact <u>www.the3day.org</u> or 800-996-3DAY for more information
> on the three-day walk.

Former president Bill Clinton makes a speech at the Democratic convention supporting the Kerry/Edwards campaign. Reporters marvel over how virile and fit he looks, following his bypass heart surgery. It has been about five weeks since his major procedure. I had mine before he had his. He is walking several miles a day. *Did I hear them correctly?* I couldn't even make it the second time around the *Race for the Cure* course recently. I don't even walk several miles a week. And, I am younger than he is. *What's wrong with me?*

MEN GET BREAST CANCER TOO

I receive an e-mail from Dan's cousin's wife, Brenda B who discloses that Vince was diagnosed with breast cancer (in his early 40's). *Why didn't we hear about it before now? Did they keep it quiet? If they did, was it because breast cancer is associated with women and not men?* She said that one day she asked Vince about a lump on his chest. He said, "Yeah, that's been there awhile." Thankfully, she insisted he see a doctor. Vince is open to telling others, and sharing his experience with me, since raising awareness could save someone's life:

> *The lump was on the underside of the left side of my chest. I first felt it when I was showering. I thought about breast cancer, exactly, but didn't want to believe it. A few months went by and I finally said something to my doctor. It was as plain as day. It was my greatest fear, and always will be…cancer of any kind. My family doctor didn't think about breast cancer at first, because breast cancer in men is unusual. He said, "I think this is no more than an ingrown hair or an oil gland stopped up. Let's remove it to be sure." He took the lump out in his office under a local anesthetic – it was the size of thumbnail, round or a little bigger. Sometime later, it grew back and he suggested a specialized surgeon to remove it. Dr. Z, at the Christiana Care Medical Arts Pavilion did a lumpectomy and sent it out to pathology. A few days later he called Brenda and said he needed to talk to me right away. I couldn't believe I had breast cancer! I had clear margins so an oncologist, or a specialist who specialized in carcinoma, rec-*

ommended radiation treatments as a precaution and no chemo. It has been two years. I have CT scans, from my neck to my pelvis, every six months.

Tip 115   If you are interested in reading more about male breast cancer, the National Institutes of Health (www.nci.nih.gov/cancer-topics/pdq/treatment/malebreast/patient) is a good place to start.

BEGINNING THE PATH TO NUTRITIONAL AND ALTERNATIVE SOLUTIONS

My sister, Deb, flew in from Colorado and is treating me to an education in nutrition, organics, herbal supplements, and complementary and alternative medicine. We go to health food stores, do some research and talk to her nutritionist, Jennifer, who is an advocate for Ayurvedic medicine. Most of us have life-altering experiences like a layoff or loss of an important job, a death of a loved one or a cancer diagnosis. Sometimes we see these events as bumps in the road and other times we see them as opportunities to make big changes. I am using my cancer diagnosis to do the latter, and I will modify my way of living and eating, my spirituality and view of life. Deb's visit is helping me to do this. She is a living example of Dr. Steven Covey's *Seven Habits*, in particular, the one that says we learn when we teach. I like to think that she is getting re-energized about her own life while she is teaching me about the possibilities in mine. Jennifer had a few life-changing events that pressed her to make significant changes in her life including an Ayurvedic approach to nutrition. Deb has one too; her sister's cancer diagnosis. She is a terrific coach I hope she utilizes my walk with cancer to pursue her dreams and passions (in case she is not doing this already).

Tip 116   The benefits of eating organic have not been proven (although, eating less chemicals from residues makes sense to me), but the benefits of eating a wide variety of fruits and vegetables have. Provided you can withstand a normal diet (depending upon your tolerance for the medications), eat a cornucopia of fresh produce.

Tip 117   If you are interested in CAM (complementary and alternative medical therapies) search the Internet. A useful website that was recommended to me is www.mindbodyhealing.com. It includes information about holistic medicine, color therapy, color light therapy, alternative healing, etc.

So, about my customized nutritional diet, I now have my own section of the fridge and an entire cabinet dedicated to organic food. Michele and Andrea come home from school and look in the kitchen for goodies to eat. They see bee pollen, almond milk and ginger roots, "MOM, are we gonna have to eat weird food now?"

They each sigh with relief when I tell them "no."

I learned some very interesting things. Certain fruits and spices help a body to detoxify. Many fruits, vegetables, seeds and nuts contain antioxidants that help the body prevent cancer. And, did you know that if produce is labeled "USDA organic" it is organically grown, but if it isn't (produce isn't always labeled), you can check the PLU (Price Look-Up) sticker? If it's got five digits, starting with "9', then the produce is organic. Four digits mean they are conventionally grown (More, p. 146).

Also, some produce is known to have lower pesticide residues than others, e.g., asparagus, avocados, bananas, broccoli, cauliflower, corn, kiwi, mangoes, onions, papaya, pineapples and sweet peas have very low residues (More, p.146).

I shop at the Albertson Acme large chain grocery store (for my family) and the Harvest Market individually owned, natural foods store in Hockessin (for me). If you are like most cancer patients, you feel betrayed by your body and begin to point fingers. Food is an easy target. It is also a feasible thing to modify. There are some known reasons people get cancer, and many unknown reasons. It is normal to want to take an active role in changing your diet in light of evidence that diet and nutrition are connected to some health problems. If you want to make drastic changes in what you stock in your cupboards, much of what you will buy won't be at your grocery store (you know, "weird food" according to my teenagers). Look for a natural food store in your area if you are interested in organic food, and natural herbal supplements and vitamins.

Tip 118 I will always shop at the health food store, but I do want opportunities to cut down on my tasks (like weekly grocery shopping), so I asked John, the manager of the Acme grocery store, to consider carrying a few items that I buy in large quantities like organic fruits and vegetables, organic juices, and cage-free eggs. Ask the manager at your favorite grocery store to consider stocking certain items you plan to buy, especially if a health food store is not convenient to get to from where you live. Who knows, your grocer may pick up a few new customers besides you.

Also, ask the manager at your health food store to order things for you in bulk (to cut down on your costs). I drink organic vegetable and "greens" juices everyday; therefore it is more cost-effective for me to buy them by the case.

Eating organics cost more. If you can't afford to go total organic for yourself or your family, minimize your chemical intake by installing water filters on your faucets, and washing your fruits and vegetables. I learned that it is safe to use a mild dishwashing detergent and water to wash the produce and use plenty of water to rinse it, but there are produce-cleaning solutions on the market that I prefer. I use Earth Friendly Products Fruit and Vegetable Wash. I believe it is worth the $5 for a 22-ounce product. I buy organically grown lettuce and broccoli, and wash the rest of my fruits and vegetables (something I *never* did before cancer).

Tip 119   At this point in your journey (if you are considering a combination of foods, sleep, herbs, meditation, yoga and natural detoxification), try reading *The Answer to Cancer Is never Giving it a Chance to Start, by Hari Sharma, M.D. and Rama K. Mishra, G.A.M.S. with James G. Meade, Ph.D.*

As far as my approach to wellness, I have chosen a conventional Western approach to fighting cancer, and a combination approach (the inclusion of complementary medicine and Ayurvedic nutrition) to maintaining a healthy lifestyle. For more information on ancient Ayurvedic principles, which is what I chose, go to www.thebalancedapproach.com.

Conventional Western (Traditional) Medicine: This system basically approaches cancer and lifestyle after cancer with some or all of the following modalities: Surgery, pharmaceutical drugs, radiation therapy and rehabilitation. We may be most familiar with modern Western medicine, but many people are becoming increasingly aware of, and attracted to, alternative philosophies of patient care, particularly east and south Asian methods, homeopathic, and naturopathic medical systems (Brown, p. 143).

Alternative and Complementary Medicine: Non-traditional therapies that combine approaches and treatments to optimize health. Whether you are a caregiver considering alternative or complementary medicine for your family, or a cancer patient looking at alternative or complementary choices for yourself, it can be overwhelming. According to Imaginis (www.imaginis.com) these medicines have become increasingly popular in recent years. But do your homework when considering these approaches; while evidence reveals that they may be beneficial to patients, extensive research is still needed. Most physicians recommend that patients who use non-traditional approaches use them only as supplements to traditional/conventional/Western options that have been scientifically proven to be effective.

Alternative Medicine	Complementary Medicine
A non-traditional therapy that is used *in place of* traditional medicine.	A non-traditional therapy that is used *as a supplement to* traditional medicine.

(imaginis.com/breasthealth/alternative.asp)

A few examples of alternative systems are Ayurveda, homeopathy, naturopathy, traditional Chinese (an approach we explored when our daughter, Christine needed support for her Tourette's Syndrome), and Native American medicine.

A few examples of approaches within systems (and treatments) are diet (like, macrobiotic), nutrition (like, organic, Ayurvedic, and vegetarian), herbology, mind-body/spiritual (like, reflexology, T'ai Chi, yoga, visualization, poetry, and prayer), and manual healing (like, Reiki). For a complete easy-to-read explanation of types of therapies as well as links to additional resources and references, go to www.imaginis.com/breasthealth/alternative.asp.

If you decide to use non-Western therapies in conjunction with standard therapeutic regimens be sure your doctor knows about them.

Update: Tuesday, October 26, 2004

Hello all,

Last week, at about 1:15 PM on Tuesday the 19th, you may have heard a sound; DING. That was my girlfriend Lisa and I, stepping into the ring for round two of chemo. I duked-it-out with "the invader." It went pretty much like the previous round with the exception of one thing. The final gift for the day from the chemo nurses was a shot of Aranesp® to boost my red blood cell count. Aranesp® is the 'cousin' to Procrit®, a product many of you asked about.

Wednesday to Sunday I put in a rough couple of days. Good thing my sister Deb was in from Denver. She cooked for me, put her arms around me while I slept on the couch, and hung out with Dan, the rest of the family and me. I felt truly lousy, but my heart was full.

Christine's college roommate, LaToya, printed a poem for me to read following my chemotherapy treatment entitled, A New Kind of Beautiful. The following are a few lines. '...He didn't ask for perfection, but perfection is what he got...Love, Hope and Happiness. Companionship, a home, a family...now she lay so beautifully, softly sleeping off today's therapy session. The pink ribbons on the back of the cars were her stamps of pride. She subtly told the world what she'd endured. He cried when he put the ribbons on, could one person be so beautiful.'

Fast forward to yesterday afternoon. I was feeling better than I had in days and insisted on doing a 'mom' thing with Michele, which was to pick up supplies for a school project. During the time we were out I began to feel itchy.

...Simultaneously, a light bulb went off in our heads. He put his hands on my shoulders and moved me closer to the hood light near the range and said, "You're losing your hair!"

When we got home, Andrea and a few friends were in the kitchen. "Mom, if you're itching, take off the scarf," she said, "Katie and Marie don't care."

As soon as I removed the scarf, Dan looked at me and asked, "Did you shave your head today? Because if you did, you must've shaved some spots closer than others. It's uneven." We looked at each other. Simultaneously, a light bulb went off in our heads. He put his hands on my shoulders and moved me closer to the hood light near the range and said, "You're losing your hair!"

'I dashed to the powder room mirror and saw a few obnoxious bald patches. "Excellent!" I shouted, "This is evidence that I'm getting an edge on the competition!" In my best cowgirl/John Wayne voice I said, "Move out invader', you're not wanted around these parts." My hand was formed into a makeshift gun. I blew the smoke from my index finger, shot at the person staring back from me from the mirror and winked.*

Andrea hugged me, "I never thought I'd say this Mom, but congratulations." Katie and Marie hugged and congratulated me too.*

"I never thought I'd say this Mom, but congratulations."

I went to the sink, washed my head and dried it briskly with a towel. I laughed at the hideousness of it. The top part rubbed off in waves so it had the effect of Bengal tiger stripes. Dreadful, but funny. Things are happening. Hooray for pharmaceuticals. The drugs are working.

It suddenly dawned on me that a thing in my eye that was bothering me might be an eyelash. I suppose my eyelashes are falling out too. Another trip to the mirror. Sure enough.

An intellectual thought popped into my head; I'm due to shave my legs, now maybe I won't have to. Oh yeah.

I took advantage of my burst of energy fueled by the good news (this is something I had been waiting for) and called a few family members. "Congratulations," was the resounding exclamation.

...I sought out my daughter, Michele, to share my good news..."See? This means, the chemo is working. It's killing stuff, even the cancer. I am winning the battle."

I sought out my daughter, Michele, to share my news. I found her in the den, sitting at the computer. I could not contain my excitement. "Hey. There you are. I've got great news. Guess what? I know why I was so itchy when we were at the store," I pointed to my head, "Yep, my hair's finally coming out." I rubbed a spot on my head and the hair wiped away. "See? This means, the chemo is working. It's killing stuff, even the cancer. I am winning the battle." Her fingers stopped typing. She continued to gaze at me. "Well?" I asked. Her fingers remained on the keyboard. She looked into my eyes, up at my head, and then turned back to the computer. With masked love and all the fervor of a fifteen-year-old, she replied, "Gross, Mom." And her fingers began to type.

Later that evening, a friend and colleague stopped by for a visit. I was so energized that I bounced from topic to topic in my usual fashion when the vigor is so high that I can't hold a thought in my head. It would be later, while I was in bed at the end of the night, when I would think about the evening's events. I realized that when Joseph walked into the den to see me sitting on the couch in my PJs without a head covering, his expression never wavered from that of a colleague who was happy to see me. His eyes registered no shock at my new appearance. For that I was grateful.

I didn't sleep well that night, because every part of me was prickly. When I stepped into a dressing area of the closet to douse myself with baby powder, I discovered that tiny hairs, all over my body, were falling out. Interesting. I wish I hadn't changed the linens on my bed yesterday. Guess I'll have to do it again today.

Love to all. Keep the faith.

DAY FIFTEEN – THE HAIR'S FALLIN' OUT

Michele willingly talks about when I showed her my hair was falling out:

The day when my Mom showed me that she was losing her hair and that "the chemo was winning" was very disturbing and gross. I guess it's okay though because my mom was excited that she wasn't dying anymore. However, I really did not need to see it. I love my mom very much and I know she'll make it through this.

Tip 120   You may hear the phrase, "Day fifteen." Apparently, that's the average day, for many chemo patients, after AC chemo begins when many women lose their hair.

My neighbor, Judy, tells a story that involves her three daughters, ages nine through thirteen:

When the girls first found out that "Mrs. Pedicone" had cancer, even before they asked what kind of cancer, pretty much the first question they asked was, "Is she going to lose her hair?" I didn't know the answer to that. In their defense, they don't understand cancer as much as they understand hair. At their age, losing your hair is like an outward sign to them. Especially for Wendi. She taught me how to french braid their hair, she does up-do's for proms, and she has beautiful hair. Later, when she said that she would [lose her hair], I told them the story about when she was buying her wig and they enjoyed that.

It has been a few days, and most of the hair on my body is gone. *Most, but not all.* I wonder why not all of it is gone. Does this mean that not all the cancer cells are gone? Dan exits the bathroom and says, "Wen, years ago you asked me to put the toilet seat down whenever I used it and I did as you asked. Now, it's my turn to ask; could you wipe the toilet seat off when you are done?" There is a look of utter bewilderment on my face. He clarifies, "There are pubic hairs on the seat." *Oh. OH! Yikes!* Yes, I've lost hair there too. *Most, but not all.*

George W. Bush is reelected and Elizabeth Edwards' breast cancer is revealed. *Cancer is not partial. It touches a well-known senator's wife and an unknown like me.* I actually consider sending her some of my e-mail updates. I believe they will help, but she's in the public eye, especially being the wife of John Kerry's presidential running mate. My e-mail might get filtered out. *Perhaps I won't bother.* There is a spokesman on television saying that she will have surgery, sixteen weeks of chemo and radiation. *Like me.* She will also shave her head as a means to take control. *Like me.* She has a near adult daughter and very young kids; a separation of years between two sets of kids. *Kind of like me. I should send her my updates. Can you imagine how powerful it would be to help?*

Well, I'm not a nail-salon-virgin anymore: Vicki treats me to my first professional pedicure and manicure, at a salon near the cancer center, just before chemo number three. *It gives a new meaning to the saying, "I'll be there with bells on," or the lines from a fairy tale, "With rings on her fingers and bells on her toes, she will be jolly wherever she goes."*

While we sit in the chemo room, in my head I'm humming the tune from West Side Story, *I Feel Pretty. I feel pretty, and witty and gay!* Within minutes of starting the Decadron® drip, I feel slightly buzzed. *There goes the song.* The woozy feelings are the harbingers of the couple of hours to come.

Once home, I see that someone brought the mail in and placed it on the kitchen counter. I go through it and find a reply to my letter to the CEO of Christiana Care Health System. Dr. Lsk:

Dear Ms. Pedicone:

Thank you for taking the time to personally express your appreciation for the care you received at Christiana Care. I have passed your positive remarks along to those who participated in your care, and I know that they will be pleased with your comments....thank you for your thoughtfulness, and we wish you the very best.

And the loop is complete. I said something positive to him and he replied in kind. I feel good.

Twenty years ago, on November 9th, Dan and I stood on the altar and said our vows before God. Twenty years ago, on November 10th, Charles and Lisa did the same. We met on our honeymoons in Hawaii and the spark of a meaningful friendship began. We want to celebrate the anniversary of that occasion, but since I am well into my treatment we dare not travel anywhere. We decide to postpone festivities. In the meantime, Dan and I decide to go to dinner.

In the bedroom, we are getting dressed for our evening out and Dan says, "I invited Roseann and AJ to meet us for dinner. Okay with you?"

CHEMO, BELCHING, AND (AHEM) PASSING GAS

Roseann is Dan's cousin. She is a twelve-year survivor of Non-Hodgkin's Lymphoma, an uncommon form of cancer (the slow-growing type she was told was incurable). Fourteen years ago, she was told they could possibly get it into remission, but that it would come back and she would eventually die from it. She opted for a bone marrow transplant on top of chemo and here she is today, cancer free. Dan must've sensed that it would be good for both of us to talk with Roseann and AJ.

And he was right. I look forward to having dinner with them.

I decide I want lobster. I think I'll be able to taste it. *Woo hoo!* While ordering, I belch. [*Brrrrb-ch-foo.*] *Oh my goodness where'd that come from! I had no warning.* No one says a word. No one notices. *Whew.*

The waitress appears and rattles off the specials. "I have a yen for lobster," I say, "Market Price? Noooo problem!" *Yens are serious. Market Price is totally, wholly and fully inconsequential when you have a yen.*

We are served appetizers; crackers and cheese, and caesar salad. *My favorite.* I order a glass of wine. We toast our wedding anniversary and salute life. The wine doesn't taste as fruity as it normally does, but ordering it feels like I'm staring at cancer, eye-to-eye, and doing something subversive or rebellious. *Okay 'invader', I'm sticking my tongue out at you. Neener, neener, neener.*

[*Brrrrb-ch-foo.*] *Gross! That was me! PeeEww, I didn't eat peppers or a sub....did I?*

Roseann speaks up, "It's been years and I can't remember, are you able to have wine while on chemo?"

"Yes, " I say, "chemo metabolizes in the liver so they suggest not to over-tax your liver by having alcohol inside twenty-four hours before or after a treatment. It's been a few days, [*Brrrreeep*] *so* it'll be okay." *Well, there it is. Can't hide that one. I'm disgusting.*

Inside my head, I make a deal with God. *Okay God, if you'll make this stop I'll go to Church more often, I won't procure a few extra sugar packets from the restaurant table tonight, I won't take extra napkins when I go to the doughnut shop, and I'll stop circling parking lots for an up-front space.*

We had a superb lobster dinner. "I am stuffed," I blurt out.

AJ and Dan nod their heads in agreement. Roseann says, "Me, too."

Two conversations are happening in parallel. AJ's back is to me; Dan is engrossed in a conversation with him. Roseann and I are chatting. She says, "I can't believe you are still awake. If that were me, I'd be flat out by now."

"I suppose I am energized by being here with you, but I am starting to feel a little [*brrrrp-fsh-haww*] drained." *Another burp – it didn't stop. Okay God, all deals are off!*

Roseann quickly and softly places her hand on mine and says, "When I had chemo I belched alot, too." *Gross, so cancer patients just sit around, belching and passing gas? If that's the case, that's another reason I'm glad I won't always be a chemo patient.*

We had a complete and lengthy discussion about how neither of us was ever able to burp, accidentally or intentionally, before we became cancer patients. "Swallow air, Aunt Roseann," her nephews would say. *We can't burp on command. We are losers in the male world. But, thanks to chemo, we can burp by chance, and at full volume too!*

A few days later, the six of us are at the kitchen table. We hear a socially unacceptable sound. Flatulence perhaps. *It is definitely not I.*

"Mom, that was you, wasn't it?"

"Girls, need I remind you that it is not proper to point fingers or talk about such things in an open forum? And, no, it wasn't me. If it happens again, please excuse yourself from the table, whoever you are, and you can count on the rest of us to not say a word." *Naturally, they can't keep straight faces. Egads, I've obviously been under the misconception that they are maturing!* Little Danny laughs because they are laughing.

As if they didn't hear my spiel, one says, "You know it couldn't have been Mom. She doesn't do that."

"And if she did, she would admit it and apologize. It was probably Dad." Dad's head perks up and so do his eyebrows.

"No, if it were Dad he'd have announced it ahead of time. Men are proud of their stuff." They all laugh, Danny too. *True, men are all too happy to discuss the magnitude, frequency and quality of their flatulence.*

"Did you guys forget? Mom's on chemo."

As I listen to the absurd conversation, my head is volleying back and forth as if I'm watching a tennis match.

"What's chemo got to do with it? Mom, does chemo give you gas?" Suddenly all eyes are on me.

"Well," I begin. "I've heard it affects some people that way. A friend of mine told me about her cousin who underwent chemotherapy. It happened to her often enough that the family jokingly gave her anti-gas pills from a joke shop. They were actually jellybeans. She would keep the pill bottle at her place setting, and whenever she would feel the urge to pass gas, she'd take a jellybean out and place it next to her plate, on the table. When she did, everyone knew to clear the room or prepare for the worst!"

"Okay, so if you had a jellybean it would be on the table, right? It was you, wasn't it?"

"NO! It wasn't me!" Again we hear the offensive sound. In perfect unison, we all look under the table. Our cat is on all fours with her back hunched, horking up a hairball! "Yuck it up, girls. Thanks for your faith in me."

So impressed are we with our kids, that Dan and I give them a sitting ovation. *Remind me to check the details of our will and any trust funds we might have considered for them.*

I do worry about our children, especially my teenage daughters, and hope they will never get any kind of cancer. About this time I begin stepping up my nagging about good health. Parents should help children to engage in healthy exercise beginning in childhood and especially during preteen and teenage years. We should also decrease the junk food, because it makes us fat (adults as well as children). Increased fat and lack of exercise leads to insulin resistance which leads to further craving of sugary carbohydrates which eventually leads to a greater lifetime of estrogens without adequate progesterone. All of which lead to increased breast cancer risk (Lee, Zava and Hopkins p. 76). Use of contraceptive hormones exacerbates problems and risks, also. There are so many reasons to eat healthy.

Update: November 15, 2004

Hello all,

It's been a little while since I've written. The truth is I've been very fatigued and a little blue. I have felt the cumulative effects of three chemo treatments. I had a difficult time recovering from number three. I didn't feel better until Wednesday, which was a solid week after the treatment. During this hazy period I began to ask myself totally irrational questions. How do some chemo patients go to work? Will I be able to go back soon? How can my manager and I plan resource hours and set objectives if we don't know how many hours in a day or week I am capable of working? Would I be able to work with focus and stamina? What is the right thing to do? My questions went downhill from there: If I take my doctor's advice and stay on disability leave for the duration of the chemotherapy treatments, will my colleagues convince themselves that they've done without me for several months and therefore would no longer need me? Will AstraZeneca feel that way? Will I be replaced? Will the college that I'm enrolled in force me to re-enroll in the degree program? Will people wonder why I can't return to work or school when other chemo patients have? Will I lose credibility? If I take the time to write about my cancer fight, will folks assume I am capable of working or taking classes?

Meanwhile, daily events occurred...

I've known my husband, Dan, since I was a little girl. We dated for ten years and we married when we were twenty-five. Last Tuesday was our twentieth wedding anniversary. I had been pondering gift ideas for this occasion for quite sometime. The night beforehand, during the wee hours when I was alone with my thoughts, I decided on the perfect gift; the promise of twenty more years. Ahhh, the gift of time. I wondered, "Is time on my side?" Intellectually I know I cannot promise twenty more years. So I promised the only thing I can promise and that is to do my part to be here for our fortieth anniversary.

On Monday, I talked with one of my surgeons during a scheduled visit. He and his wonderful staff were happy to see me as they usually are and were practically tripping over themselves to get me to notice that they were all wearing the "We're here for Wendi" buttons. I sat in a slumped position on the examining table. I was less than cheerful, to say the least. Dr. M, Marcia and Diane are so compassionate and optimistic, and I always look forward to my visits with them. This visit however, all I could do was hang my head. They definitely noticed my mood change that was at the other end of the spectrum from my usual cheerfulness. The doctor reminded me that it is okay to 'not always sparkle' and when this is over, I will again. It is certainly not unusual for critically ill people to become depressed. If I am offered and accept anti-depressant medication would it interfere with the effectiveness of the chemotherapy medicines? I decided to tough it out and stay the course. Oh brother, why can't I snap out of this? Think, Wendi. Think. I should be positive and rational... I can do this. I can be upbeat and optimistic. Ugh. But panic has set in. I'm failing at this.

One late afternoon, I fell asleep on the couch while little Danny was playing with his dinosaurs in front of a beautiful fire in the fireplace, and the girls and friends were buzzing in and out of the kitchen. Sleeping in front of the television, for me, is a rare occurrence unless I am sick. I heard Dan's voice from my chemo-induced sleep, "Why don't we go upstairs to bed. I'll watch TV from there and you can stretch out and be comfortable."

"No, no. I'd rather be here surrounded by the kids." I insisted. "I'm only resting. I'll be awake soon." Moments later, I heard Dan's voice again. I opened one eye and looked around. The fire was reduced to embers, the kitchen was dark, the house was silent, little Danny was gone from the room, and his dinosaurs were still.

Dan was hovering over the couch. "Come on," he said softly, "I'll take you upstairs."

I could see his outstretched hand...Unnnh, I can't move. Then an idea came to me. Dance. Pretend he's asking me to dance...I floated with him for an awkward waltz up the steps and into our bedroom. Then I slept.

I couldn't seem to move. I felt drugged. I wanted to get up but was too drowsy. Inside I was sulking. Please God. Help me move. My mind wanted to, but my limbs could not. It's useless. I heard myself say to Dan, "Why don't I just sleep here. You go upstairs. I'll be okay." I could see his outstretched hand. "No, come with me," he answered. Unnnh, I can't move. Then, an idea came to me.

Dance. Pretend he's asking me to dance. I took a deep breath, and imagined energy like a breeze blowing over me. My vision was blurry, but I could see enough to place my hand in his. He pulled me up and I stumbled into him. With one arm encircled around my waist and the other in front of us holding my hand, he began to walk and so did I. I floated with him for an awkward waltz up the steps and into our bedroom. Then I slept.

'Doing my part' to increase my chances consists of several choices I've made. Someone said to me recently, "That's why they call it fighting cancer!" She said, "Right now, this is your job." Here are a few items on my daily to-do list:

√ *Resting when my body signals the need*
√ *Iyengar Yoga to eliminate stress and build strength*
√ *Meditation to disconnect from cancer thoughts*
√ *Visualization to focus energy on driving cancer from my body*
√ *Practicing an Ayurvedic approach to eating, healing and living*
√ *Learning about, shopping for and preparing organic meals for myself*
√ *Measuring my intake of herbal supplements, fluids and cancer fighting foods like leafy vegetables and dark juices, and immune-enhancing foods like shiitake mushrooms and miso*
√ *Acquiring knowledge through books, articles, websites, and people about how to continue the fight*
√ *Reading the Bible and praying*
√ *Enjoying time with loved ones*
√ *Living each day to the fullest. Cliché, but true!*

I mentioned an unusual gift idea (presenting Dan with twenty more years). Our family has a pattern of extraordinary gifts. I would like to explain. As with any marital relationship, ours was not without difficult times. Several years back, we spiraled downward. We went through a rough era. The easy way out would have been to go our separate ways. We chose the road less traveled. With the help of professional counseling, our priest and other third party means, we traversed the complex path uphill. Once we reached safe ground, we celebrated by adding a cat to our brood. An interesting gift. We named him Genesis to mark our new beginning. Later, a larger extraordinary gift to ourselves, we had another baby. The girls convinced us it would be a wonderful reward. Three-of-a-kind was already a winning hand for our clan. Adding a fourth girl would have been, to a poker player, like drawing a fourth ace. I will never forget the moment we were told that the baby was healthy. And, just as vivid in my memory is when the bearer of good news told us, in the next breath, that it was a boy. Dan was beside himself. Since the girls had been going through puberty, there were days they left him scratching his head. Having a son would give him clarity again! We believe that Daniel Thomas was a present from Heaven. God helped Dan and me beat the evils that had threatened us, then rewarded us BIG. Our view of the world would never be the same. Little Danny is here.

I expect to have blue moods. I have asked, "Was Danny really a gift to us or...[hard swallow]...is he a replacement for me, and will Dan spend time in his golden years with our son [and not me]?" I do not know the answer to these questions. In the meantime, I ask Him to continue to deliver us from evil and will pray to "reward my husband for the work he's done to improve our marriage, by allowing me to stay here on Earth and grow old with him." Heck, it can't hurt to ask. Besides, Dan already stated, "IF YOU THINK YOU'RE LEAVING ME ALONE WITH FOUR KIDS, YOU'VE GOT ANOTHER THING COMING!" Smile.

As humans, we experience significant learning from troubled times, as did I in the week following this chemo treatment. Many of you have said that I have courage. Before my mini-bout with gloom, it was my sincere belief that you were wrong. Think about it, following doctors' orders doesn't require bravery. I followed orders, had surgeries and began chemo treatments for the opposite reason, cowardice. At the time, I viewed it this way; if I didn't agree to treat the cancer I would die. I do not know what it is like to die. Fear of the unknown is the worst fear of all and I was afraid. Consequently, I was not being courageous. I was being cowardly. Simple.

Regarding this, my friend, Jill, recently reminded me that I could have followed the doctors' orders without hesitation, which is not so daring. Instead, I chose to question the protocols, research cancer topics, modify my dietary regimen, be part of the decision-making process and supplement the doctors' plans with my own. I opted to give myself the best possible prospect for success. Therefore I am courageous and I accept your accolades with humility.

From Wednesday to Wednesday a week passed, the effects of the chemo continually decreased and I had a few conversations with wise friends. All lifted me from my despair. Geez, what got into me! I now can coherently say that there are answers to the irrational questions I had asked myself. In some cases the answer to those foolish questions is (to put it the way my daughters would), "AS IF!!" I now realize that I'll be a whole lot better as an employee and a student if I return later (not sooner) and in good health. I also know that not all chemo patients receive the heavy doses that I'm receiving, and therefore aren't forced out of commission. Realization. Thank goodness. And so, a bittersweet smile spreads across my face. Emotional recovery at last. Mental clarity may be temporary until the next treatment, but I acknowledge the illogical thoughts and vow to pro-hibit them from distracting me too much.

Please celebrate with me. I'm back at the top of my game for now and I've got an "invader" to grapple with!! [Mental fist to the air.] Eureeekaaaa.

So, it is not within my power to grant my first choice anniversary gift to Dan, but that's not to say I won't be sticking around. STAY TUNED IN TWENTY YEARS FOR FUTURE COMMENTARY.

Love to all,
Wendi

Brenda and Vicki receive many responses to my e-mail updates and some-times one or two make their way to my home e-mail address.   After this update, I receive a touching voice mail mes-sage from Nancy, my manager's manager. And Anne from France, a colleague writes:

> **"We really have no idea of what's going on once someone has been diagnosed unless that someone is us, or you, who documents it."**

I can only bow to your courage (and your talent as a writer). Thanks for sharing these details and your wonderful sense of humour to top it. We (in the pharma industry) really have no idea of what's going on once someone has been diag-nosed unless that someone is us, or you, who documents it. It is important to know more than treatment dosages and trial results.

Other feedback centers on the reality of my dilemma and my willingness to talk about it:

Finally, she shows us she's normal.

Glad to know she, like most of us, sees a dark side to this. Too much optimism is unhealthy.

> **Tip 121**   Cry Uncle! If you are depressed, there are medicines that can be prescribed to get you through trying times. If you'd rather not try medica-tion, try a support system. Make a list of breast cancer survivors people tell you about and their numbers. Make an

> *Cry Uncle! If you are depressed, there are medicines that can be pre-scribed to get you through trying times.*

appointment with your clergy member and ask candid questions. I went as far as to ask my priest if he was afraid to die (among other things). The main thing is, don't suffer in silence.

Tip 122   Go to www.cancercare.org where you can get free professional help through counseling, education, information and referral, and even financial assistance. This site is one of many that contains information in Spanish too. Finally, go to the library or bookstore and get any one or all of the following books: *Uplift*, by Barbara Delinsky, *Breast Cancer Survivor's Club*, by Lillie Shockney, and *There's No Place Like Hope*, by Vickie Girard. Each delivers, in surprisingly enriching ways, tips and ideas, and information on what to expect in every phase of treatment. You will find yourself smiling through these books.

HANDLING CANCER DEATHS DURING MY CANCER BATTLE

It is November 17. A friend named Ann, calls to tell me that Cheryl passed away. *Oh no. I hate cancer. &%$@ cancer.* I know that informing me was not easy for her, but I made her promise she would. I didn't want to be spared this news nor the opportunity to offer my condolences to Cheryl's family.

— XXX —

Update: November 21, 2004

Hello all,

Round four – done! On Thursday afternoon, I put on my imaginary boxing gloves and stepped into the ring again. My friend Cindy sat with me for the fourth treatment. Aren't I lucky to have had such great company during the four sessions? Dan, my sisters, Lisa, Cindy, Mom and Mom Pedicone have all been to the cancer center with me for chemo, injections, and lab work. Yes, I have many people to be thankful for and I celebrate the fabulously long list.

Long ago I decided to go with optimism and the positive stuff. I'm talking in the womb long ago. I have always been a person with a positive outlook. During my cancer battle I'm staying with that strategy and practicing two approaches: take one day at a time and celebrate small victories. With that in mind, I can say that I've succeeded in enduring eight weeks of chemo (Adriamycin® and Cytoxan®). Woo hoo! I reached the half way point. A victory. Next, is the second set of chemo infusions (eight weeks in four treatments of Taxol®). Bring it on; I'm ready! I'll take one day at a time. Barring any complications, I should be finished mid-January and ready to begin radiation afterward.

With my head held high I'll gracefully endure the side effects of the medicine because I believe they are indications that the meds are working. Besides the fatigue, I experience a constant awful taste in my mouth, which is common for patients. Most things don't taste yummy anymore. It will return to normal when I'm done chemotherapy. I think the metallic taste is one of the reasons many cancer patients lose a little weight. I have an occasional nose or mouth sore, sandpapery gums, watery eyes, some memory blips and momentary confusion, peeled fingertips, and bone aches. All are very tolerable. Last week an oncology practitioner remarked that I am tolerating the chemo better than average. I'd like to think that it is due to my positive attitude and the life-style and dietary changes I've made.

One evening, our schedules allowed for the six of us and two of the girls' high school friends to sit together for a family dinner. The girls know I have scratchy gums and that tiny food particles stick to my teeth. They exercise extreme diplomacy when informing me in front of others, "Um, Mom," Michele points to her tooth...she discreetly looks away.

I understand her discretionary signal and scratch my tooth. I mouth the words, "Did I get it?" She nods.

Next, it is Andrea who diverts my attention, "Mom," and points to another tooth.

"What? Spinach, parsley?" I rub a section of my teeth. And, Christine nods that I got it, but then points to her lip...

I begin to wipe my lip until I put my hands, palms down on the table and stand. Out loud I say, "Oh for crying out loud!" No use hiding it now...everyone knows. I laugh as I dash to the powder room. When I look in the mirror I smile big and see gunk all over my teeth! It's amazing how much food didn't get past my gums! Geez. I can hear their amusingly bawdy remarks about Halloween pumpkins and jack-o-lanterns, rugby players with missing teeth, 'shoulda worn a mouth guard', 'can dress her up but can't take her anywhere'... Nice, kids. Nice. This is what I've raised.

Now, there is a toothbrush and dental floss located in the powder room. Just for me.

Oh, I almost forgot to share a side effect I am experiencing. I get major hot flashes! Amazing how fast a body can change temperature. In the last few years, I was hoping that I'd go through menopause later than the average woman does since I had a baby at forty-one. Apparently, the later a woman goes into menopause, the less intense the side effects are. Now that I am a cancer patient however, I'm going through a chemical-induced menopause, or a temporary cessation of my female reproductive cycle. Younger women's reproductive systems usually return following chemo. Mine may not because I'm 45. That's okay because, by then I'll be through the menopausal side effects, we weren't planning any more children, and (a bonus) I probably won't suffer with migraines ever again. Hooray!

My migraines, sometimes quite severe, have been a part of me since I was a little girl. They intensified with the onset of puberty. Through the years, we were able to determine that mine were mostly triggered by my reproductive cycle (and not red wine, aged cheese, or chocolate). The migraines stopped whenever I was pregnant or nursing. Therefore, they may stop for menopause, chemo induced or otherwise!

But oh, these hot flashes. They come on quickly day and night. For example, they wake me from sleep. I kick off the covers, remove my sleep cap and use it to fan myself. In about five minutes, I cover up and go back to sleep. Ugh.

One evening, Danny and Dan were lying in bed with me and watching television. I'd dosed off. I was on my side with my hand, palm side up, supporting my head on the pillow. My palm was apparently suctioned to a smooth spot on my bald head. I awakened and lifted my head. As I did, I heard a loud TNCK to which Danny brought his eyes close to mine and excitedly replied, "Do that again Mommy!" Dan heard Danny's response to the suction sound and smiled with male pride. Oh brother, I'm outnumbered. What is it about boys and their infatuation with the ability to make noises with parts of your body…I just don't get it. "Do it again," Danny said.

Tonight, Dan and I plan to say goodbye to someone we've been praying for. Her name is Cheryl and she lost her fight with ovarian cancer. We would not miss the opportunity to offer our sympathy to her wonderful husband, Jack and their three kids, and I think I'll be okay when we do. You see, I do not believe that her fate will necessarily be mine. Cancer scenarios are unique to each individual. Though I don't understand why, the evil cancer got her, but it may not get me. This disease mystifies me. Why does it take some and not others? And, which one will I be? Before, I prayed for Cheryl, now I will pray to Cheryl and ask her to watch over me.

One of the many happy side effects of being a cancer patient is role reversal. The girls come in to my bedside and kiss me at night like I used to do to them. How wonderful. Only, they usually kiss the top of my head! I'm sure I smile in my sleep. The nighttime kisses stay with me each day.

I wish you a warm Thanksgiving with loved ones and remembrances of your blessings.

Mom calls me the morning following Cheryl's funeral. I tell her how lovely and valiant Cheryl's family was. What I didn't tell her was that I did okay facing a funeral of a cancer victim. I'd rather not discuss this aspect with her for fear that it would upset her or remind her that her daughter has cancer. Mom might not have the positive attitude that I have [*most of the time*]. Mom asks if I read the obituaries recently. Other than Cheryl's, I haven't. My parents have always read the daily newspaper faithfully and kept us kids apprised of events. This has always been helpful. Mom tells me about Ray, a high school friend of my brother's and a classmate of ours. He died of lung cancer. *What? He's my age.*

I am unable to attend his funeral, because it is all so overwhelming.

It has been three days since Ray's funeral and I have a desire to make up for my absence at the services. I visit his parents. My vehicle steers into their neighborhood. I pull up to their house unannounced and without a phone call in advance. I am received warmly. As it turns out, Ray's older sister is still in town (she lives on the west coast) and I not only see his family and his older sister, who was my close friend in high school, but I meet his wife. I realize she's his widow now. For the first time, I know what to say. I am wearing a scarf and my face is pale. I'm sure they have seen plenty of people during Ray's cancer ordeal that look like me, so I have confidence that they know I have cancer, too, and it is okay for me to say, "It sucks that Ray died." *Not my typical terminology, but hey, I am irritated.* It has been over twenty-five years since any of us has seen each other and in ten minutes we are up-to-date. We say our good-byes and I communicate my wish for his family to find purpose in his death, and his life. *Now, if only I can find purpose in an early death of a husband and father of young children. Grrrr.*

Thanksgiving is a day our family reflects upon the things we are grateful for. I have so many. Having cancer has helped me see the milk of human kindness. In fact, if it were possible to tell me that, at the end of all this I would be cured, I'd say I am glad I got cancer.

Black Friday. The day retailers get out of the red on the accounting books and into the black. The day of big sales. Several flyers and catalogues arrive in the mail. *Victoria's Secret, Frederick's of Hollywood, Venus USA* and *Body Central* are among them. Sexy, voluptuous cleavage adorns the cover of each. *Wow. Bling-bling.* Such a fascination we have with breasts, eh. When does that begin? Does it begin after birth, when we are nursed (if we are nursed)? After puberty, when breasts are budding? How is it influenced? The media? The fashion models? Mardi Gras? *I wonder.*

Staff at Andrea and Michele's high school has been supportive. I want to thank them. A letter would be good, but I want to do more – who wouldn't want a lunch provided for them? I make a list, buy deli trays, beverages and deserts and deliver them to the main office.

The girls arrive home and see me resting on the couch. They tell me that the teachers and administrators liked lunch and appreciated the letter I wrote to them. *I feel good.*

My support network is strong. It will give me strength as I enter the next phase, Taxol®.

I'm ready.

If you are going through Hell, keep going.

Sir Winston Churchill
British statesman, soldier and author
(1874 - 1965)

CHAPTER

CHEMOTHERAPHY: TAXOL®

5

(Me with Christine)

Photo courtesy of G. Thomas Murray Photography

A wise man should consider that health is the greatest of human blessings, and learn how by his own thought to derive benefit from his illnesses.

Hipocrates
Regimen in Health
(460 BC - 377 BC)

THE VALLEYS GET DEEPER WITH EACH TREATMENT

Chemotherapy keeps me in a constant peaks-and-valleys pattern. Because it has a cumulative effect, the valleys get a little lower each time. I try to remind myself that all of this is temporary and when it is all behind me, I'll emerge cancer free and my peaks will be higher than they ever were before cancer. *I just know it.*

I am blue. On Thanksgiving Day, my brother handed me a book given to him, for me: *Uplift*, by Barbara Delinsky. It is an informative book and all I want to know is how many of the women who submitted anecdotes and tips are still alive. *I am probably missing the forest because of the trees.*

Brenda sends a message on November 30:

Just a quick update from me on Wendi so you don't start to worry (I know when the updates start thinning out, you wonder what is up).

Today, Wendi starts her new chemotherapy...Taxol. She does not know what to expect...will it be worse, better, what are the side effects? But she's ready to bring it on.

She had a very nice Thanksgiving with her family and didn't have to lift a finger. Then, Friday morning (November 26), I received a call at home from Wendi. She wanted LOBSTER!!! Were my husband and I up to meeting them for dinner that evening? Why, of course! So we met for drinks and dinner at Feby's on Lancaster Pike. Wendi really enjoyed her meal, we had a nice conversation.... then she started to get tired. But it was really nice to be out.

She doesn't fool too much with the wig these days...it itches. She donned her head with a beautiful scarf and looked very nice. I did get her to take it off...she was proud to show me her bald head.

So, say a prayer that her chemo goes well today. She'll probably be feeling lousy for the next several days, so I imagine we won't get another update until next week. I plan to stop by with a hot meal soon, so if there's anything more to report, I'll let you know.

A little over a week after my first Taxol® treatment, I write to my e-mail support network.

Update: December 8, 2004

Hello all,

On Tuesday of last week, I had my fifth chemotherapy treatment, which was my first Taxol® treatment. My chemo plan is; four AC (Adriamycin® and Cytoxan®) sessions, which I completed, and four Taxol® every other week, sixteen weeks total. This means that as of last week I am past the halfway point!

With the AC sessions, I'd first receive through my medi-port, a small IV bag of a steroid called Decadron® plus an antiemetic to coat my brain barrier and prevent nausea. Then I'd receive a very large syringe of the Adriamycin®. The device looked like something you'd use to inject grain alcohol into a watermelon for a summer party!   The liquid was the color of Fruit-Juicy Red Hawaiian Punch and slowly infused manually through my port, by a nurse. The next bag was the Cytoxan®. The first bag made me feel like I had a few glasses of wine. That's why I wasn't able to drive myself home afterwards. I told one of the nurses that when I had AC I felt like I'd been to a bar. She laid her hand on mine and said, "I'm so glad I can do that for you!" During my AC sessions, I'd recline in the chair and wrap up in my blanket. I'd sip tea, read or chat with whomever was with me for the two-hour treatment. The first Taxol® treatment went differently than the ACs...*

> *The first Taxol® treatment went differently than the ACs...*

In September, when I was given a tour of the "chemo room" at the Helen F. Graham Cancer Center I noticed that some patients were alone and sleeping. I didn't understand the sleeping part. Now, I do. When I went in for round five and my first Taxol® session, I was told that it would take four to four-and-a-half hours. "They didn't tell you about this?" the nurse asked. No. Why so long? She proceeded to tell me it is delivered at a slower drip rate, there are some things I might experience with the Taxol® and that the staff would be watching me closely especially in the first ten minutes. I watched them pull up a cart with medical supplies and, [eh oh], do I see an oxygen tank? An oxygen tank? Oh brother, I must be seeing things. Breathe. Relax. I heard her say, "...difficulty breathing, tongue and throat swelling, extreme and sudden pain in your back, let us know immediately if..." Ohmygosh. Naturally, my thoughts ran away with me. Will this stop my heart? Could I go into shock? Could I die? Will I not be able to receive any more Taxol®? Will I be forced to discontinue the fight against cancer?

My pupils were probably dilated and my terror must've been apparent.

She stopped talking and said, "Oh Mrs. Pedicone, the things you may experience are not life-threatening." Thank you. I needed to hear that. She explained that it is not uncommon to encounter an anaphylactic reaction (like the ones folks have who carry Epi-pens because they are allergic to bee stings or shellfish). "The staff is prepared to react, just in case," she consoled. "We will give you three bags of prophylactic meds before starting the Taxol® bag." By now, I was so relieved since my thoughts-way-out-of-control phase was over, that I was giddy. Yessir, yessir, three bags full. I was humming in my head, Baa, baa black sheep, have you any wool... She further explained, "If you have a reaction despite the Decadron® steroid, Benadryl® antihistamine and Tagamet® antihistamine, we will stop the Taxol, treat the reaction, then re-start Taxol® thirty minutes later at an even slower drip speed." Okaaaay. Let's get started. Let's fight "the invader."

Within a few minutes of the antihistamines, I was slurring my words. I felt a cozy feeling come over me akin to the feeling I get on the occasions that I drink.

Since I've shared so much of myself in the last few months, I'm going to let you in on my experiences with alcohol because my chemo treatments put me in a similar state. Until the last few years, my drinking record was minimal; two or three times a year. Even now, I don't drink often. Some people are "mean drunks", "rowdy drunks", or "sloppy drunks." I'm, what I call, a tactile-drunk. Though I've only been in that state about three times in my life, I've established a pattern! Don't we all. After a few glasses of wine or a chocolate martini, my hard-coded internal emotions tend to become exaggerated; for example, I am basically a happy person so I smile and grin a lot when I drink. And one of my core beliefs is that one can never get enough hugs, so I become really affectionate towards folks, when I've had a few drinks. I've been known to declare, "I love you guys soooo much." Geez. "You guys are the best." Oh brother. "Let me give you a greaaaat big hug." Smooch.

One time, my brother-in-law asked Dan, "When Wendi drinks, does she overtly pledge her love for you and promise you the moon?"

"Yep," replied Dan.

"On the way home do the promises increase?"

"Un hunh."

"...And when you get her home does she pass out the moment her head hits

"Ah, yep."

"It's confirmed. They are sisters." How embarrassing.

Likewise, when I had the Taxol® treatment I told my loved ones how much I love them, and then passed out, sound asleep, soon after my head touched the pillow of the reclining chair in the chemo room. During the first few minutes of the antihistamines I felt myself dozing. My eyelids were exceptionally heavy and the upper lids seemed to be sticking to the lower lids. Opening my eyes was not easy. The task was similar to pulling a suction cup window ornament from a window. A few times, when I swallowed, it felt like I had air caught in my throat or that I was going to choke. Was I so drugged that my brain would forget to swallow or breathe? I don't think I was capable of thinking clearly. Even so, I wanted to reassure my mother, who was sitting beside me, that I was okay. I wanted to talk to her. I didn't want to look feeble and dismal and cause her to worry. If I was having any conversation with her, I was on autopilot. I slept for most of the next few hours. My mom said I talked some, but I don't recall. My friend, Kim, brought us food, but I don't remember eating my salad. Later, Kim said I said "good-bye" but I only remember seeing her then closing my eyes, and then seeing my daughter Christine sitting in Kim's place. A regular party girl, I was! Passed out in the chair. I was down for the count. So much for round five.

Side effects from the Taxol® are supposed to be less than those of the AC for the majority of patients. So far, not for me. I spoke with several women who are either a little further along in their chemo than me or freshly finished, and three out of four found Taxol® to not be any easier. Okay, so I'm not weird. Chocolate and sweets still taste like mud. I'll do without. The fatigue and flu-like symptoms are prevalent particularly in the three-to-four days following. My eyebrows, though slightly thinned before, are now tapering to nearly none. Who needs eyebrows? I have facial breakouts, like a rash. Nothing Vicki's Mary Kay cosmetics can't cover up. And now I'm experiencing an odd sensation in my hands and feet. No big deal. This is the most common side effect for Taxol® patients. There is soreness in my fingertips, heals and toes that waxes and wanes throughout a twenty-four-hour period. Sometimes I can't open an envelope or tie Danny's

...when I had the Taxol® treatment I...passed out, sound asleep, soon after my head touched the pillow of the reclining chair in the chemo room.

shoe and I limp a little. Sometimes. Not all the time. It's endurable. Honest.

The side effect that I don't like to bear is the depression I encounter in the days following each treatment. It's getting more evident with each, so I'm glad to have only three treatments left. Fear not, I am in the process of building my arsenal. I've already made appointments, for the days following infusion number six, with some friends in faith and with my priest, so we can pray when I'm feeling low. I must say, that I don't believe I'm facing my mortality...I sincerely believe there are reasons for me to stay here for many years to come. It's just that the days following treatments, I'm not my usual upbeat self.

When I was at the cancer center on Monday (I go there three days a week during chemo weeks and once a week during non-chemo weeks) I saw a woman walking around with her IV pole. I looked at the bags dangling from the hooks and immediately recognized that she was getting a Taxol® treatment (how she was standing and awake was beyond me). We talked a little. I think she was still in the why-me stage and was angered about having cancer. I told her that it wasn't long before I figured out that it wasn't helpful for me to look back or ask "why me." I suggested that she and I could already be cancer free but don't know it. "Cling to that!" I said. She seemed genuinely pleased that I'd given her a positive thought to cling to.

Recently, Dan and I went to a local restaurant. I don't know why, but I've been craving lobster. Perhaps the cravings are due to hormone changes; perhaps they are due to cancer treatment. I don't know. Anyway, we were out and I was wearing one of my pretty scarves. We saw many people who, in the course of conversations, asked if I had cancer, which is precisely my reason for being proud to show that I am without hair. One of the many wonderful things about having cancer and being around people is that the people are reminded living is finite. When I am in their midst, they sometimes feel compelled to share a touching story. I feel like a celebrity. I listen to their stories. Sometimes, I feel like an expert on breast cancer, but I'm definitely not. Sometimes, I think they expect me to be. I wish I had answers for folks, but I don't. I am, however grateful for my optimism, because I usually have some inspiration to offer people.

Since I am unable to return to work yet, my days consist of the things I do to fight, mostly resting, meditating, becoming educated, and attending medical appointments. I choose to keep little Danny home from daycare until around 10:00 a.m. so I can be with him for a few hours each morning. We cuddle-up on the couch and watch cartoons, do yoga, and eat oat meal together. The time we have in the mornings, when I don't have to share him with anyone else, is one of the many beautiful advantages of having cancer. It is so important to create warm memories for him, of us.

Were it not for cancer and AstraZeneca's benefits program that allows me to heal at home, I would miss some really "kewl" things. Like, when I watched Danny socialize the nativity. The other day, I listened to him play. He held a dinosaur in one hand, and put all the figurines in the manger with the other. He told them, "Stay in the house. You're not allowed in the yard because Tyrannosaurus Rex is coming." Visualize a Christmas tree, a manger underneath and all the ceramic characters crammed into it. He had both hands out, palms facing them and said, "You stay in the house, okay? Don't go in the yard." Then Danny was down on the floor, making monster sounds, "Grrrrrr," moving the plastic dinosaur toward the manger. Hmmm, perhaps the shepherds, the three wise men, and T-Rex followed the same star.

This morning, Danny sprang from his bed and declared, "I'm a T-Rex. T-Rexes don't have to brush their teeth."

Ah, I see. I looked him squarely in the eye and said, "T-Rexes don't, but you do. Here's your toothbrush."

He stood looking up at me with his hands at his sides, "T-rexes don't wash their hands." He blinked his eyes and waited for my response.

"Maybe they don't, but you do." His body language signaled defeat. He stepped onto his stool in front of the sink, I turned on the water for him, and began to make my bed.

Once he started brushing, I heard him call from the bathroom, "MOMmeeee, um, I dropped my toothbrush on the floor, and...and it got hair on it, and...and I brushed my teeth, and now there's hair in my teeth. See? Aaaaaa." Awww, yuck.

After trash collection the other day, I was rolling the trashcan back from the street and the wind whipped the scarf off my head. I looked ridiculous as a bald woman with swinging arms, reaching for it. It circled a bit and so did I. It floated about ten feet and so did I. The trashcan, I had been rolling, tumbled over. As I was tying the scarf onto my head, a yellowish-white, dirty paper towel came unstuck from the inside of the can and fell out. Just then I heard Danny sneeze. As any mother would, I recognized the watery sound and turned to look at him. I spotted the little-kid-sneeze-substance dangling from his upper lip. "MOMmeeee, I need a tissue," he called, frozen like a statue with his chin jetted forward, and his hands away from his body, palms facing downward. Both pairs of eyes, his and mine, went to the napkin on the driveway. While our eyes looked in the same direction and settled on the imposing article, our thoughts went in opposite directions. Faster than you could say, Eeeewww, NOooo he had wiped the hanging nose-stuff with that awful thing. He looked at me with a stream of yuck across his cheek and said proudly, " I got it Mommy!" Ugh. Heaven knows where that napkin has been.

Since my diagnosis, many of you told me about things I did to influence, help or motivate you. I had no idea I touched so many people. It's so easy to go about life and not realize. Think of a teacher or professor who affected you in a very positive way. Could he possibly recall all his students and good teachings? I feel like I am George Bailey living out It's a Wonderful Life. I am looking to Clarence to help me realize my reasons for being here. Angels, who have gone before me, like Kayla's mom, Cheryl, and Ray, are my Clarence. Danny is my Ju-ju. And YOU are the people of Bedford Falls. For all your good deeds and kind words, I thank you Bedford Falls.

God bless you all.

A colleague writes:

Hi Wendi,

I have followed the latest developments of your progress. This is tougher than we previously thought but I am confident that you will get to recovery with patience and optimism. These qualities will be so important for other women who will come on that road later. Please continue documenting your journey.

There have been many recoveries of difficult cases. You are right, an Armstrong mind is half the battle won.

However, I cannot underestimate the worry, the sadness and the physical pain that must overwhelm you at times. In those moments, Wendi, please know that I (and many others) pray for you to get the strength to go towards light. It may be little comfort as we cannot walk this road for you; but this represents how important it is for us that you get to recovery.

Two of my friends in France had stage III breast cancer. One had children like you. She was treated fifteen years ago at a time when treatments had not made such progress. The other one was treated with Taxol® four years ago. Both are now clear.

Hugs,
Anne

Brenda's friend, Melody, writes to her:

I wanted to tell you that I read bits from Wendi's progress reports to my Church Circle last night at our Christmas meeting. For our holiday program we always read something inspirational with a holiday theme. Some of Wendi's recent updates have had those little holiday references and she's certainly inspirational! ...[The reading] obviously moved everyone there. I thought they were going to applaud her at the end!

I send the next update, and then Dan and I get into the car for number six.

Update: December 14, 2004.

Hello all,

This week is a chemo week. Today, I have my sixth treatment (which is my second Taxol® treatment). Listen for the bell at 10:15 when I step into the ring. For me, maybe the bell will be a wake-up alarm at 2:30 in the afternoon when it's over and the antihistamines wear off! No problemo, I'll be fighting in my sleep!

My "anti-depression arsenal" for the next few days (the things I will do when the big "D" gets me) is to meet with Father John at St. Catherine's, keep my phone list of Christian friends on-hand, attend a support group meeting at a nearby wellness center (if I'm up to it) and visit some people at the company I'm so grateful to work for.

With regard to the latter, each morning following a treatment I typically have some energy, so I calculate that tomorrow I can splurge on a few hours of quality time with my AZ colleagues. By the afternoon, the side effects of the chemo will kick in as well as those from the Neulasta® shot, and zap that energy. I'm going to make the best of the open window of opportunity. My visit to AZ will be in the late morning. My injection is scheduled for 2:15.

Since my diagnosis, family life continues in our household. The kids have had the usual amount of disagreements, one daughter left for college, another and her boyfriend decided to break up and become independents, one spent an evening from midnight to daylight in an emergency room, another sprained her ankle and broke a finger, my son needed a doctor's care for a viral infection, and he attended his first professional dental visit. And, they've all needed uplifting emotional support for a plethora of teenage and three-year-old reasons. Being a Mom does not step aside so cancer can consume me. Thank goodness. Cancer is disruptive enough. I do not want it to interfere with a role that I looked forward to fulfilling since I was a little girl.

I am no longer afraid of having cancer, since I am deep in the throes of fighting it. I know my enemy. I am busy with the business of curing. My fear, now, is that cancer will someday return. My theory is that I need to prevent it by changing some things I was doing before. Based on the health and nutrition education I have acquired thus far, the dietary changes I have made (which are doable for me) to get through the chemotherapy, get rid of cancer and increase the risk that it won't return are:

- *Taking daily herbal supplements and vitamins made from food (not synthetic) to detoxify, destroy free radicals, and support liver function (chemo metabolizes in the liver)*
- *Consuming a handful of organic almonds each day (Almonds are high in laetrile. Some believe laetrile acts as an anti-cancer agent – whether it does or not, almonds are a healthy food)*
- *Drinking dark juices every day (grape juice, and beet and veggie juices)*
- *Sipping red clover, green and herbal teas, plus a dandelion beverage that is a powerful blood cleanser, and high in antioxidants*
- *Eating flax seed in the same form as wheat germ. I mix a teaspoonful with my yogurt or kefir.*
- *Drinking kefir smoothies. Kefir is a probiotic cultured-milk drink that is the consistency of liquid yogurt and is beneficial for your own bifidobacteria. In other words, it supports a healthy intestinal ecosystem. This is important to me since I don't want to spend another Christmas and New Year's holiday in the hospital like I did two years ago; complications from Inflammatory Bowel Disease*
- *Ingesting ginger (in the form of tea and crystallized chunks)*
- *Eating fresh veggies, especially the green leafy ones*

There are other dietary things I do regularly, and not necessarily on a daily basis. For instance, I:

- *Consume mushrooms for their immune-enhancing abilities*
- *Have totally eliminated sodas and artificial sweeteners from my diet. I drink filtered or spring water, herbal teas (hot or cold) and juices. For sweeteners, I use organic honey or Stevia. Stevia is a natural sweetener that is unrefined like cane sugar is. It comes from a plant in Paraguay.*
- *Greatly reduced my chemical intake by installing water filters on faucets, eating pesticide-free fruits and vegetables, and not using aerosol products. Not that I need hairspray anymore.*
- *Drink miso soup and eat cage-free eggs*
- *Concentrate on the good nutrition becoming army pawns that line up in my defense*

And then, there are a host of emotional and future-look and life-outlook changes I am in the process of making.

This morning, after 10:15 when the IV begins to flow, I will utilize my newfound visualization techniques. I will imagine myself, in a fancy outfit, being picked up in a limo and driven to a luxurious place. My ankles, adorned with high-fashion shoes, will step onto a red carpet. Once inside and decorated with healing jewelry that will point to my port, the medicine will enter me, reach my heart and burst outward with dazzling affects, like fireworks through my body. Rich, orchestral music will build in sound and magnificence. Radiant colors will reach as far as my fingertips and toes, and paint my system with gloriously vivid hues. The dull and ugly cancer cells will not fit into this beautiful palette. I will be illuminated and stunning when I am taken home.

> **This morning, after 10:15 when the IV begins to flow, I will utilize my newfound visualization techniques.**

You can feel the triumph too. Think about how you felt when heard triumphant music and you saw Rocky reach the top of the steps, Rudy called into to the Notre Dame game in the penultimate play of the last game of his senior year, and Ralphie, in A Christmas Story, punch out Scott Farcus! Hooooooraaaaaayyy for them. Hooray for us. Hooray for me!

Dan is driving me to "the Helen Graham." On the way, he expresses his frustration over a situation that occurred the evening before between him and one of our daughters. I listen to a bit of sounding off from him, and then I remind him that I need to concentrate on what I'm about to have done. I need to focus on my visualization techniques. His ranting moves from the topic of our daughter to another bone-of-contention and then another. All topics of his frustration. Ironically, none of them is about my cancer. He is getting louder. I break in and begin yelling, "I DON'T NEED THIS RIGHT NOW. If you are going to continue, let me out of the car."

> **"Our family issues don't stop for cancer..."**

His reply is, "Our family issues don't stop for cancer. EVERYTHING DOESN'T STOP FOR CANCER. It's not always about you, you know!"

And my reply is, "Correct, it's not *always* about me, but *right now* IT IS ABOUT ME! I'm on my way for a chemo treatment for godsake. If I don't get it, I may die. I don't want to talk about family issues on the way to chemo. If you can't drive me without talking about family issues then LET ME OUT OF THE CAR." Silence.

I think we may need some help getting through this cancer ordeal. Cancer affects the significant other, too. Not everyone realizes that. Most times I try to; sometimes I forget.

When we arrive at the cancer center, I ask him to drop me off. It is a dreary, drizzly morning and my spirits mirror the weather. My anger towards him quells once inside, and my fear sets in. *God help me.* I don't want to be here alone. I call his cell phone and he returns to the cancer center. We do not talk. The IV begins to drip. We still do not talk. We are both steaming, I suppose. And then I fall asleep.

Tip 123 In this particular case, Dan's anger pointed to a problem of what I call "the three cancer f's" - frustration, fear and fixation with cancer. Caregivers, it is not fair to become angry with us for bringing cancer into the relationship. It's not our fault.

On the other hand, it's okay to get annoyed with us sometimes for everyday (non-cancer) things – it may even make us feel normal! Treating us too delicately may make us feel fragile and dependent. It is not easy to strike the balance, which is why you need support too.

That evening, I sit down to the computer and see a note from my high school friend, Debbie, in response to the update I sent this morning (she, by the way, is a cancer survivor.):

I really enjoy being on your list of e-mailers— receiving your "updates" is wonderful.   Whenever I see an "Update from Wendi " I automatically open it first – forget all the work e-mails, they can wait. I sit at my desk and read your letter, every word, and smile, laugh, and feel your pain. But what stands out the most is that you always manage to find the brighter side – your attitude has been great…. Keep fighting – I know you are winning. Just remember – there is a light at the end of the tunnel and it is waiting for you!!

OKAY, LET'S TRY THE WELLNESS COMMUNITY

During a lovely evening with Dan's colleagues at a holiday party we meet someone who is the wife of one of them and a co-founder of the local Wellness Community. They are an organization of professionals and volunteers who offer professionally led programs to complement conventional medical treatment and are offered free of charge to people whose lives have been touched by cancer.   Dan and I visit the Wellness

Community a few days after meeting Cynthia.

The one near us, in New Castle County, is in a marvelous, historically pre-served, colonial structure with warm and friendly rooms. We discuss their support group offerings; one for cancer patients and another for pri-mary care givers. We each are given literature and a tour. I feel that our vibes (Dan's and mine) are in sync and that the Wellness Community is definitely for us. At the end of the tour, and while we are sitting with Sean, one of the counselors, Dan announces that he needs to get back to work. He hands me his literature. *Hmmm, I detect some resistance....maybe I was wrong about the vibes.*

"I've already got literature, that pack is for you," I say.

"Well, why don't you take mine home with you?" *Resistance.*

"Why don't I take mine home with me and you take yours to your office with you so you'll have it in case you want to refer to it?" I suggest.

"Okay," he says reluctantly.

And I insensitively ask him, in front of Sean, "So, what do you think about the support group? Are you interested?" *That was stupid of me.*

"We'll *[resistance]* talk about it."

That evening, the atmosphere is tense. Isn't it interesting how the human psyche can pick up feelings from other people? Deep down inside I was experiencing my own guilt for pressuring him earlier today and I sensed his emotions about it tonight. I should not have put him on the spot as I did today. He's in the den, I'm in the kitchen and out of nowhere and without context he blurts out, "I'M NOT LIKE YOU, I don't always need people like you do, I'm not into the group hug thing." *Ah, there it is. The truth. The reason the hair on the back of my neck is standing up.*

I ponder the feedback he's giving me and remind myself that he is not like me and I am not like him. We find our strengths from different sources. I apologize for putting him on the spot earlier and tell him he shouldn't go if he doesn't buy into the concept. *But I hope he does.*

So, we are standing in the entranceway of the Wellness Community talk-ing with others...

Whew! I'm so glad Dan decided to try this. *You never know unless you try.*

We step into two separate rooms; mine is the cancer support group, his is the primary care givers' support group, and both are conducted simultaneously. I thought I wanted this, now that I'm here, I'm not so sure.

Twenty minutes of my first support group experience can be described this way:

People are talking about their cancer situations. I don't want to know about other people's cancer situations. One, two, three...there are six of us. The four men seem to know each other well. They seem intelligent...I'm not smart. Why are they talking about finances, flying, poetry, painting and gardening? Why aren't they talking about cancer? So far, I'm not getting anything out of this. My ears perk up when I hear my name. Our individual contributions to the discussion overlap:

"This is Wendi. She's new to the group..."

...Group therapy and support groups are supposed to be helpful, so I'll give this a try. "Hello." I smile and make eye contact with each person in the room. "I am here because I have breast cancer. I am presently going through chemo. October 9 was when I started..."

"...I started chemo in April and finished last month," one person says. "You can get through this you know. Keep reminding yourself that it's all temporary..."

"...Temporary side effects I experience are light nauseousness and loss of appetite, "another person says. "Also, I get wired..."

"...I get wired for a day after chemo because of the Decadron..."

"...Decadron kept me from throwing up..."

"...Throwing up is the least of my worries right now," said the other newcomer to the group. "I just found out I have cancer..."

"...Cancer is horrible, yes, but it brings about good things sometimes..."

"...Sometimes I am embittered because I'm okay, but it makes my wife cry..."

"...Cry, if it helps..."

"...It helps to get answers and information. I have a list of numbers you could call..."

"...Call any of us any time."

By now all members of the group have chimed in. All, in their own way, console the distressed, discuss treatment, and what it's like to live with cancer. The conversation becomes theoretical and more appealing to me. We speak about death and the afterlife. There is philosophical talk about dying and preparing one's soul. This is the stuff most people don't like to talk about. But finally talking about it is liberating. It's like the first down-hill drop of a roller coaster ride; you approach it slowly and with great trepidation. By the time you reach the top just before the descent, the sensation in your stomach is intense. If you could go back, you might. The first few seconds of the plunge are frightening, but once you realize it's not as bad as you thought it would be, exhilaration then relief reaches you. When the ride is complete, you are glad you did it. So I am glad we are talking about death.

When both group sessions conclude, I see Dan in the library chatting with two other men. He talks most of the way home about the people he met. I am hopeful this gives him an outlet, because he is on a journey, too. Loved ones of cancer patients need support also.

Loved ones of cancer patients need support also.

A few days later, he gets word about an associate who is about to undergo surgery for a tumor in his brain – possibly a cancerous one. He asks me to send a get-well card and write in it something caring. "Oh, and tell him that there's a woman in my support group who had brain tumors and surgery, twice, and she's doing fine." *'My' support group, he called it 'my' support group. No more resistance.*

> **Tip 124** Is a support group right for you? It is if you like to talk about your feelings, are interested in helpful hints, and like being part of a group.

In talking with other cancer patients, I learned there are many types of cancer and over a hundred kinds of chemo medicines used to treat them. I used to think that chemo was chemo and you needed it to treat cancer. Period. Not only are there other methods of cancer treatment, besides chemo, there are many types of chemo products, and also there are many ways to administer chemo. Some take it orally, topically and intravenous-ly. Some intravenous methods might be for two to four hours in a doc-tor's office or cancer center, some receive it during overnight hospital stays, and some go home with an IV pole or a 'pump' they wear on a belt or backpack and withstand a continuous drip for days or weeks at a time. Also, duration of this systemic approach varies for people and cancers. Mine is sixteen weeks. I met two amazing people in my support group, for example, who have been receiving several chemo drug products for a year and a half.

And, I met a man in a retail store who has bladder cancer. Bladder cancer is not treated with chemotherapy. He receives periodic doses of TB (yes, tuberculosis). Apparently, with each infusion, his body's immune system kicks into high gear to resist the TB and while doing so, kills the cancer. He told me he's been assured that bladder cancer is easy to treat; only he doesn't particularly like receiving the treatment via the "only direct route to the bladder." *Ugh. Maybe I don't have it that bad after all.*

Suzanne Somers, actress and writer, had breast cancer several years ago. As I understand it, she decided not to have chemotherapy at all. *Not me, I want it!* She opted for an alternative therapy that included hormone balance. The idea being that when your hormones are in balance, your immune system is strong, and your immune system can fight the cancer. *But what about hormones and their association with breast and ovarian cancer? Hmmm.*

> **Tip 125** If you are interested in learning about other types of cancer treatments, go to the bookstore and spend some time in the Consumer Health/Cancer section and read. If you would like to know more about hormone balance and it's affect on the immune system, ask a clerk or salesperson to perform a search on Ms. Somers books (she's written thirteen or so I believe).

Today, Andrea tells me that Mrs. S (her girlfriend's mom with a recurrence of breast cancer) is not doing well and has been hospitalized. I wish I could help. I feel connected to Mrs. S in some way. I can't describe it. I drive by her house and stop a minute to say a prayer for her and her daughter.

CANCER PATIENTS NEED ACCOLADES AND INSPIRATION?

An untold number of people have told me that I am an inspiration. Me? Inspirational?

An untold number of people have told me that I am an inspiration. *Me? Inspirational? It is unintentional...I am simply being me.* One day I open an e-mail from our neighbor, Bob, and I read a quote as part of his closing. I think it sounds like a first-class quote. "I am grateful for my optimism, because I usually have some inspiration to offer people." Suddenly I see my name following the quote and realize it's mine! *The quote is mine. He's quoting me! Wow.*

Tip 126 If you are the cancer patient and someone applauds you, revel in it. You may feel good to hear others cheer you on.

Tip 127 Likewise, if you know someone who is going through a cancer ordeal, or whose quality of life or life expectancy is being threatened, cheer him on. And if 'cheering' is not appropriate for the situation, lift ideas from my story (of things people gave me, or did for me, during the many stages of my ordeal).

Update: January 1, 2005

Hello all,

It is time for a New Year's Resolution. 2005: I will see the coming year through new lenses.

My December memories consist of chemo evenings on the couch in a gentle haze surrounded by mellow incandescent light from low-voltage bulbs intertwined with garland and evergreens while watching holiday movies on the television. The anticipation of the holiday traditions was stronger this year than ever, especially given that there is a three-year-old among us who is beginning to understand the concept of Christmas. Due to that, I was adamant about participating in traditions. Some evenings I would subliminally stand with my fist in the air and take on "the invader." Defiantly, I decided to mark my territory. I did it with cookies. Whenever I was able to, I baked and the house smelled like a home. A who-cares-about-cancer-today home. Whenever I didn't feel up to baking, I lit cookie-dough scented candles.

I savored my time with people I care about. We spent a day in Pennsylvania with Charles and Lisa, and their children, Shaun and Caitlin. We snacked, relaxed, ate dinner and watched movies. I loved every laid-back minute of it!

One evening during the holidays, Dan and I had dinner with four other couples. The five men are childhood friends. They are the glue of these get togethers, but we women have formed our own bonds; after all we've been with these men for many years. It is always pleasurable to be together. This time, while I was not well, was no exception. Since I was among old friends, I allowed myself to drift off to sleep on the couch whenever I needed to. Ha ha, cancer didn't short circuit my merriment. Awhile into the evening came the stories. You know the ones, the fish-that-got-away stories. They get bigger and bigger each year nearing far-fetched absurdity. I used to become slightly embarrassed at the brazen embellishment of them, especially once the beverages started pouring. Oh, the basic tales are the same. The narratives, with the passing of time, are ever more grandiose accounts of the original tales. And so is our collective laughter. No couple departed until we were all replete with food, drink and cheerfulness. This year, I recognized that mounting stories are part of living and living is good. 2005: Accept absurdity when it is harmless and enjoy it.

Each year, we go to my childhood home on Christmas morning to celebrate the birth of Christ and the visit of Santa. We partake in a filling brunch, cheeses and cookies that make their perennial appearance only at this time of year, and in witty repartee. The floor around the Christmas tree was crowded and hectic as usual, but no one was accidentally thrown in the trash bag with the paper and ribbons. We emerge victorious and affirmations are doled out. Family by family goes away. After the last one is gone Mom gets to rest with another Christmas coup under her belt.

We always converge with Dan's side of the family too, usually following Christmas day. We modified some of our traditions this year and had a cozy and merry event a few days before the 25th to work around my chemo and the kids' schedules. I felt totally surrounded by love and happiness. I hope every other person there felt encircled in love also. As it should be.

On the 26th, Andrea and Michele left for England with the high school band. They marched in the New Year's Day parade and performed in Queens Park at a soccer game. Very memorable.

The holidays were hectic at times, as they often are. The December and January months can be stressful. To people who are fatigued and experience side effects from cancer or other illness in addition to the holiday season strain, I recommend envisioning an event and the what-ifs, prior to it, and deciding what would be best for you. Also, it doesn't hurt to allow loved ones to cater to you a bit. Ofttimes, it's therapeutic for them as much as it is helpful for you.

Unfortunately, Andrea and I were recently psychologically impacted by another cancer death. That's three in three months. Is this a coincidence or have I become aware of cancer deaths more now because I have cancer? I think it is a coincidence, but I certainly feel the blow more than I did before my diagnosis. Andrea goes to school with a girl whose mother had breast cancer two years ago. Her mother recovered. She and her family live in our neighborhood and Dan would comment when she power-walked past the house in the afternoons. He often said that she looked like epitome of health. The breast cancer recurred a few months back, in her lungs. Remember, breast cancer goes to bones, liver and lungs. Andrea's classmate was quiet about their ordeal but shared some details with Andrea, probably since they were in similar situations. I walked in to our computer room one evening and Andrea was sniffling in front of the screen. "Why are you crying, Andrea?"

"Mommy," she says while she points to her classmate's instant message on the computer screen, "[Her] mom has been in the hospital with breast cancer that went to her lungs, but now she's dying and they are bringing her home to be assisted by the Hospice. She probably won't make it for [her] graduation in June."

I am breathless. And, I am speechless.

One busy morning after that, we were making breakfast and getting ready for the day. Andrea received a call. Not an unusual occurrence for a teenage girl. I had no idea who was on the phone, but I knew it was one of her friends. Dan walked into the kitchen, overheard Andrea's responses to the caller and asked if she was okay. I said, "Oh Dan, she's okay. Everyday is something with girls. It's probably teenage dra..."

"Mom, Mrs. S died!"

"...ma." Didn't I feel foolish.

Sadly, Andrea's friend's mother passed away a few days before Christmas. How could this happen? Why so fast? What did she do or not do that I am not doing or doing that allowed cancer to overtake her and not me? How can it not be me? Why won't it be me? We always want to know facts about why someone died or was killed, and why it can't possibly happen to us. Haven't you read about a fatal car accident and rationalized that they must've been on a cell phone, drinking, or without seat belts? Or heard about a massive heart attack and streamlined your thoughts to say that the person must've had heart disease, high cholesterol or an existing heart problem? You always cast the blame on something they must've been doing wrong, because you want to believe it won't happen to you if you do things differently. You want to believe that you are invincible.

We hugged. Andrea cried. We were mostly silent except for when I said, "It'll be all right." I drove her to another friend's house and several girls came outside to hug me. Hug me? They are hugging me?? Andrea confided, "Mom, I know they are looking at you and me like we are next." That's a very human reaction. I might've thought the same thing if the shoes were on other feet. At the outpouring of grief, a thought came:

People are not afraid of dying as much as they are afraid of the process of dying. I recall when my doctor reminded me of an old Jewish proverb that says we are old enough to die as soon as we are born. We know we are going to die. We just don't want to know when we are going to die. Cancer is a disease that, if given a poor prognosis, tells us how many days, weeks or months we have left. I believe we become afraid that we won't be able to settle our affairs in time or say the things we should say to people we care about before the end. Or maybe we are afraid of how physically painful a terminal illness might be. My strategy to quell my own fears is to say the things I want to say, now, settle some affairs like sorting out sentimental trinkets for the kids and discuss burial wishes, and talk with Dan about what his life might be like without me. Then I plan to talk to someone at Delaware Hospice about the process of dying since many people who are cared for with hospice care are cancer patients. I believe that people who are armed with knowledge of a situation before it occurs aren't usually as afraid as they might be without knowledge. For example, you might be less apprehensive about company mergers, offshoring or the possibility of losing your job if you have a resume prepared and career ideas. Therefore, I'd really like to know what terminal illness might be like, so I can tuck away that information and use it if I ever receive a poor prognosis.

One evening Andrea and I were in her bed and we talked until dawn. She asked, "Are you gonna die?" [I think so.] "I hope not." "Are you scared?" [Ohmygod yes.] "Not very." I was relying on the idea that parents have force fields that deflect fear. And then she said that she doesn't like when I say, "'it'll be all right' because you don't know that things will be all right, Mom." I explained that it's a matter of observational viewpoint: When she hears 'all right' she wants to know that I will live another forty years; and that when I say 'all right' I mean that no matter what happens, she'll get through it. I also reminded her that no matter how old I am when I leave this world; she won't be ready to accept my death and will always miss me. My mom is eighty-two and I'm not ready to let her go. And if I make it to sixty, seventy or eighty-two, I will always miss my mom because I may experience something in those years that she experienced. We will always miss loved ones no matter how long they live; there is normally a period of time when we will be without our parents just as there was for our parents to be without us before we came along. It'll be all right.

> **Andrea said that she doesn't like when I say, 'it'll be all right'. When I say 'all right' I mean that no matter what happens, she'll get through it.**

When I was little and I was sad, my mother was there to dry my tears. When my girls were little and they were sad, I was there to dry their tears. They are not little anymore and I am still here and drying their tears. I'm grateful for that. I've already left my legacy. They will be here to dry their brother's tears if I will not be. They will be here to dry their childrens'. The years will go by and I'll never be forgotten so long as they live. It'll be all right.

In a recent support group meeting at the Wellness Community, discussion ensued about what happens to us after we pass away. There were intellectual ruminations about the string theory [whatever that is], Tao te Ching, Zen Buddhism and hidden messages in water. The conversation neared pulling Nietsche and Emoto off the bookshelf. We settled on talking about preparing one's soul, finding 'special purpose' in existence and understanding life rather than trying to comprehend death or the afterlife, when all of a sudden I laughed out loud. Dang. My ADD struck again. New thoughts came rumbling into my head like a freight train. Everyone was looking at me and I realized that my attention was disconnected from the profound conversation. Do you remember when the comedic actor, Steve Martin played Navin in The Jerk? His mother assured him that when he went out into the world and experienced life, he would discover his "special purpose." I couldn't tell the group what I was thinking about. I was recalling the point in the story when Navin met a scary motorcycle-riding nymphomaniac in the circus and she dominated much of his time for her needs. He wrote home to tell his family that he might have found his "special purpose." Why, oh why did someone in the support group meeting say 'special purpose' anyway? Geez.

All in all, the support group discussion was helpful. I concluded that in the 21st century we expect to live long, especially in first-world countries like America. In previous centuries, people knew they probably wouldn't. Perhaps people in previous centuries were more passionate in the time they had and that's why epic romances are placed in previous centuries. 2005: I will live my passions and not be limited in my creativity or thinking.

> *2005:*
> *I will live my passions and not be limited in my creativity or thinking.*

And what about the recent tsunami? Oh dear. Who am I to be afraid or pensive about something that is inevitable for every one of us when so many people on the other side of the world were swept away in a wave of water in the span of a few hours? And, aren't many of the tsunami survivors facing a sort of terminal illness now because of unclean drinking water and high risks for diseases from the dead bodies? Isn't that more frightening than what I am facing?

2005: I hope that thinking about dying will grow very old and I'll emerge from my darkness.

Tuesday, I met another oncologist who was pinch-hitting for mine while she was on vacation. I always meet with the oncologist before each chemo treatment for an examination and re-order of chemo meds. He wrote the orders. Round seven was scheduled for Wednesday. I was not looking forward to it. I don't like the Taxol treatments because the Benadryl makes me sleep. I can't stand the idea of being alone in a room with people milling about and there I will be, not in control of my faculties. I also don't like to ask a loved one to sit, while I sleep, for four-and-a-half hours. I asked anyway. When I had the AC treatments they lasted two hours and represented quality time with my attendees. The Taxol ones dispirit me. The anxiety set in. I decided however, that I would simply give in to the disquiet. I don't always have to have a strategy to thwart apprehension; why not acknowledge it and let it play out.

...I entered the world of chemo-dom armed with my slippers and little Danny's super hero blanket.

So, on Wednesday I entered the world of chemo-dom armed with my slippers and little Danny's super hero blanket. I'm so angry that I have to be here – if I could shoot guns, I'd envision cancer's a— filled with buckshot! The medicine began to drip. I could feel the intoxication envelop me. I laid in the recliner wrapped in my Spiderman cocoon. Nervousness skittered through me and loomed low in my gut. I hate this part. I looked up at my oldest daughter who was drinking tea in the chair next to me. My lips moved slowly, "Kis Teeeen...[long pause]...wa yo ra hee baaaa?"

Christine leaned toward me and asked, "What Mom?"

"Dwo ho mee ooo wayee ra ra?"

"What?"

"Doo hoo wa ra ra?"

She sat back and chuckled, "Go to sleep Mom." Whatta girl.

Later, and with as much dignity as I could muster, I gathered up the remains of my pride and ambled out with her, and my sister, on either side of me.

I felt okay that evening and even the next day. Until about 6:00. No adult was home...there was no need for one to be; I'd been fine earlier. I was in my usual spot on the couch with Danny buzzing around me. The fire was ablaze, but the heat wasn't enough. I switched on the space heater; the one that Dan bought recently for the occasions like this one when I get the chills. My body began to shake, my face turned flush, my fingers and feet started aching and I was definitely consumed. Then came the bone aches. Oh man how they hurt. My skull and ears, shoulder blades and arms throbbed. Dan walked in and realized I'd gone downhill since he left. He extended his hand and helped me upstairs. I limped and moaned on the way up. Why do we moan when we hurt? Does it help us to feel better? I slept fitfully at first then sunk into bottomless sleep. ZZzzzz.

Why do we moan when we hurt? Does it help us to feel better?

Remember the eleventh hour of the movie Toy Story when Buzz Lightyear and Woody were in the air after the deadly rocket that Buzz was taped to launched? They were trying to reach the moving van or their owner's car and all seemed hopeless. Buzz activated his gliders and they detached from the disastrous soaring spacecraft, which soon afterward exploded. The background music turned prophetic and triumphant. You knew a happy ending was inevitable. Woody nervously asked, "Are we flying?" Buzz was fortified with cool confidence and said, "This isn't flying. It's falling with style." One couldn't help but to smile outwardly at their utter faith that the good things they were hoping for were going to happen. So on Wednesday, like Buzz and Woody, I gave in to the effects of the chemo and fell "with style."

2005: I will follow some of Erma Bombeck's advice from her passage, 'If I Had my Life to Live Over.'

Christine's friend Vanessa gave me a Christmas card and wrote a quote in it that reminded her of me: "Life loves the person who dares to live it." - Maya Angelou. Thank you Vanessa. The best thing that happened to me in 2004 was, I got breast cancer. Life will love me in 2005!

Happy New Year.

PEOPLE ARE MORE AFFECTED BY MY DIAGNOSIS THAN I WOULD HAVE THOUGHT

Vicki reflects:

I sat with Wendi and her oldest daughter, Christine, during the Dec 29 chemo. As she slept, I watched and admired her strength through this life-changing ordeal. I find strength in her writings; I hope you do.

I receive an e-mail from Brigid, my colleague:

I got your latest update from Brenda, and I still feel breathless. Your experience has made me see the New Year from a different perspective."

In a conversation I have with Lisa, she shares her feelings. "You are amazing. I have such creative friends," she says (as she often does when I do something amazing).

I remind her (as I often do when she tells me I am amazing) that she has strengths that I draw from. I have always leaned on her for her quiet strength. I wished I'd said to her, years before my diagnosis when I realized I felt this way that I always believed I should be singing Bette Midler's song in Beaches, "Did You Ever Know that You're My Hero." I can't say this now though, because the main character dies in the movie. And that's not going to be my ending.

It is Sunday, January 2, 2005. Andrea and Michele have been away for eight days. I am glad they went on this unforgettable trip, but have missed them terribly, and anxiously await word of their arrival today in the States.

Life continues to run in parallel with cancer. Tourette's Syndrome (TS) made its entry into our household nine years ago when Christine was diagnosed. We, along with her, have managed through the ups and downs that no one would understand unless they have lived with someone who suffers with it. Hers has gotten worse as she's gotten older and it has been pronounced lately.

TS is caused by chemical imbalances in the brain (Serotonin, Dopamine; etc.). It manifests itself, on the outside, by uncontrollable, observable movements commonly referred to as tics. They wax and wane. People with mild cases of TS tic by blinking their eyes or twitching. People with severe cases of TS drool, blurt out words, and constantly jerk and jolt. Christine's TS is somewhere in the middle of that scale. We try to look at the bright side; she does not have a severe case, but knowing that doesn't always help us to feel better when everything she does is interrupted by tics. With the recent increase of symptoms, she voluntarily gave up driving a car about a month ago. My heart goes out to her. I imagine it is not easy to be nineteen, working to progress your life, and then being pulled back by a debilitating disorder.

During the winter break Christine has decided to try an Eastern approach to treating her TS. She has been seeing an herbalist and an acupuncturist; she has had two acupuncture treatments so far. Today is her third treatment. As I watch her lying still with her eyes closed and tiny needles protruding from her head, face, hands and feet, it evokes a feeling of all-too-familiar vulnerability. I think about the time when she was an infant. She is my first-born and the one who made me a mother. She is also the one who made me realize the magnitude of such a grand role. So grand a role that I stepped into it three more times.

She is my first-born and the one who made me a mother. She is also the one who made me realize the magnitude of such a grand role. So grand a role that I stepped into it three more times.

Time is running out before Christine's winter break is over when we can have her close to us to observe changes or effects of the Eastern treatments for TS. We observe no decrease in severity, so she moves back to the Western medicine approach. This is precisely what I have been doing, moving between the Western medicine and Eastern methods. That's why I like "the Balanced Approach" that my nutritionist is helping me to adopt. It is a blend of both and theories are based upon food being good medicine.

Tip 128 Get information about nutrition and decide what's right for you: *Breast Cancer? Breast Health!* By Susan Weed, *Eight Weeks to Optimum Health,* By Andrew Weil, M.D., *The Cancer Survival Cookbook,* By Donna Weihofen R.D. and Christina Marino, M.D., and/or *Stop Your Cravings,* By Jennifer Workman.

Tip 129 A family owned company, Rodale, is a global leader in healthy, active living information. Their magazine properties *include Prevention, Runner's World, Organic Gardening, Bicycling, Backpacker,* and *Mountain Bike.* They also publish books on health fitness, cooking, nature and more. Visit www.rodalestore.com to order books, CDs, and magazines on Women's Health, Men's Health, Organic Living, spirituality; etc.

Christine and I discussed and agreed with her neurologist on a combination of several drugs. The trick to treating TS, Obsessive Compulsive Disorder (OCD) and Attention Deficit Disorder (ADD) (she has the latter two also), is to find the combinations and dosing that bring the symptoms to milder levels for the individual. This process takes time.

I go to our pharmacy and pick up a few prescriptions. She begins a few of the meds and we go about life while watching for signs of a break.

It would be sometime in the coming months when we find the right combination of meds, they reach therapeutic levels, and her tics decrease in frequency and severity (and she is able to drive again).

THE LAST CHEMO TREATMENT – AN OPPORTUNITY

Tuesday, January 11 will be my last chemo treatment. So, I send out the following plea:

To all of you who have been traveling this journey with me,

I need your help. I have one more chemo treatment to endure and am requesting (actually, I am pleading) for everyone to send me good vibes on Tuesday, January 11. On Tuesday, please look at the clock and, when you realize that the time is anywhere between 10:30 and 2:30, pause a moment to send me good vibes, prayers, and visions of the medicine working.

Radiation, which will begin in early February, will scorch the site where the tumor was, but it won't destroy cancer cells that might be lurking anywhere else in my body. So, this last chemo treatment is the final opportunity to seek out every last cancer cell floating around and destroy it.

Please. Between 10:30 and 2:30 on Tuesday, close your eyes a moment and send me healing thoughts. If you believe in God, send me prayers. If you trust the power of visualization, imagine the medicine working harder than ever before. Whatever is your belief system; draw from it for me please. You are an important part of my artillery. This is a final opportunity and one that I do not want to miss.

I already have cancer; I don't ever want to see the adjectives 'metastatic' or 'metastasized' before it on my medical chart. I don't want cancer to recur...I DON'T EVER WANT IT BACK!

With sincere appreciation and gratitude,
Wendi

Incredibly quickly, the e-mail replies start pouring in:

Your updates have given me a new meaning of life and priorities. I have never prayed so much in my entire life. – Dottie

Jill corrects me if we miss praying to Blessed Gianna so that "Mrs. Pedicone gets better soon and comes back to work with Mommy." – Helen

Battle it hard this one last time, Wen, and beat it. – Brigid

Consider me a bazooka, no a ballistic missile. I'll be sending all I have. – Judy T

From a Christian friend and middle-school teacher:

I truly believe that you will be lifted by all the people who care about you, and by God... I will be sure to send positive thoughts your way on Tuesday as I stand in the middle of a room of horny seventh graders. Hee hee hee.

I attend my final chemotherapy treatment on January 11 and the next morning while I have my wits and energy about me, I craft an update, before my expected yet temporary collapse.

CONTINUING THE CONNECTION WITH OTHERS AND THINKING ABOUT MY SPIRITUALITY

Update: January 12, 2005

Hello all,

Thank you everyone! I am so grateful for all of you who prayed, envisioned and sent me good vibes, because I went into the FINAL ROUND yesterday with a weighty array of cancer weaponry. "Three grand essentials to happiness in this life are something to do, something to love, and something to hope for." – Addison (1672-1719). Thanks to you I received my last chemo treatment with something to hope for. After I pleaded for your help, the e-mail replies started pouring in incredibly quickly and I saved every single one. I collected them in the "Cancer Survivor" folder that I optimistically created on September 9th, the day before I left for the mastectomy [Boy, it seems like such a long time ago]. I reread all that I had saved, yesterday morning, before I left. I later found out that my e-mail plea from last week went to distribution chains connected to distribution chains and connected to distribution chains. I saw replies from Washington DC, Colorado, New York, Indianapolis, California, Texas, England and Sweden. Kewl.

Christine sat with me for this last chemo treatment. Me, well, I slept through it all. Dan and his mother stopped in, and I received a surprise visit from someone who, a year ago, figuratively sat where I was sitting. It has been a year and Mary looks great. A year from now, I will visit the chemo room of the cancer center and prove to people that they too can get through it. I will also visit the chemo nurses who delivered the goods (Kelly, Jewell, Lynn, Kernie and Paula), Toni and Mayda (the Regional Oncology office staff), Dr. N, and Kim. I am forever indebted to them.

My final chemo day was also Christine's nineteenth birthday. In trying to find the positive side to having her sit with me for four-and-a-half hours, I chose to view it as a two-way gift – she gave the gift of time to me on her birthday and I will give her the gift of being here to celebrate future birthdays. Christine will have her mom around for a long time.

Last week and for the first time since beginning chemo, I came down with something. A cold perhaps. It was regular stuff, not cancer stuff. I felt almost the same achy symptoms that I feel during chemo weeks. I resented that I was ill during one of my off-chemo weeks. I must have bad cancer karma. Even though cancer patients, quite naturally, become hypochondriacs, we do get regular illnesses like everyone else. And it is all right. But, we are not medically treated in the same way and we cannot take anything over the counter unless we check with the oncologists at the cancer center first. I did not follow orders to contact the cancer center however; I did not contact them for fear of having my chemo postponed. Am I bad. I was adamant about having it on the scheduled day.

The thing that bothered me about having a cold was the inconvenience. I expected to feel rotten every other week due to bi-weekly cancer treatments. I did not wish to feel rotten in the weeks in between, because during each week in between chemo, I would prepare for the week ahead. I would meditate, exercise, run errands, go to my medical appointments, fill the refrigerator with groceries, pay bills and do as many things a wife, mother, sister, daughter, friend and neighbor with cancer might be able to do in a week's time.

Over the holidays, our dear friends, Charles and Lisa settled on a new house in Pennsylvania. Despite Lisa's concern that I wasn't well enough to travel, I threw an overnight bag together for li'l Danny and me and headed to their place to help make their house a home. Happily, Christine came with us. I sure did enjoy her companionship. You see, I needed the emotional uplift more than anything.

Collectively, we packed things from their old house, carried them to the new one, and unpacked. Pack, carry, and unpack...pack, carry, and unpack. Me? I packed, carried, napped and unpacked. And napped again.

Spending the night there felt like old times when Charles, Lisa, Dan and I would spend entire weekends in New York together with our collective brood. It was 6:00 a.m. one morning and Lisa's kids were getting dressed for work and school. I knew they'd enjoy a good start to their day. (And I unpacked the kitchen so I knew where everything was.) What made me feel productive was to make them some scrambled egg and cheese sandwiches. As they were leaving I heard them call to me, mouths filled with warm breakfast food, "Aunt Wen, you're the best," and, "You're awesome, Aunt Wen." I smiled as I returned to bed and pulled the warm covers over me. For that day, I was the breakfast queen, June Cleaver, and woman, hear me roar!

For that day, I was the breakfast queen, June Cleaver, and woman, hear me roar!

While I am not terminal, I think about people who are. Some, who know death is near, learn to accept it and live out their final days with grace. They agree to palliative care. Palliative care means patients no longer receive treatment for the disease and caregivers do what they can to alleviate pain and keep the person comfortable. A patient can receive palliative care even if he does not have a terminal diagnosis (for example, a patient with Alzheimer's can receive palliative care and live for another ten to fifteen years). A general guideline to be accepted into a Hospice Care program is a life expectancy of six months or less. In addition to symptom management, hospice care provides emotional and spiritual support. While some accept death and go peacefully, others live out their final days fighting until the end. My first thought is that it is very noble to fight to the end. Many of us have so much to live for and believe our "will" is not yet done on Earth. I know I will feel cheated if I ever find out I am to be robbed of my desire to be part of my grandchildren's lives, doing things with Dan that golden-years couples do, helping other people, and slowing down to settle my affairs over time and not in a rush. My second thought, however, is that maybe in the final weeks, days or hours when it becomes clear that there is nothing more that can be done, I would accept my destiny and trust my faith. If believers in God or a supreme being practice a religion all their lives and seem to believe in Heaven or an afterlife, why wouldn't they finally accept that Heaven is near? People who die with hostility, and those who are close to them, who become hostile after they die, perhaps have been practicing a religion but not truly believing.

What happens to people like me who like it here and don't want to leave?

I love life. Life is good. I have always been high on life even when the chips were down. I am not wealthy but I do have material things. What happens to people like me who like it here and don't want to leave? Father John reminded me that having faith and anticipating Heaven is a challenge for those with earthly possessions and happiness. He suggested I read some verses from the books of Genesis and Psalms. And so, I am.

Tip 130 If you are an atheist or agnostic, it doesn't hurt to explore spirituality at this time. Your mind may be more open than you think. Finding a new spiritual direction or strengthening an existing one can provide enormous comfort.

Tip 131 If you believe in God, locate your Bible. A systematic reading plan for Holy Scripture is important for our life as Christians, and for you at this time. Read the Book of Genesis and Psalms. These became my favorites: Genesis 2:5-25, Psalms 6, 23, 25, 42, and 63. Whichever chapters and versus you read, do not rush through them; find a quiet place and time to read a few verses and reflect on them. Find your inner self in each or reflect on your own life, in the light of the passage; determine how you want to internalize the words. You may be surprised to find that the Bible is a how-to book.

Someone told me recently, and I am adopting her attitude, that I will always think about death and cancer, but not as much as I do now. Furthermore, I do not always want to think maudlin and self-pitying thoughts about death and cancer. I want to live normally again; with a new perspective and priorities, of course, but mostly normally like before I got breast cancer. I look forward to getting back to work, school and structure.

I wear my reading glasses more often now. I think my eyesight has been affected. I need stronger lenses too. Also, I am in a temporary, chemo-induced menopause or cessation of menstrual cycles.

The hot flashes from the chemically induced menopause force me to rapidly remove clothing or blankets and headscarves. These actions are obvious to those around me. I was standing in a greeting card section of a local store and my little man was at my side holding a greeting card. He looked up at me and said, "Here Mommy, I got this for you. You can do this with it." He bowed his head and used the card to fan it. Precious.

Most women get their periods back following chemo. I wonder if I will get mine back. Some who get cancer and receive chemotherapy when they are younger not only menstruate again, they are even able to become pregnant. My periods may return, but that would mean I'd have to go through menopause again someday. Again! Geez, more hot flashes. Swell. That's just groovy. I am told that chemo patients typically encounter problems with vision, hearing and brain functionality (we get confused and forgetful). So, I wonder, will things return to the way they were before chemo? Or did chemo advance me up the steps of the natural aging process?

Often, I forget what I'm doing in the middle of doing it, misplace things, forget names of people I know quite well and can't recall where I'm driving. It is distressing at times, but at least most of the absentmindedness is brief.

Michele reflects on my chemo brain:

'My mom always writes our first initial when she addresses notes to us, like M for Michele, or A for Andrea. One day she wrote me a note addressed to S!'

I have one single hair left where my left eyebrow used to be. What a discovery. It is quirky, I know, but I don't want to pluck it. My eyes look a little sunken and the lack of lashes (I have none) looks odd. The rash on my face is better, but the skin on my face is numb. It feels like I've had Novocain that is beginning to wear off. I can't feel little Danny's soft skin against mine, but I am always hopeful. We nudge each other cheek-to-cheek anyway, because it is good for him, and I remember what it felt like. And, I'll feel it again someday soon.

I am loath to apply makeup to my face because it irritates. I cannot put on mascara; I have only three lashes left. I don't do eyeliner because without eyelashes it runs into my eyes. I look like such a cancer patient! Really though, it is fun to see how positively awful I look (the worse; the better even) because it will serve me well for a pathetic before picture. Someday, soon enough, I'll have a lovely after picture. And, the difference will make me feel magnificent.

I do not miss shaving my underarms or legs. Thanks to the TRAM reconstruction I don't have the fold of skin that used to emerge on my lower stomach area whenever I sat down. Ladies, you know what I'm talking about. (This, I acquired after I gave birth to Danny, and I don't miss it.) I don't even miss my left breast. Most likely because my new breast mound looks good. I do, however miss my left nipple. When I get chilly, only the right one shows through my shirt. I look like a car with one headlight missing. I can hear it now; men will see me walking toward them on a beach after a cool breeze sweeps by. They will flinch and whisper to their comrades, "High beam." Notice, one beam, not two; singular, not plural. When I told my surgeon about my feelings he winked at Dan who was sitting next to me and said, "Real men don't worry about such things." Dan immediately sat ramrod straight with his hand on his chest, fingers splayed and a look on his face that said, 'Not me. I don't feel that way." I just laughed. I miss my nipple for other reasons, but I can't seem to articulate what those reasons are.

In response to my question in my last e-mail update about why we moan when we are not feeling well, I was told that we moan when we are exerting energy or pushing our bodies to an extreme. When we are in pain, groaning is like releasing the energy. My next-door neighbor, Cole, is eleven years old and practices karate. He tells me in the martial arts it is a fact that when individuals do a kick the tendency is to do it harder when they shout (and not as hard when they don't). So now I know.

I received a lovely note from someone who included a quote from the Catechism of the Catholic Church. It goes like this. "From infancy to death human life is surrounded by [their angels] in watchful care and intercession. Beside each believer stands an angel as protector and shepherd leading him to life." I am fortunate to have many, many angels. YOU all have been and continue to be my earthly angels. I am indebted.

Radiation will begin in three or four weeks. I am told it will be every week-day for six to eight weeks. I do not view it as a nuisance, rather another step toward excellent health. Hooray!

I am leaving in a few minutes for my 'day-after' shot, Neulasta®. I will say good-bye to the chemo room.

Then I will say a temporary good bye to Christine, who is returning to college.

I am not looking forward to this evening; I expect to go physically and emotionally downhill as I usually do after chemo. And I don't know which is worse. However, I seek solace in the knowledge that THIS WILL BE THE LAST TIME I SUFFER THE EFFECTS OF A CHEMOTHERAPY TREATMENT and these feelings will go away.

Thinking of myself as cancer free and grateful to you for helping me get there,
Wendi

After reading my updates, some folks have commented on how living should be high priority and the tedium of work should be low priority. I agree that work should not be as high a priority as living, but we work to live and if we do it correctly, work is a fulfilling part of life. Jill reflects and somewhat captures this:

Just a short note to tell you that you've been in my thoughts all day. It's been a busy day here [at work] and as I'm going from meeting to meeting I'm wondering 'what is it all really about?' You are battling cancer, 150,000 souls disappear in a wall of water [tsunami], and 20 [die] in a mudslide [in California]. It reminds me how fragile life is and makes me wonder what is this thing we call living? I've come to the conclusion that living is about connecting, pure and simple. Connecting to others, some we know, some we'll never know, but it's about caring, feeling, being hurt, being happy, and getting up each day to discover what new connections I'll uncover. It's why I come here [to work] each day.

Tip 132 Let's face it; from the time of diagnosis, death is always in the back of your mind. Try to determine what it is about death that frightens you and become educated. Knowledge is power.

DOING SOMETHING ABOUT MY FEAR OF DYING

I read through information that I believe will help to quell my fears of dying, from two sources:

1. HealthCare Odyssey, a local organization that provides services to terminally ill patients.
2. Delaware Hospice for Delaware and surrounding Pennsylvania counties. Their professional team works with you, your caregivers and your physician to provide the best care and comfort possible. The programs they offer are unbelievably comprehensive. Hospice care is available to anyone whose prognosis is measured in months rather than years. Patients receive care wherever they choose to live out the time they have left. Many choose to do this in their homes.

I learned an interesting detail; hospice care in the U.S. typically means home-care (care in the home) or palliative care in a hospital if the terminally ill patient has no caregiver, whereas in England it typically means in-patient facilities and almost no home-care.

One of my friends in the Wellness Community said he learned a lesson from a former member (who is no longer with us) when they were in an 'Exploring Your Mortality' session together: The notion was that when we learn to die, we have an opportunity to accept the responsibility to teach others how to die. *I will remember that. If ever I know I am going to die, I will strive to do it with dignity and teach my children and loved ones one way it is done.*

I visit my priest; Father John and we talk candidly about living, dying, faith, Heaven and the fulfillment of preparing for death knowing it is coming soon versus sudden death. I feel immensely peaceful.

The day following my final chemo treatment I go to the cancer center for my last 'day-after' shot. The nurse gives me a Purple Heart Award which is a certificate stating that I successfully completed chemotherapy. It contains salutations and the nurses' signatures. I am pleased to receive it but quite candidly, it feels like a hollow victory. No one can tell me the treatments worked or that the cancer is gone. I am tempted to ask for one more treatment, just in case. I say 'so long' to the chemo nurses wearing lab coats. I walk out with an empty feeling.

I find a toll-free Survivor's Helpline number at www.lbbc.org. I can talk to a breast cancer survivor who understands what I am facing. I think I will call 888-753-5222 one of these days.

Christine's second semester classes begin on Wednesday and I go as a passenger in the vehicle to take her to her dorm the afternoon before. I have time before the after effects of the treatment set in. Since her Tourette's Syndrome has been troubling her, she is reluctant to go back.

During the next few days I go in and out of sleep, on the couch.

It is midday Friday. I am feeling well enough to drive. My mother and I are in the car, on our way to her beauty salon. We are on a crowded road, and I signal to someone, who has been waiting awhile, to pull out in front of me. Apparently, in being kind to one person by letting him pull out, I detain another person; the woman behind me has now caught the red light. She stops in the lane next to me. As we sit at the light, side by side, she is behaving obnoxiously. She is pounding her hands on the steering wheel, bobbing her head up and down and throwing her hands upward towards the red light. I feel badly that I made her catch the light. She continues to gesticulate. *All right already! Sheesh. I made her miss the light. I'm sorry.* She doesn't stop complaining. Finally, I do something totally out of the ordinary. In an attempt to circumvent her aggravation I pull off my hat, face her with my baldhead and whisper, "Relax. Shhhhh. Relax. It'll be okay." *What has gotten into me? I don't do radical things like this.* She freezes and stares at my cancer-appearance for a few seconds; mouth agape. With her hands at rest on the steering wheel she gives me a half-hearted smile, turns her head forward and never looks at me again. The light turns green and even though she has opportunity to speed ahead of me, she never drives by my side. She hangs in her lane, behind my vehicle. I am not certain if she is embarrassed or timid. Either way, I eventually turn onto another road and ease her discomfort.

Christine's TS is brutally raging on and the tics are on the border of violent, to the point that her neurologist recommends the emergency room for scans and tests. Christine can't drive. I can't drive. Vicki takes some vacation time from work, collects me from home and Christine from college, and drives us to the ER. I feel so helpless watching her jolt. She is tired and desperately wants a reprieve. Immediately they give her a room. Dan comes in, his mom comes in and Christine's boyfriend comes in. *Aren't we a mess!* Everyone offers to stay so I can go home and rest. Cancer or no cancer, chemo or not, I'm staying. *I will pay for it later.*

And, I do. As soon as we arrive home, I go to bed with an elevated temperature, chemo face and a mild case of the shakes. *Man, cancer is so inconvenient.*

The next day Christine's tics are the same, but at least we know from testing she had last night that her problem is classic TS that flared up and nothing more.

During the weekend, I am pleased to be surrounded by my family. Christine and Jason rent a movie and we watch it together. Michele and a few friends come and go. Andrea and Mike hang around the house and play with Danny. And, thanks to our neighbors, we enjoy sit-down dinners together two nights in row.

Andrea says, "Mom, I don't know how Jason does it. Christine tics like mad and he just pats her and waits for each episode to pass." We each have people for whom we are grateful.

Our life at the present time seems almost normal some days and I don't always feel like a cancer victim.

Only when newcomers come to the house do I hide my head under a hat. It is reasonable to believe they may feel awkward. Andrea's boyfriend, Mike said he's never uncomfortable around me. We are sitting in the den and he tells me:

> *At first I didn't know what to think. I didn't know about your cancer until I started dating Andrea. Actually, she told me the first night she hung out at my house. And then, the first time we came over here, she said, 'just warning you before you go into the house, my mom's bald.' I was worried that I would have to act different, but when I met you I realized that you are a warm and welcoming person. I was happy to be a cushion for Andrea, because she usually puts all her emotions on me when she gets upset. She deserves someone to be there for her besides her friends. Sometimes Andrea needs someone to hold her while she cries. That's where I come in.*

On Monday morning I discover it is my day to begin feeling well. My spirits are rising. A peak is near.

CHAPTER

6

VACATION, RADIATION, AND DEPRESSION

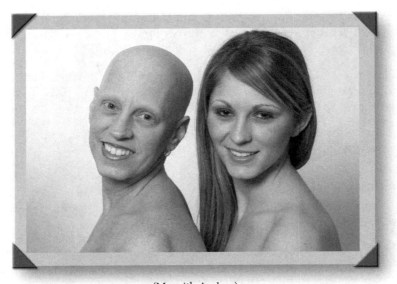

(Me with Andrea)

Photo courtesy of G. Thomas Murray Photography

Only I can change my life.
No one can do it for me.

Carol Burnett
Actress / Comdienne
(1936 -   )

Most cancer patients get a short break at the end of chemo and before the start of radiation. I have three weeks.

On the front page of The News Journal there's an article that says cancer is now the number one killer in the US. It has moved ahead of heart disease. Hmmm. Interesting. Every time I see or hear the "C" word, my brain instantly tunes in. When I read how many women in the US have breast cancer; I know one of those women is me. *Thankfully, the cancer fatality statistic on the cover of today's paper is one that I am not a part of.*

During my recent appointment with Dr. M, he suggests I stay on medical leave. The radiation, he says, does not present the side effects that chemo does; however, it makes people extremely fatigued. "Plus," he says, "This is going to be an emotional phase of your ordeal. You need to allow yourself time." Additionally, he recommended emotional support in the way of a psychiatrist and consideration of anti-depressants. *Me? Anti-depressants? No way. Uh unh. I am the eternal optimist...don't need 'em. Period. End of discussion.* As if reading my mind he adds, "It is not a sign of weakness to accept help, you know."

> "It is not a sign of weakness to accept help..."

At the conclusion of the visit, Diane looks at Dr. M and says, "Now, tell her the bad news." *Ohmygosh, ohmygosh, what bad news? I've had my share of it recently. I'm a little gun-shy. What bad news?*

He turns to me and says, "I am leaving this location and much of my practice to take up residence in the hospital to teach." *Is that all? That's not bad news. Giving me a poor prognosis would be classified as bad news. Telling me I have cancer is bad news. A career change is not bad news.* My heartbeat begins to slow to a normal pace and he continues, "I will see you for our future visits in a new office in the hospital."

"Why would that be bad news?" I notice Diane doesn't look cheerful and suddenly the magnitude of it dawns on me. Dr. M and his staff are a tight team. The team is breaking up. Once he's working in the hospital, he'll have different staff. "Oh." I said. It is relative. News is relative to where people are in their lives. I am a cancer patient; news about cancer is relative to me. She's been with Dr. M for years; news about a major change in their day-to-day working relationship is relative to her.

It is January 17 and I think I am ready to resume my college degree studies at Goldey-Beacom. The last class I attended was in August. On the morning following my diagnosis I contacted my professor with the news that I was dropping the course...and that I had cancer. Perhaps, a course in macroeconomics will be just what I need to calm my morbid thoughts.

Break time! I am halfway through class and it's time for a break. *Don't be a quitter, Wendi.* An hour earlier I realized my brain isn't functioning like it should. I'm not firing on all cylinders. I can't keep a series of thoughts in my head and I can't concentrate on the lecture. I am not certain if it is my 'chemo brain' or the subject of macroeconomics, but this I know – I'm not ready. I thank my professor and tell him I'll cancel the course in the morning. *I feel like a quitter.*

MORE THOUGHTS ABOUT DEATH

People might include the word *unselfish* in their descriptions of me. Sometimes, I can agree to this adjective; other times the guilt for the things I've done in my life that were wrong prevents me from agreeing. Nevertheless, I volunteer at Church and in my community, I recycle for future generations, I give to the United Way and many other charities, and I eat the burnt cookies on the cookie plate so others can have the good ones. Yet, I can't get past two sticking points. Sticking point number one is that I selfishly want to leave this world only when I am ready and not a day sooner. That would be after I enjoy a fulfilling career, see my children have children and careers, make a significant contribution to something, experience the golden-years with Dan, and reach a point in my life when I can rock for hours on end on a porch rocking chair without saying to myself that there is something else I should be doing. I am selfish in that I want a long life. When Christine, Jason, Dan and I watched the movie, "The Notebook," I couldn't help thinking about how much I want to die when I am old...not when I'm forty-five...not now.

I will tell you about sticking point number two, but first, the preamble: I have always accepted change; in fact I welcome it. When colleagues would become nervous about re-engineering, de-mergers and mergers, I saw these as opportunities to break out of the day-to-day and switch gears; perhaps even experience an entire career transformation. I've gone so far as to do some ad hoc informal counseling on the benefits of change. Change is healthy. Sticking point number two is that I am unwilling to change my views of what I want. (And what I want is long life.) *Am I not practicing what I have preached?* My doctor is right. I need some professional emotional support. It is not a sign of weakness to need this.

For months, folks I know through my church parish tell me I should talk to Lee, a five-year breast cancer survivor. I have been meaning to contact her, but haven't gotten around to it. Today, I run into her at a department store. We exchange information and phone numbers. At the end of the conversation I ask her what stage she was in when she had breast cancer. I believe she says stage I or II. I am instantly envious because her cancer didn't go to her lymph nodes. *I think I'm probably going to die from cancer, later if not now, because mine got in my lymph system.*

NERVOUS ABOUT RADIATION

After several wrong turns, confusion over the address, and two phone calls from my cell phone, I finally find the radiation oncologist's office. Oh my confused brain. Dr. Dz walks in wearing a crisp white lab coat. It is cold in here, and I look upon his coat with envy. I look upon any article of clothing with envy. I am wearing a paper robe and nothing else from the waist up. *I have goose bumps and one nipple standing at attention.* He goes over my pathology reports, does a clinical exam and we discuss radiation therapy for me. During the conversation I realize that it might have been beneficial for me to meet with a radiation oncologist before my mastectomy. *Might* have been beneficial – I realized early on that it is good to research treatments and get additional opinions before starting treatments, and it is also good to make a decision, go forward with it and stop second-guessing. Some patients delay treatment because they are unable to make a decision. You can drive yourself crazy second-guessing. I can live with my decisions. The only thing I might have done differently, if I had more time, would be to meet with the specialists of all three disciplines (surgery, chemotherapy, and radiology) in September before beginning treatment.

I made the consultation appointment with Dr. Dz at his North Wilmington location. I did this because I hoped to be back at work by now and planned to go to my daily treatments during lunch hour. His North Wilmington office is close to AZ. Now that I buy into Dr. M's suggestion to stay on medical leave until I get through radiation, I will be changing the location of my daily treatments to "the Helen Graham."

The amount of treatments prescribed (Dr. Dz suggests twenty-eight) depends on several variables; the size of the tumor and the risk of scattered cells. We talk about possible side effects from radiation and what to do about them. The ones I am concerned about are fatigue, the effects of radiation on my skin, lymphedema in my left arm, and radiation-pneumonitis (a sort of walking pneumonia I could get after one to two weeks – they cannot avoid radiating my left lung). I am not concerned about the fact that radiation may ruin the reconstruction. To my way of thinking, 'ruin' has different meanings and disparity. 'Ruin', to one of my surgeons, might mean a less than perfect reconstruction. 'Ruin', to me, would be things far more drastic. Dr. D, my plastic surgeon, tells me he can touch up a hardened breast mound. This, to me is one of those bridges that I'll cross IF I come to it.

Tip 133   During the weeks of radiation do not wear tight rings, watches and jewelry on the fingers and wrist of the arm that had lymph nodes removed, especially when you sleep.   Radiation increases the risk of arm swelling and lymphedema.

Tip 134   This would be a good time to read about lymphedema (if you haven't already done so).

IT IS COMMON TO TAKE VACATION AFTER CHEMO AND BEFORE RADIATION

On Saturday morning, January 22 we drive to Baltimore to board a Florida-bound airplane. Vacationing with us is Mom Pedicone and Christine's friend, Vanessa. The temperature is in the low 20's. The forecast is calling for a Nor'easter snowstorm. When we are taxiing down the runway the flurries begin. *Oh boy, we are gettin' outta Dodge!*

I estimate that I've stepped onto an airplane over fifty times in my life. And most times, I'm desperately scared. I have tried, unsuccessfully, to get over my fear of flying. A few years ago, I bought a videotape designed to help people do this, and I have looked at statistics. I am able to rationalize that the risk of a car accident is far greater than that of a plane crash, but [*and this is an important 'but' to me*] the survival rate of a commercial airplane crash is bleak. I acknowledge my fear and happily, I never let it stop me from seeing the wonderful places I've seen in the world. Before the plane takes off it dawns on me that being afraid of cancer might have a positive effect on my fear of flying. However, rather than stay wide-awake and test the theory, I take two Benadryl and conk out. *Why Benadryl? Because it shouldn't stop any chemo medicine, that might be lingering in my body, from killing cancer cells...after all, they gave it to me as a precursor to Taxol.*

During the beginning of the week, we visited relatives. James and Linda had a family bar-b-que, poolside with Aunt Sharon and Uncle Leon, Dan's sister Tina showed us her new home, and Uncle Earl and Aunt Lue treated us to dinner and a relaxing visit.

We also shopped, lounged and went to a few theme parks.

I can't believe how often thoughts of leaving this world pop into my head.

In Disney's Animal Kingdom I am deeply moved by the artists and the music in the Festival of the Lion King. As I look at the innocent young faces in the audience who are mesmerized by the singers and dancers; I get chill bumps and begin to whimper. "Please God," I say under my breath, "Let me live to see another generation of children marvel at this."

Oh, my fractious thoughts. One moment I am laughing, the next I am down in the dumps.

Disney's Epcot Center: Soon after Andrea's schoolmate lost her mother to cancer, a few of Andrea's friends told us they bought us a star. *A star? Which star? Tom Hanks? Glenn Close? Halle Berry? I've never heard of such a thing.* They bought us a star in the galaxy and named it after me. *Isn't that neat? What a clever idea!* Unwrapping the certificate, surrounded by her friends, was a very touching moment for us. We have a lovely framed record hanging on a wall in the kitchen. It says star number Ursa Major RA 9h 39m 59s D68 39 has been designated by the International Star Registry to the name Wendi Pedicone. As I look at the planetarium in one of the Epcot Center exhibits, I wonder if our star is there.

The Magic Kingdom: The Peter Pan ride is fun [*and I should tell Peter Pan it's time to grow up because Wendi has cancer.*] At the end of the evening, we watch the fireworks over Cinderella's castle and I ponder the possibility that this could be my last time to see this spectacular display. *Ugh, will these thoughts EVER stop?*

Have I reached the height of self-centeredness by thinking I am so important that my children shouldn't live without me?

And, there is no respite from the fatigue. But, it is okay. This week, I napped everywhere, as soon as my body told me it was necessary. *Certainly, there is a Sleepy or Seven Dwarfs analogy here.*

When I was little I'd say a bedtime prayer my mom taught me: "Now I lay me down to sleep, I pray O Lord my soul to keep…" I always skipped the line that says, "…If I should die before I wake, I pray O Lord my soul to take." I didn't want to face the idea of dying.

Shamu has been waiting for us at Sea World, so we oblige him and the other killer whales by watching the captivating show. *I wonder if Shamu will recognize me; I look different than the last time I visited Sea World.* Christine, Vanessa and Michele convince me to go on Kraken, the dreaded looping rolling coaster. Dan reminds me that it is my turn to ride. You see, the last trip to the Florida theme parks was when we brought the girls as a final big event before the baby was born. That was almost four years ago. I was seven months pregnant. And, I was very famous then: I was written about on many, many signs at the parks, "...no pregnant women or children under ten years of age..." Dan and I made a pact at that time that when we came back, it would be my turn to ride the rides.

So, here we are, about to board the intimidating ride. We are told to remove all loose accessories, jewelry and hats. *Oh brother, I don't want to make other folks feel awkward when I remove my hat. I am not embarrassed, in fact I am proud to show the world that I am fighting a war with cancer, but I don't want to embarrass anyone else.* I don't want to lose my hat; just before take-off we place our lose items on the exit side of the ride, my hat included. Christine and Vanessa remind me that I can put the hood of my sweatshirt on. I do. As we do the loop-de-loops I repeat my familiar mantra aloud, "I've had major surgery. Whoa! That was a big drop. I've had... [Oooooh]... major... [*Aaaaah*]... surgereeeee...[*What a flip!*]." The ride is so extreme that the hood doesn't stay on my head. Oh well. The automatic snapshot taken at the largest drop shows me next to the girls, looking positively ghostly. *Hee hee hee.* I buy it anyway, because it is a perfect depiction of what I look like, in January 2005, on a roller coaster!

At our timeshare, Danny is anxious to show me that he knows how to use the key card and open the door to our suite. We step from the living room into the hallway and he begins turning the access card in his hands and inserting it into the slot. Three older adults walk by and I realize that I forgot to cover my head. Instinctively, I shield myself by putting my arm over top and around my crown (yeah, like *that's* gonna suffice.) I looked at them, and then downward and said, "I forgot my hat." One of the women said, in a Virginian accent, "It's quite all right, your smile is so pretty we don't care if you have a hat or not." The gentleman said, "If I remove my hat, you'll see I have no hair on my head either. Bald is beautiful." *What sweet people.*

The day before our return trip home, we visit MGM Studios theme park. Dan takes the kids on the dreaded Tower of Terror. *Ooooh, they are entering, the Twilight Zone.* A woman reaches out from the crowd and embraces me in an exuberant hug. Instinctively, I know that there's a special reason for this incidence and I return the embrace. Her name is Roxanne. Before this moment, she was a complete stranger. She is from Canada and, three months ago finished chemotherapy for breast cancer. We compare notes and circumstances. She had lobular breast cancer; I have in situ and invasive. She is 48; I am 45. She is vacationing after treatments and so am I. She's not back to work yet; neither am I. She had the Canadian standard of chemo; I guess I had the American standard. *What's the Canadian standard and why would women in different countries get treated differently? If there were a standard that works there, wouldn't it work here too?* Roxanne introduces her family and I introduce mine. She saw me a few days before and recognized the appearance of a cancer patient. We exchanged e-mail addresses and hugs (you can never get enough of them). *I'm going to contact her and find out more about the country standards. I want whichever one works. Canadian, American or whatever.*

I thoroughly enjoyed this vacation, the visits, the theme parks, the non-snow, and the pinnacle of the week was meeting Roxanne.

On the flight home, I am feeling brave and forego the Benadryl. I have thought about dying so often this week that I don't want to think about it now. Besides, how frightened of a two-hour flight can I be when I've faced a cancer diagnosis?

Update: February 2, 2005

Hello all,

Several weeks have passed since I wrote an update to you. The last one was Wednesday, January 12, the day after concluding my chemotherapy treatments. Typing Brenda and Vicki's e-mail addresses in the "To" field and hitting the "send" button on the January 12 update to you were the final things I did before leaving to get my 'day-after' shot, Neulasta®.

The shot. Anxiously, I sat in the chemo room with my outer sweater on my lap, waiting for my injection. The nurse was at my side, flicking the syringe. Oh brother, this is gonna hurt. Geez, what a coward. I am so yellow. "A pinch and a burn," she said. I know the drill. As usual, the serum cramped my muscle and burned going in. My coping strategy for the ten seconds of discomfort has always been to remind myself that this pain is nothing compared to the intense pain of the reconstructive surgery. Certainly, I can handle this. When the nurse injected me in my right tricep I mutely repeated, "I've had major surgery. I've had...[Oww]...major...[Eeeep]...surgery. Oooooh." Once finished, she rubbed the site, and I berated myself. What a chicken! A friend, who is a pancreatic cancer survivor, told me she still gets nervous over something as simple as a dental filling which doesn't make sense to her since she's been through a whole heck of a lot more pain when she underwent major surgery and all that goes with it. I know what she's talkin' about.

Pulling my sweater on, I covered the yellow stripe that ran the length of my back.

What happened next was the feeling that a solemn cloud floated over me. I surveyed the chemo room while I stood. This was my last time. The final final. The tears are coming...fight 'em, Wendi. Fight 'em. Don't upset any of the chemo patients. They are still receiving chemo. They might not understand the emotion. Heck...I don't understand the emotion. I did a mental salute; stood at attention. Ten-hut. The nurses applauded me, but quite candidly, this felt like a conquest undeserving of fanfare. Completing chemo felt like a victory with a void, because no one can tell me the treatments worked or that the cancer is gone. No one can tell me that I am the victor. Words could not half convey the emotions that were screaming in my head. In my head, I moved in the direction of groveling. I wanted to ask: May I have one more treatment please? Just in case?? Let me come back in two weeks. I promise I'll be good. How about I stay right here, with the other patients? Oh, please don't make me go. I feel safe here, fighting cancer. Please let me stay. Instead, I looked at them and smiled wordlessly. It's time for me to go. I gripped the certificate they gave me and said good-bye to the chemo room, lowered my head and walked out. I felt empty as I left the cancer center.

I will, however return for blood work and monthly examinations to determine if the cancer returns. Sounds re-active to me. Can't we do something pro-active? Unfortunately, there is no test we can take to predict cancer. Because the only way to check for cancer has always been to find evidence of it after it appears, we'll look for evidence. I will:

- *Do my monthly breast self-exams of my right breast and report changes to my doctors (Other unrelated incidences of breast cancer sometimes occur in people. Can you believe that?)*
- *Continue getting annual mammograms to my right breast*
- *Attend monthly appointments with my oncologist so she can manually feel for changes in my liver and listen to my lungs (in case this specific incidence of breast cancer moves to my organs)*
- *Report unusual pains in my bones so they can do x-rays or bone scans (in case this incidence of breast cancer moves to my bones)*

In the meantime, I will continue to look in the mirror at least once a day and say, "I am cancer free." And I will try to believe it. I am told that believing it gets easier to do with the passing of time.

Lately, I have learned to estimate my energy and use it when it is important to. It is like watching the gas gauge on your dashboard or the battery indicator on your cell phone; you use it freely when you have plenty of fuel or battery power. Likewise, you use it sparingly when it's low. Finally, you start planning when and where to refuel.

It was essential to me to be with Christine when she went back to college on the afternoon of my Neulasta® shot, so I used some of my energy for that. Winter break was over; it was time for her to go. A few hours after having left the cancer center, Dan, Danny, Christine, her friend, Vanessa, and I piled in the SUV headed for Immaculata, Pennsylvania. Her Tourette's syndrome flared up recently and, during the break, became aggressive. In the vehicle she was jolting and jerking uncontrollably, and she hardly spoke. When asked why she was so quiet, she said she was feeling anxiety about going back to school without having her TS under control.

So, she and I were experiencing similar feelings on the same day: We were both being required to do something we didn't want to do. Wrapped in a blanket and holding a pillow on my lap, I rested in the passenger seat. I felt reasonably okay, but I knew that by nightfall I'd be out of sorts, so I peacefully savored the hour with her.

I felt safe in the knowledge that my family watched over me that evening. They always do, but it was especially meaningful to me that night. I was acutely aware of the arrival of the fever and bone pains. They came on so fast this time. I began to whimper. I surrender. Uncle! I said goodnight to my mom, and my mother-in-law took a turn at walking me up the steps while I shivered. She pulled the covers over me and I settled in for the long night that lay ahead. The phone rang and my fitful sleep was interrupted. According to the clock, it has been an hour since I went to bed. Christine's Tourette's syndrome was on the warpath and she needed me. Thank God I don't have to hold my role, as a mother, at bay. During troubled times, there's no place like home…and second to that, your mother's voice over the telephone. She was crying. My maternal function took the lead role and cancer was forced into the back seat for a while; my baby girl needed me. I talked through some relaxation techniques I have been practicing since I got cancer. Eventually she began to calm down. And so did I. Each of us, in our own beds, miles apart, with phone receivers resting across our faces, was drifting to sleep. Weren't we a pair!

The next few days were a blur. I stayed in my familiar place on the couch for most of each day. I utilized the downtime to sit with my laptop and write. Writing keeps me sane.

Each morning, I would awaken and vow that it would be the day I would begin to feel better, but I could not get the mind-over-matter thing to work. The melancholy moods had me stifled. Depression gripped me heavily – perhaps due to the cumulative effects of the treatments, or perhaps because I knew this was the last chance for the medicine to actively fight the cancer cells in my body. I am truly scared about my future. So now what do I do? Will cancer find its way into my life again? Is there nothing I can do? I simply wait and see? Ugh. No one can tell me I am cured. No one can tell me it's gone.

Whenever I realized it would not be a good day, I gave in to the misery and looked forward to the next morning with high expectations of feeling better.

Soon, I will call the toll-free Survivor's Help line number I found at the Living with Breast Cancer website. It states that I can talk to a breast cancer survivor who understands what I will be facing once chemo stops. According to the professionals at the Wellness Community, where Dan and I attend support group sessions, it is common to experience emotional difficulties at this time.

Over the course of a few days, I rooted through my box of things and paperwork I have collected since my diagnosis. I found copies of special reports from www.philly.com: Cancer Chronicles – Philadelphia Inquirer. I enjoyed reading about the reporter's personal cancer journey as well as some reflections from readers who wrote in.

The kids and I were talking over the weekend. We reflected on some funny situations. When the girls read my last update, they laughed at what Michele said about my chemo brain. Andrea capitalized, "Oh yeah? Last week Mom called me Adrienne and another time she called me Angela. Mom's losing it."

Christine added, "Mom forgot my phone extension at IU. She's called it fifty times probably, but suddenly forgot it. Four girls at IU told me, "Your mom called. She sounded confused; she thought she called your number. Mom's definitely losing it."

There were more stories, like putting foods to be kept refrigerated in the cupboards, forgetting what something is called, and burning range covers after turning the wrong dials. Okay girls, so I'm the brunt of your jokes, eh. Thaaaaanks. I simply must re-adjust my will.

On Monday morning I arose with high hopes. I sat on the side of the bed and realized the shakes were gone. Dare I hope? My feet touched the floor and I felt no pain in my heels. Could it be? Ahhhh, today is my day! I metaphorically stepped outside myself and looked. Here is what I saw: A prisoner who had been lying for days in a curled position. I saw myself in a hole in the ground with filth and dampness surrounding me. What covered the hole and kept me in total darkness had been lifted. I knelt on unsteady knees and placed my hands over my eyes to shield the bright sun. I had not seen a flicker of light for days. My head came up out of the hole. Through squinting eyes, I saw people standing over me. Their hands were extended, ready to pull me out. My loved ones were smiling. I climbed out and felt fresh air in my lungs. The air tingled my skin. Oh, it was magnificent and glorious. I was overjoyed to be out of the gloomy and dank surroundings.

> ...What covered the hole and kept me in total darkness had been lifted...Through squinting eyes, I saw people standing over me. Their hands were extended, ready to pull me out.

Given that I was feeling better and able to drive, I brought Christine home from college for an EEG on Wednesday. Her girlfriend came too and stayed at the neurologist's office while I went to an appointment with one of my doctors. It began to snow flurry. After our appointments, we three met Dan for a wonderful lunch at a jewel of a place called Edda's, in Trolley Square. It has been there for quite sometime, but is under new ownership. It's a bistro that features Mediterranean cuisine and the usual stuff that we Americans like. The food is prepared in unique and yummy ways. I appreciate simple pleasures even more than I did before I got cancer, the meal, the company, the snow; all good stuff, all simple pleasures. Snow was sticking on the ground and it was coming down more persistently now. When the three of us arrived home, Andrea and Michele each had a friend over. I needed a nap, but it seemed a perfect time to serve mugs of hot chocolate with marshmallows and fresh-baked cookies. And so, I did. We pulled the vertical blinds back from the sliding glass doors to watch the snow build up on the deck. Then, three out of seven of us dozed to the sound of MTV and the smell of warm snicker doodles. Life is wuuuuunderful.

Two of my physicians recommended I take a vacation. My oncologist said it is common for patients to celebrate and rest during the break between chemo and radiation. I wasn't sure if you would understand or not that I was taking a holiday (since I am still on medical leave). I hope you do. We went to Florida to visit relatives, treated the kids to some theme parks and relaxed at our timeshare. It was very cathartic. Looking back, I needed it even more than I realized. On my Florida vacation, I slept on a bench at Disney's Magic Kingdom, closed my eyes in a gift shop at Sea World, catnapped on Uncle Earl and Aunt Lou's bed, snoozed on cousin Linda's couch, and dozed at my sister-in-law's new home. Wasn't this what George Washington did? "George Washington slept here", "George Washington slept there." Next I'll cut down a cherry tree.

Since I started Taxol® treatments, my fingernails became discolored and ridged, but I never lost any. I know some people who did. Gross. A few of the nail beds under my fingernails had receded, but they are already growing back. My fingers are still tender, so others help me pull zippers and open jars. I think I see the start of tiny hairs on my head; however it may be wishful envisioning. My taste buds are returning to normal. In fact, this last week, I ate more than I generally would have. It all tasted so good. I am certain I gained a few pounds as a result.

Before I left for vacation, I met with a radiation oncologist for a consultation. Today, Dan and I are scheduled for a planning session with the radiation oncology team. Since I have some reservations about this form of treatment, I have many questions to ask.

During my state of unrest after the last chemo treatment, I pulled out greeting cards I received as far back as September. I marveled at the ones with exquisite artwork, smiled at the humorous ones, and became absorbed in the motivating verses that were in the inspirational cards. And, in all of them, the handwritten notes moved me. While reading them I felt blanketed by a peculiar occurrence, like I was in a time warp: The thoughts of utter gratitude I had the moment I read each card for the first time, returned. Oddly, so did my original mood, physical state, and the essence of my then emotions. For each, I was flashed into the particular instant in time when I first opened the card. Awesome. The human mind is powerful. I can only describe this as a supernatural, kind of déjà vu.

As I studied and appreciated each card, I was bowled over by all that transpired in several months. So far, I've had three surgeries and sixteen weeks of chemo. I have one surgery and possibly six weeks of radiation to go. Wow. All of this just to live? You'd better believe it, baby!!

Happy Groundhog Day,
Wendi

Mark, a colleague says, in a voice mail message:

I just finished reading your update. A big part of me just waits until the next one. It is wonderful sharing your adventure...Hang in for the radiation and be the fighter that you have been to date...The days are getting longer, so spring is coming and life renews...You're definitely on the road to finding your way back to work. Getting back to a normal routine must seem like a wonderful goal...Keep those updates coming – we all really appreciate them.

Anne, another colleague writes:

I have read with much emotion all your letters since the beginning of your journey. I had told you how much I would like to be with you at the end of this project, as I was at the end of other projects with you at AZ. And here I am, here you are, but this project cannot be wrapped because this project is called "life." I read your last message and heard your anxiety. It was heart breaking. There is so much we take for granted day after day; and you were part of it and the cancer took you away. For me, the end of your chemo trip is like having you back on these shores. I rejoice that you are back. So much has changed and so much has been tested. But you are the same, our Wendi full of life and questions and desire to do more, do better. Warm wishes.

Tip 135 Go to www.breastcancer.org and click on the Emotional Recovery and Renewal tab. There's a wealth of information and advice.

THE CONNECTIONS BECAUSE OF CANCER ARE AMAZING

Dan is building a fire in the fireplace and from his stack of newspaper he uses as fire starter I see a picture in a January issue that piques my curiosity. It says that Mrs. Gore, wife of the late W.L. Gore, founder of W.L. Gore Incorporated, has died. I touch my abs and know that, thanks to them I have a Goretex® patch there. It prevents me from having a hernia by holding my organs in. *So many things impact me now, that wouldn't have before cancer.*

I receive an e-mail from my newfound chemo friend, Patty. During a few of my chemo rounds she attempted to talk with me. Each time I unintentionally snubbed her (I fell asleep). When we finally did get to have a real conversation, we were amazed to discover that we have a great deal in common besides breast cancer. She and I will probably keep in touch long after breast cancer treatments end and I won't refer to her as 'my new-found chemo friend'. 'Friend' will suffice.

Today is February 3; three days before Super Bowl Sunday. The Philadelphia Eagles are NFC champions. *Hooray Eagles!* Currently, they are in Jacksonville, Florida awaiting the 39th Super Bowl game and the chance to play the AFC champions, the New England Patriots. On the cover of the local paper, there's a picture of a Philadelphia Eagles Assistant Coach, his mom, his sister, and grandmother.

In an e-mail to me, Patty writes:

> *Did you see today's News Journal? On the front page is an article about [Assistant Eagles Coach, Mike Reed] and his Mom. I sat next to [his mom] several times during treatments never knowing who she was until my most recent visit when she told us she was going to the Super Bowl! She is the sweetest person. You never know who you're sitting next to…on the bus, on the train or during chemo!*

Well, maybe Patty sat next to an author too and never knew it. At the urging of many recipients of my e-mail updates, I've decided to write a manuscript. I have high hopes that it will be inspiring and unique enough to become a published book.

Wouldn't it be magnificent to provide people with a (hopefully) wonderful reading experience and help breast cancer patients get through their treatment by telling my story? What a dream. I have already made some decisions: If this book comes to fruition, I want it to be multi-dimensional; it will include the compassionate things others say about my journey, about cancer, and about me. And, what will be exceedingly beneficial is the mention of resources. *Yes, good idea.* I will incorporate the names of books and pamphlets I have read, which served (and continue to serve) as informational aids. Websites and phone numbers will appear in the book, also (barring legalities, of course). Oh, I am excited. Wow.

Several times, I look at [Mike Reed's mom's] photo in the newspaper. [She] doesn't look like a chemo patient. She looks healthy. She's got short hair, a pretty face and a vibrant smile. Her face doesn't show any signs of a cancer treatment ordeal. Perhaps she and Patty sat together much earlier. After all, Patty, like me, is undergoing sixteen weeks of chemo. Maybe her short hair is her post-chemo do. Or maybe it began growing back during Taxol®. Hair can begin growing back as early as three weeks after the last AC treatment. As a patient with no hair, eyebrows or eyelashes, I don't want to see a beautiful, striking woman with cancer. I want her to look like me. Whenever I pick up a book about a cancer survivor and there are photos in it, I want to see a cancer look, which is what I did today. *Am I a behaving like a martyr?*

If someone asks if I have breast cancer, how do I reply? In past or present tense? Do I say I have breast cancer? *What if it's gone?* Do I say I had breast cancer? *What if it's not gone?* And what do I do when I am filling-out a questionnaire and it asks me to rate my health? Do I check the box beside *Excellent, Good, Fair or Poor?*

Dr. M reminds me that good health is not the absence of disease; it is feeling well. As soon as I begin to feel excellent, I will say that I am in excellent health.

I go for my last weekly blood draw. As usual, each of the techs engage in pleasant conversation with me, and one takes two vials, tapes the site when she's done and smiles a genuine smile. I bid them all a 'see you soon', because I will be returning for occasional blood work. There's more in store for me at "the Helen Graham." It's not just a center to treat the sick; it's a place to maintain the healthy.

Dealing With the Gloom

Two weeks ago, I met a woman whose breast cancer recurred in October as breast-lung cancer, eight years after her breast cancer. Then, two months ago she got another kind of breast cancer in her other breast. *Ugh.* What if my breast cancer recurs as lung cancer? What if it recurs as bone or brain cancer? And, what if I get breast cancer again? I still have a breast so it could happen. If it comes back as lung cancer will I have trouble breathing? That would be horrible. Even as a kid I hated when friends dunked me in the pool and I couldn't breathe.

These thoughts…oh, these thoughts. They are fleeting, but they accumulate and frighten me. Will I always think like this? How do I keep them from affecting me? Or my family? Am I a whack job?

I express some of my gloomy concerns to Jill. (Not all of them though – geez, I don't want to bring her down with me.) The conversation is therapeutic. She tells me that the what-ifs will happen whether I worry about them or not. *What if* I get breast cancer again in my right breast in eight years? And, *what if*, in eight years, I am watching Michele receive a Master's degree, Andrea get married or Christine give birth? What if, in twenty-eight years, I am sitting on a porch in a rocking chair with Danny's baby on my lap?

A heckuva thing happened to me the other day; I saw a psychiatrist! Well, I'll admit, it wasn't a chance meeting; it was planned. As I am learning, it is not a sign of weakness to accept emotional help at this crucial turning point in treatment. Frankly, I don't feel fragile, but I do feel powerless to ward off the morbid thoughts. When you deal with something life-threatening that could come back, fear is a major factor. I suspect it will be with me for a long time; that it will subside gradually, but recur from time to time. Hopefully, the psychiatrist can get me through the emotional impact of breast cancer and the completion of chemotherapy to eradicate it. She prescribed an anti-depressant. I filled the prescription...just in case.

Some days, I feel like I am in limbo, hanging between contentment and fear. I don't want to live a deceptive veneer of normality. I want to BE normal. And happy. And without fear.

I recall something I read that says anti-depressants can serve a temporary medical need, since depression is one way to deal with pain of treatment for and healing of a physical illness. They are not just for ongoing psychiatric or emotional situations. *Oh brother. This is not an ongoing condition...is it? I hope it is temporary. Lord knows I'm trying to get over this.*

Some people tell me they cry when they read my updates. I feel a little guilty about that; my intention is not to sadden folks. However, if they feel a little of my pain whenever I am in low places, they will also share in my joy whenever I reach the summits. I am pleased to give joy.

More often, they tell me they feel moved. They say they are honored to be part of my 'updates' distribution list. Another associate writes:

> I close my door when I see your updates in my mail. I read them in private. They are that good. The way you courageously share with us is inspirational.

Tip 136 Some people enjoy reading creative-style writing. If you are one of them, check out a book by Judy Hart called, *Love, Judy: Letters of Hope and Healing for Women With Breast Cancer.* She, like me, takes folks on her journey by writing letters. I, like Judy, feel that the recipients of my updates are part of my journey. Another author who writes messages to her family and friends, and shares lighter moments of her treatment is Patty Gelman who wrote *Humor After the Tumor.*

I feel glum. I take advantage of a wonderful resource; the Junior Board Cancer Resource Library at "the Helen Graham." *Comprehensive. User-friendly. Cancer-focused.* I sign out a book that looks like a promising source for my emotional state: *After Breast Cancer: Answers to the Questions You're Afraid to Ask,* by Musa Mayer. I place it on my nightstand for times when I wake up in the night and my thoughts become filled with fears and concerns.

I also place a book on my nightstand to read in tandem with '*After*', and it is called *Why Me? Why Now? Finding Hope when you have Breast Cancer,* by Lorraine V. Murray. I found it amongst my collection of cancer-related books. The receipt is inside. I bought this book on November 14? Why I haven't read it until now is beyond me. *Or, maybe it's another of God's coincidences.* The author weaves her tale about how she was able to face cancer by putting "Christ in the driver's seat." Part III is entitled, Recovery. Hmmm. This might be a timely book.

> **Tip 137** *After Breast Cancer: Answers to the Questions You're Afraid to Ask,* by Musa Mayer is a great resource for cancer patients and caregivers when the cancer patient is at least half way through his or her treatment plan. It includes common fears after treatment ends, stories and advice from other survivors, follow-up testing, facts about recurrence, how your risk lessens over time, and ways to reduce your "worry time."

Knowing that I can give a lift to someone, will perhaps give me a lift too. Dear Diary, today I vow to do something special that will make someone smile: I buy a bag of truffles individually wrapped in pretty colored foils. I place them in the mailbox out front and put the red flag in the *up* position.

> **Tip 138** If surprising people makes you happy – do it. Most importantly, do whatever brings you joy. Many things contribute to your healing: Fun and humor are two of them.

> **Tip 139** Caregivers as well as cancer patients should make time to feel good. Read, watch *Comedy Central TV*, have lunch with friends, knit, paint, play golf, do quilting, do gardening, see a

Broadway show, go skeet shooting, have a theme party by gathering friends and watching episodes of *Friends, Sex in the City* or *Sopranos*...WHATEVER is your mecca, do it!

RADIATION – HERE WE GO

I am refocusing my battle with "the invader." So, let's talk Radiation Therapy 101. I'll call it RT. This form of therapy uses radiation to kill cancer cells. In my case, RT is being aimed at two places; where my malignant tumor was and where the cancerous lymph nodes were. The goal is to target those areas while minimizing exposure to surrounding normal, healthy tissue and organs. A large machine called a linear accelerator will beam radiation to the sites from outside my body. Each RT treatment will take only a few minutes and be painless. Kind of like an x-ray. RT doesn't sound threatening probably because most of us have had x-rays, but I recall reading about studies that show emergence of other kinds of cancers, like leukemia and skin cancer, to be higher in patients who received RT than those who didn't. I'll have to do some research to educate myself about this. Still, it seems that the benefits far outweigh the risks. If I get another form of cancer from RT years from now, perhaps by then there will be a cure. So, I'll cross that bridge IF I come to it.

During the consultation visit two weeks ago, I asked the radiation oncologist if he would recommend radiation for his wife or daughter if they were in my situation. He energetically rattled off several variations of *yes*.

Tip 140 If you haven't already, this is a good time to weigh the risks and benefits of radiation: Read what the cancer websites tell you (my favorites are www.cancer.org and www.breastcancer.org) and ask, ask, ask your radiation oncologist. Additionally, arm yourself with an understanding of the radiation treatment process: For caregivers as well as cancer patients, I found these books to be helpful: *Just Get me Through This!* By Deborah A. Cohen and Robert M. Gelfand, M.D., *Radiation*, pages 168 to 181, and *Uplift!* By Barbara Delinsky (*Radiation: Soaking up the Rays*, pages 41 to 56). Both books are not only informative, but they are, believe it or not, fun to read.

It is Wednesday. I have thought about it; I am going forward with radiation therapy. Dan and I meet at "the Helen Graham" for the simulation appointment. This is the second step before actual RT begins. According to a guide published by Christiana Care, prior to receiving treatment, most patients have a simulation CT scan to record images of the parts of the body to be treated. Mine is today.

In seven to ten days, they will have my RT prepared and will call me for the simulation check. The day after that, I will start my first treatment. At this time, the plan is to have twenty-eight.

> **Tip 141** Write in a journal or notebook. Keep track of your radiation appointments, symptoms, side effects, lab test results and any medications you are taking. This information may be helpful for your radiation oncologist to know.

Super Bowl Sunday, woo hoo! Most everyone is full of football, half time, and television commercial mania. And so am I. Sporting one of my nifty, breast-cancer-pink Eagles hats, I am prepared for the event...

...Okay, so the Eagles didn't win. Life is full of disappointments. We should accept them and get over them. Lord knows, I've worked at getting over my disappointment of having cancer. Congratulations, Patriots! I am genuinely happy for Patriots fans and my colleagues at AZ who are located at the Boston site, for I am sure they are dancing in the streets, and in their homes, and at the pubs.

Dear Diary, I will do something special that will make someone smile: I keep my promise to myself...[and my diary]... and, on our way home from our Super Bowl get together at Charles and Lisa's, I decide not to use the EZ-Pass lane. Instead I use a pay toll lane and pay an extra dollar for the car behind me.

This morning, Dan and I quarrel. He leaves for work and I sit and stew. I conclude that I have been a little grumpy.

> **Tip 142** Caregivers, forgive your loved one if she is occasionally irritable or unkind. If, however, she is bad-tempered for a prolonged period of time or with severity, gently talk to her about it,

> or offer to find support for her. She may be experiencing clinical depression, in which case talk-therapy and/or medication can help.

Later in the day, I have a fateful telephone conversation with Andréa G, my colleague and a sister-in-faith. I explain that I haven't been in touch with people very much because I've been so blue and I haven't wanted to share the melancholy moods with anyone. She told me, "Did you ever think that you might be robbing someone of the chance to help you?" Wow. No. *That's what I love about the human race...we have so many viewpoints. Like flavors of ice cream. Andréa's optimistic viewpoint cheers me.*

Then, Andréa generously offers to three-way God into our telephone conversation. I'm envious of the way she can talk with Him. In the past, she has prayed openly with me for peace and healing during my surgery and my cancer treatments. *She is able to talk so freely with God.* Today, she prays for my gloom and for Christine's struggle with Tourette's Syndrome.

Dear Diary, I vow to do something special that will make someone smile: So, I am on my way to buy a helium balloon and write on it, "Today is my last chemo treatment." Next stop: To visit Patty at "the Helen Graham."

GENETIC COUNSELING – A GIFT TO MY CHILDREN

I was going to bring Danny with me, but he said he wanted to go to daycare. I took him to Miss Sheri's and thank goodness I did because I have been here for two hours chatting away with Patty, a physician friend of hers, and her sister. This feels great. Among other things, Patty is concerned about cancer and her children. She tells me about genetic counseling and a blood test she received to determine if she is a carrier of a cancer gene (or something like that). *BRCA was it?* I have my children to consider too. I go downstairs and make an appointment with the genetic counselor. *Cool.* She can see me at the end of March. This is the first week of February. Hmmm, that's a long wait. Her services must be in demand.

I can wait. What if I test positive as a carrier and my children have a 50/50 chance of getting cancer? The upside to that question would be that my children would hopefully do monthly exams and pay attention to body and skin changes. The downside would be that my children might get cancer. And, what if I test negative as a carrier? Will my children become lax? Will it matter if my daughters have gene mutations, alterations or duplications and they decide to use oral contraceptives at anytime in their lives? I think I won't stress over these questions; much will be revealed to me in the consultation.

Tip 143 Write down your questions about upcoming consultations, even if they are months away, and keep them in your binder for future use. That way, you don't have to try to recall them. I found some information about genetic tests, BRCA1 and BRCA2 genes, and gene abnormalities in Dr. Kaelin's book, *Living through Breast Cancer*, on page 18. And, if you have concerns about oral contraceptives and cancer risk (breast, ovarian, cervical, etc.), then search the National Cancer Institute's site or type the following address: http://cis.nci.nih.gov/fact/3_13.htm.

I recently finished reading Gilda Radner's book, *It's Always Something*. She was a member of the first cast of *Saturday Night Live's* Not Ready for Prime Time Players, and she died of ovarian cancer. I am glad I read her book, but am thankful I did not read it any sooner than now. I don't think I would have been emotionally able to read it while I was in a positive mindset and actively fighting cancer with chemo; it would have negatively impacted my focus. Gilda courageously shared the details of her journey in her book as I am in my updates and in my manuscript. I am not a celebrity, though.

In an e-mail update I talk about how cancer patients are advised to keep a journal. I tell my friends, colleagues and loved ones that my writing sessions are often rambling, but helpful.

Tip 144 If writing keeps you sane, honor the rambling.

Maybe it is not long life that I want (although it would be nice to see my children and their children grow), rather it is a fulfilling life that I want. I believe I can have a fulfilling life if I can get these awful thoughts and fears out of my head.

I am sure many of my friends and family are tempted to tell me I will be physically and emotionally okay, but I need to find my own way and reach these conclusions in my time. Which is why those folks, who have left messages, sent e-mails, and mailed cards, may be wondering why they haven't heard from me. I am in such a funk. Some days, I just don't have much to say, or I do but am limited in the time I have because of fatigue.

I AM BLOOMING – MY HAIR IS GROWING IN

Today is Wednesday, February 9, almost one month since my final chemo treatment. I notice tiny white hairs sprouting from my eyelids. I think I am getting eyelashes! *Woo hoo!*

I hope they don't stay white.

Thursday morning – I awaken with a bit of a migraine. *Hmmm.* The first one since September. Since my migraines were triggered mainly by the onset of my monthly period, does this mean my periods will be returning? *Egads.* Get out the razor; I'll be shaving my underarms soon. Here we go; migraine meds, sanitary protection and, I suppose, in a few years another menopause...a real one this time. *Yeesh.*

'Let-down' is the term that describes the feeling a nursing mother feels when her milk fills her breasts moments before or just after her baby begins suckling. I swear I just felt 'letdown' in my left breast. *Weird, because it's not a real, functioning breast. There are no milk ducts or breast tissue.* I wonder if what I felt was the return of nerves and sensation. Dr. D said over the next year the nerve-endings would change so that my breast mound will no longer feel numb to the touch.

Why can I look forward to a year from now and think about some sensation in my breast, and then wonder if I'll even be here in a year? *How paradoxical.*

After Breast Cancer is a book that is helpful to read. It is a different kind of book for women diagnosed with breast cancer (Mayer, p. xi). It is about dealing with uncertainty and preparing for readiness during the vulnerable post-treatment period when everyone expects cancer patients to get back into the swing of life. I highly recommend it.

> **Tip 145**   Even if you are not struggling psychologically after treatment ends (and especially if you are), read *After Breast Cancer*, by Musa Mayer. I care about you, so please read it.

LETTERS, LOTS OF NOTES, AND MORE LETTERS

Last week, at my cancer support group meeting, I expressed my concerns about not being here for my children, especially when they reach milestones in their lives (graduation, career choices, marriage, births; etc.). The group talked about preparing for the future even if you got a clean bill of health or heard the word "cured." A person could have a car accident and be gone in an instant, so we all should think about preparations. That's precisely why folks who are in excellent health have wills, powers of attorney, money for burial expenses, and life insurance. Addressing my concern about the emotional well-being of my children, Jim (one of the members of the group) gave me an idea. He told me I should consider writing letters for those milestone events. I think it's a great concept, but the thought of any one of my children reading a letter from a deceased mom on her or his wedding day would make them too sad. Maybe. Plus, I have to come up with something all-encompassing and inspirational. The task seemed too large so I procrastinated.

Until today. I have a conversation with Jack, who has been without Cheryl for several months now. He tells me that she wrote each of their kids and him a letter, to be opened when she died. He said, with strong emotion in his voice, that they treasure those letters. So, I am modifying Jim's suggestion based on Jack's sentiments – I will write random letters to my loved ones and they don't have to be awe-inspiring (and therefore, the task will always be easy). I write my first batch, on yellow legal paper (nothing fancy), and in my own handwriting (not typed). They are short. In fact, the one to little Danny is about what he wore to daycare today for a Valentines Day party, what PBS cartoons we watched this morning, and how much I can't wait to see him this afternoon. For Michele, I talk about how excited I am that she's getting her driver's permit tonight. I write letters to Dan, the kids, my sisters and my brother. And, as things come up, I'll keep writing letters and stuffing them under my mattress. *I'd better consider a fireproof box.*

WILL, LIVING WILL, POWER OF ATTORNEY, AND HEALTHCARE POWER OF ATTORNEY

Tip 146 Cancer reminds us all that we should have our affairs in order, but not just for cancer. Everyone should have his or her affairs in order. If you haven't already, do some practical planning by making an appointment with an attorney to document a will, living will, power of attorney, healthcare power of attorney; etc. Consider life insurance options, too, especially if you have dependents. As for the emotional planning, try writing letters, recording voice messages on tape or recording yourself on video. Cancer or no cancer: Do what you think your loved ones will appreciate having long after you are gone. And then, because you took such care to prepare for a time when you won't be around, you'll probably outlive them all! Murphy's law.

RADIATION SIMULATION CHECK

Today is my third appointment to prepare for radiation. It is my simulation check to verify that the treatment planned for me will be delivered as prescribed (Christiana Care pamphlet, p.5). Using x-rays and laser lights (red beams of light) the therapists check and record the targeted areas (under my left breast and my left armpit) and the exact positions for the treatments.

I am feeling a little anxiety about radiation and its side effects; my family cannot help here so I do not burden them with my worries. I go to www.breastcancer.org, search on 'radiation' and click on 'open chat room'. Anyone can go to this site and talk to people around the world, twenty-four hours a day, seven days a week. I get testimonies from people who are pleased they had radiation therapy. Also, I talk to a few breast cancer survivors from the list I created months ago, and ask them to confirm their conviction in this form of treatment.

I am convinced enough to begin. Tomorrow is my first radiation treatment. Before I go to bed, I brush my teeth with toothpaste my dentist prescribed. It has a large amount of fluoride in it, which will help during radiation. (Some dentists are of the opinion that when radiation affects bone, it can also affect teeth. It is a precaution that I found easy to take.) I am ready for radiation in as many ways as I can think of, even down to my toothpaste.

> **Tip 147** Inform your dentist of your radiation treatments and request prescription-strength fluoride toothpaste. Mine recommended SF 5000 Plus, by Cypress Pharmaceutical, Inc.

Michele received her "blue slip" from her Drivers' Education teacher. It's time to get her driving license. What a major step! Oh, how I wish I could take her to Delaware Motor Vehicle, but I just don't have the energy. "It's really okay, Mom," she said. *I hope she means that.* Unlike when we took Christine and Andrea, Dan will take Michele without me.

Tuesday afternoon, February 15, time to go to my appointment. *One of twenty-eight. I can do this.* I have the portable CD player and the CDs, which became my friends during chemotherapy (*For People with Cancer,* by Belleruth Naparstek and *Getting Ready,* by Bernie S. Siegel, M.D). I write about this experience in my March 3rd Update.

Tonight, at the Grammy Awards, the Lifetime Achievement Award is given to the late Janice Joplin. Melissa Etheridge sings Ms. Joplin's song *Take Another Piece of my Heart.* She wows the crowd with her powerhouse singing, high energy and baldhead. She's my hero. *How does she have so much energy? She must be finished with chemotherapy. How is she finished so soon? She was diagnosed with breast cancer a few weeks after me. Maybe she did not have the Taxol®. I wonder if, when her performance was complete, she went backstage and took a nap.*

Update: February 17, 2005

Hello All,

"Courage is not a lack of fear, but the ability to act while facing fear." Author unknown.

Good quote. So, how do I act? Never before have I questioned myself as I have recently. I think courage has escaped me. As you may have been able to tell in the previous update, a great deal of change took place in the weeks following the end of chemotherapy; I moved from calm to scattered to panic.

While we were in Florida resting between chemo and radiation, I met a woman named Roxanne. She is from Canada. She finished her treatments three months ago. Among other things, we shared our fears. I told her I was worried about my future and couldn't stop the morose and gloomy thoughts. "…and I feel weepier now than I ever did," I confided. One thing Roxanne said to me, that has been sticking in my mind, was that my state of mind is similar to post-traumatic stress syndrome. Her analogy was, "Fighting cancer is like a car accident. When it's over is when you realize the magnitude of what you've been through, and you break down." She looked me squarely in the eye, "You've had your car accident."

Such is post-traumatic stress syndrome; I suppose Roxanne's correct, I have had my car accident.

Some days, I have had very little focus. I've been fatigued. I had intermittent negative thoughts that I kept in my head, away from my family. No need to bother them. I don't sleep well some nights; my thoughts are so active. There have been mornings when I was able to predict the coming twelve or fourteen hours as lying around in my flannel clothes and going to bed that evening in the same outfit I woke up in. If I didn't have children or a husband, I might not have bothered to get dressed in daytime attire at all. In retrospect, I have had days filled with non-productivity; I didn't write about my journey or compose e-mails. I neglected to return phone calls. I could not find motivation to pay bills, do yoga, cook a meal or take a shower.

But, in between those times, I have actually managed positive thoughts, energy and some fun events. It hasn't been depressing all the time.

Which leads me to my next bit of news; I started seeing a psychiatrist. Me! The eternal optimist. Can you believe it? I have been wrestling with the notion of going public with this news versus keeping it under wraps. I decided that it would be best to be frank. Taking anti-depressants (which I am also doing), in my case, is for a medical condition, not a psychiatric situation. Depression, to a cancer patient, I am reassured, is a common way to deal with the pain of treatment and healing. This is a temporary situation that I am in.

Then, the time to refocus my battle with "the invader" came. And not a minute too soon: I needed my warfare fix.

After I wrote the previous update to you, Dan and I went for my radiation therapy (RT) simulation appointment on Monday. (This was kind of a dry run before the real thing). We were at the cancer center when a medical staff member, Kathy, lead me to the dressing room to...[what else]...undress from the waist up. There's been a lot of this going on. I hope that when I return to work you'll excuse me if I inadvertently walk into an office and start undressing from the waist up. Then she led me around the corner to an extra wide and heavy looking door with a "Danger" sign on it. Behind it were two more staff members standing beside a sizable machine in a large, stark room. The intimidation I felt made my mouth do an involuntary impersonation of a kissing fish.

...Behind it were two more staff members standing beside a sizable machine in a large, stark room. The intimidation I felt made my mouth do an involuntary impersonation of a kissing fish.

They greeted me and helped me to lie down. Once I was in a horizontal position, the doctor, whom I met during the consultation a few weeks ago, appeared. Where did he come from, I wondered?   Man, I'm so skittish these days. All at once, the four professionals became a well-oiled team.

Each, quickly and efficiently, performed purposeful steps that contributed to the intended outcome; a CT scan, a mold and body markers.

Their gentle tones had a calming influence over my apprehension. Eventually, the echoes of the immense room were reduced and I concentrated on their soft voices as they explained what they were doing.

I was carefully positioned, such that I was facing the ceiling, my legs were straight, ankles uncrossed (so as not to twist the spine), my right arm was under my right hip and my left hand was under my neck, my left elbow extended outward from my body. There was a blue pillow supporting my head, it felt similar to a beanbag. All at once I felt it being pressed around my left elbow, and it began getting hard. Kathy explained that air was being sucked out of it so it could become permanently shaped. Afterward, it felt like a soft cardboard egg carton. Or, dried paper mache. This would become my mold. Someone would write my name on it, and when I get my radiation, I will lay in it. My mold. It'll hang on the rack with the other molds, waiting for me to use it each day.

I was told, "Breathe normally and do not move." I saw the backs of two lab coats and two nursing shirts walking away in a single file.   "We'll be back," was the last thing I heard. They were gone. I don't see a door. How did they exit?

A question popped into my head, "Why am I staying, but they are leaving?"   A second question came racing behind the first one, "Will this become a dangerous place?"   And, another "Isn't it a bit extreme for everyone to depart?"   HellOOOooo? Anybody here?

It was the worst of times. It was the best of times. Ugh. I have been through craziness lately and my rational thinking is affected. Oh brother, Wendi. Don't be so edgy. Hygienists and x-ray technicians leave the room when x-rays are taken; CT scan technicians do the same. Ah, there it is; the voice of reason. Ease up and don't be so jumpy.

There I was alone in the room, and I knew I'd be okay.

The table underneath me was perpendicular to a five foot round doughnut-shaped device. It's a CT scan machine. No big deal. I've had two or three of these since my diagnosis. The table moved into the round opening in the center. I held still, as they told me to. I didn't breathe normally though. I held my breath as long as I could when the machine was running. I've got to do what I can to get good pictures so the radiation will be accurate. Then, out of the blue, a tickle in my throat began...[don't cough]...and then grew. Ahem. Ah, ah, ahem. No satisfaction. The urge to cough sadskwas upon me. I allowed a tiny one to escape. And another. No satisfaction. I decided to hold my breath. The cough was coming, it's coming. Hold it. Then, my eyes began watering. Tears were imminent. Hold it in. Teardrops threatened to spill. And they did.

The troops returned. Again, I didn't see where they came from. Sheesh, am I in the Oval Office? The therapist saw my watery eyes. She patted my shoulder and said, "It's okay. Radiation can be upsetting."

I quickly corrected her assumption, "I'm not crying. I didn't want to screw up the CT scan. I didn't want to move. I was fighting a coughing spell." We chuckled and she handed me a tissue. I blew my nose.

Next, I was on my back once more. The technicians were placing "markers", and "reference points" on my upper abdomen and chest areas. The technicians explained what they were doing, as they were doing it. Tattoos? Did I hear them say, tattoos?

It felt like someone was sticking me with a safety pin over and over, or snapping a rubberband on my skin. Ouch.

Tattoos. I now have three! I have joined the ranks of people with body art. Well, my tattoos qualify...kind of. Good grief, actually they are so tiny, they look like black freckles. Two are located on each side of my abdomen and one in the center, a few inches above my belly button. The markers will allow the therapists to aim the radiation at the exact same position for every treatment. Fascinating.

The preparation that goes into an individualized radiation treatment plan is scientific, precise and intense. I understand that four people, in a subsequent planning session, studied the images taken during this simulation. The regimen of twenty-eight treatments will go like this: The Radiation Oncologist who developed the treatment plan will supervise the process for the duration of the treatments. I will meet with him every week. The Radiation Therapists will position me for the treatments and run the machine that will deliver the radiation. I will see them every weekday, twenty-eight times. Working behind the scenes, the Radiation Physicist will be responsible for the equipment and the Dosimetrist, under the supervision of the oncologist and physicist will calculate the amount of radiation being delivered to the cancer. I believe the Dosimetrist is also the technology person; I think this person had the responsibility of putting the plan into the computer.

On Tuesday, I officially began RT. This form of treatment uses radiation to kill cancer cells. In my case, radiation is being aimed at three places; where my malignant tumor was and where the cancerous lymph nodes were (my left armpit and collarbone). The goal is to target those areas while mini-mizing exposure to surrounding normal, healthy tissue and organs. Like, my heart. Please don't radiate my heart. A large machine called a linear accelerator beams radiation to the sites from outside the body. Each RT treatment takes only about fifteen minutes and is painless. Kind of like an x-ray. I will go to the cancer center every weekday for the next five and a half weeks.

I am relieved to be back in the arena fighting.

There is an element of anxiety in our society about radiation in general, possibly caused by movie industry fright flicks, radiation warning signs that appeared after WWII, and misunderstandings about nuclear power plants and meltdowns. I had concerns, but I now know that radiation, for the purpose of treating cancer, is used safely.

Meanwhile, tiny white buds have appeared where my new eyelashes will be. Tiny green buds are poking up from the ground where our daffodils will grow. Spring is sprouting and so am I.

The "chemo line" on my fingernails is growing out. There is a distinct line on each. The part of the nail above the line is discolored and ridged. The new part of each nail, below the line, is smooth and pink.

I know that life is happening for all of you while I am in treatment. I won-der who celebrated Mardi Gras, and how? And, what did folks do for Valentine's Day? At AZ, is the individuals'-objectives-process complete yet?

I know I have been uncertain and gloomy. I also know that it has reflect-ed in my writing, but don't get glum. An emotional part of my story is being lived here. So glad you are staying on for this part of the voyage. Knowing you are at the other end stimulates my positive sentiments and gives me peace. Many times, advice for cancer patients is to keep a jour-nal. I have and I do. The writing sessions are often rambling and expan-sive. My updates to you are abbreviated versions of my copious prose. Thank you for giving me reasons to write. Thank you for reading.

Stay with me please; I know that with you, I'm gonna make it after all. Strong mental image: Mary Tyler Moore spinning around with delight on a crowded city street and tossing her hat in the air. I'm humming the tune from the Mary Tyler Moore Show (1970-something, wasn't it?). Are you? ...*You're gonna make it after all..."* ? *Da, da, da, da, dah!*

I hope you had a wonderful Valentine's Day with loved ones!

Love to all,
Wendi

In case you are wondering, I didn't flash anyone during Mardi Gras. I didn't think a mastectomized-breast would get any beads.

My emotional recovery is proving to be a bit challenging. Writing the February 17 update was difficult. In hindsight, I had to do my own personal rewrites, because my thoughts were disjointed. It was impossible to keep my ideas together in a coherent fashion. I later realized that it was the stage of my illness.

Dale, a fellow rugby mom, writes (in response to my update):

There is a physiological, chemical reason for all of the negative feelings. That, combined with facing this change, accepting it and figuring out where you are going...your strength must come from different sources: religion, family, medication and even a psychiatrist. Call in the reinforcements I say! They are there for a reason and accepting their gifts makes you strong. Keep at it.

Susan, a colleague says:

This has been an incredibly long ordeal. I'm glad you're able to make some lemonade out of the lemons.

One week after the Grammy Awards, On NBC's Dateline, Stone Philips interviews Ms. Etheridge. She confirms that she felt her energy drop after the second verse of Janice Joplin's song. Ah hah. Okay then. She was paying attention to her gas gauge. Ms. Etheridge says she knew that her adrenaline could carry her through for two-and-a-half-minutes.

I agree with Mr. Philips. "Her performance in front of millions of people on music's special night was more than a musical act; it was an act of courage."

When asked about the chemotherapy, she and her partner, Tammy Lynn Michaels agreed that it was the closest to death that she's ever been. Together they survived the "in sickness and in health" vows.

As she is speaking, she exudes radiance. She says she was grateful "to be able to throw my head back and scream the last six months out of me..." *Hooray for you Melissa!*

Danny is sitting on my lap watching the show. He looks at Ms. Etheridge and then at me and says, "Look Mom, no hair just like you."

GIVE IN TO THE FATIGUE – YOUR BODY NEEDS REST

The quality and pace of my daily life are changing; to say that the radiation makes me tired is somewhat of an understatement. I knew to expect some fatigue after ten to twelve treatments. *But geez, I am beat...and after only five treatments...I'll look to the positive side of this and say that my body must be working harder than the average person's.* First, there is the time and energy required to organize and attend daily treatments. And, there is a physiological reason for the fatigue: the main purpose of radiation is to destroy stray cancer cells that might have been missed during surgery, but it also bombards healthy cells on a daily basis. The human body kicks into high gear to repair the damaged cells and uses a lot of energy to do so (Cohen and Gelfand, p. 179).

Some days I bring my camera to Primus One. I've seen pictures of chemotherapy in books, but none of radiation therapy. *It's pretty interesting stuff.* I take photographs of the blue body molds and the white net face molds.

It is Wednesday, February 23. A few nursing students at the University of Delaware attend our cancer support group meeting at the Wellness Community. We conducted ourselves as we usually do. I think they learned a lot from being with us. I hope they carry the experience with them once they graduate and go on to become nurses.

I enjoy my Wednesday night support group meetings and the people in them. Dan stopped going to the cancer caregivers' support group meetings. He, on the other hand, did not get as much out of his experience (though I will say he gave it a shot with an open mind), so he decided to discontinue.

Since my eyelash buds are prevalent and eyebrow hairs are beginning to emerge, I apply a little eye makeup for the first time in months. Today is Dan's birthday, *and a perfect time for a little eye makeup.*

GET OUT AND DO THINGS

We go to our favorite pub and restaurant, Six Paupers in Hockessin.

Several times, during my ordeal, we've gone to "Paupers" and seen friends. It has been a place I could go for an hour or two, have a glass of wine, a chocolate martini, cranberry juice or just plain water. One of the bartenders, Joseph, serves us beverages and places a few shot glasses on the bar in front of us, in an upside down position. This signifies we have drinks in the queue, bought for us by friends at the bar. Several people gather round to wish Dan happy birthday and while they do, they urge me to remove my hat. They tell me, "Make believe that we are at the Grammies." *Wow. Melissa Etheridge really broke ground for us cancer patients with no-hair days!* Even though I keep my hat on, it is comforting to know that if I removed it, I am surrounded by accepting people.

While we are on the topic of baldness, I brag that my head feels like a peach. Joseph-the-bartender smiles and says, "Begin with the fuzz!" *How many times has a bartender said that to his bar patrons!*

Update: March 3, 2005

Hello all,

The other day, Dan handed me a page of the March 1 News Journal with an article written by a radiation oncologist for Bayhealth cancer centers. It started with, "Perhaps no word in the English language engenders more fear than the word cancer." Man, oh man, you and I know what he's talking about, don't we? The radiation oncologist said that "every cancer survivor should realize that cancer is a chronic disease, one for which oncologists have excellent, effective therapies. Much like heart disease and arthritis – also chronic diseases – cancer can often be stabilized."

Dear diary, I will try to believe his words and the theory of cancer being stabilized.

Radiation, for me, will be complete on March 24. As I am nearing the end of my total cancer treatment plan (mastectomy, chemo and radiation), I am searching for ways to view this ordeal in retrospect and going forward (past and future). But, maybe I shouldn't look back. Perhaps a forward look is my best bet. So for the future, I should view my cancer – and that of anyone else I know who is finished with cancer treatment – as a chronic, treatable ailment...one that we should be wary of and take precautions to prevent [as in, a recurrence]. Perhaps I will think of a recurrence as a flare-up. After all, aren't flare-ups what happen with many chronic illnesses? So, if I ever have one, and I hope I don't, I'll try to see it as something I'll need to battle again, and not something that will take my life. Recently, I read in Parenting Magazine that twenty-two percent of women with breast cancer that spreads to their lymph nodes, as mine had, don't

*survive past five years. Well, I'm counting on being one of the 78 percent.
I think the odds aren't so bad.*

*Each day, at least once a day, I face myself in a mirror and say four words,
"I am cancer free." I then imagine what it looks and feels like to be healthy
and free of "the invader." I convince myself that I am [cancer free]. I say
it while I'm in the car. I say it in the radiation changing room. I say it in
the kitchen.   In a box, with a fox, in a room, with a broom...just kidding...got a little carried away. Obviously, little Danny has heard me say
the four words. He was playing with his dinosaurs a few days ago. They
were having an open dialogue...you know how sociable dinosaurs can
be...and "Mr Seratops" said to "Mr. Saurus", "My mommy is cancer
free."   Cool beans, Danny. Go Dino's.*

**... At times, I
feel like a rose
without a bloom,
but other days I
recognize signs
of emotional
recovery...**

*These days, I am still struggling with disturbing
thoughts. At times, I feel like a rose without a
bloom, but other days I recognize signs of
emotional recovery, e.g., I am preparing
meals, and volunteering for small tasks in
the girls' spring sports. And, I am focusing on a project: putting my updates into a
manuscript. Thank you, all of you, for
encouraging me to do this. Since I go to the
cancer center everyday, I oftentimes visit the
Christiana Care Junior Board Cancer Resource
Library to relax and read. I've concluded that there
is a market for a manuscript like mine, though it's a double-edged sword;
sadly, my manuscript could help many, many people. There are too many
people with cancer.*

*This would be a good time to thank Pfizer Pharmaceuticals for Zoloft®. It
does seem to be helping. When I'm feeling upbeat, I test myself and try
thinking dismally. Isn't that awful? Why do we question when something
is working? I discovered that my dark thoughts don't take me down as
deeply as they did before. And, I come up and out of the darkness faster.*

*Allow me tell you about radiation.   My first treatment was Tuesday,
February 15. It went like this:*

*Dan and I headed for the Radiology Oncology department at the cancer
center for my 6PM appointment. I was tense. If he was nervous, it wasn't
showing. We were sitting in the waiting room when the attendant called
my name. I followed where she was leading me, away from Dan. We were
about to go through a door, but not without looking over my shoulder to*

see him watch me go. He gave me the same slow wave and half smile that he did on the morning I had the most important surgery of my life. Rewind to six months ago; I will never forget that September morning walking through those double doors and over the brass plate, and then glancing back to see Dan standing there where I left him, trying to look brave.

Fast forward to March; in the changing room, there was a stack of freshly laundered robes that we radiation patients get to wear everyday. I reached for one and immediately recognized a familiar scent. It is utterly amazing how, in an instant, I had a strong recollection of something. What was it? Ahah. The scent of the freshly laundered robe brought back my sentimental memories of the four times I was in the maternity ward after having my babies. The robe reminded me of the gowns the labor and delivery nurses gave me after my babies were born. Having babies; oh, such magnificent times. Call me crazy, but I miss pregnancy and giving birth. How I wished I were putting on a hospital gown for a reason like bringing new life into the world, and not for cancer. How I wish I were using my breasts once again for nursing my babies and not viewing them as an enemy that I needed to cut away just to live.

Next, I was in the "Primus One" room scrutinizing my radiation protocol on the computer monitor or whatever parts of it I might comprehend. Yeah right, like I'm gonna understand it. In the upper left hand corner of the screen was my picture...for verification. Safety, always patient-safety.

The plan is: each day, four rounds targeted at three key places (two rounds angled at where the tumor was, below my left breast, one to where the cancer-positive lymph nodes were removed, under my left armpit, and one to where the nodes under my collar bone were removed).

The technician asked me to verify my birth date...(more verification). I was tucked in to my pillow-mold, while the therapists lined up the coordinates according to the plan and my position on the table (and my tattoos). "Can I scratch my nose?" I asked.

"Tell me where the itch is and I'll scratch it," the technician replied. Wow, it's really, really important not to move! So, there I was, lying perfectly still with one technician scratching my itch while another went about the business of radiation set-up. She taped a meter on me (to calculate the amount of radiation I receive – more verification). They left the room for the first detonation. The machine hummed and whined. It sounded like electric hair clippers that change pitches or the way a metal detector changes sounds when it detects metal. Bam! Zap! Take that!

They returned…[using that Oval office method I told you about in my last update]…checked my position; changed the location of the meter and left. The machine moved to reach me from another angle. It hummed. It whined. Bam! Hi-YAH!

In they came; checked, changed and left. The machine moved into position. It hummed. It whined. Bam! Cancer cells are now excrement! They are burnt like a newlywed's first self-cooked meal.

For the final hit, the machine moved to my right and came close to my face. I looked into its one eye and spoke out loud, "Oh helloooo. Nice to meet you. Helping me, eh? Have at it…do your thing." The machine hummed…whined. Bam! Woo hoo!

It was all over in less than ten minutes.

…If other patients or medical staff members are ever on the other side of my dressing room hearing the deep-breathing noises I make, I wish to say that I'm not having an asthma attack, nor am I having… [ahem]…closet sex. I am taking a walk down memory lane! …

Afterwards, I walked to the changing room to remove my gown and, before placing it in the laundry bin, I held it to my face and breathed deeply, the way a person smelling fresh sheets on a breezy summer day would. I did this several times, and I do it every single time I have a treatment. Ode to the newborn days gone by. I allow myself these 20-second luxuries that I call flashbacks, because I enjoy remembering the days my children were born. If other patients or medical staff members are ever on the other side of my dressing room hearing the deep-breathing noises I make, I wish to say that I'm not having an asthma attack, nor am I having…[ahem]…closet sex. I am taking a walk down memory lane!

On my way out the door, I reached into the basket on the counter and took a small tube of the provided ointment called Aquaphor® by Beiersdorf, Inc. I currently use the ointment once or twice each day to eliminate the possibility of burned or blistered skin, but never within four hours before a treatment so it doesn't actually cause a burn. At the time of this writing, I've had about a dozen treatments…no pigment changes yet.

So far, I have no side effects from radiation other than extreme fatigue. Radiation is not a systemic (total-body) treatment like chemotherapy, so why would a local treatment make my whole body tired? Simple: Radiation kills bad cells and in the process damages good cells. The body goes into overdrive to repair the good cells. An interesting tidbit; the radiation oncologist told me I may see an "exit tan" on my back where the radiation goes through me. Intriguing, huh?

My daily treatment times have been moved from 6 p.m.; they are now at 10:00 a.m. To date, I've had twelve. During the treatments, I use visualization techniques from Bernie S. Siegel, MD, to prepare and heal. On his CD, Dr. Siegel talks about a patient who experienced no burning on her skin. When asked, "How is this possible?" she said that, in her mind, she gets out of the way and lets the radiation do its thing. I follow the advice.

What's more, I lie still and try to amuse myself. Amusement is a nice supplement to visualization. I look at the blue pillow molds hanging in rows on the racks. I try to determine if the impressions of each one are of legs and hips, arms and shoulders, or shoulders and heads. I like to bring them to life by imagining who the people are who rest in these molds for their daily radiation treatments. There are rows of white net facial molds too for radiating head or throat, I suppose. Apparently, these are placed over the patients' faces and anchored down to keep patients still. Immobility is imperative for radiating brain tumors (and more importantly, NOT radiating healthy parts of the brain). Geez, I pity the claustrophobic person!

Besides the daily treatments, I have weekly events. One is to see one of my radiation therapy oncologists, Dr. Dz or Dr. Kp. And, for him to see me. And another is when the technicians set the machine to take pictures and check the precision of the radiation. Additionally, they look to determine if the treatment angles and depths need to be adjusted because things swell, become reduced, or shift. I asked one of them, "If you are radiating my chest and armpit, why did you put the tattoos on my abdomen and not my breast area?"

She told me that abdominal skin is un-moveable skin. Breast skin moves when your breasts lay to one side or the other. Therefore, they put the tattoos...beauty marks...on the abdomen. Okay, now I know.

The technicians are all so considerate. They introduce themselves, answer all my questions and smile a lot.

At this morning's treatment, I decided to forego my cancer reading books and selected a magazine on the table in the waiting room. Ah, good, Self Magazine. "Burn Belly Fat Without Working Out." Hmmm, that article appeals to me. "Look-Beautiful Tips." Hmmm, that one sounds interesting too. Where did I end up? On the page that starts with "Healthy

Breasts for Life; a 22-Page Bonus Handbook." Sheesh, I don't think I'm ready to give up thinking about breast cancer or my bosom buddies, yet.

As a patient relying on drugs, I appreciate, and wish to acknowledge, the work on behalf of everyone at the following pharmaceutical companies: Endo (Percocet®), Merck (Emend® and Decadron®), Pharmacia (Adriamycin®), Mead Johnson Oncology Products a Bristol-Myers Squibb Company (Cytoxan®), Ortho Biotech (Procrit®), Amgen (Neulasta® and Aranesp®, cousin to Procrit®), GlaxoSmithKline (Tagamet®), Pfizer (Benadryl®), and Bristol-Myers Squibb (Taxol®).

I wish I were a candidate for AstraZeneca's hormone therapy drugs. But, I'm not. The hormone receptors on my cancer cells were negative. (From my pathology report: ER and PR status = negative.) I have one less future treatment option than women whose ER and PR status is positive. C'mon AZ Discovery and Development groups...keep plugging away! People like me are counting on you.

On Monday, my oncologist, Dr. N, wrote a script for me to have a bone scan. I've been having unusual pains in my right shoulder blade and at the base of my scull. Cross your fingers that it's nothing serious. I don't want to hear that cancer has traveled to my bones. I will go to Nuclear Medicine for the scan next week.

Furthermore, I need to make an appointment with an ENT (ear, nose and throat) specialist. I have pulsing and pinging deep inside my left ear. Please don't let it be a brain tumor.

I met with one of my surgeons, Dr. M, on Tuesday. Remember him? He was the person who had the unfortunate task of breaking the breast cancer news to Dan and me months ago. He has been a staunch ally against "the invader." Looking at the information from all my medical reports, he told me I should consider more time to finish treatment, rest and heal. However, I asked him not to sign papers for more disability. Even though I need more time, it's only a little more time that I need, and with medical bills I incurred, I can't afford long-term disability at 60 percent of my pay. Besides, I want to get back to my job, and contribute to the company that discovered my tumor. I believe that I am almost ready.

Because I anticipate added fatigue during the rest of my radiation, I am taking a few more weeks off using banked vacation and 2005 vacation days. Unless something changes, I plan to be back in the office on Monday, April 4, for half days, and Monday, April 11, for full days. Hooray, a piece of my previous, regular life again.

So many things will be different in April; my routine, my looks, the weather... And, most importantly, I'll be leaving my cancer winter behind. I'm patting myself on the back for that! Viva la Wendi.

Oh, how I look forward to wearing conventional clothes and I anxiously anticipate a time when paper-covered tables and disposable paper gowns aren't part of my everyday mix. When I was in Dr. M's examination room yesterday, he was looking for a piece of paper to write on. I was tempted to say, "Why don't we just tear off a piece of the gown you gave me?"

Love to all,
Wendi

After this message was distributed via e-mail, my sister Vicki gets a reply from Don in North Carolina. He is the father-in-law to one of her colleagues, Michelle:

'Shell' forwarded the e-mail to my wife, Karin, and she to me. I am in tears as I write this.

Please thank Wendi and give her my/our best. I found myself relating to a number of the emotional situations she is passing through. I am sure you know of the book, The Breast Cancer Husband by Marc Silver. As I was reading Wendi's note, I was recalling parts of the book.

Don's wife, Karin has breast cancer. He filled in some details on her progress and asked to be added to my "Updates" distribution list. I like the way he concluded his e-mail, "...a hell of a way to meet people on the Internet. Quite a community."

Today, I went to the chemo room to have my port flushed (it takes a few minutes and should be done once a month) and am now in the radiation waiting area, wearing my hospital gown and expecting to hear someone call my name so I can have my thirteenth treatment.

Tip 148 Place jellybeans in a jar, corresponding to the number of treatments you will have or use an advent calendar approach to counting down until you are done. It feels great to see the beans disappear from the jar or the X's on your calendar.

It is Saturday, March 5 and my sister, Deb, is due to arrive any minute from Denver. My kids are excited. I am ecstatic. We have a busy week ahead. In addition to daily radiation treatments, I will need to go to scheduled appointments with the psychiatrist, radiation oncologist, ENT (ear, nose, throat specialist for the pinging in my ear), Nuclear medicine professionals and my surgeon.

Deb is coming at a good time; I need some food coaching because my new balanced approach to nutrition has regressed a bit. She is coming to re-energize me by shopping together at Harvest Market, cooking together with Ayurvedic recipes and special spices, and practicing a restorative sequence from the Iyengar yoga method. She should change her profession from an IT manager to a life coach, because she's a natural!

RADIATION – A FEW MINUTES EACH DAY

First thing Monday, we go for radiation. Little Danny didn't want to go to daycare, "I want to stay with Aunt Debbie, pwease, pwease, pwease." How can we resist! Mom comes with us and afterward we go shopping at the Harvest Market health food store so Deb can begin a week of healthful cooking.

On Wednesday, the radiation technicians treat Deb to a learning experience; they invite her in to the room.

Tip 149 Caregivers: Ask the radiation technicians to show you the radiation room. Mine were excited to invite my sister to learn more about my treatment. I sensed their pride when they encouraged her to walk in with me while I got settled on the table and into my blue pillow. When my treatment was over and I walked out of the room, I saw Deb standing at their computer! They offered her the opportunity to observe what they were doing to deliver my treatment and to watch me on the camera screen.

Next stop: across the medical campus to Nuclear Medicine. I get my injection of radioactive material, as I did in August (just two days after my diagnosis). Then Vicki meets Deb and me for lunch and laughter. They take me back across the campus for my bone scan.

I am lying on my back, completely still, while a large machine travels slowly from head to toe, all the while staying about three inches from my body. If there is any cancer in my bones, the radioactive isotopes would attach to it and illuminate it. The scan is finished in thirty minutes.

THE GOOD NEWS STARTS POURING IN

Thursday morning, March 10, exactly six months from the date of my mastectomy, I hear from Dr. N's nurse, Kim at "the Helen Graham": Ring, ring. "Hello? Yes...unh hunh...okay...thank you." She tells me there are no signs of cancer. And, there are no signs of osteoporosis either. *A bonus. I can use a bonus.* Vicki writes:

> *Yesterday, Wendi, our sister in from Denver, Deb, and I spent the day together. One of the items on our list was to go with Wendi for her bone scan. The mood after the scan was definitely subdued. I am sure it brought back lots of feelings from the first time prior to surgery.*
>
> *This morning, Wendi called me full of energy, very upbeat! She blurted out the results of the bone scan...It's a beautiful day!*

Brenda sends out an update too. She fills them in on the details and concludes the e-mail with, "*...She was so excited and upbeat in her voice mail...it was great to hear from her and hear the great news! Keep praying for our girl...we love you Wendi!*"

Deb and I are together when the replies start pouring in to my e-mail address. You see, everybody on the e-mail lists have become part of my journey. We get Vicki on the phone and all three of us cry as we read them out loud. *And, I'm humming the tune from White Christmas in which Rosemary Clooney and Vera-Ellen sang, "Sisters, sisters, there were never such devoted sisters... God bless the misters, who come between me and my sisters..."*

It is Sunday, March 13. I am a little blue since Deb went back to Denver. I'm in bed, doing a BSE (breast self-exam) and I find a lump in my right breast. Fear strikes my heart and burns in my stomach. This is more than the peek-between-your-fingers kind of fear...it's the kind that starts out that way, but doesn't stop when the movie is over. Oh brother, this is a downer.

First thing Monday morning, Dr. M agrees to see me right away. I postpone my radiation treatment by an hour so I can see him first. "Mrs. Pedicone, this is a cyst..." *Oh boy! This is an upper.* "...Because of your situation, we are not going to leave any lumps in you," he says. (Isn't it an amusing way to say that!)

Marcia will schedule me for surgery after I check with the radiation oncologist to be sure the lump is not within the field of radiation I am receiving. (Skin that is being radiated does not heal well. If the cyst were within the field, we would have to wait a few weeks to have the surgery).

A POSITIVE ATTITUDE IS HELPFUL

When I leave Dr. M's office, I head for "the Helen Graham" for my daily radiation treatment and weekly examination by Dr. Kp, my radiation oncologist. He and I have an uplifting discussion and he tells me he's pleased with my spirit. He talks about that point to the important role that attitude plays in how patients manage during treatment. Dr. Kp e-mailed the reference: The NCBI (National Center for Biotechnology Information) published a paper comparing 'quality of life in breast and rectal cancer patients.' Breast cancer patients, despite better prognoses, appear to suffer more psychological problems than rectal cancer patients. Gender, age and therapy did not seem to explain these differences. The negative public perception of breast cancer may play a role.

This means to me that public hype around beauty and female breasts make it difficult on women whose breasts are affected by cancer, and therefore the trend is that they do not do as well during treatment as people who have an equally or more difficult type of cancer (rectal cancer), even though the breast cancer patients start out with better prognoses.

Following my radiation treatment on Wednesday, I drive to an imaging location in Glasgow for an MRI. My ENT believes I do not have cancer in my brain but has agreed to order the MRI to give me peace of mind. Thank you Dr. T!

MRI

At the imaging center, they perform several modalities (MRI, CT Scan, mammogram, x-ray; etc.) After dressing in, what else, a hospital gown, Kathy and Kim wearing, what else, lab coats, help me to relax on the formidable magnetic machine. They give me earplugs (it gets loud inside the doughnut part of the machine) and place a Darth Vader looking white mask over my head and fasten it down so I cannot move my head. I can't wear anything with metal, nor can I take a camera into the room because of the high electromagnetic energy that will produce detailed views. I close my eyes and listen to the sounds. I can describe one as being similar to a loud sewing machine. Rat-a-tat-tat. I can describe another one as sounding like a loud gong of a rich grandfather clock that strikes 40! Believe it or not, I fell asleep. When the lab coats return, they slide the table forward and tell me to continue to stay still. Kathy pats my shoulder while Kim injects me with "Gado." Magnevists® brand of gadolinium (thanks Berlex Laboratories) is the stuff that will highlight cancer metastases. The table slides back into the spiral machine and I listen to the sounds before drifting off to sleep. I can always use a nap.

When I am finished, they give me my films so I can hand carry them to my ENT. They are about 2′ x 2′ and have x-ray type images of my head. I sit in the car and look at one film. There are all sorts of dots in the images. I panic. Since I am untrained at reading these, I put them away. Let's let the doctor do this.

In the early evening, Dr. T calls me at home to tell me I'm in the clear! I don't care to ask what all those dots were...they weren't cancer; that's all I care about.

The next morning I call Dr. N's office to let them know that my ENT ordered this test and what his opinion is. Kim tells me I can consider myself in remission and disease-free. I immediately sit down on the kitchen chair, because I feel like I'm going to pass out. I celebrate my good news with little Danny who is the only other person at home with me. Then I prepare to make a few phone calls that I know will set off a fabulous chain reaction of good news. I have a feeling that within a matter of minutes, hundreds of people are going to rejoice. This is their good news too!

CURED UNLESS SOMEONE PROVES DIFFERENTLY

Once I received word of a clear MRI, I had written an e-mail to one of my radiation oncologists, Dr. Kp to share the wonderful news of remission. He responded:

> *Actually, I avoid the term remission. To me, it suggests the early days of chemo when those therapies were used almost exclusively for leukemias and lymphomas and the patients were told that they were "in remission" when all their blood counts had normalized and there was no objective evidence of disease activity even though both patient and physician knew there was no hope of a cure.*

> *In the classical sense Wendi, you are in remission as you have no objective evidence of disease, but I prefer to frame it differently: How about if we just say you're cured unless proven otherwise!!*

I like the sound of that!

Vicki and Brenda communicate-out. Brenda adds other details to our AZ colleagues:

...She's still very tired from radiation, but that will end soon. We can expect to see her back to work on April 4 (half days that week).

...Your prayers have worked. It's been a long journey for Wendi, but she's on the other side of that miserable disease now!

Immediately after their e-mails go out, I receive many, many e-mail responses praising my 'fighting spirit'. The content of all of them can be summed up in the following one that was sent from Geoff, a colleague in the UK:

It is no surprise given the gauntlet you threw down to "the invader" from the start! Warm wishes and prayers for continued good health. Cheers.

This morning, Miss Sheri gives me a hug when I share my news. Danny will be celebrating St. Patrick's Day with his daycare buddies and I am off to radiation.

Once there, I see someone approach me and realize it's Dan sneaking up on me to plant a kiss on my lips. I love him. My name was just called. "Come with me while I get changed."

In the dressing room he hands me a wrapped box with a gold bow. In it is a pair of dainty gold shamrocks "to commemorate this day," he says. While he's talking, I breathe in the scent of the hospital gown before putting it on. He looks at me like I'm crazy. We walk together to say hello to the radiation nurses who are waiting for me. Proudly, I wear my new earrings into Primus One and fit myself into my blue pillow.

Things we do to celebrate this day: We go to McGlynns Irish Pub to witness the wearin'-o'the green and partake in the fun. Then to Six Paupers Restaurant and Pub where people hug me. The bartenders serve me celebratory desserts and a few men kiss my head.

Andrea and a friend stop in to congratulate me. As I did with Dan and everyone else I've spoken to today, I in turn congratulate Andrea. This is, after all, her victory too.

It is early, yet I have expended my energy. I feel like a gorilla dragging my knuckles on the ground.

I will never forget this day.

Update – March 21, 2005

When I heard I had advanced stage cancer, I thought my life was over.

I was prepared to fight, but I had doubts about winning the battle. I didn't think I'd ever hear that I was "cured unless proven otherwise" (as my radiation oncologist has framed it). I am not at the end of my cancer journey yet, but the end is VERY near. I want to take this moment to thank you for being a vital part of it. And, I want to congratulate YOU for the victory!

Over the previous few weeks, I'd felt like I was on the verge of something big...a light at the end of the tunnel, perhaps? Signs of spring were beginning to show, daffodils had broken through the soil, I could hear the occasional bird chirping, my eyebrows were returning, tiny white eyelashes were evident, my return-to-work date had been decided, I passed the halfway point of my daily radiation treatments, and I held prescription scripts to begin getting tested for cancer metastases. And, there were telltale signs of our family's future; Christine's Tourette's Syndrome had settled down to the point where it looked like she'd be able to drive a car again; Andrea was getting acceptance letters from the colleges she applied to; Michele's rugby season was about to begin; Danny started talking about his birthday party when he turns four; Dan was preparing to start a new project at work; and our FAFSA paperwork and taxes were almost done. Yes, SOMETHING was about to give.

True story: On the morning of St. Patrick's Day, I awakened from a nightmare and a hot flash. I hope the hot flashes go away soon. My nightmare was one I actually didn't want to end...until it was over. Somehow I was aware I was in a terrible dream, but that the ending would be good. I dreamt that I was in another century and was among about a dozen people who were about to meet our deaths by a firing squad. We were innocents being persecuted by a misguided king. One by one we were interviewed. Interviewed? Hey, it's a dream; they don't have to make sense! As my turn for the interview approached, fear struck my gut and my heartbeat quickened. The moment came. On the count of three I heard a deafening sound but no pain. In my dream, I somehow became aware that the shooters shot the king!

When I awakened I reiterated the dream to Dan so that it wouldn't fade from my memory. I also discovered where the gunshot sound in my dream originated; one of the cats had knocked over a picture on the nightstand.

And, now I ask YOU, do you suppose the mad king was "the invader"? I like to think so. Was my nightmare a prophecy? You decide.

And now, my recollection of the rest of the events of a day 'that will live in infamy' – Pearl Harbor Day? No, St. Patrick's Day 2005...

Feeling sweaty from head to toe, and gooey from the Aquaphor® ointment that I used on my radiated skin, I hopped into the shower [on the morning of St. Patrick's Day]. Because I noticed tiny hairs on my legs, I shaved them for the first time in five months. I'm a woman again.

... What did I just hear? No way, it couldn't be. Disease free?

I called Dr. N's office [on the morning of St. Patrick's Day] to discuss the MRI results from the evening before. I was standing in my kitchen when I was told I "could consider myself disease-free." Disease free? When our conversation was over and I got off the phone, the room began to spin. What did I just hear? No way. It couldn't be. Disease free? I sat down, out of sheer necessity, and stared into space. Little Danny's voice broke my trance. "Mommy, are you okay?" I hugged him for an extra long hug. Again, his voice. "Mommy, I can't breathe."

All at once, I wanted to throw my head back and shout, scream, hug myself, call somebody, send a text message, open the front door and howl, breathe, look at Heaven and shout "thanks", do an Indian dance, do the Rocky-at-the-top-of-the-steps dance, do the Mexican hat dance, race like in Chariots of Fire, do jumping jacks, jump, play jacks, make monkey noises, oo, oo, ah ah ah, get down on the floor and jump like a frog, stand up and walk like an Egyptian, call people and tell them my news, sing... Ba ba ba da da do do do.... La la la. IMAGINE, all these thoughts in a single second and I didn't know which one to do first! Ahhhhh! Wow, WOW! Eeeeheeee!!!

All at once, I wanted to throw my head back and shout, scream, hug myself...do an Indian dance, do the Rocky-at-the-top-of-the-steps dance, do the Mexican hat dance, race-like in Chariots of Fire, do jumping jacks, jump, play jacks, make monkey noises, oo, oo, ah ah ah, get down on the floor and jump like a frog, stand up and walk like an Egyptian...

"Danny," I said, "I have an idea...let's do our Cancer Dance!" He knew the drill. We'd done this before. So, while many of you were getting your day started on the morning of St. Patrick's Day, Danny and I were stomping around our kitchen with our hands in scary monster fashion, growling

aloud. Roarrr. "Louder Danny, let's growl louder!" ROARrrr. "We can do better than that...use your outside voice." ROOOAAARRRRR! Oh, blessed release!

WWWwwwweeeeee! I did it, I did it, I really, really did it. I beat "the invader", yes I did. Ahhhh.

Now, I know that I didn't do it alone. With sincere humility, I thank you, all of YOU.

Then, I made a few phone calls and set off a spectacular chain reaction. IT WAS TIME TO REJOICE!!!

Later that morning, Dan surprised me by showing up at the cancer center. What was he doing there; he was supposed to be at work. When Rick, an owner of the company Dan works for, heard our news, he told Dan, "You're not allowed to stay at work another minute." So Dan left to be with me.

My mother and I had previously planned a simple lunch that day and we kept our date. While we were in Burger King, I saw a striking woman at a nearby table. This would be my opportunity to pay forward a compliment I'd received a few weeks ago. Rewind to a day when I walked into "the Helen Graham" and heard a pleasant voice speak in my direction, "Well, hello Miss Fashion Plate." Even though she appeared to be talking to me, I looked over my shoulder. Softly, she said, "There's no one behind you, I'm talking to you." And she added, "You look so lovely with your hat and scarf. My brother and I admired you the moment you walked in." Me? I had a dumb look on my face and my index finger pointed at my chest. A fashion plate? Nah, I wear some of the same things so often that my daughters tell me my wardrobe is one big uniform. Anyway, her flattering remarks made me feel so good, that I knew I would have to pass them on to someone else.

Fast forward to the day I received my great news; my chance arrived. When Mom and I finished our Burger King whoppers, I walked over to the striking woman whose table was near ours and said, "Excuse me, I just wanted to tell you that you are very beautiful. I hope I just made your day."

"Why, thank you," she said. She asked me a few questions since she could tell I was fighting cancer and we concluded our conversation when she cheerily said, "You have such bright eyes and a nice smile. Stay the course with your fight and good luck!"

I smiled all the way to the car. I buckled my seat belt, buckled my mom's seat belt, and adjusted the rearview mirror. And saw two sesame seeds on my upper lip. Yeesh.

Later, Dan and I went to McGlynn's Irish Pub to meet everyone with last names that begin with "O" and "Mc." Oh, you know them. I was Wendi O'Pedicone, he was Dan McPedicone, and we met Someone McSmith...you get the picture.

We stopped home for a few minutes before getting Danny from daycare and going back out for more festivities. This was a glorious day! Woo hoo!! I was upstairs when I heard the girls and a few friends come in from school. They were in the kitchen when I was walking down the steps. I lost my footing and slipped. I must've squealed and made a noise because they came running and shouted, "What happened? What happened?" I was about to tell them, when I lost my footing again. Doh! Once I recovered myself Dan looked at me and said, "You could've just told us!"

Were comical things happening to us that day? Or, were we in the mood for comical things?

Andrea and a girlfriend of hers, Dan, Danny and I sat in a nearby restaurant-and-pub called Six Paupers where folks who know us (and even many who don't) wished me well. Dan walked around with Danny in one arm and shook people's hands with the other...

Andrea and a girlfriend of hers, Dan, Danny and I sat in Six Paupers where folks who know us (and even many who don't) wished me well. Dan walked around with Danny in one arm, and shook people's hands with the other. John-the-bartender and Joseph-the-bartender served me celebratory desserts. And I indeed ate them! Many days I look at some foods as poison, because I'm scared they will cause cancer, but that day, I would have eaten anything. God gave me that day to express my joy!

Danny announced, "Daddy, I have to go potty." Dan took him outside the restaurant because it was easier than going into the crowded restroom. They returned and Dan confided that he celebrated our victory with Danny by cross peeing in the grass! This was OUR day to exult in any way we wanted to! Whatever floats a boat, I like to say! Merriment, and freedom from fear, can make a person do silly things.

The night was young. It was early, but I had quickly expended my energy. I was spent. "Don't worry about it, Mom," Andrea said, "Peace out." "Peace out" is a good thing.

I'd say I was on the couch by 7 PM and in bed by 8:30. I was sleepy, but nothing could have gotten me down that day. Not even the news I had received from my surgeon's office about an upcoming surgery. You see, last Sunday night, I did my monthly BSE on my good breast and found a lump. Can you believe it? My friend Chris put it this way, "It must've been like you were watching a movie...didn't you feel like saying, no-way, that can't happen?" And I couldn't bring myself to tell Dan and the kids. I kept my fear at bay. Early Monday morning I called the doctor's office and begged them to see me. Which they did. Dr. M said, "Mrs. Pedicone, it is a cyst. Let's get rid of it." Oh man. Man, oh man, oh man what a relief. Then came the news a few days later that I was disease-free, "cured unless proven otherwise." So you see, NOTHING could've gotten me down...not even a lump in my right breast.

I am scheduled for surgery this Thursday, but I'm not requesting any prayers or crossed fingers, because I don't want to overuse the God-network or the superstition-system! This time, it'll be a simple surgery and I don't feel the need to build an arsenal. I won't even be nervous about a pathology report to come a week later. Well, maybe only a little nervous. I'm sort of gun-shy I suppose. Yeah, yeah, I will feel better upon hearing the confirmation that it was truly only a cyst.

This Thursday is my final radiation treatment, but I will not be saying "good-bye" to my radiation friends: Lisa-to-the-second-power (there are two Lisas), Michelle, Kathy, Rose, Linda, Tracy, Beth and Dr. Kp, and a few others who are nameless to me (I don't know their names, but I certainly recognize their smiles). There's no way I could've been with these individuals day after day, under my circumstances and not create a bond. We are forever linked. And when there's a connection, you can't walk away nor say "good-bye." Therefore, I will say "see you soon" and I plan to visit them in the future.

I will celebrate Thursday as it marks the closure of another phase. It will be the last time I breathe in the scent of the hospital gowns. It will be the final time I position myself in the blue pillow. It will be the last time the technicians wearing lab coats will align my tattoos with the red beams of light, and the last time they'll position the radiation table under me. I will close my eyes and smile when I hear them say, "Lateral negative three point two, vertical one point two, and longitudinal negative twenty three point five, for the last time." ...For the last time.

In twenty years, if my children write a book and they describe me, would they describe a time I hugged them when they cried or laughed so hard with them that we nearly wet our pants? Or would they write about the morning I looked haggard because I stayed up all night baking treats for their school events, paying bills, and creating their Halloween costumes? Or would they only write about the day I was "psycho Mom" when they argued about cleaning the dinner dishes one too many times and I went fanatical and swiped everything that was on the dinner table, with one sweep of my arm, onto the floor? And if they wrote about the time I had cancer would they write about how I courageously fought "the invader?" Or would they only remember how night after night I sat on the couch after having done nothing all day and answered "no" each time one of them asked me if I could go to a movie with her [no], read a book to him [no, Daddy will read it to you], go shopping with her [no, I don't feel up to it], or go to her basketball game to watch her play [no, I'll try to make it to next week's game]? Kids. We never know how they see us in retrospect. do we?

In twenty years, if my children write a book and they describe me, would they describe a time I hugged them when they cried, or laughed so hard with them that we nearly peed our pants?... And if they wrote about the time I had cancer would they write about how I courageously fought "the invader?"

In twenty years, how will I feel about my kids? Would I be disappointed if, when they stepped up to a microphone, they didn't say what I hoped they would say, "I'd like to thank the academy..." but instead said, "Would you like a hot apple pie with those fries?" What things will I remember about them? How will I view what they did for me while I fought "the invader?" We never know how we will see them in retrospect, do we?

It's been six-and-a-half months. I am still reading the get-well and greeting cards from my basket in the kitchen. I am still thinking about how much has occurred. Now hear this: In a not-very-authentic-but-I'll-try Manhattan voice (for the fun of it), hear me saying, "Enough about me already!" Let me tell you about YOU and what YOU have done for my family and me in six months:

✗ *YOU donated money to the Susan G. Komen Foundation, the Lance Armstrong Foundation, and the Wellness Community...*

✗ *YOU gave me bracelets, charms, a robe, slippers, potted plants, flowers, restaurant and take out certificates, store gift cards, money to supplement my medical expenses, tee shirts, stuffed animals, candles...*

✗ *YOU sent flowers, dish-gardens, hanging plants and fruit baskets...*

✗ *YOU sent me virtual bouquets of flowers from VirtualFlowers.com and e-Cards from BlueMountain.com...*

✗ *YOU sent me edible gifts from CookiesbyDesign.com and FruitFlowers.com...*

✗ *YOU gave me a lovely butterfly clock that was your idea of the gift of time, and spring...*

✗ *YOU gave me hats, bandanas and headgear for the cause, and designer accessories; pink Eagles hats and Ford breast cancer awareness scarves...*

✗ *YOU sent me pink tee shirts from the breast cancer walk in Denver...*

✗ *YOU knitted me a hat and a few scarves to keep my neck warm in the winter...*

✗ *YOU wrote me a poem...*

✗ *YOU helped little Danny make me a canvas bag with his hand prints...*

✗ *YOU wrote me prayers, sent me prayer booklets, gave me a saint medal and a prayer box, prayed for me and enlisted your children to pray for me...*

✗ *YOU gave me pink Christmas ornaments with pink ribbons and "survivor" written on them...*

✗ *YOU sent me books about cancer, literature to help my teenage daughters and Dan get through this, and books to help little Danny understand...*

✗ *YOU gave me magnetic pink ribbons for our vehicles, pink ribbon and guardian angel pins, earrings, a glass guardian angel and Kiwok, the warrior...*

✗ *YOU had a star named after me...*

✗ *YOU gave me tapes and CDs to use in meditation and healing, magazines, and novels on CD when I needed to escape cancer...*

✗ *YOU left me empathetic and humorous voice mail messages, and told me you were thinking about me…*

✗ *YOU baked us cookies, pastries, pies, breads, brownies, muffins, and cupcakes, and gave us plates of holiday cookies and candy…*

✗ *YOU drove me to doctor appointments and tests…*

✗ *YOU offered other 'chauffeur' services for my family and me…*

✗ *YOU cleared the snow from our driveway…*

✗ *YOU prepared roast chicken, vegetable soup, minestrone soup, pea soup, wedding soup, chili, roast beef, beef stew, lasagna, baked ziti, meatballs, applesauce, fruit salad, garden salad, pasta salad, ham, pasta, tacos, scalloped potatoes, Jell-O deserts, chicken and stuffing, sloppy joes, green beans, sides, eggs and quiche…*

✗ *YOU sent packages and left things on my doorstep and in my garage…*

✗ *YOU gave me stamped thank you cards to send…*

✗ *YOU visited me in the hospital and at home…*

✗ *YOU brought me a video-recording of the IS Town Hall, a banner and a book full of get-well wishes…*

✗ *YOU picked up groceries for me and took me grocery shopping…*

✗ *YOU brought me a walker to use…*

✗ *YOU cleaned my house, stocked our refrigerator, washed our clothes, polished the silver and washed the windows…*

✗ *I thank YOU for all that you have done and I VOW TO PAY IT FORWARD and give others a hand-up, so long as they need it and I can give it. Promise.*

You'll be hearing from me soon. Happy first day of spring!

Love to all,
Cured-unless-proven-otherwise (me)

THE FINAL RADIATION TREATMENT

Today is March 24, the day of my outpatient surgery to remove the cyst in my right breast.

It is also the day of my last radiation treatment. I have a busy day ahead of me. The cancer center has more in store for me in the way of follow-up and maintenance visits, so I'll make it a point to stop in to say 'hello' to these outstanding folks and to the office staff in the reception room who made it a point to remember my name from the first day forward.

My mother and I go to the cancer center at 7:00 a.m. The radiation technicians give her 'the tour' and graciously show her the Primus One room. In the last few weeks, they have buzzed around my family members like true hostesses.

This day, I pick up the Christiana Care 2004 Annual Report of the Helen F. Graham Cancer Center. There are exciting advances in treatment strategies. As you survive each day you'll realize that tomorrow holds promising new treatment options for cancer patients. For example, in the case of radiation, there are systems being developed to deliver radiation inside the breast, directly to the tumor site, that will ensure all cancer is removed and preserve healthy breast tissue. (2004 Annual Report, p. 27) One such method will be a small balloon catheter inserted under the skin directly into the spot where the tumor was removed and the cancer is most likely to recur. A radioactive source will be delivered inside the balloon that will inflate to the shape of the tumor cavity. *Isn't that fascinating?* This strategy can be applied to riskier areas like the brain; radioactive iodine in a balloon that conforms to the shape of the tumor bed and minimal exposure to surrounding healthy tissue (2004 Annual Report, p.41). Once a patient has had external beam radiation in a particular area (as I had), he cannot have it again in the same area. This new form of therapy allows more radiation if the tumor returns in the same spot. To any of you who are considering a medical career, this is exciting stuff!

"Come on back, Mrs. Pedicone," they call. This is it. My last treatment. I notice that Lisa pulls the masking tape off the blue pillow that identifies it as mine, and Linda doesn't hang it on the rack when the treatment is finished – a few subtle reminders that I am done; my battle is over. I do not feel the same emotions I did when I completed my final chemo treatment, but I do feel a little weepy. Linda says, "It's normal for patients to feel emotional on the last day. Believe it or not, we feel the we feel the same." She explains that they don't use the "G" word (good-bye) when patients complete radiation treatments; instead they say things like, "see you at the mall," or "see you in the grocery store."

Since January 12, I had a vacation from cancer therapy, went to "the Helen Graham" for 28 radiation treatments, encountered depression and came out on the other side disease-free.

Following a mastectomy and chemotherapy, and since January 12, I have vacationed from cancer therapy, gone to "the Helen Graham" for twenty-eight radiation treatments, encountered depression and come out on the other side disease-free. Today, March 24, 2005, it feels as though I am truly leaving my cancer winter, and "the invader", behind me.

I'll see you at the mall.

CHAPTER **SURGERY NUMBER FOUR**

7

(Me with Michele)

Photo courtesy of G. Thomas Murray Photography

They always say time changes things, but
you actually have to change them yourself.

Andy Warhol
(1927 - 1987)
The Philosophy of Andy Warhol

This morning I had my final radiation treatment. Shortly, I will be leaving the house to have minor surgery to remove a lump in my right breast. The lump does not have anything to do with the cancer that was in my left breast. After it is removed, if news from pathology states that the lump is cancerous, it would be a separate incidence of breast cancer and not a recurrence of the cancer that was diagnosed in August.

At this time, what do I say if someone asks about breast cancer and me? Am I ready yet to say I *had* breast cancer? Shall I consider myself a breast cancer *patient?* Or, a breast cancer survivor? And when I am filling-out a questionnaire and it asks me to rate my health, what box shall I check? Shall I check the box beside *Excellent Health, Good Health or Poor Health?*

Today, March 24, is another milestone. It is the day I find myself in the exact same place where I began my treatment ordeal. I am on the seventh floor of the Wilmington hospital location of Christiana Care awaiting a surgical procedure that has very little to do with my breast cancer that was diagnosed seven months ago. My two moms (Mom Pedicone and Mom Fox) brought me here so Dr. M can remove the cyst in my right breast.

I will be awake for this procedure and so I dress in – what else – a hospital gown. And, I don a dopey-looking oversized shower-cap-looking covering for my head. *Not one of the cool-looking ones you see on TV. However, wearing it is a fashion risk that I'm definitely willing to take.* Dr. M turns on his iPod and the lovely music relaxes me. "Do you like this song?" he asks. "I have over 1200 songs recorded on my iPod." *Neat.*

A while back, Dr. D, my other surgeon, sent me a link to the iTunes Music store where he apparently created a list of what he called, "Dr. D's Plastic Surgery OR." It is "an eclectic mix of classic and obscure tunes meant to keep the OR rockin' and cuttin' in harmony." And, Dr. M has done the same. *My doctors...you gotta love 'em!*

As Dr. M cuts out the cyst, I cannot feel the procedure, but I feel the skin being pulled and it makes my left breast feel tight. The left breast looks a little burned and is tender like sunburn. None of this hurts; it's just a little uncomfortable. *No problem...I can handle this procedure; after all I've had major surgery!*

When I return from the procedure, and walk into the waiting room to tell Mom Pedicone and Mom Fox that I am done, I do not see them in the seats they were sitting in when I left. Ironically, they are sitting in the exact two seats that Dan and I sat in on the morning of my mastectomy. I find it remarkably interesting that I am here on the very last day of my radiation treatment (and the very last day of my total cancer battle). How is it that I ended up with a cyst and had to come back here? And, isn't it amazing that the only available day for surgery to remove it was today?

I walk up to my moms and say, "I'm done." They both smile at me as they collect their things and prepare to take me home. While they do I steal one final look at the room. *Breathe. In through the nose. Fffff. Out through the mouth, fffffsshhh.* How ironic it is that my battle with cancer started in those two chairs on September 10, on the morning of my mastectomy, and it ended in those two chairs today, March 24, on the same day of my final cancer treatment.

Life is peculiar and mystifying. I look down at my breasts resting inconspicuously under my purple sweater. The right one is the surviving part of the team. It nursed my babies, has made me feel sensual, and this week gave me a little scare. The left one is a mound that replaced the breast that seven months ago betrayed the team and nearly killed me.

Life is peculiar and mystifying. I look down at my breasts resting inconspicuously under my purple sweater. The right one is the surviving part of the team. It nursed my babies, has made me feel sensual, and this week gave me a little scare. The left one is a mound that replaced the breast that seven months ago betrayed the team and nearly killed me.

I had my last radiation treatment this morning and the cyst in my right breast has been removed. I am alive and I choose to live well from this day forward.

CHAPTER

8

LIFE AFTER CANCER

(Dan, me, and my wig)

Photo courtesy of G. Thomas Murray Photography

A man should not leave this earth with unfinished business. He should live each day as if it was a pre-flight check. He should ask each morning, am I prepared to lift-off?

Diane Frolov & Andrew Schneider
Northern Exposure, All is Vanity, 1991

March 25, 2005 I am now a 'cancer survivor'.

If someone asks, I will say I *had* breast cancer. I will familiarize myself with the phrase breast cancer survivor. And when I am filling-out a questionnaire and it asks me to rate my health, I will check the box beside Excellent.

It is now officially spring. Some days we have warm, seasonal weather and other days, signs of winter linger.

How Does Cancer Start? And, How Can I Avoid a Recurrence?

My radiation treatments are complete, visits to the cancer center are winding down and I'll shift my focus from beating cancer, to avoiding a recurrence. It is time for me to learn more about nutrition, hormones, chemicals, and genetics.

But first, how did my cancer start? Cancer is the overgrowth of cells. For some reason, cancer forms when cells start growing in large numbers in an abnormal fashion. Some cancer cells can grow in an area of the body for ten or more years before there is evidence that something is wrong (Every Woman, p. 45).

According to Joan Edwards, *Strategies for Promoting Cancer-Free Living*, uncontrollable reasons for cancer may include: mutations (abnormal changes) in cells that we inherit, conditions that affect our body's immunity, and hormones within our body. There are controllable causes of cancer (tobacco, alcohol, and exposure to sun). Reduce your cancer risk by living a healthy lifestyle in mind, body and spirit. Specific cancer-related factors that are in your control include: weight, nutrition, activity level and exercise, tobacco use and exposure, alcohol use, sun exposure, receiving regular health checkups, and tuning into your body (Every Woman, p. 45).

As I drive to the bookstore, the radio is playing Tim McGraw's song, Live Like You Were Dying. Good advice, Mr. McGraw. I'll do it. *But don't expect me to go seven seconds on a bull named Fu-Man-Chu.*

Hormone Therapy and Hormone Replacement Therapy are Different

I enter a bookstore and see the best sellers and new releases facing me.

The first one that catches my eye is *The Sexy Years: Discover the Hormone Connection*, by Suzanne Somers. Even though she is a breast cancer survivor, it is not a book about breast cancer. It is a book about living well after menopause with natural and properly balanced Hormone Replacement Therapy (HRT). It says on the cover, "Say good bye to mood swings, sleep deprivation, fatigue, weight gain, and loss of libido and say hello to the best time of your life!"

Since my menstrual period has not returned and my estrogen receptor cells tested negative, according to Ms. Somers' book, I may be a candidate for bioidentical HRT.

Tip 150   The key here is the negative status. If you've had breast cancer and your ER status is positive, taking estrogen is not a good idea. To learn more about whether it is right for you if you are a recovering breast cancer patient, talk to your oncologist (you will see this recommendation on every label of HRT products), and go to www.breastcancer.org and read the Hormonal Therapy section, because there is information regarding the difference between HRT and HT (tamoxifen, Arimidex®, etc.). HRT is for menopause.

If you've had breast cancer and your ER status is positive, you may be a candidate for Hormone Therapy to prevent recurrence because HT blocks the effects of hormones on the cancer cells that have hormone receptors (HER-2/neu positive). HT is an adjuvant cancer treatment.

If you think HRT is for you, Ms. Somers suggests going to your doctor and asking for your baseline hormone levels through lab work (estradiol, progesterone and follicle-stimulating-hormone levels). Tell your doctor that you want to be prescribed bioidentical estradiol (Estrace or Gynodiol) and progesterone from compounding pharmacies. She talks about how often they should be taken in order to mimic your body's natural cycle. To learn more about bioidentical HRT, read the section that begins on page 79 of her book.

Tip 151   There is a great deal of information available on HRT choices for post-menopausal woman. You may want to start your information-gathering and decision-making by asking your oncologist and PCP (primary care physician). They may recommend genetic counseling first however, because it would be helpful to know about your BRCA1 and BRCA2 genes (read further in this chapter about my experience with genetic counseling and the knowledge I gained).

GET ON WITH THE BUSINESS OF LIVING

I make my way to the health section of the store and find cancer books. One in particular, *What your Doctor May Not Tell You About Breast Cancer* (Lee, Zava and Hopkins) says, "Experts agree that environmental risk factors such as diet and exposure to toxins and pollutants account for about 80% of breast cancers" (p. 318). Chapter 17 is titled "How Nutrition affects your Breast Cancer Risk" and chapter 18 is "Protecting the Present and the Future." Both interest me, so I buy the book. There is a table of "Do's and Don'ts of the Anti-Cancer Diet" on page 352 that I can see myself copying and placing on my fridge.

Tip 152   Now would be a good time to read books that will set you on a new path to your new future. I recommend, *Excuse Me, Your Life is Waiting*, by Lynn Grabhorn, *Now, Discover Your Strengths*, by Marcus Buckingham and Donald O. Clifton, *Happiness is a Choice* by Barry Neiel Kaufman, and/or *Help Me To Heal* by Bernie S. Siegel, MD.

Tip 153   If you haven't already, donate to a cancer charity in some way. Make a contribution to one of your favorites (mine are the American Cancer Society, BreastCancer.org, Dr. Susan Love Research Foundation, Lance Armstrong Foundation, Susan G. Komen Breast Cancer Foundation, The Wellness Community, and my church). You could contribute as a way to thank someone. Make a donation in someone's name; your caregiver or spouse, your children, a physician or even a group of nurses or technicians. If you are financially overwhelmed by bills and co-payments you made during your battle with cancer, then do something that costs nothing. If you are a healthy cancer survivor or caregiver, sign up for a 'Race for the Cure' or '3 Day Race' in the US, or other fun events in your country (like the one a UK colleague of mine told me about - The Polar Challenge - building Europe's First Breast Cancer

Prevention Centre. Or become a volunteer (look on your favorite cancer website and do a search on the word 'volunteer' or 'advocacy', or click on the 'contact us' link and ask how you can help). Sad to say, these things may help someone you love.

Tip 154   eCards offer messages of hope to those with cancer. If you know someone with cancer, you may be at a loss for words. You want to reach out and be supportive, but you may not know how. Something as simple as a card and your personal message can help remind people that they're not alone. Go to www.talkingwellness.org to send free eCards and offer them words of comfort and encouragement. Each card has been written by a celebrity—and illustrated by an artist—some of whom have been touched by cancer.

Tip 155   Don't let embarrassment keep you from getting screenings for cancers such as breast cancer, or even colon cancer. If you have read this book, you'll know why. Your physician or many of the websites suggested in this book will help you to get a mammogram. In the case of a colonoscopy, contact your physician, visit the Colon Cancer Alliance at www.ccalliance.org, or call the help line, 800-464-HELP in the U.S. and ask for Screening for Life (promoting breast, cervical and colorectal health). In the case of colon cancer, did you know:

• It is the second leading cause of cancer deaths in the US
• Using Delaware as an example, rates of death are 46% higher among African Americans in Delaware than other Delawareans.

Please do not ignore these, and other, statistics. Do self-exams, pay attention to your body's changes and signals, and follow cancer-screening guidelines. The statistics tell you why.

I saw a television commercial recently about the Cancer Centers of America. I recall reading something about them. They are places people can go to who are newly diagnosed, end-stage and every stage in between. Patients stay three to five days a month to get treatments and wellness education. The mission is to take a total approach to treatment including nutrition, naturopathic and conventional medicine, mind-wellness; etc. They are located in the U.S. in Illinois, Oklahoma and Washington State. If I find myself in a situation with a recurrence and poor prognosis, I will probe further to determine my options.

Tip 156   You may want to explore the Cancer Center of America concept. Go to www.cancercenter.com or call 888-744-8442.

At my Wednesday night support group meeting, a group member's wife gives me a few magazines. One is *Cure*. *Cure* is dedicated to Cancer Updates, Research & Education. What a wealth of information! The articles present current information about many cancers and cancer initiatives. One of the issues she gave me is a Survivor's Issue, Winter, 2004. In it are a few pages dedicated to the 2005 National Patient & Survivor's Forums (there are three in 2005). I am considering attending the one in July in Washington, D.C. entitled Focus on Advocacy. When I decide, I will register online at www.curetoday.com. I begin reading two articles that catch my eye, *Living with Uncertainty, and Facing Fear of Recurrence.*

Tip 157   Subscribe online for *Cure* magazine at www.curetoday.com, or send a query to The Cancer Information Group at their Dallas, Texas location via fax number 214-820-8224. It is $20 for an annual subscription and free for cancer patients and their caregivers.

According to estimates from the American Cancer Society, 1.37 million new cases of cancer are expected to be diagnosed this year [2005] – this does not include the more than one million cases of basal and squamous cell skin cancer that are expected to be diagnosed.

Below are some statistics I will share with you (because many people have asked me for them) – But don't let them frighten you: Any one of us could very well be part of the "survival" percentages! I plan to be!

Stage	5-year Relative Survival Rate
0	100%
I	98%
IIA	88%
IIB	76%
IIIA	56%
IIIB	49%
IV	16%

Overall Survival Rate	
After 5 years	85%
After 10 years	71%
After 15 years	57%
After 20 years	52%

(www.imaginis.com)

Estimated Breast Cancer Cases/Deaths Worldwide		
Region	New Cases (2000)	Deaths (2000)
Eastern Africa	13,615	6,119
Middle Africa	3,902	1,775
Northern Africa	18,724	8,388
Southern Africa	5,537	2,504
Western Africa	17,389	7,830
Caribbean	6,210	2,310
Central America	18,663	5,888
South America	69,924	22,735
Northern America	202,044	51,184
Eastern Asia	142,656	38,826
South-Eastern Asia	55,907	24,961
South Central Asia	129,620	62,212
Western Asia	20,155	8,459
Eastern Europe	110,975	43,058
Northern Europe	54,551	20,992
Southern Europe	65,284	25,205
Western Europe	115,308	40,443
Australia/New Zealand	12,748	3,427
Melanesia	470	209
Micronesia	62	28

Source: J. Ferlay, F. Bray, P. Pisani and D.M. Parkin. GLOBOCAN 2000: Cancer Incidence, Mortality and Prevalence Worldwide, Version 1.0. IARC CancerBase No. 5. Lyon, IARCPress, 2001.

These statistics regarding estimated breast cancer deaths worldwide are a few years old, and even though technology has advanced since they were published, I consider them distressing (unless they are near zero – the numbers are worrisome).

I find an article on the National Institutes of Health website dated August 31, 2004, called, "Scientists Estimate Probability of Death from Breast Cancer and Other Causes Following Diagnosis." It doesn't contain much that I haven't already read and includes comparisons of black and white women. It says that patients with ER-negative tumors were more likely to die from their cancer than those with ER-positive ones. *I think I should stop reading the statistics at this point.*

Tip 158   The Dr. Susan Love Research Foundation is dedicated to ending breast cancer in the next ten years. "The Website for Women" is a wonderfully informative site www.susanlovemd.org. Consider getting involved in some way and join the movement.

THE TRANSITION BACK TO WORK

It is April 15 and I have completed two weeks of half-days at work. I am doing well. Each day this week I rested after I arrived home from work and took only one nap (the first week I took two naps; each afternoon and early evening). I see this as a physical weaning process and an important part of my re-entry to the world of work. Next week, I begin full days at work. Should I feel fatigued, I will close my office door, pull out my pillow of pink ribbons that a friend's daughter, Ellen, made for me and nap for ten or twenty minutes.

As far as the work goes, my manager and I have had several weekly meetings to ensure there is time set aside to discuss my needs. I have been familiarizing myself with key things I need to know about AZ, my department's activities, and my clients. Once I have a comfort level with the current status in all three areas, I can begin working with my manager to set new objectives and begin delivering against them. When I told my manager that I felt unproductive with regard to accomplishing tasks, she told me I should view this "catch up" time as an investment into the future when I will be able to deliver. She reminded me that once I am up to speed, contributions and productivity would happen.

It is Monday and Janet, a colleague, stops by my office and says, "I am part of the Hispanic Network Community here at AZ y'know," and she continues, "I found your e-mail updates to be very informative and I know that that there is a tremendous need for information that you provided in them within the Spanish-reading-only community. I am often troubled by the stats that indicate our high risks but are they due to ethnic genetic configuration or lack of the knowledge, resources, and healthcare? When you got breast cancer and communicated to us via e-mail, it prompted me to do a little research of my own." Janet told me that according to the Intercultural Cancer Council (www.iccnetwork.org/cancerfacts/) only thirty-eight percent of Hispanic women have regular screening mammograms, and breast cancer is the leading cause of cancer death among Hispanics.

Before she left she said, "You couldn't have possibly said it better – having the knowledge, the education and the information is power and I am passionate about finding a way, perhaps through the Hispanic network here, to make information available to Spanish-speaking cancer patients and their loved ones. We do, after all, work for a company dedicated to breast health."

Tip 159   The National Hispanic Medical Association represents thirty-six thousand licensed Hispanic physicians in the US. Their mission is to improve the health of Hispanics and other underserved populations. If you are a caregiver and your Spanish-speaking loved one needs access to health services, go to www.nhmamd.org or call the NHMA at 202-628-5895 for more information, or call Comprehensive Cancer Centers of Nevada to talk to someone in the breast cancer support group in Las Vegas that meets twice a month. Their number is 702-952-3374.

Even though I may not take up cooking again until the next decade, the wonderful people who provided quality care deserve to be formally thanked. So this week I carried in two trays of my home made lasagna to the cancer center. I delivered them to the Hematology Oncology group (the staff who cared for me during chemo) and Radiation Oncology. It felt good to be able to treat them to a little lunch surprise. Then I wrote a letter about them to Dr. Lsk, the CEO of Christiana Care Health System. I consider every lab coat at the cancer center part of my support network.

Susan, my life coach, reminds me, "A strong network that supports your vision, healing, and continued growth is a gift that facilitates the healing process." She's right. I think it is time to reach out to my e-mail network:

Update – April 18, 2005

To all,

Man, it's great to be back to work. And, oh yeah, it's great to be alive and well too!

For two weeks, I have been at work on a half-day schedule. Looking back to the first morning, and subsequent few mornings, I realize I began each day on overdrive! I was so excited to see people at AstraZeneca and to have a piece of my pre-cancer life back that I dashed in, wearing a ridiculously huge smile, and packing extreme energy. I functioned on pure adrenaline. Full throttle! Slam-dunk! And-one! People visited me; I visited people. To say it felt fantastic is an understatement.

By mid-morning, however, the adrenaline rush wore off. Wendi slithered downhill. It's okay though. I've learned to give in to the fatigue. I stayed put in my office at my computer and began acclimatizing myself to the world of work. Um, that would mean reading through a large amount of e-mail and Strategic eBriefs, for starters. When people stopped by, I stayed seated as much as I could to preserve energy. Kind of like driving to the gas station on "E" and shifting the car into neutral while going down hill so you use as little fuel as possible. I would become aware, over the next few days and weeks, of the fact that friends and colleagues saw a dazzling new me [and that's great] and yet sometimes, underneath I would get overwhelmed and they wouldn't know it; I was unable to handle everything coming my way [and that's okay].

So, Monday April 4 was the beginning of my new-regular life. Yesss. I need to feel pieces of ordinary again. On that morning, Dan left for work, the girls kissed me good-bye and headed for school, and little Danny and I got ourselves ready for the day. I was weepy while doing so – not a sad weepy, a wonderfully sentimental weepy. Returning to work was a momentous occasion…a huge milestone. I felt like doing "TA DA" out loud! Hmmm, can I do "TA DA"? It feels a little self-serving. Shouldn't I be more humble? Hmmm. Dare I say it? Sure, why not.

> *Returning to work was a momentous occasion…a huge milestone. I felt like doing "TA DA" out loud! Hmmm, can I do "TA DA"? It feels a little self-serving. Shouldn't I be more humble? Hmmm. Dare I say it? Sure, why not. TA DA!!*

TA DA!!

When I dropped Danny off to daycare, Miss Sheri hugged me when I told her all that that day meant to me. I got into my car and waved good-bye to my little guy and his pals and drove off. Rewind to nineteen years ago: A few weeks after Christine was born. I was dreading my first day back to work. I couldn't bear the thought of leaving my new baby. The day eventually arrived; Dan and I carried her into Sharon's daycare. Then I cried. I remember walking down Sharon's driveway with Dan's arm around me while I wept. He got into his car; I got into mine. I dabbed my eyes and drove off. But, once I was on my usual route to work the tears stopped and I felt blanketed by comfortable familiarity. And when I arrived at work, it felt like I was never gone. I wished I hadn't spent so much time worrying about it.

Fast forward to Monday, April 4: I was nervous about my first day back only because I was different. When I arrived on the AZ campus, most things were so wonderfully typical of the way they were when I walked out in September that I began to cry. Yeesh, what a day it was going to be. It had been months since I had eyelashes and could wear mascara, and I was about to make it run.

I parked the car, got out, looked at the building against a backdrop of vivid sky-blue and took a deep breath. Thank you, God. Rebirth comes in many packages...that day was packaged for me. I'm pretty sure I was walking a foot off the ground. I bounced up the stairs, dashed through the hall and joyfully set my things down in my new-old office. And did a private TA DA!

It was decorated with "welcome back" stuff, ribbons and flowers, and "we're here for Wendi" buttons. Ahhhh, Wendi is in the HOUSE!

During the first re-entry week I focused on my relief to be back and the future of my new world. But, thoughts about death occasionally crept in. Like, on day three, I got a migraine. I took a Zomig® for the first time since September. That night, Dan and I went to bed early, but I stayed awake until midnight. You see, I rationalized that if the medicine didn't work, then it would be because I had a brain tumor. I drifted to sleep eventually but awakened twice during the night. The headache is still here? Oh no, it must be a tumor. The medicine will work on a migraine but not on a tumor. If I have a headache and the medicine won't help, it must be breast/brain cancer metastasis.

Thankfully, Thursday morning I awakened migraine-free and, I assume, brain cancer-free. Scare's over...for now.

When Pope John Paul II passed away that week, it meant more to me than the death of a leader. It was a reminder that people die, we all will die, and someday I will die. Am I ready to have faith in the lessons I learned when I was fighting "the invader"? I listened to every news report, and scanned newspaper and magazine articles for details of the Pope's final moments. Was he aware he was about to die? What did he say? Was he brave or scared? Since he achieved so much in his life, was he accepting of death?

My mother's brother, my uncle, was placed in ICU (Intensive Care Unit) at Christiana Care's Christiana Hospital during the week I returned to work. I took my mom to visit him. They are both in their 80's. When she saw him, did she think about death? If I make it to 80-something and my siblings are looking at me in a hospital bed, will they be thinking about our mortality? Or, will they be thinking about the wonderful life we had? Or, egads, maybe they'll just be thinking about my hospital gown. So, my mother and my uncle may have been simply enjoying each other's company, and perhaps I was the only one in the room thinking about end-of-life.

My mom and I visited another brother of hers, and his wife, my aunt. They are 83 and 86 – wow – and reside together in an assisted living community. Among many topics, we four talked openly about death. I have a feeling that dying is going to be like the times I was afraid of something, did it, and then looked back and said, "Gee that wasn't so bad…wish I hadn't wasted so much time worrying." Therefore, I have decided that if I ever know that death is imminent, I will close my eyes and expect to see my Dad, all my loved ones who have gone before me, and a vision of God waiting. I will pray that Dan and the kids will not view it as me giving up the fight. And, I will pass on to the other side and say, "That wasn't so bad. I wish I hadn't worried so much about it."

Somewhere along the way, in that week, something happened to my thinking. I made a few decisions. I decided that it is okay to desire old age. And, it's okay to feel cheated if ever my life is about to be cut short. And, I determined that when the time comes, I will seek solace in knowing that I did everything in my power to live and give as long as I could. I won't feel like there was something more I should say to anyone because, in seven months I've said and written a great deal to everyone. I've done some other things too: I, along with Dan, updated my will, living will, power of attorney and healthcare power of attorney. I documented items the kids said they want in the event of my death; I discussed my wishes for their future with people who will continue to be in their lives; and I wrote, in my own hand, casual and numerous short notes to my kids, Dan, and my siblings about my thoughts on day-to-day occurrences (like how pleased I was for something he or she did that day, and even how hurt or disappointed I was about something she or he said to me). Finally, I've come face-to-face with many of you, for the first time in seven months, who followed my progress through my written updates. It is staggering to see the people I touched. I am at peace knowing there are so many who know my heart. I will be able to leave this world trusting that I brought understanding and goodness to others.

A neighbor of mine is losing her husband. She told me Friday that he is in the hospital and "it is only a matter of time." For the first time, I felt I knew what to say in this situation. I said, "He has lived a long life and not everyone gets to live that long. He was able to see three generations of offspring during his time on Earth, has a strong faith in God and has loved ones who are waiting for him when he passes onwards to them. We, along with all your other neighbors, will look after you, and your children and grandchildren will continue to help you; he shouldn't worry. Soon he'll be on the other side, and while I'm sure you'll miss him terribly, knowing he will be there waiting can give you comfort for when it is your time." And I meant every word.

On my third day back to work, people who donated money for breast cancer research earned the enviable right to wear jeans for the day, woo hoo! – I wanted to say to each person I saw, "Thank you, I am one of the people you are wearing your jeans for!" And, I ran into Rose, another breast cancer survivor at AZ. Last year, I noticed she was wearing scarves on her head. I didn't know what to say to her or how to approach her. I figured I was respecting her privacy when I said nothing, but it may have been my subconscious excuse for not knowing how to approach someone who looked to be battling a disease. I can only speak for myself when I say that once I got cancer I appreciated when people approached me, acknowledged my head and said, "Are you fighting something like cancer?" Statements like that pre-empted many enriching conversations. I wouldn't have missed them for the world.

I have a new perspective on everything, and got many opportunities to flex my new perspective muscles during my first week of new-normal life. For example, when Prince Charles and Camilla Parker-Bowles got married, I couldn't think of any reason why two people who are in love shouldn't be together – no matter what happened in the past. They are good for each other, and whatever happened in the past is history. I appreciate that their union has an impact on a society of people, but life goes forward. Call me romantic, but on the evening they married, I didn't think of them as titled figures that had an affair. I imagined how content they must have felt to finally be able to go to sleep and wake up together as a couple with nothing to hide.

My new perspective is not really new though – it sounds cliché but I'll say it anyway; life is too short to fret over some things. Why, just yesterday I was twenty-eight years old, the day before that I was fifteen; today I am forty-five, how old will I be tomorrow? Life speeds by and we have to remember to slow down and step away from the tedium – to live life's precious moments. Look under life's rocks: Smile with an old person, wear a fifty-cent bubble-gum ring to work, don't grimace when something breaks, make yourself available to hold your child's hand when he asks you to – reach for pieces of life and you won't have regrets.

I have a new perspective on everything...

By the second week of half days at work, I found I was able to stretch my awake time a little more each day. On two occasions, I stayed at work until 3:00 instead of leaving around noon. Just because I could! One of those mornings I discovered that our refrigerator compressor went kaput and we lost most of the food in the fridge and all of the food in the freezer. Instead of getting upset, I followed the attitude that a colleague had. She said, "Gee, your life is back to normal like the rest of us!" I like her way of thinking.

On the home-front, life for the teenagers is returning to the way it was before my cancer. Twice I've heard, "My parents live just to ruin my life." Hmmm. And now, like before I got sick, there are some days when none of my daughters can locate the laundry room even though she has to pass through it to go out the garage door. And, how about when neither of them can remember the proper setting on the dishwasher that we've had for six years, but they can IM (Instant Message) in fabulous colors and fonts, and employ multi-lingual skills for a whole new language; POS (parents over shoulder), G2G (got to go), TTYL (talk to you later), and IDK (I don't know). Dan and I hear anecdotes about how meticulously one of them completed her research paper, how participatory one is in her class and how fast one of them can carry the rugby ball to the "uprights." Gee, Dan and I look at each other and marvel at how comatose they can be when vacuuming is on the agenda and the trash begs to be carried out. Teenagers – most of them show their love to parents only when they have to, bury it until a future point in time, and allow it to surface once the teenage years are behind them. I know; I was a teenager once. But, thanks to cancer, I've seen their love. Thanks to my victory over "the invader", I plan on being here when it resurfaces.

I have been receiving catalogues in the mail for spring attire and summer swim wear. It is no coincidence that nubile maidens with lovely racks and heads full of hair grace the covers of each. Geralyn Lucas, author of Why I Wore Lipstick to my Mastectomy, says that these exquisite young ladies have "cleavage and hair bling." Both are things most cancer patients have that are out-of-stock or back-ordered. While the women in the catalogues are beautiful, we, who have given up our breasts and hair for the chance to live, are true beauties.

I talked with Dr. M who reminded me that my next milestone is two years. Eighty percent of advanced stage breast cancer recurs in two years. I believe I can be part of the twenty percent. Recently, Christine found five-year survival rates on the Internet (www.imaginis.com). For women in stage IIIB there is a forty-nine percent survival rate within five years. Sixteen percent of stage IV women survive five years. Oh dear, only sixteen? I was in between those two stages – and the site didn't list statistics for stage IIIC – so my chances are somewhere in the middle of forty-nine and sixteen. I firmly believe I can be part of the smaller percentage of survivors and last the five-year mark. But, my expectations are definitely managed back a bit; therefore I will live like I have five years left, or less, and each year beyond that will be a coup. I will imagine myself as a swash-buckling captain of the seas, standing tall and proud, facing the wind… And as a general, riding tall in the saddle after the battle was won… And as a suffragette promenading to the voting booths for the first time…

Today marks the completion of my half-days at work; I have moved onwards to full days. I can do it. I am ready. With the understanding that I know I have from my compassionate colleagues, I will re-enter the work world as a full time employee and aspire to become a full time contributor.

As for my future, I will…

- *Forgive myself for my wrong doings, and hope others forgive me also*
- *Pay forward the love and encouragement I received (and continue to receive)*
- *Advocate at the top of my lungs about how to survive and live with a life-threatening illness*
- *Be reminiscent of the need to appreciate life (and help others to do the same)*
- *Try not to waste time worrying about things I cannot change*
- *Do cool things with my daughters that will be unique to each*
- *Play with Danny instead of saying, "Mommy doesn't feel well today"*
- *Spend healthy-time with my husband – the man who has been waiting patiently in the sidelines for expressions of my love and attention – and love him like I am in an epic romance novel, with flowing hair and heaving breasts*

- *Let God help me manage my life*
- *Gladly celebrate my one-year cancer anniversary, and two-year non-recurrence and five-year survival goals*
- *Joyfully celebrate my next milestone birthday: My 50th. Instead of thinking that a birthday brings me one year closer to death, I will see it as one more year I cheated it*
- *Not worry too long before investigating an unusual health symptom*
- *Shout hooray when a health symptom is not cancer and turns out to be something really small by comparison, like bronchitis, a liver infection, arthritis or a broken bone*
- *Not feel guilt when I buy expensive gifts for people, leave large tips for wait staff and dip into the retirement fund for vacations*
- *Breathe in the scent of flowers like I am sensing their perfume for the very first time*
- *Enjoy the benefits of a rainy or stormy day as well as a sunny one*
- *Sing in the shower, dance and say, Ta Da!*
- *Treat myself gently and take good care of me, because your warm thoughts will stay with me for the rest of my life*

Finally, I have decided to view each birthday as a curtain call – and I expect to have many. How does a performer feel when he has given the performance of his life and is called out for numerous curtain calls? I vow to find out. So, this year on June 15, I will celebrate my forty-sixth birthday and my first curtain call. I will listen for the applause from within my heart and take a very deep bow.

*In closing, pause for a moment and imagine yourself standing up. Next, imagine me standing by your side. It is with joyful tears in my eyes and a lump in my throat that I close this update. I wish you life's joys, enlightenment and clarity, and many curtain calls of your own. Enjoy the applause that you deserve and life has to offer. As for me, **I will never forget** the discoveries I made*

It is with joyful tears in my eyes and a lump in my throat that I close this update. I wish you life's joys, enlightenment and clarity, and many curtain calls of your own. Enjoy the applause that you deserve and life has to offer. As for me, I will never forget the discoveries I made during my cancer journey, the extraordinary lessons I learned along the way, and the incredible outpouring of love and support I received.

during my cancer journey, the extraordinary lessons I learned along the way, and the incredible outpouring of love and support I received.

Very gratefully yours,

Wendi
Breast Cancer Survivor

Ta Da!

It felt good hit the Send button on that e-mail and many people wrote back to say it felt good to receive it.

It is Wednesday night, nearly midnight and I am unable to sleep. A few hours ago, I attended my weekly cancer support group session at the Wellness Community. I think I have survivor's guilt. *What a strange phenomenon.* I do not feel out of the cancer woods yet, but I've got something that most of my friends in the group don't have at this time and that is the absence of evidence of cancer. A section was dedicated to the concept of survivor's guilt in Vickie Gerard's book, *There's No Place Like Hope.*

Tip 160 If your cancer, or that of your loved one, was diagnosed at stage III or IV, meaning cancer had spread to the lymph nodes, you would benefit from listening to anything that Musa Mayer communicates on the topic of living with metastatic disease. Go to www.advancedbc.org/musa.html.

SO, WHEN DO I START THINKING OF MYSELF AS A PERSON WHO USED TO HAVE CANCER?

A few of Andrea's friends stopped by; one of them has never met me. From the other room, I can hear her say to him, "Come, meet my mom. Don't mind her short hair, she had cancer." When my hair was gone and my illness was apparent in the way I looked and dressed, our daughters were careful to forewarn kids just in case they didn't already know or understand. Now that I have hair growth, I wonder how long it will be before I stop looking like a person who recently finished chemo, and I begin to look like a person with very short hair.

For those of you who may be on a similar journey and would like to make a comparison to mine; I weighed 155 pounds at the time of my diagnosis, and my bra size was 36B. My hair was medium blonde. Since my surgery, chemo and radiation I weigh 140 pounds, my bra size is 34B and my hair seems to be coming back slightly lighter in color, thicker, softer and wavier. People tell me post-chemo hair is usually curly for the first year. For me, that remains to be seen.

I recall many people I've talked to who told me they were survivors, and they would state a number of months or years. When did they start counting? What is my number? Am I an eight-month survivor (since my diagnosis)? Or, am I a one-month survivor (since my 'cured' diagnosis)?

Meet Karen. She is a colleague and breast cancer survivor who was about a month ahead of me in treatments. *So, she could be a nine or two month survivor.* We kept in touch, by the use of e-mail and telephone, throughout our ordeals, but haven't seen each other as cancer patients or survivors. One day, during my second week at work, she comes to my office to greet me. We are both overcome with emotion, marvel at our new hair-dos and then quickly move on to swapping war stories. Even now, after our ordeals are behind us, we continue to learn about life after cancer. Her hair is growing back and I notice she has facial fuzz like I have. "Do you know if that will go away?" I ask her. "I don't know," she replies. I confide in her that I use an electric razor to shave my face. *It's unattractive. I hope it goes away.* She tells me about an after effect that some chemotherapy patients encounter that is unpleasant – toenail fungus. *Ewwww.* I hope I don't get that. She and I are looking forward to wearing sandals and flip-flops this summer so we hope we don't get toenail fungus. She said that treatments for nail fungus are either an oral medication or a topical preparation. *Groovy.*

I go home at the end of the workday, remove my toenail polish and check my feet. I have only one toenail that is thickened and yellow. *If that's all I have, I can live with it. No big deal.*

> **Tip 161**   Having other cancer patients to talk to, whether in organized therapy or as part of your informal support network, is important after cancer and not just during your ordeal. Small things can become large things in your mind, so talk them out with others to keep them in perspective.

Dan and I have been invited to an upcoming party. I can't wait. There, we'll see friends and some people whom we haven't seen in the last eight months, before I was diagnosed with cancer. I am truly looking forward to mingling with everyone as well as the opportunity for Dan and me to test our newfound perspectives on life. You see, there will be former friends there who hold some resentment for us because of misunderstandings that occurred years ago. We are realistic in knowing that not everyone in this world will like us, but the bitterness is uncomfortable, not only for us, but for others. The party is certainly not about Dan or me; it is about a couple that deserves to celebrate an important milestone, but we all bring our own thoughts, feelings and energy to events that affect the outcome. Dan and I have agreed to demonstrate in our actions that it is time for all of us to put the past where it belongs, in the past. We hope the party can be a catalyst for a positive change. As evidenced during our battle with "the invader", we already have a strong network of friends so we aren't in search of more relationships, but it would be nice to try one more time to purge the animosity that exists among a few people who were once part of our lives. Perhaps we can all find it possible to simply smile in each other's company, or more. As survivors of a cancer ordeal, Dan and I have the choice to go on living in ways never possible before by making the most of our time, and deeply valuing family and friends. As it should be.

As we would find out in the next few months, the effort was well worth it.

Tip 162   As Melissa Etheridge put it – eliminate poison in your life. Work through issues with people if, and only if, you think the outcomes of your effort will be worth your time and energy. If not, put them behind you. Living a healthy life and surrounding yourself with positivity is vital.

April 21, 2005 – Today is my son's fourth birthday. I can't believe it. Why, it seems like only weeks ago that the five of us were rushing to the hospital to deliver him. I remember my daughters' voices coaching me through labor, "That's one minute and thirty-six seconds Mommy", "Keep pushing Mommy," and "You can do it Mom." And there he was…and now he's four! He happily went off to daycare this morning with fancy cupcakes I made, ice cream and other party stuff. I look forward to the celebrations that we have planned for him tonight and this weekend.

GENETIC COUNSELING DETAILS

Today is also my appointment with the genetic counselor at "the Helen Graham." In the mix of transitioning from a patient at home to an employee at work, I inadvertently missed my appointment last week with her. Enter Richard. He is, I think, an official jack-of-all-trades at the cancer center. I do not know his specific role or job title, but he greets people by first name in the reception area, doles out materials and information when folks request them, and organizes appointments and paperwork. I am pretty sure his job title is 'Knower of All Things'. When I realized I missed my appointment with Ms. C, I showed up in the Reception Area and he quickly rescheduled me. *It must've been the tears in my eyes.*

The purpose of my genetic counseling educational session today is to determine the risk of breast and ovarian cancer for my siblings, mom, my children and me. Yes, I could be at risk for future occurrences of breast cancer that would be unrelated to this bout with it. Plus, I could be at risk for ovarian cancer if I test positive for an alteration in the two most common genes associated with hereditary breast and ovarian cancer – the BRCA1 or BRCA2 genes (chromosome seventeen and thirteen). These two genes are tumor suppressors and everybody has them. Alterations or mutations in these genes increase risk of cancer and account for approximately eighty percent of familial cancer cases. Gene mutations may be inherited or acquired during a person's life. Some people have genes that are good or ones that are altered.

What will I do with this information? Well, if I test positive, I may opt for a prophylactic mastectomy (removal of my other breast), and surgical removal of my ovaries and fallopian tubes (called Salpingo-oophorectomy). Salpingo-oophorectomy reduces the risk of ovarian cancer by ninety-six percent. Additionally, I may be able to enter a clinical trial (if one is open) for special screening.

If I test positive and the assessment of Dan's side of the family turns up a measure of risk, our children will fall into a high-risk category and therefore screened earlier and more extensively. Screening for breast cancer for them would mean mammograms beginning at an earlier age than the average age for mass screening of forty, most likely at age twenty-five. Ovarian cancer screening is not offered to the general public since the incidence of ovarian cancer is two percent or less; thus according to guidelines for mass screening it is not cost effective and yield would most likely be low. However, screening for high-risk individuals, such as those with BRCA1 or BRCA2 alterations or family history of ovarian cancer, should start at age 30. The ovarian cancer screening protocol would include transvaginal ultrasounds with color Doppler and blood tests measuring CA-125 levels.

Once all the genetic information is assembled and an assessment of risk is made, Dan and I will sit down with our daughters and discuss it.

Tip 163   If, at the end of the genetic assessment process, you receive an easy-to-comprehend document, store it with all other important papers, such as your will, life insurance policies, birth certificates, etc. If documentation you receive is not easy to comprehend, write down the basic facts and store them. As soon as your daughters and sons are old enough to understand about the role genetics play in their lives, explain the assessment to them or schedule an appointment with a genetic counselor who can.

Soon, I will have a tube of blood drawn and it will be sent to Myriad laboratories in Salt Lake City, Utah (currently, the only laboratory that does this specific type of genetic/DNA testing). It pleases me to think that, through risk assessment, I may be able to help my siblings, children, nieces and nephews, and not just myself.

Perhaps that's why I got cancer – so I could have the choice to see and do good things because of the lessons I learned after I got it. One of the good things I am doing is to gain knowledge and therefore protect my family. And, in this regard, my children will have subliminal sentries watching over them. That satisfies my maternal instincts.

After my two and a half hour education session with Ms. C, I am fatigued and need a nap. Then I will need to get my notes in order, because I have some homework to do. Following up with relatives who have had cancer will be of utmost importance to my assessment.

Subsequent steps of this multi-step process are to have a follow-up session with Ms. C regarding my findings and to have blood drawn. She explained that a positive result would be a true positive, whereas a negative result could be a false negative because of limitations in the ability to test the gene. (Current BRCA1 and BRCA2 analysis is thought to miss approximately fifteen to thirty percent of alterations, primarily deletions, duplications and rearrangements of the genetic alphabet). Currently, looking for them would be like searching for a misspelled word in an encyclopedia, and everyone's misspelled word is different. The good news is that in about a year new technology will likely be available so that false negatives could be virtually eliminated.

According to FORCE (Facing Our Risk of Cancer Empowered) and NSGC (National Society of Genetic Counselors), genetic tests – like other medical tests – can provide important, even life-saving information. The benefits of testing need to be weighed against the concern about genetic discrimination. Most states have laws to prevent insurance companies and employers from discriminating based on a hereditary risk for disease.

Tip 164   If you test positive for genetic abnormalities that increase your risk for diseases, you may want to research the most current laws in your state regarding genetic discrimination. There are also federal laws that offer some protection against genetic discrimination. The HIPAA protects people with group health insurance against being denied insurance, having their insurance canceled, or having their rates individually increased due to any preexisting condition. Contact the Department of Health and Human Services at www.hhs.gov/ocr/hipaa or call 866-627-7748.

Learning about my genetic information and its impact on my family feels like an epilogue to my ordeal. It is one of the post-cancer things on my list of things to do.

I will have another surgery in the future to have my medi-port removed and finish the reconstruction that was done on September 10 (as part of my mastectomy). Dr. M and my radiation oncologist suggested I wait because radiation can have effects on reconstruction as far out as six to twelve months after radiation is complete. Apparently, the radiation after-effects are better for TRAM reconstructions than implant reconstructions, but they are possible. Dr. D, my plastic surgeon tells me that if I experience 'hardened' reconstruction or uneven scarring on the front side, he can touch it up with tissue and fat taken from other parts of my body via liposuction. To that I say, "Oh, turn me over and take it from the back side!" *Wouldn't you?*

And, if I test positive for BRCA1 and BRCA2 the final surgery will also include a prophylactic mastectomy and/or a salpingo oophorectomy. *So many choices for this final surgery; door number one – nipple and medi-port, door number two – lipo, and door number three – girl parts extraction…I may choose all three and be a winner!*

My new-old-regular life is coming together now. Despite my public and private fears, I am becoming comfortable with referring to myself as a 'breast cancer survivor'.

My next annual mammogram (to my right breast) is already scheduled, thanks to CHS at AZ and their reminder program; only my mammograms will no longer be on-site. My mammograms, from this point forward, will include more specialized diagnostic imaging, and will be performed at the cancer center.

Tip 165   No excuses. Do not forget your annual mammogram. Go to the American Cancer Society website and use the interactive tool that will send an e-mail message each year reminding you or a woman you love to "Please, schedule your mammogram today." When you click on the link I provide at the end of this tip, you will be able to choose an e-mail address, month, and day that you would like an e-mail reminder sent. http://www.cancer.org/docroot/PED/content/PED_2_3x_Mammogram_Reminder.asp. Then talk to your PCP (Primary Care Physician) and schedule it.

Today is April 26. I am ready for the second monthly follow-up with Dr. N. I enter "the Helen Graham" feeling well, not sickly, and wearing business attire, not jeans and slippers. Most everyone who knows me there notices I look different. During the examination I express my fears of recurrence and small doubts about five-year survival. She reminds me that new developments are happening everyday that improve my chances. She tells me to watch the newscasts today.

GOOD NEWS TODAY ABOUT ANOTHER WAY TO FIGHT BREAST CANCER – HERCEPTIN®

All major broadcasting stations are heralding news about Herceptin® and its use in treating breast cancer recurrence and improving survival in certain women. Herceptin® is an immunotherapy treatment, a monoclonal antibody that selectively binds to the protein coded by the HER-2/neu gene to block tumor cell growth and signal the immune system. Basically, it helps the immune system fight metastatic, HER-2/neu positive cancer. Unfortunately, Herceptin® will not work for me since I do not have the over-expressed cancer gene, [*imagine, there's some part of me that is not over expressive!*] but it is breakthrough news and it serves as a reminder to me that there is hope. Your PCP or oncologist can discuss after-breast-cancer options with you that improve your chances, so ask.

Tip 166   There is a wide range of benefits to participating in clinical trials. When you enter a trial, consideration is given to the timing of the trial and that of your needed treatment. Most pharma companies have an extensive detailed transition plan worked out for when the trial is scheduled to end and when it ends early.

Women, who were taking Herceptin® as part of a clinical trial, had such success that the clinical trial was discontinued. This is great news overall for breast cancer, but whenever a trial stops sooner than expected, it can set off a chain of events that you and your doctor – if you are part of a trial – will need to work through. Since Herceptin®, for example, was already available in the marketplace, most oncologists were pleased with this type of data because the product is obtainable. True, the patients who were in the trial would no longer be getting free Herceptin®, but their physicians would be able to keep the patients on the drug, they would need to write a prescription. (The patients' insurance plans would then pick up the costs.) In some cases, however plans could take a couple months in order to review the new indications and data to determine coverage. There are various options; the company that makes the drug, your insurance company and the physicians will work together to recommend the best course of action in order to avoid compromising your treatment.

In cases where the product isn't currently available in the market, the company might have a gap between when the trial stopped and when it is approved by the FDA (usually anywhere between six and ten months, depending upon the complexities of the manufacturing process and the expected demand). Again, there are various options for continuous treatment if a cancer trial does turn positive.

Herceptin® targets specific cancer cells whereas chemotherapy drugs target more than just cancer cells. Scientists hope to make all cancer-fighting drugs specific, like Herceptin®.

Tip 167   Breastcancer.org has a section dedicated to Research News whereby each month, experts examine recent research, advances, important updates and changes in how breast cancer is treated and diagnosed. Go to the section periodically and see for yourself that there are reasons to be optimistic.

TAMOXIFEN

Hormonal therapy is a form of systemic treatment for breast cancer. The goal is to protect your whole body from cancer cells that may have escaped the original tumor. Hormonal therapy can be very effective in lowering the risk of recurrence for women with ER positive or PR positive breast cancer, because it uses drugs to block the effects of hormones (such as estrogen) that have the potential to promote the growth of breast cancer. According to breastcancer.org, tamoxifen is the hormonal therapy that's been around the longest—nearly thirty years. It blocks the effect of estrogen on breast cancer cells, and keeps the cells from growing. Tamoxifen can reduce recurrence by forty to fifty percent in post-menopausal women, and by thirty to fifty percent in pre-menopausal women. It also lowers the risk of a new breast cancer developing in the unaffected breast. And it can slow down the progression of advanced disease. There are several brands of tamoxifen available: Nolvadex® is one; alternative brand (trade) names are, Valodex® and Istubal®. Doctors recommend that it be taken for five years.

But in recent years a new type of hormonal therapy has been developed for post-menopausal women with ER positive breast cancer called aromatase inhibitors (AIs). Authorities say it works by blocking the production of estrogen in muscle and fat tissue. This is the main source of estrogen in women beyond menopause, after the ovaries stop making significant levels of estrogen.

AROMATASE INHIBITORS

There are currently three aromatase inhibitors used to treat breast cancer: Arimidex® (anastrozole), Femara® (letrozole), and Aromasin® (exemestane). There are some key studies that show benefits of aromatase inhibitors in lowering the risk of recurrence. Five years of tamoxifen therapy reduces the risk of breast cancer recurrences by fifty percent, and the risk of breast cancer mortality by twenty-eight percent, in women who are estrogen receptor positive (Lancet 351: 1451-67). In the ATAC trial (Arimidex, Tamoxifen, Alone or in Combination) there was a seventeen percent reduction in the risk of recurrence with Arimidex® and tamoxifen in the population with cancers that expressed ER or PR with a median of sixty-eight months of follow-up (Lancet 2005:365: 60-62). These are exciting statistics. Conversely, women with early breast cancer who do not take hormonal treatment after completion of surgery with or without radiation, have a greater than one-third chance of recurrence. Go to breastcancer.org for more information and results from trial studies. Talk with your PCP or oncologist about hormonal therapy.

Tip 168   Women whose tumors are hormone receptor-positive (ER or PR positive) are likely to respond to adjuvant treatment. (Adjuvant means "in addition to.") And, adjuvant hormonal treatment, such as Nolvadex® or aromatase inhibitor treatment, such as Arimidex®, Femara®, and Aromasin® helps reduce the risk of recurrence.

A colleague at AZ and a two-time breast cancer survivor gave me an easy-to-understand analogy which she got from a doctor at the MD Anderson Cancer Center in Texas. It goes like this: Cancer genes that are ER positive are like locks. Estrogen is the key that fits the locks. You don't want the key to go into the locks. Tamoxifen fills the keyholes to prevent the key from going into the locks. Faslodex® alters the key so it doesn't fit the locks. Arimidex® dissolves the key. The process involves a five-year plan.

Experts emphasize the criticality of adherence to the five-year plan using this form of therapy, because the more you stick to the program, the more benefit you'll gain from the treatment (breastcancer.org). So, stay on track with it and take the medications as prescribed, year after year, in order to get the best results.

Tip 169   Women whose tumors are ER negative (like mine) should watch for new classes of medications under study that target cell function that is independent of estrogen. Breastcancer.org says one promising new class of drugs, called farnyseal transferase inhibitors (FTIs), works by weakening other chemical signals (NOT triggered by estrogen receptors) that stimulate cell growth, and that are NOT triggered by estrogen receptors.

Tip 170   Despite your fears and doubts, continue to build good health. Treatment continues to progress at a quick pace, especially in recent years. This is great news for improving health and survival odds. Caregivers, remind your loved one that he or she should be checked regularly. View cancer as a chronic illness much like heart disease or diabetes, and get on with life. Go to www.breastcancer.org for tips on Building Long-Term Health.

Follow up appointments with my oncologist will be: three one-month visits, several three-month visits, a few six-month visits and then annual visits. This seems to me to be one part weaning-process and one part health-indicator. To my way of thinking, as the visits decrease in frequency, the passing of time occurs; as time passes, chances of recurrence decrease.

Andrea calls me from work and tells me she ran into a friend from school. Her friend says that her mom was just diagnosed with breast cancer. I immediately contact her mom to remind her that she and her family can get through this and to offer my phone numbers and e-mail address. I hope she reaches out if she needs support. She works at AZ, just like me. Last month, AZ CHS called her for her annual mammogram (just as they called me). She tells me her mammogram showed no abnormalities (mine didn't either), and my jaw drops when she says that the nurse discovered the lump in the clinical, hand-to-breast, exam that was performed immediately before she went in to the imaging room! Amazing. I believe it is worth the effort to repeat a tip from the first chapter of this book:

> **Tip 171** Doctors recommend routine screening mammography because it helps find breast changes early. But not all changes show up on mammograms. Studies have shown that using BSE, mammography and a clinical breast exam by a doctor or nurse increases your chance for early detection and can reduce deaths from breast cancer (Breast Health p. 6).

Defining the "New Normal"

As for me, I smile every day. I thank God for his many blessings…every day. As often as I can, I remind myself to take deep breaths and breathe away stress, because the world will continue to turn on its axis even when I trade a task on my to-do list for something of greater meaning. I try to recognize my spin-patterns (when a 'what-if' thought grows out of control and goes round and round in an endless loop) and I break them. Instead of going back to doing things 'normally', the way I used to before breast cancer, I seize opportunities to redefine "normal."

In life, we do things that are sometimes inefficient, and oftentimes we stop doing inefficient things only because we are forced to (too tired, sick, can't). Why don't we recognize and change them by choice?

Jill, my manager and my friend, said, "You have different parts of yourself that you hadn't met before cancer. And they are good. Your priorities are different now – more qualitative than quantitative. You're seeing life through different lenses. It's like when I became a mother. The baby was born, I had time with him at home on family medical leave, and then I returned to work and expected to – even hoped to – get my former life back, so I could feel 'normal.' I yearned for my life to be exactly the way it was before [my son] was born. But it couldn't be the same because my life was changed. My priorities were different. And that's okay. I want to support you as you follow the path of redefining what normal is. And don't be afraid to meet the new you."

My naturopathic sister, Deb, agrees and suggests I try eliminating the word "normal" altogether and using "natural" instead. She says to find what is natural for me.

So, this is what it is like to be a breast cancer survivor. *Cool.*

My daughters are searching the Internet for information and find an inspirational and informative website by Dr. Siegel for Exceptional Cancer Patients: ECaP-Online.org. It is so helpful that my family is involved in my cancer journey. I am ready to be an exceptional cancer patient.

A FEW WELLNESS IDEAS

Soon, I plan to begin a chiropractic wellness program, the idea being that if my vertebrae are properly aligned, my brain can evenly distribute nerve impulses throughout my body. As I am learning, identifying possible subluxation (malposition of bones in the spine that causes nerve interference) and treating it can improve the function of my nervous system. A high performing nervous system will enable my body to work properly, and regulate my body's responses to physiological conditions, stress, and other psychological conditions. According to a physician named Henry Windsor, MD, data suggests that organs supplied by pinched nerves revealed pathological changes (disease). The more severe the pinched nerves the more serious the organ damage. Even Hippocrates said, "look well to the spine for cause of disease." I want to be healthy. *I need to be healthy – I've got the rest of my life ahead of me.*

Tip 172   If you are interested in chiropractic wellness consult your phonebook and ask chiropractic offices if they use new chiropractic technology like the ProAdjuster by Dr. Pisciottano.

Now that I am back to work and in a routine, I've added time for spiritu-al wellness into my schedule. I may not make it to church on Sundays, but every morning I spend a little time with God by having a discussion with Him about my daily life and the people who surround me. I believe He hears me.

FIGHTING DISEASE USING STEM CELL RESEARCH – A MORAL DILEMMA

I eagerly anticipate the future. Not only do I want to live in it, but also I want to see what cancer treatments and cures will be developed. According to Leon R. Kass, a fellow at the American Enterprise Institute and chairman of the President's Council on Bioethics, scientists and patients' advocates are eager to garner support for this promising field of research, and will be urging Congress to overturn current limits on feder-al funding for embryonic stem cell research.

A civilized society is unable to witness human afflictions from disease and sit idly by when there is the promise of cures dangling in front of us. Yet, no decent society can afford to treat human life, at whatever stage of development (such as the controversial embryonic stage), as a mere natu-ral resource to be mined for the benefit of others. It is definitely a moral dilemma. Fortunately, there are a growing number of reports beginning to suggest a method of producing the same kind of cells, but without destroying embryos (Kass, p. A13). Recent scientific reports suggest there may be ways to research stem cells without having to destroy human embryos in the process.

One way is through fusion. By fusing an adult cell with an existing embryonic stem cell, scientists have reported progress toward producing cells that are genetically identical to the adult cell but that retain stem cell properties. This has advantages of cloning-for-research but without the need for eggs and without creating embryos. These fusion experiments could be carried out using any of the twenty-two human stem cell lines that are eligible for federal funding under the Bush policy and that are today available from the NIH (Kass, p. A13).

The topic of stem cell research will hit the Senate floor in the near future. Let's hope there are mutually beneficial solutions for scientific research and life advocacy groups, to fight disease.

Mother's Day is a few days away. In my heart, I will honor my Mom, my Mother-in-law, and all the wonderful mothers I know. I will also honor me. There were moments during my battle with "the invader" when I wondered if I would be here to celebrate this Mother's Day. And, even though I continue to have moments when I wonder about future Mother's Days, I will face them one at a time. All my life I wanted to be in the role of Mom. I have been in the role for nineteen years and continue to look for ways to improve it for my family and me. This Sunday will not be about the role, but celebrating myself in it.

The most important thing I am wishing for in my life is for Dan and I, together, to observe our children as they achieve their dreams; be they to have children of their own, to have successful careers, to travel, to live simply, to have enriching relationships, or all of the above. *Or, none of the above.* Whatever their dreams are, I want to be here, alive, old, feeble and gray. The second most important thing I am wishing for is to courageously accept God's will and my fate, if it comes to pass that my first wish is not going to be granted.

Since it is a few days before Mother's Day and my life-after-cancer has begun, I will close my journey here, with a poem as a happy tribute to everyone (because everyone has a mother).

My Mother
By Ann Taylor Gilbert and Jane Taylor (London 1783 – 1824)
(Writers – memoirs and poetry)

Who fed me from her gentle breast
And hushed me in her arms to rest,
And on my cheek sweet kisses pressed?
My mother.

When sleep forsook my open eye,
Who was it sung sweet lullaby
And rocked me that I should not cry?
My mother.

Who sat and watched my infant head
When sleeping in my cradle bed,
And tears of sweet affection shed?
My mother.

Who taught my infant lips to pray,
To love God's holy word and day,
And walk in wisdom's pleasant way?
My mother.

And can I ever cease to be
Affectionate and kind to thee
Who was so very kind to me, -
My mother.

Oh no, the thought I cannot bear;
And if God please my life to spare
I hope I shall reward thy care,
My mother.

When thou art feeble, old and gray,
My healthy arm shall be thy stay,
And I will soothe thy pains away,
My mother...

Happy, happy Mother's Day to everyone!

Wendi
Breast Cancer Survivor

CHAPTER

9

FRIENDS AND FAMILY: IN RETROSPECT

(Clockwise from left: Michele, Dan, Danny, Andrea
Christine, and me in the middle)

Photo courtesy of G. Thomas Murray Photography

The unexamined life is not worth living for man.

Socrates
Greek Philosopher
(469 BC - 399 BC)
in Plato, *Dialogues, Apology*

Some people who were part of my journey graciously penned their thoughts in retrospect after my ordeal was over.

Sue F was one of them:

When Wendi asked me to add my thoughts about her fight against breast cancer to her book, I was really flattered, then found myself procrastinating. At age 60, I know myself well enough to realize there was a psychological reason behind my failure to put words to paper since I'm really quite blabby. Finally, I forced myself to do some soul-searching and came to an understanding, which I would like to share since there are probably other people who respond to physical threats in the same way.

First, though, let's go back to the beginning of Wendi's journey. Between the tears, I prayed and reasoned with God that Wendi was far, far more valuable with us because she sets such a wonderful example of how life should be lived. She teaches us daily the impact of goodness, love, compassion, understanding, thoughtfulness and kindness on those who are lucky enough to know her, and in the energy she projects we find ourselves trying to become better human beings. Surely, He wouldn't want to waste this asset; these qualities are far too rare on earth.

Between the tears and prayers, there were the busy times: cooking, delivering food from coworkers, visiting, going to lunch. It was at a luncheon when Wendi had almost completed her chemotherapy that I noticed a mental withdrawal on my part. I came back to work depressed and thinking that, while I really wanted to support Wendi in probably the most important battle of her life, I was uncomfortable with the conversation that consumed our luncheon. I found myself printing off her e-mailed updates but putting them in my briefcase to read later and, in some cases, not reading them at all. This, plus the procrastination over a contribution to her book, made me stop and really examine my behavior. What kind of a friend was I that my support of Wendi was less than 100%? Why was I closing down in her time of need?

Then it hit me: it is fear!

I have suffered from lab coat syndrome for many years, worrying that doctors would diagnosis some awful problem on my wellness visits. I avoid articles about strokes, heart disease, cancer, Alzheimer's, Parkinson's, etc. and I suffer from panic attacks driven by the fear of becoming sick and dying. Wendi's battle with breast cancer has made me face my old enemy and I have obviously been trying to run – to avoid having to talk or think about a subject which scares me – and over which I have no control. I feel that recognizing this behavior may help readers, both patients and her network of family and friends, understand how some people react to life-threatening illness.

And so, while I am still uncomfortable dwelling on the disease for any length of time, I feel strengthened in understanding my own shortcomings and committed to helping Wendi, my dear friend, a cancer survivor.

Donna, a pharmacy technician at the store that fills my prescriptions, tells me what it's like to work at a pharmacy and know that one of your customers has cancer:

Until the customer says something [about having cancer], we can't talk about it or acknowledge it because of the customer's right to privacy (the HIPAA privacy act). So I kept my thoughts in my head. Once I knew you were on the meds, I watched the changes in you. Seeing your sister and family come in to get your medicines indicated to me how you were doing – everybody came together to help you – it was unreal. I appreciated observing your family and seeing how they interacted with you and you interacted with them. I realized that your situation involved them too. And when you came in, to see you dragging would make me wonder; did you have a chemo treatment today? I would look at you and feel sad.

As soon as you talked about your cancer, I felt like I became more involved with your positive attitude about it. Because of your overwhelming freeness and openness, I learned about how the meds helped you. You were teaching me (because I don't always know what all the medicines are for). It was unreal to learn how it all goes together – it opened my mind – it helped me to see what my cousin [who has cancer] is going through. Seeing you come in feeling good on some days was interesting and I would feel relieved.

I loved when I got to rub your hair! No one has ever offered that before.

Mary, a colleague, who was part of my journey, sent me an e-mail:

I know that you like to share so much about your life and experiences that you and your family have been through the past few months... so I wanted to tell you about an experience I had this past weekend.

My daughter (almost 4) and I were in the bathroom at the movie theatre and there was a lady standing beside us at the sink. Lauren kept staring at her. She had a bright red hat on and I could tell that she had no hair underneath. Prior to meeting you and following your journey through your cancer ordeal, I probably would have felt self conscious about not knowing how to talk to the lady or how to act. Instead, I said to her "I think my daughter is loving your beautiful red hat." My daughter piped up, "red is my favourite colour." The lady responded that she wears a lot of hats these days because she's going through chemo. We then spoke for a few minutes about my daughter and her grand kids before parting ways.

I'd like to say thank you for making me realize that everyone craves that little bit of normalcy in their daily lives, like speaking about their children/grandchildren, especially when the rest of one's day may be not so normal. I will never again hesitate to speak with someone I see who may need a little bit of conversation and "normalcy" in her day.

Jim, a communications professional, whom I previously worked with, and a colleague @FoxPress™, writes:

I will treasure the times Wendi and I worked together at AstraZeneca; the projects we collaborated on always became interesting and fun rather than just ordinary work. I think it was the shared experience of September 11, 2001 that ensured we would always maintain contact with one another, because we were working on a task together when someone came in our office to tell us a plane hit the World Trade Center. Neither of us will ever forget that fateful day as we watched the newscasts in stunned silence.

My reaction was eerily similar when I got the e-mail from her that said she had breast cancer – I was shocked, in disbelief and had a terrible feeling that all was not right with the world. How could something like this strike such a warm and kind person?

We missed our 2004 September 11th anniversary phone call because Wendi was in the midst of recuperating from surgery; I know that we'll take up the tradition again for 2005.

Sharry, Kayla H's grandmother, writes:

A sweet, bright-eyed, eleventh-grader named Kayla never knew her mother. She died when Kayla was eight months old from metastatic malignant melanoma. Kayla's grandfather and I brought her home from the hospital to stay with us because her father was so busy taking care of his sick wife and three other small children. Some say that Kayla's mother (Cindy) "lost her battle with cancer." We disagree. We feel that, in the end, Cindy no longer gave it a place to grow. She won and now she's in the arms of the Lord. She is in Heaven for those left behind to help them fight their battles here on Earth.

For the last seventeen years we have loved Kayla and taught her to love herself. She has helped fill the gaping hole left by her mother's death. When Kayla was in the fourth grade, she was an average student. She was not excited about school or her life. Then, out of the blue came an angel named Wendi. She became Kayla's mentor. Wendi and her beautiful family went to school programs, lunches, and purchased a computer and supplied the Internet for her. They became a very important part of Kayla's life. Wendi made Kayla feel like she was someone special and important. I know that without Wendi's input Kayla would not be the honor student in a nursing program that she is today. I feel that Cindy is looking down at Wendi with gratitude and praise and she is saying, "job well done." Bless you Wendi.

Before Wendi got cancer, Kayla always thought that if you got a horrific disease there would be no hope for it and it would be deadly. She struggled with the fact that Wendi was so sick. But she's seen Wendi triumph over this. The way Wendi wrote about her experience left me breathless. I know there's a God and I'm still upset with Him for taking my daughter and leaving her four small children [without a mother], but I also know He was there for Wendi.

Sheri, Danny's daycare provider writes:

I will share an anecdote and a few conscious things I did to help little Danny and his friends deal and cope more easily at daycare:

The first thing I consciously did was to be very open and available to answer questions and talk about comments brought up in conversations with me and between Danny and the kids. I listened for questions directed to Danny from the children about why he was late to daycare or why his mommy wears hats. I would follow cues from Danny on how to help him answer. I wanted him to know things would not change and I would take care of him while mommy was at the doctors. I was always available for him with extra hugs and snuggle time. Sometimes he seemed oversensitive or would react with unusual intensity to a situation or minor injury. Another thing I did was to read "Helping Children Cope with Separation and Loss", by Claudia Jewett. There was a lot of helpful information, which gave me insight into what Danny might be experiencing and how to help him cope and understand.

One morning Danny came into daycare and another child asked him why his mommy wore hats all the time. Danny said mommy wore hats because she did not have hair. He seemed very comfortable and confident with his answer. The other child asked the perfect three-year-old question, "Why?"

Danny and the other children were eating breakfast, so I let the conversation progress. Danny answered that medicine made mommy's hair come out. Of course, the next question was, "Why?" Danny answered very matter-of-factly, that the medicine that made the bug in mommy go away made her hair go away too. This seemed to answer the why questions and everyone continued to eat breakfast. I gave Danny a huge hug from behind and we all sat and talked about what we were planning to do that day. This was how most of our conversations went.

Most of the time Danny was confident and capable to answer his friends' questions and when he was not or became frustrated I was there to help with the answer. This seemed to work for all the children including Danny.

Dan says:

In retrospect, it was devastating. I thought many things; what tough luck – we've been through rough times, we worked hard to get through them and then this? Sour grapes. After all we'd been through and we got dealt a blow like this. I felt like, woe is me. So, what should we do? Jump off a bridge? Throw in the towel? In the beginning the bad news kept coming. It was one thing after another. Finally, you reach the point when you say to yourself, "We'll do what we need to do and get through it." Then came decisions to be made. It's not my body so I wasn't sure how much to interject. It wasn't going to be me who would sit there in pain from surgery or have scars. How could I tell her what kind of reconstructive surgery she should get? It wasn't going to matter to me what she looked like afterward. I'll love her no matter what.

I worked hard to support my wife in things related to her cancer, and tried not to treat her differently in things that were not. I didn't want her to feel as though she was altered so she would not feel self-conscious. I think I needed that for myself too. It is wonderful to be on the other side [of the cancer], to be able to appreciate things more, and enjoy each day more. I try to stay on top of her health needs and nutritional needs...and those of my own. Now, I take vitamins, go to bed earlier, and read about healthy living. I know I come off badly if I'm tired. I get miserable and drag everyone else down. So, I understand that she gets tired easily and I remind her that she shouldn't fight it – "Why don't you go upstairs and take a nap. We can handle things without you for awhile." I try to be supportive in that way. We live a little bit wiser. I hope Wendi doesn't have a recurrence of cancer. I know that is one of her fears. If it happens we'll deal with it. Maybe it will be like adding another experience to our portfolio. Maybe it will be like the work I do; when you build your first building you are shaky, the second one you are less shaky and in some areas more confident.

I listen to people who tell me they had cancer and how technology has made it easier to go through. I always try to share with Wendi what I hear out in the world – the stories of their battle scars – because she has an alliance to them. I also look ahead. My eyes are open; the light is bright on the other side of the tunnel. We've refined our togetherness and our differences, respect one another, and are back to the business of raising our family, and teaching the kids right from wrong and how to work together as one big team. Wendi and I can stand united. It's nice to have two people raising children rather than one.

I am different. Now, I don't mind if I don't have a lot of extra money in my pocket...I'm happier now to just putz around in the garage and hang around the house. I ask myself, what do you choose to do with your life? Put in time? Or make sure to have a bar-b-que, take the kids on vacations, and do things more than just work. I prioritize things so that I can look back on my life and hers, and see that we've been places, done things, and enjoyed ourselves.

I'll look back on Wendi's cancer episode as a negative experience for my partner and me...We go forward from here.

Christine, my eldest says:

If someone asked me what it was like to have a mother with cancer I would say: There were a lot of times when Mom was resting, so we had to learn how to get along without her. We had questions and worried a lot, but we always had to think positively, pray and hope that everything was going to be okay. We had to pitch in taking care of Danny because he didn't truly understand what was going on. We took turns playing with him, acting as mom, watching him, and keeping him from waking her up.

Now, I think cancer was an obstacle or a test that God set for us; it brought us closer and we all came through it together.

Andrea, my seventeen-year old writes:

First and foremost when a person tells you something as traumatic as my mother told me, make sure you hold and comfort him or her. I regret not holding my mom tighter when I first found out. I ran out of the house. Another piece of advice would be to surround yourself with caring people who love you and support you. I had a great number of friends and an extremely supportive boyfriend, Mike, who would listen to my worries. My mother's diagnosis was life-changing in many ways. My school became very different. My teachers were very favoring and sensitive towards me. If I had trouble with something, they were more willing to help and they became more lenient when it came to handing in homework. In some of my classes, whenever the word 'cancer' came up in what we were learning, I felt as if other kids were looking at me. Whenever my teachers would say the word, they would look in my direction, I always got a knot in my throat and felt that I was getting sympathy I did not need or want. At work I always felt a warm welcome from the nicest ladies: Sue, Cindy, Barb and Stacy. They seemed like extra mothers. When my mom was sick and tired, they helped comfort me and give me advice. My home life was definitely the most changed, although we had neighbors and friends making us dinner, it was not the same as walking into the house and smelling my mother's home made cooking. Our mailbox was always full of cards and gifts and she let us open them. Our doorbell was always ringing, and whenever I pulled into the driveway there were often cars in it that were not familiar. I only wish that if I am ever diagnosed with any illness that I have as many people thinking of me as my mom did. My mother is the most popular person I know. My mom, the survivor, is a celebrity to many. When you experience something negative you may always see who your true friends are; my mom did. Her journey has allowed me to see her in a more insightful way. Instead of worrying about herself, she worried about keeping a sense of normalcy in the household. I wish I were like that.

My brother was never aware of the extent of my mother's condition and he might never understand how much easier he made her recovery. My mother sees him as a blessing from God for the wonderfully small things he did and said to take part in her survival with cancer.

My mom and my brother made up The Cancer Dance and did it together. She gave him something that he could use and understand in their time of need. Some people need religion and some people need literature, but together my young brother and my mother needed only The Cancer Dance.

Peace out.

Michele, my sixteen-year-old says:

In the beginning, when my parents told me Mom had cancer, I was sure my mom would die, because of other [cancer] deaths. My mom is the center of our family. Something without a center falls apart. I thought my Mom would die, the family would fall apart emotionally and we'd sell the house, and it would be a slow painful process. I shared my feelings with my friends and not my family...my friends were outside sources.

They tell you that you should look to an outside source for support, some-one who's not involved.

When my mom had her surgery, I didn't want to go see her in the hospital because I didn't want to see her like that. Just as I thought it would, it scared me when I saw her. One of the first nights my mom was back home, I slept on the couch next to her. I wasn't as afraid when I was near her, and I wanted her to know she wasn't alone.

I didn't like to see my mom without hair because she looked like a true can-cer patient, and people with cancer die. But after awhile, I stopped think-ing she would. I saw her day-by-day and she never looked bad enough to die.

If someone asked me what it was like, I would say it was kind of surreal. It never actually felt like it was happening, because normally when I pic-ture a cancer patient, I picture someone lying around looking like death. And that wasn't the case at all. My mom and family seemed to cope with it well. As her daughter, I felt just as protected and secure as always.

It felt good to tell my friends my mom was in remission. I wrote about it in my Live Journal, only I didn't know how to spell the word. I think I wrote that she was in "reminission."

I believe that she's fine now and free of cancer.

It's over and we made it.

For the true nature of things, if we will rightly consider, every green tree is far more glorious than if it were made from gold and silver.

Martin Luther
Monk, Doctor of Theology
(1483 - 1546)

Epilogue

Life is just a mirror, and what you see out there,
you must first see inside of you.

Wally 'Famous' Amos
Father of the Gourmet Cookie Industry
and Motivational Speaker
(1936 -)

Like most painful things I have experienced in my life, my memory of the difficulties I had during my walk with cancer has already faded. What I can recall is that I got through it with help from an untold number of loving family members, friends, neighbors, colleagues, and lab coats. Hanging out with lab coats has saved my life. And I will continue to hang out with them for the rest of it.

My recollections of the past seven months are sparse, which is why I am so grateful that I sent out e-mail updates and kept a journal. Someday, I will read my book and, I believe, I will be surprised at what occurred. Right now, I can remember only a few incidences, some peculiar and some not so peculiar.

I remember that in the beginning, I couldn't collect my thoughts and I did irrational things ranging from simple to complex. I was afraid for my family and for me. And, aside from the fear, there was the mountainous task of getting rid of the cancer. I didn't know what to do first or whose advice to follow, because there were several medical professionals involved – AZ Health Services, my GYN, my PCP, my surgeons, and my oncologists. So, I did whatever Marcia told me to do, because she was Dr. M's assistant and Dr. M diagnosed me. I sucked in information from books, websites, articles and conversations, but I recall that deciphering it was not easy.

And then there were dumb things I did that I can remember, like when I inappropriately and unnecessarily told people about my cancer. Like the time I was talking on the phone with someone about an overcharged item on a bill. The person was very accommodating in his mission to fix the problem and interpreted it as the company's error. But then I went into a speech that concluded with, "I am particularly grateful for your help because I just found out I have breast cancer." Geez. Now what did that have to do with it?

One day I pulled the breast cancer card to get my daughter out of a commitment because she didn't want to go and I wanted to be with her. I pulled it again to get a tele-marketer to stop calling me, "I have breast cancer, I just had a mastectomy, and I am about to start chemo...don't call me anymore." Click.

But after those early days, I got down to the business of fighting "the invader", and now I am hard-pressed to be angry about having had it. I have deep beliefs that the good reasons for me to have walked with cancer are infinite.

Sure, I'll feel really cheated if I can't be around when my children graduate, get married, or even experience sadness in their lives. I'd like to be here if they need me. And I may feel a little resentful if I don't get to live out my golden years with Dan.

But this I know; if, someday, I die from cancer, then I will die from the very thing that became my catalyst for a happier and healthier life from 45 onwards.

Therefore, I will not forget to focus on today. The "today" that occurs each and every day. In the movie, Along came Polly, Ben Stiller plays Reuben. Reuben's father says to Reuben's has-been friend, "It's not about what happened in the past or what's gonna happen in the future, it's about the ride!" I will remember that.

I will never lose my newfound closeness with my husband for we have grown closer together after our months as one on the battlefield.

Recognizing ways that my children show me love will become my specialty. And when they accuse me – and they surely will – of choosing favorites, I'll playfully smile and be prepared with one of my standard "duh" replies: "Because she is my favorite," or "Because I don't love you as much as I love him."

Actually, I am truly guilty of choosing favorites amongst my children; my "favorite" has always been the one who wet her pants in grade school, cried when no one would play with her, shivered in the nurse's office while the school called and said, "guess who has a fever and vomited at recess today", became embarrassed when I scolded him in the grocery store, stood frozen and with watery eyes while I told her I had breast cancer, made my heart heavy when he asked why his sisters were crying, laid in the ER all night, and jerked and tic'd so badly that she couldn't fall asleep. Yes, I'm guilty of choosing favorites.

I will not judge people. I will always give others the benefit of the doubt. Like, when someone cuts us off on the road or runs a stop sign – perhaps they are on their way to the hospital for an emergency. There's always room for a shift in the paradigm.

The lighter side of life with cancer will always appeal to me. Even though I do not see myself using them, I will smile when I hear the "T" or the "B" words for breasts. And terms like "Boob-b-gone, Uni-boob, Boobs-r-us and One-boobed-woman" will delight me.

In February, Ms. Etheridge said in her interview on Dateline, "I'm completely grateful." When asked about being cancer free, she replied, "Yes. In every detectable way and every knowing way (in my heart and mind)."

Me too.

Here is one final bit of advice that I will give you, dear reader, although it doesn't come from me. It comes from Anne Frank, the legendary teenage Holocaust victim who stole the hearts of most everyone who read Anne Frank's Diary, "Go outside, to the fields, enjoy nature and the sunshine, go out and try to recapture happiness in yourself and in God. Think of all the beauty that's still left in and around you and be happy!"

Here is one bit of advice that I will give to you, dear reader, although it doesn't come from me. It comes from Anne Frank, the legendary teenage Holocaust victim who stole the hearts of most everyone who read "Anne Frank's Diary", "Go outside, to the fields, enjoy nature and the sunshine, go out and try to recapture happiness in yourself and in God. Think of all the beauty that's still left in and around you and be happy!"

Love to all,
Wendi

For an update on my progress, visit me at my website, www.FoxPress.com.

God made my life complete when I placed
all the pieces before him.

When I got my act together he gave me a fresh start.

God rewrote the text of my life when I opened
the book of my heart to his eyes.

Psalms, 18:20, 24
Scripture reference from *365 Day Brighteners*™
Celebrating God's Grace
Published by Garborg's®

PHOTOS AND ILLUSTRATIONS

Me at 2 years old

14 years old

Dan and I
at 21 years old

Our wedding day in 1984

35 years old - great breasts huh!

Danny's birthday, April 2001.

Christine and I, in June 2004
(before I was diagnosed). Little did I
know "the invader" was present.

Dan and Michele, 2004
"Geez Dad!"

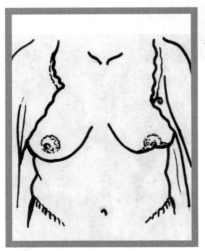

Sketch of my breasts following my lumpectomy. Notice the misshapen left one –
the tumor and surrounding tissue was
removed, therefore a portion underneath
was noticeably missing.

Sketches courtesy of Anthony Carbone, Sr.

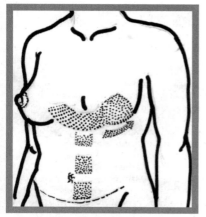 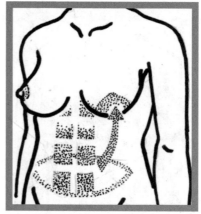

In the case of a skin-sparing modified radical mastectomy and TRAM reconstruction, which is what I had, the nipple and breast tissue is removed and the skin is spared. Then tissue from the lower section the abdomen is surgically sectioned and tunneled upwards underneath the skin, folded at a ninety degree angle under the breast to be replaced, and fitted into the empty breast skin to form a breast mound. Healing from this surgery was intense for the first week and very uncomfortable for the second and third, but looking at the results, I would do it again.

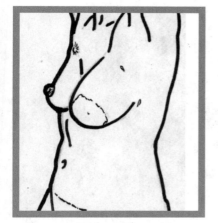 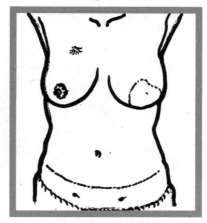

These are sketches of the scarring you can expect if you or your loved one undergoes the same surgery I had. (Read Chapter Three starting from page 100 when I describe my post-surgery observations!) I can tell you that the scars fade substantially in time. At one year post-surgery, my tummy is wonderfully flat, and the scar around my belly button is hardly noticeable. (Since the abdominal tissue was tunneled underneath my skin, the skin had to be reattached around my naval.) The bell shaped line on my breast mound is very light, and the top portion of it will be covered when I undergo plastic surgery to reconstruct a nipple. The horizontal scar line from hip to hip hasn't faded yet as much as the others have, however it falls below my underwear and bathing suits; not many people see it! The two dots below the horizontal scar represent two of the drains. Since I finished treatment and my hair grew back (everywhere), they are naturally camoflaged. The two dots above the breast mound and near my left armpit represent the other two drains and are covered by my bathing suit tops. They can't be seen anyway unless I lift my arms.

The marking above my right breast represents my chemo port. Admittingly, it does look conspicuus if I wear a strapless bathing suit or top. It will be removed in the future.

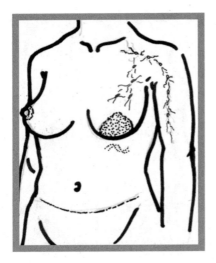

Post TRAM reconstruction: Fifteen lymph nodes that tested positive for cancer were removed during the mastectomy/reconstruction. They were in my breast, near my collar bone, shoulder, and armpit. Notice the bell-shaped gray area on my left breast (which is actually considered a breast mound). It represents some of the skin from my abdomen that was used to replace the nipple, areola, and skin that was cut away. Typically surgeons remove the nipple and areola only. My surgeons removed more skin in order to eliminate the scar from the lumpectomy. Hence, the bell shape. Also notice the lines underneath the breast mound. They represent the muscle that was turned in order to bring it from the abdomen to the breast. This area is slightly puffy and protrudes noticebly (when someone knows to look for it). In the future, as part of the nipple reconstruction, the plastic surgeon will liposuction some of the fatty tissue that gathers there, and the puffiness will not be as apparent.

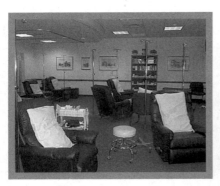

The chemo room at the Helen F. Graham Cancer Center.

This is my view from the Race for the Cure in October 2004 at the Wilmington River Front. The hooded sweatshirts you see are members of the Lady Colts Wilmington Rugby Team (one is my daughter, Michele).

This is Brenda holding a sign at the Race for the Cure - I walked by, read the sign, saw my name on it, looked up at the person holding the sign, and realized it was Brenda!

(L to rt) Vicki, me, and Deb - my head was shaved, but the stubble hadn't fallen out yet.

October 2004 – me in my wig in front of a poster in the Immaculata University dining center.

The special IV needle going into my medi-port - the tubing is taped to my clothing.

Lisa and me while I was hooked up [to chemo].

The day after my 3rd chemo treatment, trying to be a Mom, with little Danny on my back.   Don't I look wasted with nose and mouth sores, watery eyes, dry lips and a complexion that pales to everything?!   Fear not, the effects of treatment are temporary and the outcomes last a lifetime.

Andrea and me after the 2nd or 3rd chemo treatment (I still had eyebrows and eyelashes - woo hoo!)

This is me on January 11, 2004 at about 10:30 a.m. It was my last chemo treatment (and the day many people on my journey had a moment of silence knowing it was the final opportunity for chemo to kill the cancer cells). You can see that I am listening to my CD and wrapped in my "Spiderman cocoon."

Vicki and me at chemo...too bad you can't see my newly manicured fingernails and my pedicured toenails.

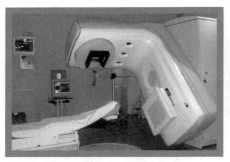

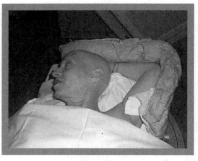

This is the table and radiation machine (by Siemens Medical Systems, Inc.) in the Primus One room at the "Helen Graham" - notice my pillow at the top of the table.

Me in my pillow mold. (I am wedged in so snugly that I am unable to turn my head and smile for the camera.)

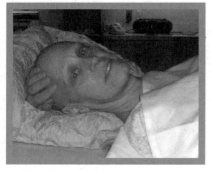

Another angle of me in my pillow mold. Now I can smile for the camera!

The racks of radiation pillow molds and white net facial molds.

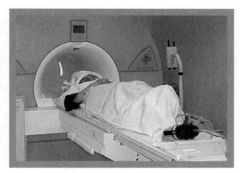

Me in my white "Darth Vader" mask getting an MRI of my head to check for cancer metastasis to my brain.

Little man Danny
(Photo courtesy of Colleen Burg)

My friends, Rhonda and John, who are also colleagues and owners of RhonJohn Communications, Inc.

Some of my colleagues at AstraZeneca (l to rt): Brenda, Jill, Joseph, Sue S, Sue F, and Andrea (with me in the middle).   *Photo by Monica Brunsberg taken from the article in the Delaware Business magazine 2005, "Juggling Cancer and Careers" by Sara Streeter.*

The door to my office on the day I returned to work!

Jim, my friend and FoxPress™ colleague, and his wife Laurie

MY FAVORITE READING RESOURCES

100 Questions & Answers
Brown, Z., and Leffall, LaSalle D., Jr., MD with Platt, E., (2003). Sudbury, MA: Jones and Bartlett Publishers, Inc.

After Breast Cancer: Answers To The Questions You Are Afraid To Ask.
Mayer, M. (March 2003). Sebastopol, CA. O'Reilly and Associates, Inc.

Be a Survivor™
Lange, V. MD (June 2005) Los Angeles: Lange Productions

Bosom Buddies: Lessons And Laughter On Breast Health And Cancer
O'Donnell, R. and Axelrod, D. MD, FACS, with Semler, T.C. (1999) New York, NY: Warner Books

Breast Cancer? Breast Health! The Wise Woman Way
Weed, S.S. (1996). Woodstock, NY: Ash Tree Publishing

The Breast Cancer Husband: How To Help Your Wife (And Yourself) During Diagnosis, Treatment, And Beyond
Silver, M. (September, 2004). Emmaus, PA: Rodale

Breast Cancer Survivor's Club.
Shockney, L. (1996). Midvale, UT: Windsor House Publishing House, Inc.

Dr. Susan Love's Breast Book
Love, S.M., M.D. (1990, 1991, 1995, 2000). *Cambridge, MA. Perseus Publishing*

Holding Tight, Letting Go
Mayer, M. (1997). Sebastopol, CA. O'Reilly and Associates, Inc.

Humor After The Tumor
Gelman, P., Prometheus Books

It's Not About The Bike: My Journey Back To Life.
Armstrong, L., (2000). New York, NY: The Berkeley Publishing Group

Living Through Breast Cancer
Kaelin, C.M., M.D. MPH with Coltrera, F. (2005). New York, NY: McGraw-Hill

Love, Judy: Letters Of Hope And Healing For Women With Breast Cancer
Hart, J. (1993). Emeryville, CA. Conari Press

My Mother's Breast: Daughters Face Their Mothers' Cancer
Tarken, L. (1999). Dallas, TX: Taylor Publishing Company

There's No Place Like Hope
Girard, V. (2001). . Lynnwood, WA: Vickie Girard and Compendium, Inc.

Uplift
Delinsky, B. (2001). New York, NY: Simon and Schuster, Inc.

What Your Doctor May Not Tell You About Breast Cancer
Lee, J.R. MD, Zava, D. Ph.D., and Hopkins, V. (2003). New York, NY: Time Warner Book Group

Why I Wore Lipstick To My Mastectomy
Lucas, G. (2004, October). New York, NY: St. Martin's Press

MY FAVORITE NUTRITION BOOKS AND WEBSITES

www.thebalancedapproach.com

The Cancer Survival Cookbook
Weihofen, D. R.D., M.S., & Marino, C. M.D., M.P. (1998). New York, NY: John Wiley & Sons, Inc.

Eight Weeks To Optimum Health
Weil, A., M.D. (1997). New York, NY. Alfred a. Knopf, Inc.

Stop Your Cravings
Workman, J. M.S., R.D. (2002). New York, NY: The Free Press.

www.rodalestore.com

MY FAVORITE LISTENING RESOURCES (AUDIO BOOKS AND CDs

For People With Cancer.
Naparstek, B. (1993). Los Angeles, CA: Time Warner Audio Books

Getting Ready: Preparing For Surgery, Radiation, And Chemotherapy With Minimal Side Effects
Siegel, *B.S., M.D., (2004)* Hay House USA, Australia and South Africa

MY FAVORITE CHILDREN'S BOOKS

Sammy's Mommy Has Cancer
Kohlenberg, S. (1993). Washington, DC: Magination Press

What is Cancer Anyway
Carney, K.L. (1999). *Barklay and Eve series, book 5.* Wethersfield, CT: Dragonfly Publishing Company

The Hope Tree
Numeroff, L. & Harpham, W.S., M.D. (1999). New York, NY: Simon & Schuster Books for Young Readers

MY FAVORITE WELLNESS BOOKS AND WEBSITES

The Answer to Cancer; Is Never Giving it a Chance to Start
Sharma, H., MD & Mishra, R.K., G.A.M.S. with Meade, J.G., Ph.D. (2002). New York: SelectBooks, Inc.

The Bible
Psalms and Revelations

Excuse Me, Your Life Is Waiting

MY FAVORITE CANCER AND HEALTH INFORMATION WEBSITES

www.asco.com (American Society of Clinical Oncologists – meets annually in May)

www.breastcancer.org

www.breastcancercare.org.uk/home (UK)

www.bro.org.se/english.html (Sweden)

www.cancer.gov

www.cancercareconnection.org

www.cancer.ca/ccs/internet/niw_splash/0%2C%2C3172%2C00.html (Canadian Cancer Society)

www.hurricanevoice.org

www.imaginis.com

www.laf.org (Lance Armstrong Foundation)

www.lbbc.org (Living Beyond Breast Cancer)

www.nbcam.org (National Breast Cancer Awareness Month)

www.nih.gov (National Institutes of Health)

www.nlm.nih.gov/medlineplus/breastcancer.html (National Library of Medicine)

www.komen.org (Susan G. Komen Breast Cancer Foundation)

www.wellnesscommunity.org

www.yme.org

ACKNOWLEDGEMENTS AND DEDICATIONS

My view of *Acknowledgments and Dedications* is that mine should be a thank you, and so they are. This book is dedicated to:

Brenda and Lynne, who sat me down one night and convinced me to put my fingers to the keyboard and turn my updates into a book.

Mark P, Joseph L and Deb, who gave me how-to-write-and-get-published books to undertake this project.

Jim, without whom the book would not have gotten published and printed as soon it did.

Rhonda and John, without whom the book would not have artwork with panache and a professional cover, and FoxPress™ would not have the very cool triumphant pink lady logo.

Brigid, Dr. Bill, Sue F, Andréa, Nancy, Dr. Ann, Sue S, Cathy S, Meryl, Steve, and Susan D-S for offering edits and feedback with regard to my manuscript.

All the recipients of my e-mail updates, and those who told me I was inspirational.

Gin who called me 'the amazing Wendi'.

Vicki and Brenda who maintained the e-mail distribution lists and mailed out my updates.

Sue S and Jill, who apprised me, while I was out, of departmental and 'people' events at work.

My neighbors and colleagues, who prepared meals for my family as I traveled this journey.

Sue F, who wore a path to our driveway to bring food and goodies.

Every single person who sent cards and stayed in touch with me throughout my ordeal.

Rachel, who reconnected with me, and Karen, my grade-school friend who kept in close contact even though we were miles apart.

My surgeons, Dr. M and Dr. D, and their staff.

The nurses, technicians, physicians and administrative staff at all

Christiana Care Health System facilities, especially the Hematology & Oncology Group and the blood laboratory on the second floor of the Helen F. Graham Cancer Center, the Radiation Oncology Department on the first floor of the Helen F. Graham Cancer Center, the Xray groups, and staff on the fifth floor of the Wilmington hospital location.

The Junior Board Cancer Resource Library on the first floor of the Helen F. Graham Cancer Center where I spent at least thirty hours resting after radiation, reading and doing some of my research.

Cynthia and Sean and the Wellness Community of Delaware, and to my friends in the Wednesday night cancer support group there: Art, Chris, Hannah, Jackie, Jim, Kathy, Lynn, Mary and Pete. And, in memory of Larry, who was with our group until his walk with cancer ended and he passed away earlier this year.

Kayla H, who, when she was eight months old, lost her mom to cancer, and learned more about her mom's ordeal as mine unfolded.

Miss Sheri, who received little Danny at daycare with open arms no matter what time we got him there.

Dan's employer, EDiS, who allowed him to be flexible with his time.

St. Catherine's parishioners who prayed for me at Masses. To Father Hynes whose persistence enabled me to attend healing Masses and opened up opportunities to have meaningful one-on-one conversations with him.

AstraZeneca, my employer who, through its health program, discovered my cancer, and through its HR and Benefits departments, and the support of Rob, Nancy and Jill, welcomed me back to the job I vacated seven months earlier. To my OE team and SPKS team for standing behind me, and supporting me in many personal and professional ways.

Janet, a friend, colleague and member of the AZ Hispanic Network Community, who offered to translate the *"Lab Coats"* manuscript in order to help the Spanish-speaking population.

My professors at Goldey-Beacom College who wrote to me, visited me, prepared meals for my family, and welcomed me back to school when I *thought* I was ready, and then again when I *was* ready.

Jeff and Diane who sometimes hung out with Dan and me at Six Paupers.

All of Dan's friends and his support network, and those who kept him company during the times when he needed to take a breather from what was happening at home, especially; Chris, Dusty, "Dr. Tim", "57-Bob", Gary, John C, John D, James, Phil, and Tim.

My caregiving team:

My chemo companions – Dan, Lisa, Vicki, Mom Fox, Kim, Cindy, Christine and Mom Pedicone.

My mom and mother-in-law for partnering and interchangeably being mothers to me.

My siblings, who found amazing and unique ways to support me.

My friend, Lisa.

God.

My daughters, Christine, Andrea, and Michele, who used creative means to help me, and themselves, get through the difficult times.

My four-year-old son, Danny, who loved me unconditionally, even when I was ill, weak, and unsightly.

My husband, Dan, for reasons too numerous to mention in the *Acknowledgments and Dedications* section of this book.

References

American Cancer Society. www.cancer.org.

American Society of Anesthesiologists. (2005, April). *Patient Safety.* www.asahq.org.

Breastcancer.org. (2005, April 27). *Building long-term health.*

Breastcancer.org.(2005, April 27). *Staying on track with hormone therapy.*

Brown, Z.K. and Leffall, L.D. Jr., M.D. with Platt, E. (2003). *100 questions & answers about breast cancer.* Sudbury, MA. Jones and Bartlett Publishers.

Junior Board Cancer Research Library at Christiana Care. (2005). *Cancer Information on the web at* www.christianacare.org.

Junior Board Cancer Research Library at Christiana Care. (2005). *Breast cancer Information on the web.* www.christianacare.org.

Cancervive video. (2002). *Daughter to Mother: Teenage girls whose mothers are living with recurrent breast cancer share their experiences.* Aventis Oncology. www.livewithit.org.

Christiana Care pamphlet. *Breast health – A woman's guide.* Pamphlet 05CAN31.

Christiana Care pamphlet. *A guide to radiation therapy.*

Cohen, D.A. and Gelfand, R.M., M.D. (2000). *Just get me through this! A practical guide to coping with breast cancer.* New York, NY. Kensington Books.

Delaware Breast Cancer Coalition, Inc. (2000, September). www.dbcc.org.

Dickson-Witmer, D, MD. Christiana Care, Helen F. Graham Cancer Center. *2004 Annual Report*

Discovery Channel University. (2001). *Donna's story: Living with breast cancer.* Films for the Humanities & Sciences. 2001 Discovery Communications, Inc. www.films.com FFH 12029.

Edwards, J. (Winter 2004). *Preventing cancer? Strategies for promoting cancer-free living.* Every Woman magazine. New York, NY: Profile Pursuit Inc.

Engel, J., Kerr, J, Schlesinger-Raab, A, Eckel, R, Sauer H, and Holzel, D. (2004, September 12). _Comparison of breast and rectal cancer patients' quality of life: results of a four year prospective field study._ Munich Field Study, Munich Cancer Registry, Ludwig-

Maximilians-University, Search results by National Center for Biotechnology Information at the U.S. National Library of Medicine.

Genetic information, privacy & discrimination. Brochure by FORCE: Facing Our Risk of Cancer Empowered, www.facingourrisk.org, 16057 Tampa Palms Blvd. W., PMB #373, Tampa, FL 33647 and NSGC, www.nsgc.org, 233 Canterbury Drive, Wallingford, PA 19086-6617.

Giordano, S., Gupta, D., et. al., _Cancer,_ (July 2004). _American Society of Clinical Oncology annual meeting,_ June 2004, Abstract #777 (article found in www.breastcancer.org/male_bc_rise.html).

Imaginis Corporation. _The breast health resource._ www.imaginis.com.

Jibrin, J.R.D. (2004, November). Body & Mind: Nutrition, _More Magazine._ p.146.

Junior Board Cancer Research Library at Christiana Care. (2005). _Cancer Information on the web at_ www.christianacare.org.

Junior Board Cancer Research Library at Christiana Care. (2005). _Breast cancer Information on the web._ www.christianacare.org

Kaelin, C.M., M.D. MPH with Coltrera, F. (2005). _Living through breast cancer._ New York, NY: McGraw-Hill.

Kass, L.R. (July 2005). _Another way with stem cells,_ July 14, 2005 (article found in _The News Journal)._

Lancet 351. (1998). _Early breast cancer trialists' collaborative group: Tamoxifen for early breast cancer: An overview of randomized trials. p. 1451-1467._

Laskowski, R.J., MD, MBA. (2005). Christiana Care, Helen F. Graham Cancer Center. _2004 Annual Report._

Lee, J.R. MD, Zava, D. Ph.D., and Hopkins, V. (2003). _What your doctor may not tell you about breast cancer: How hormone balance can help save your life._ New York, NY: Time Warner Book Group.

LBBC webpage www.LBBC.org Living Beyond Breast Cancer

Loef, J., Instructor of "Write to Heal" journal-keeping workshops.

NABCO – National Alliance of Breast Cancer Organizations. www.nabco.org. A non-profit education resource on breast cancer in the US.

Paik, S., et.al., (2004) *A multigene assay to predict recurrence of Tamoxifen-treated, node-negative breast cancer.* N. Engl. J. Med. 351: 2817-2826.
Parenting Magazine (2005, December/January). Time Inc. Tampa, FL. p. 119.

Pingry, P.A. (1997). *Best-loved poems.* Nashville, TN: Ideals Publications.

Shah, S, MD.(2005).Christiana Care, Helen F. Graham Cancer Center. *2004 Annual Report.*

Self Magazine (October, 2004). The Conde Nast Publications, a division of Advance Magazine Publishers Inc. New York, NY. p. 91.

Somers, S. (2004). *The sexy years: Discover the hormone connection.* New York, NY: Random House, Inc.

United Health Foundation (2005). UHFtips.org.

Workman, J., M.S., R.D. (2002). *Stop your Cravings.* New York, NY: Simon and Schuster, Inc.

Y-ME National Breast Cancer Organization.

DISCLAIMER AND PERMISSION TO PRINT

This book is designed to provide information on cancer (mostly breast cancer), support for cancer patients, support for primary caregivers, and inspiration to anyone who faces something that threatens his or her quality of life. It is sold with the understanding that the publisher and author are not engaged in rendering medical or legal services. **If medical, legal or other expert assistance is required, the services of a competent professional should be sought. This book is meant to educate and should not be used as an alternative for certified medical care.**

It is not the purpose of this book to reprint all the information that is otherwise available to cancer patients, caregivers and medical professionals, but instead to complement, amplify and supplement other sources. **You are urged to use this book as a guide and read all the available material, learn as much as you care to, and tailor the information to your individual needs.** For more information, see the many resources throughout the book, in the *Suggested Reading and Listening* section, and in the *References* section.

Research about cancer is ongoing and subject to interpretation. **We have exerted every effort to ensure that the information presented is as accurate as possible at the time of publication.** There is no guarantee that this information will remain current over time and there *may be mistakes*, both typographical and in content. Therefore, this book should be used only as a general guide and not as the ultimate source of cancer information. Appropriate professionals and experts should be consulted before adopting any processes, procedures or treatments discussed in this book.

Quoted material from family, friends, colleagues, medical personnel and other professionals is approved. References to books, CDs, magazines and other media are reprinted with permission. Graphics and tables are reprinted with permission.

Many designations used by manufacturers and sellers to distinguish their products are claimed as trademarks or are copyrighted. Where those designations appear in this book, FoxPress‰ was aware of a trademark or copyright claim, and the designations have been noted.

The purpose of this manual is to inform, support and educate (by reading tips, quotes from professionals, and resource information) as well as entertain (by following the story). The author and FoxPress‰ shall have neither liability nor responsibility to any person or entity with respect to any loss or damage caused, or alleged to have been caused, directly or indirectly, by the information contained in this book.

Glossary of Acronyms Used in This Book

Note: This is a glossary of acronyms used in this book. For a glossary of medical words and cancer terms, go to the glossary at www.breast-cancer.org, or refer to the book called *100 Questions & Answers About Breast Cancer* (Brown, Leffall Jr., Platt) pages 229 to 236.

AC = Adriamycin and Cytoxan
AI = Aromatase Inhibitor
ASAP = As soon as possible
ATAC = Clinical Trial: Arimidex, Tamoxifen, Alone or in Combination [trial]
AZ = AstraZeneca Pharmaceuticals
BP = Blood Pressure
BRCA = Breast Cancer [gene 1 and 2]
BSE = Breast Self-Exam
CAM = Complementary and Alternative Medical therapies
CAT Scan = Computerized Axial Tomography (also called CT Scan)
CBC = Complete Blood Count (red and white blood cells)
CBE = Clinical Breast Exam
CEO = Chief Executive Officer
CHS = Corporate Health Services at AZ
CIO = Chief Information Officer
CT Scan = Computerized Axial Tomography (also called CAT Scan)
DCIS = Ductal Carcinoma In Situ
EDiS = The company Dan works for
ENT = Ear, Nose and Throat
ER = Emergency Room
ER negative/positive = Estrogen Receptor status (negative or positive)
FP = Family Physician
FTIs = Farnyseal Transferase Inhibitors
GYN = Gynecologist
HER-2/neu = Hormone Expression Receptor status (negative=normal and positive=overexpressed)
HIPAA = The Health Insurance Portability and Accountability Act
HRT = Hormone Replacement Therapy (for post-menopausal women)
HT = Hormone Therapy (to treat ER positive breast cancer)
IBD = Inflammatory Bowel Disease
ID = Invasive Ductal Carcinoma
IL = Invasive Lobular Carcinoma
IM = Instant Message (cell phone)
IM = Intramuscular

IU = Immaculata University
IV = Intravenous
IS = Information Services [department at AZ]
LGFB = Look Good…Feel Better [program for cancer patients]
MRI = Magnetic Resonance Imaging
NIH = National Institutes of Health
OE = Organization Effectiveness [team in SPKS]
PCP = Primary Care Physician
PR negative/positive = Progesterone Receptor status
   (negative or positive)
RT = Radiation Therapy
SPKS = Strategy, Performance, & Knowledge Services
   [department within IS at AZ]
TB = Tuberculosis
TS = Tourette's Syndrome
TNM = Tumor, Nodes and Metastases
TRAM Flap = Transverse Rectus Abdominis Flap
UTI = Urinary Tract Infection

Andrea = Our second daughter
Andréa = A colleague on our OE team in SPKS
Anne = Colleague
Betsy = The nurse at AZ who discovered my tumor
Betsy the chemo nurse = Nurse at the cancer center
Brenda = Friend and colleague at AZ
Brigid = A friend and communications colleague at AZ
Cammy = Kala's mother and our neighbor
Charles = Lisa's husband
Christine = Our oldest daughter
Cindy = A friend and one of my chemo companions
Cynthia = Co-Founder of the Delaware Wellness Community
Dan = My husband
Danny = Our son (and fourth child)
Deb = My oldest sister
Diane = One of Dr. M's office assistants
Dr. C = GYN
Dr. D = Plastic Surgeon who did the TRAM reconstruction
Dr. Dz = The first Radiation Oncologist to see me before I changed
    locations
Dr. K = Primary Care Physician
Dr. Kp = My Radiation Oncologist
Dr. Ln = High School Principal
Dr. Lsk = CEO, Christiana Care Health System
Dr. M = Surgeon who performed the mastectomy
Dr. N = Oncologist
Dr. P = A Senior Physician in Oncology Department at AZ
Dr. T = My ENT
Father John = My priest at St. Catherine of Siena Church
God = My creator
Janet = Colleague, member of AZ Hispanic Network Community
Jason = Christine's boyfriend
Jennifer = My Ayurveda nutritionist
Jim = My friend and someone who helped me get the publishing
    work done
Jill = My friend and manager of our OE Team
Joann = A friend and colleague is IS
Joseph = A colleague on our OE team in SPKS
John = A friend and colleague, and partner in RhonJohn
    Communications, Inc.
Joseph = A colleague on our OE team in SPKS
Judy H = My neighbor who, along with her husband and daughters,
    helped our family

Kala = Michele's close friend, our next door neighbor
Karen D = A colleague at AZ who was ahead of me in her cancer treatment
Kathy = One of the RT nurses
Kayla H = my mentee and an important person in my life
Linda = One of the RT nurses
Lisa = My closest girlfriend, married to Charles (Dan and I met them on our honeymoon)
Lorraine = One of my cousins
Marcia = One of Dr. M's office assistants
Marie = A colleague in Sweden
Michele = Our third daughter
Mike = Andrea's boyfriend
Miss Sheri – Danny's daycare provider
Mom = My mother
Mom P = My mother-in-law
Ms. C = My genetic counselor at the cancer center
Nancy = Jill's manager (my second-line manager) and the Executive Director of SPKS
Patty = My newfound 'chemo' friend
Rhonda = A friend and colleague, and partner in RhonJohn Communications, Inc.
Rick = One of the owners of the company Dan works for
Rob = The CIO at AZ and an internal client of SPKS
Roseann = One of Dan's cousins and a fifteen year Hodgkin's Lymphoma survivor
Sean = Facilitator at the Wellness Community
Sharry = Kayla's grandmother (and mother of Cindy who died when Kayla was eight months old)
Sue C = A nurse at AZ
Sue F = A friend and colleague in our department, SPKS
Sue S = A colleague in our department, SPKS
Susan = My life coach
Ted = A colleague of Dan's whose wife led us to the Wellness Community Delaware
Terri = Dan's sister, twin to Tina
Tim = Wendi's twin brother
Tina = Dan's sister, twin to Terri
Vicki = Another sister
Vince and Brenda = Dan's cousin who had male breast cancer, and his wife
Vincent = Dan's brother

TRANSLATION TABLE OF DRUG TRADE NAMES AND GENERIC TERMMS

I would hear medical professionals refer to drugs in many ways. Sometimes I got confused about the difference between tamoxifen and Nolvadex® letrozole and Femara®, and paclitaxel and Taxol®. I realize it might be helpful for you to understand (as I needed to understand) that there are trade names and generic terms for every drug:

Trade Name® generic term (Pharmaceutical company)

Adriamycin® doxorubicin hydrochloride (Pharmacia, acquired by Pfizer)
Aranesp® darbepoetin alfa (Amgen)
Arimidex© anastrozole (AstraZeneca)
Aromasin® exemestane (Pfizer)
Benadryl® diphenhydramine hydrochloride (Pfizer)
Compazine® prochlorperazine (GlaxoSmithKline)
Cytoxan® cyclophosphamide (Bristol-Myers Squibb)
Decadron® dexamethasone (Merck)
Emend® aprepitant (Merck)
Faslodex® fulvestrant (AstraZeneca)
Femara® letrozole (Novartis)
Herceptin® trastuzumab (Genentech)
Neulasta® pegfilgrastim (Amgen)
Nolvadex® tamoxifen citrate (AstraZeneca)
Percocet® oxycodone and acetaminophen (Endo)
Procrit® epoetin alfa (Ortho Biotech)
Tagamet® cimetidine (GlaxoSmithKline)
Taxol® paclitaxel (Bristol-Myers Squibb)
Zofran® ondansetron HCl (GlaxoSmithKline)
Zoloft® sertraline (Pfizer)

RELATIONSHIP TREE
(Some of the Many People Mentioned in the Book)

This tree illustrates my family, and *some* of the *many* people who are mentioned in this book and who supported my family and me:

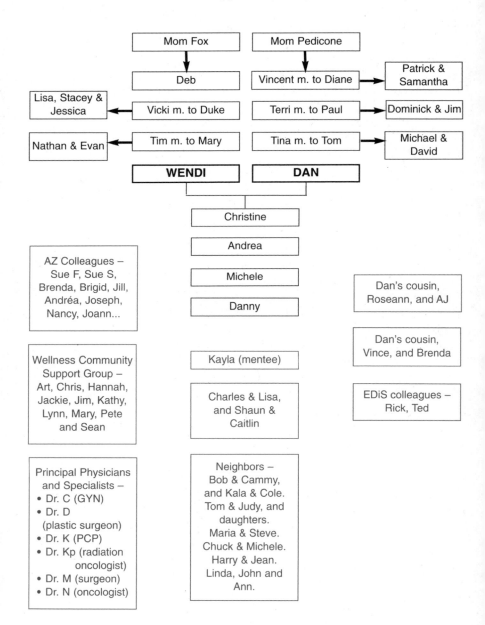

Topic	Pages listed

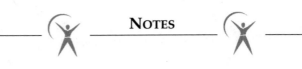

Every effort has been made to ensure that the information presented is as accurate as possible at the time of publication. I would love to hear from you regarding updated information, your experiences with this book, and how you feel it could be improved. I may not be able to respond individually to all comments and suggestions, but I'll take all of them to heart and appropriately incorporate them into future editions.

Your feedback is important to me. Check all that apply:

Your book was helpful to me. I am a:
- ☐ Caregiver
- ☐ Cancer patient
- ☐ Medical professional
- ☐ Other: _____

The feature(s) in the book that was helpful was the:
- ☐ Story
- ☐ Resource information
    - ☐ Tips
    - ☐ Suggested books, websites, CDs; etc.
- ☐ Other: _____

☐ Your book was not helpful
☐ I wish the book included: _____

_____

Other feedback I would like to offer: _____

_____

_____

Please send feedback to: Wendi Fox Pedicone c/o FoxPress™ , PO Box 1601, Hockessin, DE 19707-5601, via fax (302) 239-7529, or complete the feedback form at www.FoxPress.com. Thank you!

cut along dotted line